LIBRARY LIT. 14- The Best of 1983

edited by

BILL KATZ

The Scarecrow Press, Inc.
Metuchen, N.J., & London
1984

ISBN 0-8108-1717-9

Library of Congress Catalog Card No. 78-154842

Copyright © 1984 by The Scarecrow Press, Inc.

Manufactured in the United States of America

CONTENTS

Introduction

PART I: LIBRARIES AND LIBRARIANS

Electronics, the Cost Disease, and the Operation of Libraries (William J. Baumol and Sue Blackman) — 3
Theory vs. Practice in Library Management (Richard De Gennaro) — 25
The Erosion of Library Education (Wm. R. Eshelman) — 34
National Library and Information Planning (Maurice B. Line) — 43
Hooper and the Primal Tribe (Karl Nyren) — 61
Library Technology: The Black Box Syndrome (Norman Stevens) — 67
Computer Searching: A Primer for the Uninformed Scholar (Stephen K. Stoan) — 77
Libraries and Information Services in China (Luo Xingyun) — 85
The Neurochemical Bases of Library Use ... Or, Why We Love Harlequins (James Benson and Daniel O. O'Connor) — 102

PART II: COMMUNICATION AND EDUCATION

Public Library Reference Service: Myth and Reality (Mary Lee Bundy, Amy Bridgman, and Laura Keltie) — 113
Young Adult Reference Services in the Public Library (Mary K. Chelton) — 124
Too Many Books? Publishers' Problems and Collection Building (Audrey Eaglen) — 137
The Elusive List Price and The FPT Factor (Connie C. Epstein) — 142
The Golden Age of Science Fiction Is 12 (David G. Hartwell) — 150
Doin' Da Missin' Books Boogie: Thoughts on Axioms, Flexibility, and Attila the Hun (Carol M. Hastings) — 166
Not Yet Gutenberg! (Estelle Jussim) — 169
Sublimity Versus Circulation: For a Critical Method of Poetry Selection (J. B. Miller) — 179
The Nonesuch Press (Ashley Montagu) — 188
A Portrait of Working Women in Federal Government Periodicals (Joe Morehead) — 195
Bibliographic Control of Library and Information Science Literature (Guy A. Marco) — 204

The Muse in the Stacks: A Survey of Poetry in Public
   Libraries (Darby Penney) — 221
Information Technology and the Myth of Abundance
   (Anthony Smith) — 227
The Community of the Book (Samuel S. Vaughan) — 245

PART III: THE SOCIAL PREROGATIVE

Access and Dissemination Issues Concerning Federal
   Government Information (Marc A. Levin) — 275
A Backward and Forward Look at The New York Times
   Information Bank--A Tale of Ironies Compounded ...
   and an Analysis of the Mead Deal (Jeff Pemberton) — 289
The Rise and Pause of the U.S. Freedom of Information
   Act (Harold C. Relyea) — 305
Censorship in the Early Professionalization of American
   Libraries, 1876 to 1929 (Frederick Stielow) — 326
Island Trees v. Pico: The Legal Implications
   (Robert D. Stone) — 342
Are School Censorship Cases Really Increasing?
   (Kenneth I. Taylor) — 351
A Walk on the Wild Side: A Conversation with "Sex
   Positive" Publisher Joani Blank (Celeste West) — 363

Notes on Contributors — 371

INTRODUCTION

Here is the fourteenth collection of what some of us consider the best writing in library literature published from approximately 1 November 1982 through October 1983. We have selected 30 articles from a wide variety of periodicals. The process begins with the editor examining 180 to 200 journals. The choices are by no means limited to library publications, but may include other types. Excellence rules no matter where it appears.

Given the initial choices, the jury selects the 30 winners. Here it should be noted that throughout the year various librarians do suggest nominations for inclusion, and these are always part of the considered final list. Librarians are invited to send citations for articles they think should be considered. These to the editor at: School of Library and Information Science, State University of New York, 135 Western Avenue, Albany, NY 12222. Please limit selection to material published between 1 November 1983 and 1 November 1984 for the next, 15th edition.

Practicing librarians, teachers, and editors, the jury members make their choices in several ways. First and foremost they consider originality of thought, depth of research, and grasp of the subject matter.

In library literature, as in all fields, there is a considerable amount of repetition (in itself not bad, but hardly suitable for this compilation), and an effort is made not to cover the same material twice. Conversely, there is nothing wrong with one or two people looking at the same data, the same experience, and coming up with different conclusions, hence different and valued articles.

Consideration is given to scope. The jury tries to cover topics of interest to all librarians, not simply those dedicated to research, or to getting through the day behind the circulation desk. Various types of library service are dutifully weighed, and selection is made of the best articles which do justice to those areas. Still, it is hardly a rule that all sections and divisions of the profession must be viewed in any one volume.

Style, or, if you will, the ability to express oneself clearly and with some wit and authority, is regarded favorably. Even the best research is lost when the author (or the editor) fails to offer up an exact and lucid report. This is equally the case of a librarian observing and writing about activities from the front lines of library service. At the same time judicious account is taken of someone who may not write like Henry James or Ann Tyler, but who has an important idea to express. No jury member insists that everyone write as a professional author, but there is no excuse for sloppiness either.

Here it seems worth repeating that librarians write no worse, possibly much better, than most; and the day is long gone when librarians need apologize for their journals. Anyone who scoffs at this conclusion need only take a cursory glance at an issue of an endorsed medical, legal, English, or undertaker's journal to see librarians owe no one an apology for their style.

Other matters which are deemed important range from the timeliness of the message to its appropriate place in the stream, or flood tide of writing on the subject. Then, too, an effort is made to strike a balance between sources of publication so that everything in here is not out of only two or three journals.

Finally, though, and this seems most important of all, the jury and the editor determine what is best by intuition, experience, and luck--to quote the introduction from the thirteenth collection. This may annoy those who long for a methodical approach, for a scientific method of selecting the best and the better, but anyone who has considered manuscripts will be glad to admit to the fault of less than objectivity, of working on hunches as well as reasoned criteria.

The 1983 Jury

John Berry, editor of the Library Journal; Mary K. Chelton, co-editor of VOYA (Voice of Youth Advocates); Arthur Curley, Deputy Director of the Research Libraries of the New York Public Library; Wm. R. Eshelman, President, Scarecrow Press; Pat Schuman, President, Neal-Schuman Publishers; and the undersigned.

--Bill Katz

Part I

LIBRARIES AND LIBRARIANS

ELECTRONICS, THE COST DISEASE, AND THE OPERATION OF LIBRARIES*

William J. Baumol and Sue Anne Batey Blackman

The age of electronics may bring with it profound changes in the operation of libraries. Some of these changes may be adopted because they will expand the capacities of the individual institution and permit improvements in library services. But other changes may be forced upon libraries by financial pressures--by cost relationships which leave the librarian no alternative. It is the second of these sources of change that will concern us here.

In this article we examine trends in the costs of conventional library operation and trends in the costs of the electronic devices which may pervade the libraries of the future. We also describe some alternative scenarios for the use of computerized facilities by libraries. Then we present some evidence on the rate of adoption of electronic techniques which has so far occurred and, finally, offer some analytic material which seeks to account for the observed developments in this area.

We begin our investigation with a hypothesis that seemed to follow indisputably from the underlying technological relationship between libraries and electronics. For reasons which will be reviewed in the next section, library costs have until recently been rising at a compounded rate significantly greater than the rate of inflation in the rest of the economy, and the underlying problem can be expected with some confidence to continue in the future. At the same time, costs associated with computers have exhibited a persistent downward trend of astonishing magnitude. The conclusion that appeared to follow inescapably from these observations is that even if electronic library operation is now more expensive than traditional methods, the latter must soon catch up and, indeed, ultimately cost substantially more than computerized methods. When that happens librarians will find themselves with little choice: Traditional methods of library operation will have to give way to the computer.

---

*Reprinted by permission of the authors and publisher from the Journal of the American Society for Information Science, 34:3 (1983) 181-91, © 1983 by John Wiley & Sons, Inc., Publishers.

This "technocratic" view of the future is a radical departure from today's libraries. It envisions at least partial replacement of the written page by the television screen. And that television screen is to be located not at a central library, but at the reader's premises. Rather than handling a technical journal physically, the reader can command the library's central computer to transmit a particular article (or a particular page of an article) via his own television screen. Or he can first ask the computer for a bibliography relating to a particular topic, and can then summon up items from that bibliography at his convenience.

When a particular item is likely to be needed repeatedly or annotation is required, hard copy can be made from a page of the television screen with the aid of an attached photocopying unit which produces a copy automatically charged to the user's account. For such material no local library need be involved. A central memory bank, perhaps operated by the Library of Congress, will be able to serve the needs of all scholars and the delays engendered by interlibrary loans will become a thing of the past.

With these developments the publication of technical journals and reference books is likely to vanish, for materials such as statistical tables will be more accessible, more easily kept up to date, and less difficult to store in electronic rather than printed form.* This is not to say that all book publication will cease. Those works whose subject matter requires the aesthetic qualities of the printed book will undoubtedly survive the electronic revolution, but little else will continue to be the same.

This, then, is the technocratic vision of the library of tomorrow. Curiously, there is a sense in which none of it can be classed as science fiction. The requisite hardware has all been invented, and prototypes are already available.† Given the desire and the requisite funds, it _can_ all be realized.

On this view of things, it is only temporarily prohibitive costs or conservatism that impede the widespread adoption of electronic techniques, and librarians who will apparently have little choice in terms of overall mode of operation are best advised to plan how to adapt themselves to the inevitable electronic future.

---

*The transition to this brave new world will undoubtedly bring with it a number of curious problems. What will replace the refereeing process that precedes publication in a technical journal and serves as a rough attestation of quality? What, indeed, can be taken to constitute "publication" and serve as evidence of the merit of an author seeking academic tenure?

†Indeed, at least one library, that of Clarkson College, is reported already to be well on its way to achieving such a mode of operation. See ref. [1, p. C1] and ref. [44].

This, as already indicated, was the hypothesis with which our study began. As we will see, however, neither the facts nor the underlying relationships turned out to support the hypothesis. What emerges is much less categorical in its implications and suggests that the choice of techniques of library operations is not nearly as open-and-shut as the initial hypothesis indicated. For, paradoxically, the astonishing rate of decline in computer costs can be expected in the future to limit the rate of decrease of the overall cost of electronic library operation.

1. The Cost Disease of Library Operation

Libraries are among a set of activities in our economy which are especially vulnerable to a debilitating "cost disease" which causes their costs to rise far more rapidly than costs in the rest of the economy. The source of this cost disease is in the technology that characterizes the affected activities. It is important to understand the relationships involved in order to recognize the persistence of the phenomenon and the likelihood of its continuation in the future. Baumol and Marcus [2] explained the cost disease in the following words:

> Consider two economic activities: in one activity, the quality of the end product is directly dependent on the amount of labor expended per unit of production; as a consequence, it is difficult for technological progress to effect any significant decreases in the quantity of labor input. In the other activity, however, cumulative savings in the labor input occur steadily.
> Examples of both types of activity can be easily provided. Among relatively inflexible labor-content activities, one can list education, medicine, live artistic performances, legal services, fire protection, and certain library services. Examples of industries that have benefitted over the years from labor-saving innovations are even more numerous: telecommunications, electric power, automotive production, and electronics, to name a few. The examples show that the distinction is a very real one. Moreover, while from time to time, breakthroughs have increased productivity in some activities of the first category, these advances have rarely been followed by a steady stream of labor-saving innovations as has typically been the case in manufacturing. This result has not been a matter of accident. The difference is inherent in the nature of the two types of products and the technology of their supply. The first category consists largely of services requiring personal attention, in which the quality of the end product depends primarily on the amount of human effort devoted to it. Such products are not easily standardized or automated. In many cases, the quantity of labor involved per unit of output is virtually fixed by the

nature of the product; e.g., a performance of a trio scored for one-half hour clearly requires a one and a half man hour performance.

Now, the evidence indicates that wages in the labor-inflexible industries have often lagged behind those in the rest of the economy, but have generally caught up over longer periods. For example, while right after the war school teachers' wages had fallen behind those in industry, [by the end of the 1960s] the gap [had] been closed. Economic pressures simply do not permit growing divergences in real wages in different economic activities, for, if growing disparities were to persist, labor would move into the increasingly better paid occupations, and the resulting shortages would force wages up in the activities where they had lagged. A good deal of evidence shows that things do work out this way in practice.

The implication of the analysis for the cost behavior of the service and manufacturing sectors is straightforward. With costs of labor rising at comparable rates, but labor requirements falling cumulatively and steadily in the one sector while remaining fairly constant in the other, a differential in cost behavior becomes inevitable. Costs of the service sector must rise steadily and cumulatively relative to those in the remainder of the economy at a percentage rate directly related to the differential in their productivity.

If wages in the economy rise at a rate of 5 percent per year, and productivity in manufacturing increases by 4 percent per annum while productivity in the services remains almost unchanged, costs of manufactured goods will go up at an annual rate of 1 percent, but those of services will rise at 5 percent. The difference in the technologies of the two sectors forces this differential upon them, and, with occasional exceptions, we can expect such a differential to persist year after year.

The empirical evidence supports this conclusion. In one personal service after another, costs per unit of output have risen over 4 percent more rapidly over [much of] the postwar period than the rate of increase in price level. The _relative_ costs _per unit_ of these services have doubled every fourteen years and quadrupled over less than three decades. Understandably these sectors have faced budgetary difficulties that have grown more critical with the passage of time.

[To apply this discussion to our central topic we must recognize that] conventional library operation is a fairly inflexible labor-content activity; its success requires personal services and depends heavily on the amount of human thought and attention devoted to it. The preceding analysis [may] thus help [to] explain a significant portion of the [pressures] upon library budgets. (pp. 52-54)*

---

*For a contrary view, see White.[3] White measures (cont.)

To see how well library cost data compare with this cost disease analysis, we will divide the postwar era into two subperiods: the period before 1970 in which inflation was, by and large, extremely moderate and library funding was relatively abundant, and the subsequent period in which all of that changed.

2. Library Costs in the Fifties and Sixties

Much of the postwar period before the 1970s was a time of relative prosperity for the libraries. Of course, they have never enjoyed an overabundance of funds. Still, before the baby boom began to subside and before the Vietnam War and OPEC had produced their inflationary consequences, colleges and universities found themselves in easier financial circumstances than anyone could remember, and their libraries were among the beneficiaries. Libraries unconnected with educational institutions also enjoyed reduced economic pressures at that time.

The statistics confirm that, measured both in terms of cost per student and cost per volume held, library costs over the period rose at rates significantly exceeding the rise in the general price level, that is, far faster than the economy's overall rate of inflation.* For a sample of 58 university libraries, between 1951 and 1969 expenditure per volume held grew at 6.3 percent per year, while expenditure per student served grew at an annual rate of 6.1 percent.[2, p. 47] In contrast (although this now seems hard to believe), the wholesale price index (used as a measure of the overall inflation rate) grew only 0.9 percent per year. Put in a different way, measured in dollars of constant purchasing power, library cost per volume held and per student grew at compounded rates of about 5.4 and 5.2 percent per year, respectively. These are very substantial rates and imply that, if continued, real cost per volume held or per student must double in less than 14 years!

One may well suspect, however, that this enormous rate of

---

productivity in public libraries directly in terms of circulation relative to labor time and an index of other inputs. White concludes that from 1951 to 1963 library productivity rose about as fast as it did in the economy as a whole, although it then began to fall, perhaps because of overgenerosity of budgets.

*It is necessary to calculate some sort of cost per unit of library operation (however one may choose to define that concept). The period under discussion was one in which both number of students served and number of volumes held was increasing rapidly. Should it have proven that the total budget of a library, while expanding, was doing so at a rate significantly slower than the growth rate of the student body or the number of volumes stocked, then one would have to conclude that in substance costs were actually declining. As crude indices of unit costs, cost per student and cost per volume held were, consequently, calculated.

increase is not entirely attributable to the cost disease. The relative prosperity of the libraries during the fifties and sixties may well have encouraged costly improvements in standards of library operation. Real incomes, college-age population, and university enrollments were all rising during this period; with relatively stable book and journal prices and increasing budgets rapid growth in library collections and staff was possible, and stable prices also permitted construction of new facilities.[4, p. 7] In 1951 only 14 research libraries in the U.S. and Canada had collections exceeding 1 million volumes; by 1973-1974 there were 76 with more than 1 million volumes, 25 with more than 2 million volumes, and 14 with more than 3 million volumes.[5] Library cost increases may also have been exacerbated by other special problems of the period, such as the rapidity of the surge in number of students and the explosion in technical publications. It is therefore of some importance to determine what happened to real costs during the decade of the 1970s, and we will turn to that shortly. First, however, we will examine the trends in computer costs in order to see what they suggest about the financial prospects of electronic operation of the libraries.

3. Trends in Computer Costs

The rise in the real cost of conventional library operations in the 1950s and 1960s seems very substantial. Yet it involves a rate of change that is extremely moderate in comparison with the costs of computer hardware. The rate of decline of hardware prices per unit of computing capacity is simply sensational. While there are no cost figures which are both representative and precise, because the components in question are so heterogeneous, the following excerpts are suggestive of the magnitudes involved.*

> The increase in computational power and memory for a fixed price has been approximately exponential over time. Cost-effectiveness doubles every two years--this means, for example, that the cost effectiveness of computing has increased by a factor of more than a million since World War II. It seems likely that this doubling will continue through the 1980's. One crucial factor has been the astonishing increase in the number of active elements on a single silicon chip. (Lipson,[6] p. 23)

> The cost/performance of electronics is improving at a

---

*It is noteworthy that most of these calculations apparently make no correction for the effects of inflation. This means that if adjusted to reflect constant purchasing power the decrease in computer costs would have been even more remarkable; for example, if in a year when inflation proceeds at an annual rate of 10 percent, the cost of an electronic component declines, say, 18 percent (unadjusted for inflation), in constant dollars the (real) rate of decline will be closer to 28 percent!

rate variously estimated at from 20-25 percent per year. (Triebwasser,[7] p. 176-177)

The most significant ... future development involving [data] communications modes will be the drop in the dollar cost of transferring a bit of information from here to there. The carrier component of this cost has been calculated as declining by about 15 percent per year since about 1960, and is forecast to continue at that rate into the 80s. (Ferreira and Nilles,[8] p. 51)

Kubitz,[9] who provides a detailed description of trends in the electronics industries, estimates that computer performance per unit cost has been increasing at 25 to 30 percent per year (p. 135). Burns [10] offers the following breakdown of the rate of cost change for various components over the next decade: People (labor) up 6 percent per year, communications down 11 percent per year, computer logic down 25 percent per year, and computer memory down 40 percent per year.

This is just a small part of the cost evidence available. We can easily provide other quotations offering similar and sometimes identical estimates. But what all these observers seem to suggest is that the cost of the computer components relevant for library operations is likely to continue to decline about 25 percent per year even without adjustment for inflation, which means that the real decline will probably be considerably higher.

Our empirical observations so far would seem to imply that the widespread conversion of libraries to electronic techniques should be fast upon us. During the 1950s and 1960s library costs rose at a rate exceeding 5 percent per year in constant dollars, while computer costs have plummeted at a rate of 25 percent per year, even without adjusting for inflation. Simple extrapolation of these cost trends would at first glance imply that in fairly short order a thoroughgoing electronic overhaul of library operations will be transformed from a luxury into a financial necessity.* But we will see next that things have not worked out quite as might have been expected.

---

*It is helpful to see what these figures mean if extrapolated into the future. If we adopt the exaggerated premise that unit costs of an unspecified electronic library operation are ten times as high as manual costs, simple arithmetic confirms that if the cost of conventional operations continues to rise at 5 percent per year while that of electronics falls 25 percent per year, then within eight years the disparity in costs virtually will have been wiped out. By the ninth year electronic operation will have become the less expensive alternative.

4. The Cost Disease and Library Costs in the 1970s

Earlier, we deliberately broke off our story at the end of the 1960s, since the advent of the next decade clearly would bring with it a new era in library financing. The seventies were, as we know, not a particularly fortunate time for the libraries, which were faced by sudden and sharp decreases in funding.

Before examining the actual consequences of the new stringency, it is important to note how the cost disease generally behaves in periods of inflation. During inflationary periods the cost disease has, characteristically, departed from its usual pattern. Historically, whenever the economy's price level has been steady or declining, the costs of the services have generally risen relative to the price level in the rest of the economy. That is, the constant dollar cost of services has always risen in such circumstances. However, during inflationary periods, at least as far as nonprofit institutions like universities, orchestras, and libraries are concerned, matters have been quite different. Per unit expenditures, rather than outpacing the rate of inflation, have tended to lag behind it, so that in terms of dollars of constant purchasing power the unit costs of these services have actually fallen.*

---

*Data for the orchestras bring this out most clearly because there exist data on orchestral costs going back to the first half of the 19th century. Financial figures for the New York Philharmonic since 1842 show that costs rose more quickly than the general price level except for the periods of inflation associated with the Civil War and World Wars I and II (Baumol and Bowen [11, p. 190]). More recent figures indicate that the behavior of orchestral costs during the 1970s has not been identical with that in earlier inflationary periods. Data provided by the American Symphony Orchestra League (ASOL) indicate that between 1973-1974 and 1979-1980, inclusive, in constant dollars cost per attendee actually rose some 2.6 percent per year, though cost per performance declined at an annual rate of 1.6 percent.

The apparent inconsistency of the behavior of cost per attendee and cost per performance is explainable largely by special conditions and new practices in the orchestras. In recent years 52-week annual contracts with musicians have become common, and this has led to a proliferation of small scale chamber concerts each involving only a small number of an orchestra's musicians and aimed at smaller audiences.

The rise in cost per attendee is attributable to the surprisingly felicitous experience of the arts during the 1970s in terms of financial support both from private and public sources. The evidence indicates that giving to the arts in the U.S. (and a number of other countries) rose far faster than the price level during this period. For example, for the orchestras during the period 1973-1974 to 1979-1980, financial support rose more than 5 percent per year, compounded, measured in constant dollars.

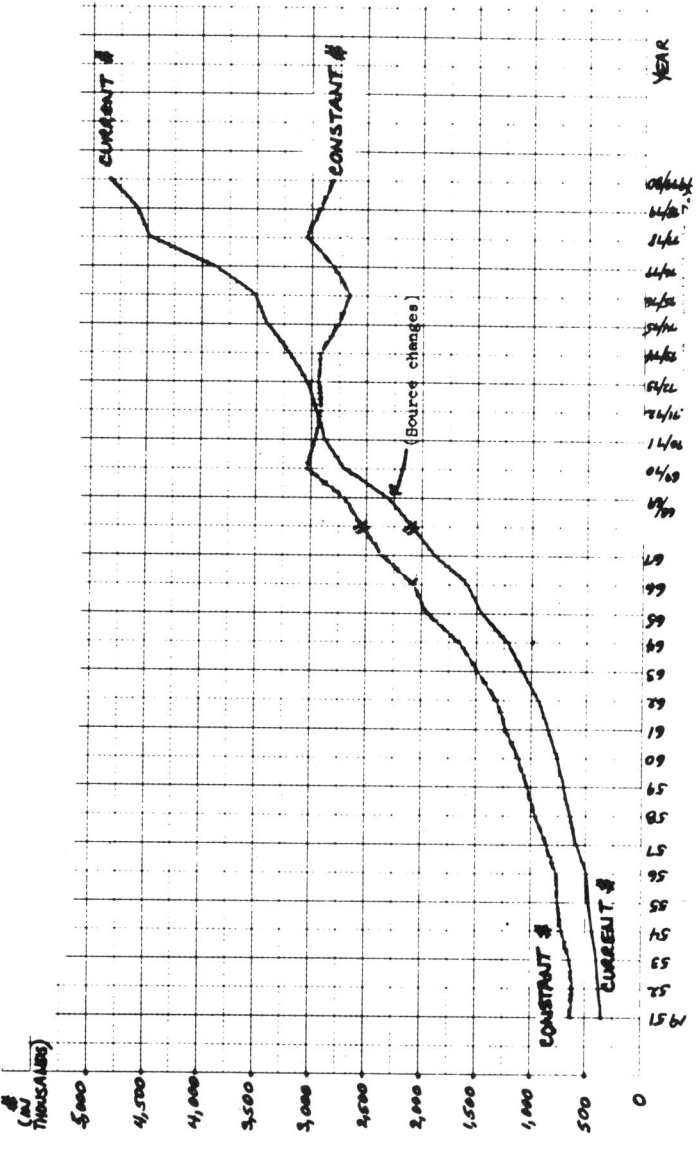

FIG. 1. Total library operating expenditures, median ARL university library, 1951-1980, in current and constant dollars (source: see Appendix A).

The explanation, presumably, is that inflation has eroded these nonprofit organizations' sources of funding. As a result, they have been forced to adopt cutbacks in service, reduce the real compensation of their staffs, and even skimp on quality. It is in these ways that the activities subject to the cost disease have been able to reduce their costs (measured in constant dollars) during inflations.

In light of all this, it should come as little surprise that library costs did not manage to keep up with inflation during the 1970s. Figure 1 shows total expenditures between 1951 and 1980 for a median member library of the Association of Research Libraries. The curve marked current dollars, which is uncorrected for inflation, shows a fairly steady rise from $350,869 in 1951 to $4,783,864 in 1979-1980. But when the figures are translated into dollars of constant purchasing power matters change substantially. While total outlays still rise until 1969-1970, after that they level off or even decline slightly. But this patterns holds only for total cost. When measured per student served and per volume held, unit

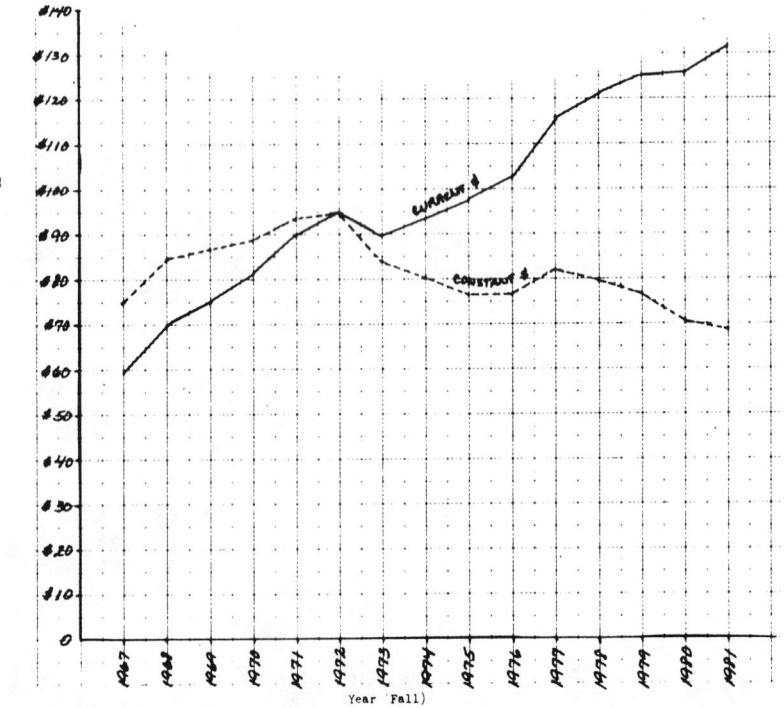

FIG. 2. Total operating expenditures per student served, U.S. college and university libraries, 1967-1981, in current and constant dollars (source: see Appendix B).

costs in constant dollars actually fell. Figure 2 shows per student costs of U.S. academic libraries. In constant 1972 dollars, funds per student increased steadily from $75 per student in 1967 to $94 in 1972. But since then they have declined almost every year until in 1981 the figure had dropped to $69 per student. Finally, Figure 3 shows the trends in library expenditures per volume held. It tells the same story--a more or less steady rise in real cost per volume from 1951 to 1970, with the cost figure more than doubling over that interval. But between 1970 and 1980, cost per volume held, in constant dollars. fell almost without let-up, declining about 40 percent over the ten year period.

The conclusion to be drawn from these cost trends is that for the libraries the cost disease has been suspended during the recent period of inflation. Since many economists feel that inflation is here to stay for a while and the financial stringency besetting the libraries also seems likely to continue, this may suggest that the cost incentives for the adoption of electronic library operations may have been blunted, if not eliminated entirely. But such a conclusion is premature. There are at least two reasons why such a revised view may not be justified.

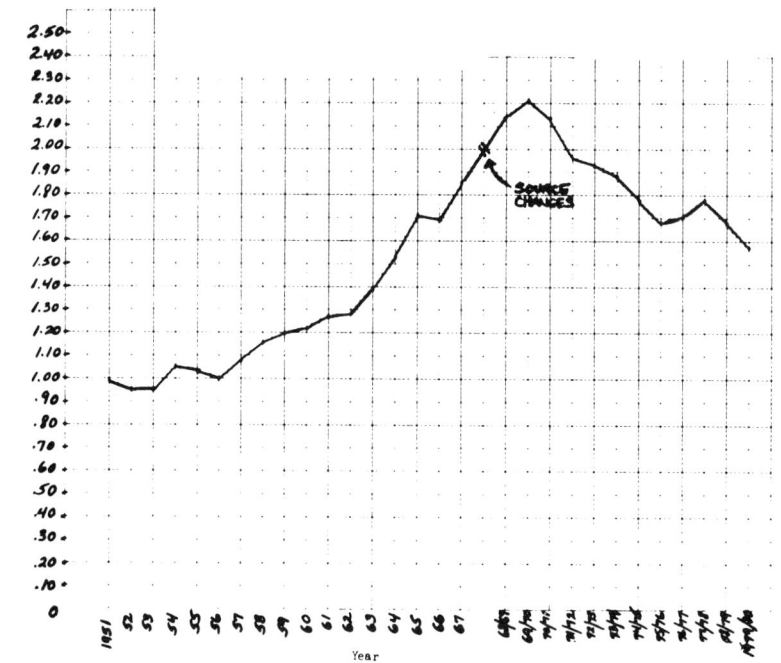

FIG. 3. Total expenditures per volume held, median university library, 1951-1980, in constant dollars (source: see Appendix A).

First, the suspension of the cost disease occurs, apparently, not because inflation in some way increases the technological efficiency of conventional library operations, but because the financial stringency which accompanies the inflation imposes painful and much-regretted economies upon the libraries. In such circumstances, if it turns out that electronic operation is less expensive, then the motivation for its adoption should surely be enhanced and certainly not reduced. The suspension of the cost disease during inflation is no reprieve from pressures for the libraries to economize. The second reason for this conclusion is related to the sheer magnitude of the decrease in computer hardware costs. Even if the cost disease for conventional library operation is halted, if hardware costs are dropping at 25 percent per year, then the date at which the cost superiority of electronic library operation occurs would seem merely to be postponed for a few years.*

There can be no doubt, then, that computers and electronics generally will play a role in the libraries of the future. But the transformation of the libraries into futuristic automated institutions has not occurred at the pace that might have been expected back in the sixties. In the next section, we will look at what libraries have actually done to computerize their operations.

5. How Libraries Have Automated

Certainly few, if any, major libraries are still run as they were in the 1950s, essentially as handicraft enterprises. The trauma of the transformation to computerized record keeping, circulation procedures, and the like has achieved the status of a "shared experience." But, by and large, the changes have been fairly conservative in character. The bulk of the library computerization process that has occurred so far has not radically transformed library services, but has enabled libraries to do basically what they always did, albeit more efficiently and less labor-intensively than before. Cataloguing procedures, circulation techniques, and record keeping, rather than the form of the reading matter and the place and manner of its delivery, are the items that have been primarily affected.

Automated systems are still mainly the preserve of large libraries with big holdings and enormous clerical tasks, or very

---

*Our earlier hypothetical extrapolation (see Section 3, second footnote) enables us to illustrate the point. It will be recalled that we started from the assumption that electronic operation is initially ten times as costly as conventional operation. We calculated that with the cost disease raising conventional library costs as it did before the onset of inflation, in only nine years the costs of electronic operation will have become lower than conventional costs. But even if the cost disease is suspended completely, the same sort of calculation shows that the catchup period is extended only to 11 years.

innovative, technical-oriented libraries, but more and more libraries are installing computerized systems.* Automated circulation is a particularly active area. The development of low cost minicomputers, microprocessors, and "light pens" able to read and transmit data from bar-coded labels has spurred the adoption of these systems. The typical online inventory circulation system provides instant access to a database of library holdings and can provide patron receipts, bibliographies, print out a variety of statistical and managerial reports, trap delinquent borrowers, compute fines, and determine book and patron status. Minimum costs today for such systems are high, but the development of microcomputers is predicted by some observers to reduce costs dramatically, and system sharing and increased vendor competition have helped make these systems accessible to smaller libraries.

Another significant development in library automation in the last ten years has been the emergence of online bibliographic utilities --organizations that maintain large online bibliographic databases and provide customer libraries with various cataloguing-related services and products. The groundbreaking and still dominant online utility is OCLC, Inc. (formerly Ohio College Library Center). Under the aegis of OCLC, more than 2000 libraries interact daily with more than five and a half million records. There are now a number of utilities besides OCLC, including RLIN (owned and managed by the Research Libraries Group), geared to large academic research libraries, UTLAS (University of Toronto Library Automation Systems), serving Canadian libraries, and WLN (Washington Library Network), a Pacific Northwest regional utility.

Other developments in library automation include computerized ordering and receipt of materials, payment systems, search techniques, and theft detection. Some particularly innovative libraries around the country are trying out video techniques, one of the newer areas of library automation. Video disks have tremendous potential for low cost storage and retrieval of information, and may some day replace microfilm and microfiche. The optical disk may represent the most significant electronic breakthrough for libraries (Kubitz [9]).

In investigating how and why libraries have automated their operations, we found that the motivation was often not financial but service-oriented and designed to obtain better control over the library collection. According to Bahr [12] only a few libraries can justify automation of circulation on the basis of cost alone. Apparently, some libraries have saved money by automating (see, for example, Druschel,[13] Berger and Cerutti,[14] and Saffady [15]), some have spent more (see, for example, Mosley [16]), and some

---
*Apparently, a rule of thumb for adopting automated circulation systems is that libraries with fewer than 200,000 transactions per year can easily handle their workload manually; for larger libraries it is more efficient and economical to automate.

have spent about the same for an automated system as for a manual system (see Frohmberg and Moffett [17]). A Mitre study of 193 public libraries reported that one third of the libraries had found automated circulation to be less expensive than a manual system, one third found it more expensive, and one third found the cost to be the same (Simpson [18]). In 1979 the Association of Research Libraries reported that:

> In general, while the promises and potentials of automation are high, it seems that automation has not had as much impact upon library procedures and performance as was predicted in the 1960's. Only a few librarians report having truly integrated multifunctional systems and there is little evidence that automation has resulted in large-scale redefinition of library tasks. However, academic libraries have benefitted from the use of automated systems. Some of these have been economic but the most important have been performance-based. (ARL Statistics, [19] p. 114)

Thus, the switch to automated libraries so far has not brought with it enormous cost savings and some observers are quick to point out the problems. Mick [20] contends that:

> ... computer hardware and software vendors offer the seductive temptations of reduced labor costs and increased production through automation, but although system performance may improve, overall costs rarely go down. (p. 37)

Price [21] is also skeptical:

> In the halcyon days of the early 1960s there was a plethora of promises about the marvelous things computers could do for libraries--and everybody else, for that matter. Unfortunately, performance seldom, if ever, lived up to the promises. Tickets for the automation bandwagon command a high price, and all too many found themselves saddled with ill-conceived and poorly planned automation, which, contrary to the promises, increased costs, degraded performance, and generally caused problems. (p. 84)

Veaner, [22] too, claims automation has failed to achieve the cost advantages that were promised:

> With automation we have still failed to realize significant staff savings (especially in cataloging) ... as computers and systems become more sophisticated, they require an ever increasing staff of highly sophisticated and expensive software people for maintenance and development. The rise of this personnel component of the computer far offsets any personnel savings in actual library

operations.... For every decline in [computer] hardware costs, there appears to be a correspondingly greater increase in the cost of staff required to support that hardware.... (p. 6)

6. Electronic Library Operation: The Paradox of Increasing Costs

Clearly, electronic library operation has not marched rapidly toward overwhelming cost superiority. This has been so despite the continued decline in the cost of electronic components at a rate of perhaps 25 percent per year. As we will see, the explanation for this curious behavior sheds quite a different light on our general subject.

Paradoxically, the extraordinary rate of technological progress in the field of electronics, and the probability that this rate of progress will continue, implies that the remarkable decline in computation costs is likely to "self-destruct," conceivably leaving this activity vulnerable to the cost disease. How is this possible? The answer lies in the labor component of electronic operations.

Computer hardware (the mechanical, magnetic, and electronic designs, structures, and devices of a computer) is only one component of an automated system. Also required is the human labor devoted to operation, creation of software (the programs and data), and the performance of other tasks, including those peculiar to the operation of a library. In the early days of automation, computer hardware was the relatively expensive component and dominated the entire cost structure. But as hardware costs have fallen dramatically, they have assumed less and less significance in the total, and software (i.e., labor) costs are becoming more important.

Dramatic evidence of this phenomenon is available. For example, Kubitz [9] reports "the major factor in the decreasing cost of computing is the falling cost of the electronics. To use a computer, however, it must be programmed. The cost of software ... has been increasing. In 1973 software represented 5 percent of the microprocessor system cost; in 1978 this increased to 80 percent ..." (p. 143). Schindler [23] also writes, "Having risen from 50 percent of total system development cost in 1975 to 80 percent this year, software is expected to exceed 90 percent by 1980" (p. 88). There is some dispute about the prospects for the software-hardware cost ratio, as we will see in a moment. But we may note first that if those figures are roughly correct, they have profound implications for the likely course of computer costs. Accepting the ratio of cost shares as 90 percent software to 10 percent hardware for the sake of argument, assume that in a year real labor costs rise 5 percent, while real hardware costs fall 25 percent. Then, a computer operation which costs $100 ($10 in hardware and $90 in software) in 1981, will rise to $102 ($10--25 percent plus $90 + 5 percent) in 1982 (in constant dollars). That is, while the same spectacular rate of cost decrease may continue to apply to the hardware, that very process will have reduced the share of total cost to which

APPENDIX A. Total Operating Expenditures, Median ARL Library, 1951-1980, in Current and Constant Dollars; and Total Operating Expenditures Per Volume Held.

Year	Total expenditures, median university library, current dollars[a] (1)	GNP implicit price deflator (1972 = 100)[b] (2)	Total expenditures in constant dollars; [(1) ÷ (2)] (3)	Volumes held, median university library[a] (4)	Expenditures per volume held, in constant dollars [(3) ÷ (4)] (5)
1951	$ 350,869	57.27	$ 612,657	615,963	$0.99
1952	354,322	58.00	610,900	642,154	0.95
1953	370,446	58.88	629,154	664,496	0.95
1954	434,652	59.69	728,182	691,752	1.05
1955	458,160	60.98	751,328	732,268	1.03
1956	476,543	62.90	757,620	758,568	1.00
1957	563,249	65.02	866,270	804,577	1.08
1958	633,511	66.06	958,993	824,545	1.16
1959	698,148	67.52	1,033,986	862,921	1.20
1960	767,104	68.67	1,117,087	917,256	1.22
1961	849,988	69.28	1,226,887	965,131	1.27
1962	931,653	70.55	1,320,557	1,031,781	1.28
1963	1,072,618	71.59	1,498,279	1,080,902	1.39

1964	1,214,947	72.71	1,670,948	1,091,396	1.53
1965	1,455,411	74.32	1,958,303	1,146,552	1.71
1966	1,582,758	76.76	2,061,956	1,219,432	1.69
1967	1,871,480	79.02	2,368,362	1,277,422	1.85
1968/1969	2,293,112	84.64[c]	2,709,253	1,268,159	2.14
1969/1970	2,698,072	89.04	3,030,179	1,370,902	2.21
1970/1971	2,776,105	93.69	2,963,075	1,390,167	2.13
1971/1972	2,855,735	98.01	2,913,717	1,486,412	1.96
1972/1973	3,026,243	102.96	2,939,241	1,522,964	1.93
1973/1974	3,243,492	111.16	2,917,858	1,553,192	1.88
1974/1975	3,366,697	121.83	2,763,438	1,549,589	1.78
1975/1976	3,490,754	130.56	2,673,678	1,592,582	1.68
1976/1977	3,863,299	137.58	2,808,038	1,656,275	1.70
1977/1978	4,467,578	146.67	3,046,006	1,707,493	1.78
1978/1979	4,605,041	157.41	2,925,507	1,741,760	1.68
1979/1980	4,783,864	170.06	2,813,044	1,792,048	1.57

[a]Sources, 1951-1967: see ref. [26]; 1968/1969-1979/1980: see ref. [19].
[b]Sources, 1951-1973: see ref. [27]; 1974-1980: see ref. [28].
[c]In column (2) starting with 1968/1969, the implicit price deflator is calculated by averaging one year and the next to accomodate data change to academic year figures, e.g., 1968/1969 is calculated by averaging the GNP implicit price deflators for 1968 and 1969.

these savings apply to a very small proportion of the whole. As a
result, the component of the cost which is subject to the cost disease
will take over, and computation cost, instead of continuing to fall,
will actually begin to rise, even in constant dollars. We call such
an activity <u>asymptotically stagnant</u> because it is characterized by
initially spectacular cost decreases, which automatically extinguish
themselves because the component of cost which manifests the rising
efficiency to which the savings are attributable necessarily soon
accounts for only a small part of the total cost. The more spectacular
its initial cost performance, the sooner that felicitous state
must come to an end.

Now the future is yet to determine whether the field of electronics
itself is really an asymptotically stagnant activity. Computers
are now being designed to take over a considerable portion of
the task of software creation, with the job becoming progressively
easier and less time consuming. There are those who suggest (see,
for example, Schindler [23] and Spencer [24]) that such changes may
even be able to reverse the trend in the share of software costs.
Not all observers agree with this assessment (see, for example,
Heines [25] and Kubitz [9]), but if it does transpire that software
costs can be reduced and held to anything like their initial share of
the total, the cost per unit of computation may be able to resume
its downward march.

Casual observation suggests, however, that no such remission
can be expected for electronic library operation. This is so
because even in the most sophisticated of automated libraries there
are associated labor-intensive activities which do not seem susceptible
to any considerable retrenchment. Some conventional books
and other physically printed or written items will continue to be
held in the electronic library, and these must be handled along
more or less conventional lines. Librarians will have to be available
to make decisions and to disseminate information too unstandardized
for computers to handle. Tasks as mundane as repair and
building maintenance do not seem about to be eliminated. Automation
may reduce these residual labor costs somewhat, but it seems
inconceivable that there will not be a substantial residue of labor-intensive
activities which strongly resists a steady rate of cost reduction,
and this means that eventually this component of library
cost must increase to a significant proportion of the whole. With
that, the electronic library, like the conventional library, becomes
fully vulnerable to the symptoms of the cost disease.

Acknowledgment

The authors are extremely grateful to the Division of Information
Science and Technology of the National Science Foundation whose
Grant No. IST 79 15235 made possible the writing of this paper.

APPENDIX B. U.S. College and University Libraries, Total Operating Expenditures per Student Served, 1967-1981 (Current and Constant Dollars).

Year	(1) Current dollars[a]	(2) GNP Deflator (1972 = 100)[b]	(3) Constant dollars[c]
Fall 1967	$ 59.29	79.02	$75.03
Fall 1968	69.86	82.57	84.60
Fall 1969	74.95	86.72	86.42
Fall 1970	81.25	91.36	88.93
Fall 1971	89.88	96.02	93.60
Fall 1972	94.76	100.00	94.76
Fall 1973	89.38	105.92	84.38
Fall 1974	93.24	116.41	80.09
Fall 1975	97.50	127.25	76.62
Fall 1976	102.60	133.88	76.63
Fall 1977	115.92	141.29	82.04
Fall 1978	121.05	152.05	79.61
Fall 1979	125.32	162.77	76.99
Fall 1980	125.46 (estimate)	177.36	70.73
Fall 1981	131.85 (estimate)	191.17 (2nd Quarter)	68.97

[a] Sources for 1967-1976 total operating expenditures per student and number of students served, 1977 and 1978, see ref. [29]. Sources for 1977-1981 total operating expenditures, see ref. [30]. Sources for number of students served, 1979-1981, see ref. [31].

[b] Sources for 1951-1981, se refs. [27] and [28].

[c] (1) ÷ (2).

References

1. Kleiman, D. "Futuristic library does away with books." The New York Times, October 21, 1980; C6 and C1.
2. Baumol, W.J.; Marcus, M. Economics of Academic Libraries. Washington, DC: American Council on Education; 1973.
3. White, L.J. "Is productivity stagnant in public libraries? Some evidence for public libraries." New York University Graduate School of Public Administration, 1978, unpublished.
4. Drake, M.A. "Academic research libraries: A study of growth." Purdue University, West Lafayette, IN; 1977.
5. De Gennaro, R. "Austerity, technology, and resource sharing: Research libraries face the future." Library Journal. 100(10):917-923; 1975.
6. Lipson, J.I. "Technology and science education: The next 10 years." Computer. 13(7):23-28; 1980.
7. Triebwasser, S. "Impact of semiconductor microelectronics." Computer Technology: Status, Limits, Alternatives. New

York: Institute of Electrical and Electronics Engineers, Inc.; 1978: 176-177.
8. Ferreira, J.; Nilles, J.M. "Five year planning for data communications." Datamation. 22(10):51-57; 1976.
9. Kubitz, W.J. "Computer technology, A forecast for the future." In F. Wilfrid Lancaster, Ed., Proceedings of the 1979 Clinic on Library Applications of Data Processing. The Role of the Library in an Electronic Society. Urbana-Champaign, IL: University of Illinois Graduate School of Library Science; 1980; 135-161.
10. Burns, C. "The evolution of office information systems." Datamation. 23(4):60-64; 1977.
11. Baumol, W.J.; Bowen, W.G. Performing Arts: The Economic Dilemma. New York: Twentieth Century Fund; 1966.
12. Bahr, A.H. Automated Library Circulation Systems, 1979-80, 2nd ed. White Plains, NY: Knowledge Industry Publications; 1979.
13. Druschel, J. "Costs analysis of an automated and manual cataloging and book processing system." Journal of Library Automation. 14(1):24-49; 1981.
14. Berger, P.W.; Cerutti, E. "The management of online reference search services in federal libraries." Science and Technology Libraries. 1(1):81-107; 1980.
15. Saffady, W. "The economics of online bibliographic searching: costs and cost justifications." Library Technology Reports. 15:567-653; 1979.
16. Mosley, I.J. "Cost effectiveness analysis of the automation of a circulation system." Journal of Library Automation. 10(3):240-254; 1977.
17. Frohmberg, K.A.; Moffett, W.A. "Research on the impact of a computerized circulation system on the performance of a large college library, Part 1: The main library." National Science Foundation Grant 78-10821, Oberlin College, Oberlin, OH; April 1981.
18. Simpson, G.; et al. Automated Circulation Systems in Public Libraries. McLean, VA: The Mitre Corporation; 1978.
19. ARL Statistics. Washington, DC: Association of Research Libraries, various years.
20. Mick, C.K. "Cost analysis of information systems and services." Annual Review of Information Science and Technology. 14:37-64; 1979.
21. Price, D.S. "Cost analysis and reporting as a basis for decisions." In J.L. Divilbiss, Ed., Proceedings of the 1976 Clinic on Library Applications of Data Processing: The Economics of Library Automation. Champaign, IL: University of Illinois; 1977.
22. Veaner, A.B. "What hath technology wrought?" In F.W. Lancaster, Ed., Problems and Failures in Library Automation: Proceedings of the 1978 Clinic on Library Applications of Data Processing. Urbana-Champaign, IL: University of Illinois Graduate School of Library Science; 1979.
23. Schindler, M. "Computers, big and small, still spreading as software grows." Electronic Design. 27(1):88; 1979.

24. Spencer, Jr., R. F. "VLSI and minicomputers." Computer Technology: Status, Limits, Alternatives. New York: Institute of Electrical and Electronics Engineers, Inc.; 1978: 13-25.
25. Heines, J. M. "Courseware development and the NSF." Computer. 13(7):31-34; 1980.
26. Dunn, O. C.; Seibert, W. F.; Scheuneman, J. A. The Past and Likely Future of 58 Research Libraries, 1951-1980: A Statistical Study of Growth and Change. West Lafayette, IN: Purdue University, University Libraries and Audio Visual Center; 1965 and 1968.
27. U.S. Dept. of Commerce, Bureau of Economic Analysis. The National Income and Products Accounts of the United States, 1929-1974, statistical tables, a supplement to Survey of Current Business.
28. U.S. Dept. of Commerce, Bureau of Economic Analysis. Survey of Current Business, various years.
29. Samore, T. "College and university library statistics: Analysis of NCES survey." The Bowker Annual of Library & Book Trade Information, 23rd ed. New York: R.R. Bowker; 1978: 243-248, 236; 25th ed. New York: R.R. Bowker; 1980: 372.
30. Samore, T. Personal correspondence, October 29, 1981.
31. Edles, N. Personal communication, November 4, 1981.
32. American Libraries. "Understanding the utilities." 11(5): 262-264; 1980.
33. Atkinson, H. "Personnel savings through computerized library systems." Library Trends. 23:587-594; 1975.
34. Abelson, P. H.; Hammond, A. L. "The electronics revolution." Science. 195(4283):1087-1091; 1977.
35. Caswell, H. L.; et al. "Basic technology." Computer. 11(9): 10-19; 1978.
36. Council on Library Resources, Inc. 24th Annual Report. Washington, DC; 1980.
37. Christian, R. The Electronic Library: Bibliographic Data Bases, 1978-79. White Plains, NY: Knowledge Industry Publications; 1978.
38. Cohen, J.; Leeson, K. W. "Sources and uses of funds of academic libraries." Library Trends. 28(1):25-46; 1979.
39. De Gennaro, R. "Escalating journal prices, time to fight back." American Libraries. 8(2):69-74; 1977.
40. Dowlin, K. E. "The electronic, eclectic library." Library Journal. 2265-2270; November 1, 1980.
41. Dunn, O. C.; Tolliver, D. L.; Drake, M. A. The Past and Likely Future of 58 Research Libraries, 1951-1980: A Statistical Study of Growth and Change. West Lafayette, IN: Purdue University, University Libraries and Audio Visual Center; 1973.
42. De Gennaro, R. "Research libraries enter the information age." Library Journal. 104(20):2405-2410; 1979.
43. Drake, M. A.; Olsen, H. A. "The economics of library innovation." Library Trends. 28(1):89-106; 1979.
44. Ferrell, T. "Libraries face up to the new technological imperatives." The New York Times. June 29, 1980; 20E.
45. Fiske, E. B. "Traditional library use threatened." The New York Times. August 12, 1980; C1 and C4.

46. Gorman, M. "Network!" American Libraries. 11(1):48; 1980.
47. Holton, W. C. "The large-scale integration of microelectronic circuits." Scientific American. 237(3):111; 1977.
48. King, D. W.; et al. "Statistical indicators of scientific and technical communication updated to 1975." The Information Age in Perspective: Proceedings of the ASIS Annual Meeting. 15:177-179; 1978.
49. Kennedy, R. A. "Bell Laboratories library network." April 15, 1980. (Based on a chapter in Industrial Information Systems, Jackson, E. B.; Jackson, R. L. Stroudsburg, PA: Dowden, Hutchinson, and Ross; 1978.)
50. Lancaster, F. W.; Drasgow, L. S.; Marks, E. B. "The role of the library in an electronic society." In F. W. Lancaster, Ed., Proceedings of the 1979 Clinic on Library Applications of Data Processing. Urbana-Champaign, IL: University of Illinois Graduate School of Library Science; 1980.
51. Lancaster, F. W. "Whither libraries? or, wither libraries." College and Research Libraries. 39(5):345-357; 1978.
52. Lancaster, F. W. "The dissemination of scientific and technical information: Toward a paperless society." University of Illinois Graduate School of Library Science Occasional Papers. 127; April 1977.
53. Markuson, B. E. "Granting amnesty and other fascinating aspects of automated circulation." American Libraries. 9(4):205-211; 1978.
54. McCarn, D. "Trends in information." Information Utilities. American Society for Information Science, 1974.
55. Mayo, J. S. "The Role of microelectronics in communication." Scientific American. 237(3):192 and 208; 1977.
56. Noyce, R. N. "Microelectronics." Scientific American. 237(3):63-69; 1977.
57. Nelson, B. R. "Implementation of on-line circulation at New York University." Journal of Library Automation. 12(3):219-232; 1979.
58. Oldham, W. G. "The fabrication of microelectronic circuits." Scientific American. 237(3):111; 1977.
59. Pobst Reed, M. J.; Vrooman, H. T. "Library automation." Annual Review of Information Science and Technology. 14; 1979.
60. Roistacher, R. C. "The virtual journal: Reaching the reader." In F. W. Lancaster, Ed., Proceedings of the 1979 Clinic on Library Applications of Data Processing. Urbana-Champaign, IL: University of Illinois Graduate School of Library Science; 1980.
61. Terman, L. M. "The Role of Microelectronics in data processing." Scientific American. 237(3):163; 1977.
62. Yencharis, L. "Technology survey predicts big jump for computer hardware and software." Electronic Design. 27:40 and 51; 1979.
63. Advanced Technology/Libraries. 10(4):2; 1981.

THEORY VS. PRACTICE IN LIBRARY MANAGEMENT*

Richard De Gennaro

In a memorable scene in the movie <u>Little Big Man</u>, Dustin Hoffman, in the title role, plays the part of a Western gunfighter. Little Big Man has built a great reputation as the fastest draw and the straightest shooter in the territory. The camera shows him drawing his guns and blazing away with astonishing speed and accuracy at rows of bottles and tin cans behind the ranch house. His only problem is that he has acquired all his skills as a gunfighter on that makeshift target range. He has never actually killed a man or even faced one in a real gunfight. The first time he goes eyeball to eyeball in the old saloon with a real live, mean, ready-to-kill gunslinger, our hero loses his nerve, is paralyzed with fright, and is unable to draw his guns. Fortunately, Little Big Man's opponent spares him--but that is not what usually happens in real life.

Little Big Man knew the theory and technique of gunfighting, but he lacked courage and experience, and without those essential qualities, his knowledge and skills were useless. Well, they were useless in a gunfight, but they would be useful to him as a consultant or teacher. If he applied himself to studying and researching the history and techniques of gunfighting, he could become an authority on the subject. That is something, but it is not the same as being a successful gunfighter.

What is true of gunfighting is equally true of other fields. Military theorists don't necessarily make good field generals. Political scientists are not necessarily good politicians, and few economists are millionaires. Management professors and management consultants are not necessarily good managers. Without belaboring the point, we need to remind ourselves from time to time that there is a big difference between theory and practice, between thought and action. One is not better or more important than the other, but they are different.

In an essay entitled "Leaders of Men," Woodrow Wilson wrote:

---
*Reprinted by permission of the author and publisher from <u>Library Journal,</u> 108:13 (July 1983) 1318-21. Published by R.R. Bowker Co. (a Xerox company). Copyright © 1983 by Xerox Corporation.

> Those only are leaders of men, in the general eye, who
> lead in action.... The men who act stand nearer to the
> mass of men than do the men who write; and it is at
> their hands that new thought gets its translation into the
> crude language of deeds....[1]

Wilson was discussing the nature of leadership and the differences between great literary and political figures, but he also gives us much insight into the nature of and differences between theorists and practitioners. He says theory is rational and elegant, but when practitioners apply it in the real world, it becomes crude and messy--and vital and effective. In Wilson's view, the true leader is the thinking person in action--and Wilson achieved that status himself, later in his life.

In a self-interview entitled "75 Years and Two Cents Worth" <u>American Libraries</u> editor, Art Plotnik, gives us another useful insight into the important differences between theory and practice and thought and action:

> If I've learned anything in 15 years of librarian watching,
> it's that the best judgements, the fairest policies, are
> made de facto by practicing librarians on the front lines.
> These are bright people; humanistic people. That's why
> they're in the field. They can handle such moral quandaries as when and when not to charge user fees, and do
> so more realistically than those in secondary librarianship.
> Secondary Librarianship?
> Yes, those having no direct contact with day-to-day library services are part of what I call secondary librarianship. That includes library journalists, ALA staff, NCLIS, the Council on Library Resources, U.S. Education Department, network staff, library educators, and members of a hundred other bureaus, agencies, and services. I believe most of us are dedicated, necessary elements of the profession; but the day we start thinking we know more about librarianship than those in primary service will be the day our usefullness ends.[2]

That is a perceptive and courageous observation. It could only be made by a secondary librarian who is confident of his own valuable contribution to librarianship.

Forcing theory into practice

The practice of librarianship, like the practice of business, used to be a very practical and pragmatic activity. There was a time when there were no library schools and no business schools, and beginners learned by doing on the job. Then came the library and business schools and beginners were given formal courses laced with potentially useful theory and practical skills; and they were better prepared in a shorter time. Then in the last 15 to 20 years another change began to occur. The business schools, with library schools right behind them, began to put increasing stress on operations research, new management systems based on quantitative analysis, and acronyms like PPBS (Planning, Programming, and Budgeting System) and ZBB (Zero-Base Budgeting) became buzz-words.

Along with these new quantitative systems came a rash of new systems and theories from the behavioral sciences. We had Management by Objective, new systems for participative management, and a host of others. It was frequently said and widely believed that these new management systems and theories were going to change management from an art to a science and usher in a new era when management could cease to be full of risk and uncertainty and organizations would work with mechanical and electronic precision. Theory was going to merge with and become practice.

It didn't happen that way. In libraries, the practitioners were either skeptical of the usefulness of these new systems and theories or they found them simply too complex and too costly to implement. Where they were implemented, they frequently did more harm than good. We librarians are a modest lot and we thought maybe the fault was in ourselves and not in the systems and theories. We were told and believed that these same systems and theories which came out of our most prestigious business schools, were working well in American business and industry, but they have not been working very well, as anyone knows who reads the papers these days. For example, the lead article in the Business section of the New York Times on May 30, 1982, "Management Gospel Gone Wrong," reported the new ideas of Robert Hays and William Abernathy, two professors at the Harvard Business School, on the real causes of the decline of American business. Hays and Abernathy wrote an all-time bestseller article in the Harvard Business Review entitled: "Managing Our Way to Economic Decline."[3]

Challenging the "B" schools

These two scholars are challenging what is taught in the best business schools, passed on by the most prestigious consultants, and practiced in our leading corporations. They are saying that we shouldn't be blaming excessive government regulations, greedy labor unions, the declining work ethic, the Japanese, or the energy crisis for the ills of American industry. Instead, they put the blame squarely on American management doctrine as it is being promulgated by the elite business schools. They say that American managers have lost sight of the basics and are neglecting production--the factory floor and the assembly line--in favor of finance and marketing. That, plus excessive management concern for short-term profits, goes far to explain the current decline of American business. The business schools, they argue, have imbued a generation of business leaders with the wrong ideas.

This serious indictment is causing a lot of soul-searching and debate among business leaders and the faculties of business schools. Many of them agree, but others say that the Hays-Abernathy view is too simplistic and is yet another false gospel coming from our most prestigious business school.

Hays and Abernathy are not the first nor the only ones questioning the "Gospel of Scientific Management" as preached by the business schools. In my own 1978 LJ article, "Library Administration and New Management Systems," I argued that management was an art, not a science, and that the new complex management systems were not working in business and would not work in libraries.[4]

Theodore Levitt, another Harvard Business School professor, published similar criticisms in a 1978 Fortune article, "A Heretical View of Management Science." The opening sentence reads: "There is only one way to manage anything, and that is to keep it simple." That sets the tone of the article and is, incidentally, the best piece of management advice around. If you add to that Bert Lance's dictum, "If it ain't broke, don't fix it" (which Levitt also cites), you have two commonsense rules of management that will carry you a long way.

The essence of Levitt's heretical view of management "science" is contained in this paragraph:

> Still, as a corporation gets better managed and more concerned with the quality and practice of management itself, its top people develop a powerful propensity to manage differently. They are encouraged in this by a rapidly expanding retinue of eager sycophants, equipped with new "scientific" tools and decision-making modes, who promise to free the manager from the inescapable uncertainties, risks, and traumas of running an enterprise. "Experts" trained to the teeth in the techniques (but not necessarily the practice) of management, are enlisted to do even better what people of native shrewdness, sound good sense, and abundant energy did quite beautifully before.[5]

Admiral Hyman G. Rickover is another articulate critic of the "management science" mystique. In a Columbia University address excerpted in the November 25, 1981 New York Times, (p. 23) he said:

> Our universities should emphasize the importance of a solid grounding in substantive learning and downgrade "management" science.
> What it takes to do a job will not be learned from management courses. It is principally a matter of experience, the proper attitude, and common sense--none of which can be taught in a classroom.
> I am not against business education. A knowledge of

accounting, finance, business law, and the like can be of value in a business environment. What I do believe is harmful is the impression often created by those who teach "management" that one will be able to manage any job simply by applying certain management techniques, together with some simple academic rules of how to manage people and situations.

Henry Minzberg is the author of The Nature of Managerial Work (Harper, 1973) and another all-time best selling article in the July-August 1975 issue of the Harvard Business Review entitled "The Manager's Job: Folklore and Fact." Like Rickover and Levitt, Minzberg concludes, from his studies of what managers actually do, that management, leadership, and entrepreneurship cannot be taught in the classroom any more than swimming can be learned by reading about it.

Library managing

My own experience as a manager on the job and in the classroom, as both a teacher and student, has convinced me that business and library schools cannot really teach students how to be managers. What they can and do teach are a variety of theories and insights about management along with a range of useful techniques and skills that are used largely by management teachers, consultants, specialists, and staff people who work for or around managers. What they teach is what some critics call "a bag of tricks." On the quantitative side, they range from decision theory to statistical and systems analysis, and to complex systems like Zero-Base Budgeting. On the behavioral side, they range from Management by Objective to the many versions of McGregor's Theory Y.

Managers are generalists

In the library environment, these theories and systems are still only of marginal usefulness. When they are used at all, it is more by people in staff positions, such as personnel and financial officers, and systems people, than by line managers. Even among staff people, the knowledge of and ability to use those theories and techniques is almost always less important for success than good judgment and common sense. With some jobs, for example, computer programmers and technicians, technical skills are of overriding importance, but this is not the case in most library jobs. Most managers are generalists. They may have come from the ranks of the specialists, but to succeed as managers, they must become generalists.

In that 1978 LJ article I said that the new management systems contained many useful concepts, ideas, and techniques, but as comprehensive systems they are all too theoretical, complex, and simplistic, to be applied successfully by ordinary library managers in the day-to-day work world. Few managers have the time or the specialized knowledge and skills required to make these systems work, and those that do can probably manage as well or better without them.

In the hands of ordinary managers (most of us), the quantitative systems can produce misleading and wrong solutions, while the behavioral systems can be used to manipulate and exploit people. The real danger with both types of systems is that they offer mechanistic formulas for dealing with complex realities. They keep us from managing in practical, realistic, and commonsense ways.

Peter Drucker says that the most important qualities a manager must possess are integrity of character, courage, and vision. These are not qualities a manager can acquire. Managers bring them to the job, and if they don't bring them, it will not take long for their people to discover it and they will not forgive the manager for it.[6]

Drucker says somewhere else that it is better to do the right thing than to do things right. He also says that Management by Objective works if you know what the objectives are, but 90 percent of the time you don't. To identify the right objectives, to know what the right thing to do is, and then to have the courage to decide to do it in the face of uncertainty, and have the trust and confidence of your people so they will follow you--that is what management and leadership are about. They depend on character, courage, and commitment, not on techniques and tools. To be a leader is to have a vision, a goal, and a determination to reach it.

The success or failure of a manager is decided not in the normal day-to-day operations of an enterprise, but during those rare times of crisis when critical decisions have to be made. If a manager in a time of crisis, lacks the courage to stand up for principles, or to make or stand by the hard decision, he or she will lose the trust of the staff and the right and ability to lead them.

Entrepreneurs & time servers

Just as management specialists are different from managers, so managers are different from entrepreneurs. There are not many entrepreneurs in the library field, but there are some. I think of people like Fred Kilgour, the founder of OCLC, and Eugene Garfield, the founder of the Institute for Scientific Information, and some library and network directors who behave more like entrepreneurs than managers or administrators. Good entrepreneurs are usually poor managers and vice versa. The personal qualities required to found a new enterprise or chart a major new direction are very different from those required to manage a stable organization. Entrepreneurs are constantly experimenting and trying new ideas. They have healthy egos, enormous self-confidence, and a single-minded determination to succeed. They are risk takers, even gamblers.

Most truly good managers possess to some degree many of the qualities of successful entrepreneurs, but they are usually more practical and prudent. They know what can and cannot be done. Entrepreneurs don't recognize the traditional boundaries and limitations. They don't know that the thing they are trying to do can't be done, the way the conventional managers do, so they just go ahead. Sometimes they succeed. Entrepreneurs make the significant advances. If library and business schools have failed to teach practical management, they have not even tried to teach entrepreneurship.

At the other end of the management spectrum are the time servers. Their idea of success is to maintain a stable organization and survive until they retire. At their best, they keep the organizational machine oiled and running. At their worst, they create backlogs of problems and unfinished business.

The need to reexamine

If the management professors and business leaders who invented those dubious and sometimes troublesome scientific management theories and systems are beginning to question their validity and applicability in the practical world of business, then we librarians ought to begin questioning their use in the world of libraries. It is time for a thorough reexamination of all the theories, assumptions, and received ideas that have shaped the way we have thought about and managed libraries in the last several decades.

We need to reexamine our ideas about what the real needs of our users are and what it takes to satisfy them. Contrary to the folklore of our profession, the real needs of all but a small fraction of library users are not for enormous and comprehensive collections of books and journals. The goal of amassing large collections comes from an earlier time when books and journals were fewer in number and less expensive. In the last two decades, the number of titles being published has exploded along with their prices. The task for libraries, now and in the coming years, is to learn to be selective and to build lean, quality collections from the mass of printed and other materials that are gushing forth from the world's publishers. We also need to further develop our capabilities to gain effective access to materials that we do not and cannot have in our local collections as well as to resources in electronic form.

Just as American business is going back to basics, rediscovering the importance of the factory floor and production, so we librarians need to go back to basics and rediscover that our main function is serving users, not building collections. It is not our main function to devise and implement new cataloging codes, or online catalogs, or national networks. Like collection building, these are all means of serving users and not ends in themselves. We have sometimes forgotten this in the excitement of implementing new technology in this time of rapid change.

There is no necessary or significant correlation between the size of a library's collections, staff, or expenditures and the effectiveness of its services or the degree of user satisfaction. Some of our largest libraries are the most difficult and frustrating to use. In library matters, we tend to equate quantity with quality. The bigger the numbers, the better the library. In the past we have accepted that premise without much question. Now, diminishing financial support and expanding technology are forcing us to put quality and user satisfaction ahead of growth and large numbers as the goal of library management.

It's the results that count

During the last two decades the management scientists have dominated the management scene. They have had their chance to show what they can do and it has not been much. Now it is time for the practicing general managers to reassert their primacy in the art of management. The management scientists are Woodrow Wilson's thinkers and writers. The general managers are Wilson's "men of action." They have been very busy managing their companies and their libraries. They have neither the time nor the aptitude to write and theorize about management. They express themselves in action.

During these last two decades the people of action, the managers, have allowed themselves to be intimidated and upstaged by the people who write--by the theoreticians. There has been such a tremendous increase in the amount of theory and writing about management that it tends to overshadow and diminish the importance of practice. Theory is supposed to improve practice. The test of the value of a theory or a technique is how well it can be applied by practitioners. Sometimes we say something is good in theory, but bad in practice. That cannot be. If it is bad in practice, it can't be good in theory.

From the time of Machiavelli, managers have used and appreciated the theories and advice that was offered to them by the thinkers and writers. In recent years many new and inexperienced managers have relied too heavily on managing by the book and have damaged their organizations in the process. Practical managers cannot avoid the uncertainties and risks inherent in their jobs by using or misusing these faddish scientific management tools.

Yes, managers learn from theory as well as from experience. The more experienced a manager is the more he or she can learn from theory. Experience teaches managers when (and when not) and how to use the growing variety of theories and techniques that are available to them. But theories and techniques have no value unless and until they are used to enhance and facilitate practice. In the end it is the results that count.

I do not want to disparage the management courses that are offered at library and business schools, and particularly not the people who are teaching them. My point is that there is a big difference between theory and practice in management, between the textbook professional manager and the practical general manager, and between the specialist technician and the generalist. What is being taught in management courses is not general management, but the theories and techniques that are used by management specialists. These management specialists serve useful, and sometimes not so useful purposes, but what they do is not management and should not be confused with it. Practical management is far more human, subtle, and complex than the tools and techniques of management science.

References

1. Wilson, Woodrow. Leaders of Men. Ed. by T.H. Vail Motter. Princeton Univ. Pr., 1952, p. 19.
2. Plotnik, Art. "75 Years and Two Cents Worth," American Libraries, January 1982, p. 6.
3. Abernathy, William & Robert Hays. "Managing Our Way to Decline," Harvard Business Review, July-August 1980.
4. De Gennaro, Richard. "Library Administration and New Management Systems," LJ, December 15, 1978, p. 2477-82.
5. Levitt, Theodore. "A Heretical View of Management Science," Fortune, December 18, 1978, p. 50.
6. Drucker, Peter. Management. Harper, 1974, p. 462.

THE EROSION OF LIBRARY EDUCATION*

Wm. R. Eshelman

Just as war is too serious a matter to be left to the military, library education is too important to be left to the educators. Yet that is just what has happened in the past two decades, and with disastrous results. The American Library Association's Committee on Accreditation (COA) allowed the number of schools with accredited programs to increase from 33 in 1965 to 69 now, producing a glut of disappointed graduates, spreading competent faculty too thinly across the nation, and creating a spurious demand for faculty with Ph.D. degrees.

The COA response was that the limitation of programs is outside its scope and beyond its authority, ignoring the plain fact that by more rigorous interpretation of the Standards it could reject new programs unless they clearly measured up to the average program, rather than the weakest.

Fairness demands that the library practitioners accept a share of the blame since, for the most part, they stood by and grumbled while COA "stayed the course." Working librarians put their faith in the COA, assuming that its membership would be kept in balance, and that it would vigorously enforce "The Standards for Accreditation" adopted by the ALA Council in 1972.

Lopsided COA

From time to time the membership of COA has had the semblance of balance, but the 1982/83 COA is the most lopsided in many years. The current ALA President, Carol Nemeyer, was faced with five vacancies to fill in order to keep the 12-member COA at full strength. Her new appointees were a library school dean and two library school faculty members, plus the two mandated public members. One of the public members, a sociologist, was for many years a member of the faculty of the Graduate Library School at the University of Chicago.

---

*Reprinted by permission of the author and publisher from Library Journal, 108:13 (July 1983) 1309-12. Published by R.R. Bowker Co. (a Xerox company). Copyright © 1983 by Xerox Corporation.

When these new members are added to the continuing members COA has the following composition: two library school deans, one former dean, and one associate dean; two professors of library science; two academic librarians; one library trustee; the two public members; and, as chair, a former academic librarian now a university vice chancellor. There are, thus, only two working librarians currently on the COA, both of whom are from academic libraries.

Analyzing the experience of the library educators on the committee shows that two once worked in special libraries, one in an academic and another in a public library, and one has had both public and academic library experience. Of the two deans, one has neither library experience nor a library degree.

An accreditation committee so overbalanced on the side of library educators--particularly deans or directors--is subject to charges of logrolling, conflict of interest, and unfair competition. While members of COA do abstain from voting on the schools with which they are now affiliated, other allegiances are not taken into account. For example they continue to vote on schools where they once held appointments, or on those with which they may be negotiating for a new position.

With falling enrollments library educators stand to benefit from fewer schools in their own geographic area. Deans and directors are particularly cognizant of this competitive reality. Another argument against a dean or director serving on COA or on a site visit team is the subtle influence they could exert on those faculty members serving with them. Such faculty persons cannot but be aware that one day in the future they might want to join the faculty of that dean's school.

A new COA

To avoid these problems, and to contribute to ending the erosion of library education, COA needs a different composition. Seven of the 12 members should be working librarians, including one recent library school graduate; three should be library school faculty; and the two public members would complete the committee. The chair of the committee should always be a working librarian or a public member. Such a COA would be far less vulnerable to charges of conflict of interest, and more likely to make the hard decisions that our profession so desperately needs.

Proliferating programs

A glance at recent library history helps us to understand the task that the profession faces in restoring the library community to health. In 1965 the National Inventory of Library Needs called for 100,000 new librarians, to which the Special Libraries Association added its guesstimate of 18,000. This figure was based on the assumption that all libraries were to be brought up to "standard." It was not compiled by using the number of budgeted positions open, the number of retirements realistically anticipated, or the number of new positions soberly envisioned in approved long-range plans. It was a fantasy.

Those affluent years (which we are now paying for) saw new public library branches built, new campuses for burgeoning systems of higher education, and school libraries mandated in state after state. As enrollments rose, library educators pushed for the establishment of new library schools. A compliant COA gave its stamp of approval to some 30 new Master's degree programs.

The push for Ph.D.'s

Library directors, many of whom made up the ALA leadership, saw no harm in this proliferation, since the annual trek they had been making each spring to library schools in order to recruit new staff had lost all its charm. They longed for the days of an employer's market. As new library schools were established the demand for faculty members grew apace, but it became ever harder to appoint people who lacked the Ph.D. The state-supported universities, hungry for recognition, demanded this symbol of respectability. Federal dollars underwrote doctoral studies; by 1972 there were 19 library schools offering doctoral degrees. The number of Ph.D. and D.L.S. degrees conferred that year was 112, up from 17 awarded in 1968.

Reminiscent of Gresham's Law, the practitioner-professors, many of whom were successful in teaching from their experience in the field, were replaced by persons with new doctorates but with little or no library experience. The rationale for this practice, in the words of Russell Bidlack, is "that continuing research into library problems, along with frequent visitation of exemplary library programs, should enable the educator to keep abreast of issues and developments in librarianship regardless of recent work experience."

Applying the Standards

The appalling number of new graduate librarians who could not find positions was a problem that cried out for solution as the Seventies began. Calls for the ALA/COA to limit the number of library schools with accredited programs were answered with the assertion that the COA could only rule on whether a program proposed for accreditation met the Standards. It could not declare a moratorium on the accreditation of new programs, went the official COA line, much less disaccredit the weaker ones in schools already on the list. The COA did, however, direct each school to warn prospective students, early in the recruitment stage, of the depressed job market.

The COA has great latitude in interpreting the Standards; it has, on occasion, insisted on petty technicalities. Its denial of accreditation to the program at Dalhousie University was overturned on appeal by the ALA Executive Board. Library educators (long dominant on the COA and its site visit teams) were indignant at having their professional judgment reversed by "non-educators." They succeeded in getting the procedure amended so that appeals are now simply referred from the Executive Board to the COA for reconsideration. The COA's power was exerted on the minority-friendly library department at California State University/Fullerton. The mere threat that COA would interpret the Standards strictly was enough to convince an unsympathetic top academic administrator to jettison the program.

Notwithstanding COA's disavowals, it is possible to hold each school rigorously to the Standards. For example, the requirement in the Standards for "sustained productive scholarship" could, if interpreted strictly, winnow out a goodly number of the 69 programs now accredited. If it had wished, the COA certainly could have controlled the proliferation of the Seventies.

By 1974 the slackening of demand for librarians had become stagnation; retrenchment followed. Toward the end of the decade taxpayers in California passed the ill-advised Proposition 13 and soon after voters in Massachusetts passed a similar measure. Cities teetered on the brink of bankruptcy. OPEC put us all in early morning queues. Libraries were caught between decreased funding and increased costs. After the book budget had been slashed unmercifully, staffing came next. Then hours of service were cut due to lack of staff. Nearly one quarter of the 1979 library school graduates were unable to find jobs after four months of searching. Library schools at the University of Oregon and at Cal State/Fullerton were closed; Alabama A&M was accredited and almost immediately disaccredited.

The status of the schools

The current library school situation looks like this: The school at the State University of New York at Geneseo has announced its closing, the University of Mississippi's program is being phased out, and the program at the University of Minnesota has suspended admission of new students. The program at Emporia State University has been disaccredited and the programs at Western Michigan University and Rutgers-The State University of New Jersey are seeking to have their two-year "conditional" accreditations upgraded. Recently programs at the University of Missouri and Wayne State University were targeted for closing by their administrations, but won reprieves; San Jose State University is considering a plan to revert to an undergraduate program only, perhaps in information science rather than librarianship.

The University of Southern California's school lost enrollment

Table 1
Library School Enrollments, 1979 and 1981

	Full-time 1979	Full-time 1981	Part-time 1979	Part-time 1981	Total, F.T.E. 1979	Total, F.T.E. 1981
Alabama	36	41	36	18	56	50.16
Albany	70	67	98	71	113.97	89.44
Alberta		(60)		(21)		(65.6)
Arizona	69	65	41	41	86.9	85.5
Atlanta	32	37	11	8	37.34	41.67
Ball State		(2)		(23)		(26.49)[1]
B.Y.U.	5	6	71	63	38.67	38.42
British Col.	122	112	2	5	123.33	113.67
Buffalo	81	82	75	71	117.5	110
UC/Berkeley	100	76	56	58	137.25	116.5
U.C.L.A.	122	138	3	11	122.67	140.75
Case Western	85	52	71	79	105.5	86.58
Catholic	38	44	295	269	180	172.5
Chicago	40	30	27	19	54	40.33
Clarion	12	31	15	21	18.66	40.66
Columbia	78	50	87	101	119.75	97.67
Dalhousie	60	61	3	4	61	63
Denver	49	51	114	76	126.5	90.5
Drexel	54	54	192	184	157	158
Emory	38	33	20	26	46.33	48
Emporia		(33)		(78)		(59.1)
Florida State	91	87	66	87	(125.64)	
Geneseo	38	35	89	42	77.3	55
Hawaii	23	27	58	52	55.9	53.25
Illinois	94	70	36	35	112	87.5
Indiana	75	52	79	134	114.25	109.5
Iowa	52	43	16	15	59.11	49.44
Kent	45	42	206	194	104	81.79
Kentucky	65	48	55	81	83.7	102.27
Long Island	19	13	202	194	107	90
Louisiana	55	33	55	42	79	50.33
Maryland	115	61	130	195	201.7	169.33
McGill		(112)		(19)		(120.25)
Michigan	87	64	188	156	175.8	142.33
Minnesota	46	22	89	90	90.5	67
Mississippi		(15)	(54)		(38)	
Missouri	43	46	47	53	59	72.24
Montreal	147	158	22	12	154.33	162
No. Carolina	116	86	48	63	138.75	116.25
N.C. Central	25	31	27	30	41.75	50.25
No. Illinois	9	12	39	35	23.91	26.5
No. Texas	22	50	101	89	68.5	94.33
Oklahoma	22	23	37	62	42.3	66.38
Peabody	23	26	75	19	50.87	43.5
Pittsburgh	89	81	93	81	126.2	113.4
Pratt	54	51	97	133	115.2	128.3
Queens	12	12	61	68	42	43.75
Rhode Island	47	36	103	97	96.33	80.6
Rosary	53	53	162	162	125	125
Rutgers	82	53	194	189	183.75	154.1
St. John's	24	33	58	45	52.96	56.86
San Jose		(75)		(134)		
Simmons	67	57	360	260	187	147
So. Carolina	39	31	75	57	60.3	61.2
U.S.C.	43	20	76	70	100.1	45.5
So. Connecticut	53	42	149	105	120.98	87.87
So. Florida	19	31	151	121	80	83.75
So. Mississippi		(25)		(66)		(54.5)

	Full-time		Part-time		Total, F.T.E.	
	1979	1981	1979	1981	1979	1981
Syracuse	39	36	80	78	75.66	72.25
Tennessee	44	37	49	54	69	59
Texas	(68)		100	50	(123.67)	
Texas Women's	30	34	125	102	74.75	78.66
Toronto	172	165	53	19	189.6	171.2
Washington	76	99	29	17	88	108.4
Wayne State	89	28	62	100	119	68
West Michigan	39	30	194	55	110.3	56.44
West Ontario	146	133	87	82	167.75	153.5
Wisc/Madison	90	63	71	54	123.23	89.6
Wisc/Milwaukee	39	56	79	73	73.23	80
Total[2]	3649	3240	5390	4877	5922.38	5336.92

1. Clearly an error.
2. Schools reporting only one of the two years omitted in total; these figures are in parentheses.

Table 2
Changes in Full-Time Enrollment

Schools Gaining Most		Schools Losing Most	
North Texas	28	Wayne State	61
Washington	23	Maryland	54
Clarion	19	Case Western	33
Wisconsin/Milwaukee	17	Rutgers	29
U.C.L.A.	16	Columbia	28
South Florida	12	Wisconsin/Madison	27
Montreal	11	U.C./Berkeley	24
St. John's	9	Illinois	24
Rhode Island	7	Minnesota	24

so drastically that it could no longer justify the amount of space it occupied. Forced to give up its new building the USC program moved in with the School of Education. The Rutgers program has merged with school of Communication, and the newcomers have taken over the building designed for library education and ousted the library school faculty.

Undergoing somewhat less trauma are the following schools, each of which has recently appointed a new dean or director: Brigham Young, Hawaii, Long Island, McGill, Minnesota, Montréal, Oklahoma, Rosary, Eastern Michigan, and Wisconsin. Programs getting along with acting deans or directors are Ball State, Catholic, Case Western, Maryland, Mississippi, Northern Illinois, Rutgers, Southern Connecticut, Texas, and until recently, Washington. Louisiana State is actively seeking a new dean and the deans at Columbia and Michigan are about to retire. Full-scale internal reviews are underway at Texas, Emory, and Columbia.

Table 3

Changes in F.T.E. Enrollment

Schools Gaining Most		Schools Losing Most	
North Texas	25.83	U.S.C.	54.6
Oklahoma	24.08	Western Michigan	53.86
Clarion	22	Wayne State	51
Washington	20.4	Simmons	40
Kentucky	18.57	Wisconsin/Madison	33.63
U.C.L.A.	18.08	Michigan	33.47
Missouri	13.24	So. Connecticut	33.11
Pratt	13.1	Maryland	32.37

Marketplace winnowing

As everyone knew it must, given the vacuum of leadership in the library community, the winnowing of library schools is being done in response to market forces: i.e., falling enrollments. The decisions to continue, merge, or close library schools are being made based on economic factors, not on qualitative ones. From 1979 to 1981 in the Master's programs the full-time equivalent (F.T.E.) enrollment dropped 10 percent, as can be seen in the Table 1 summary. Although academic administrators rely on F.T.E. figures and monitor them closely, some critics argue that the drop in full-time enrollment is more significant. It is down 11 percent. Of the 60 schools that reported to the Association of American Library Schools in both those years, 34 show a decline in full-time enrollment, 23 a gain, and three held steady (see Table 2). Six schools had from two to 15 full-time students enrolled in 1981/82, surely too few to achieve the "critical mass" that Dean Herbert S. White, of Indiana University, among others, believes necessary. When part-time students are included (thus making up F.T.E.s), the picture is even bleaker: 38 schools declined, 20 gained, and one held steady (see Table 3).

Unplanned retrenchment

It is likely that six to eight library school programs will be phased out or relocated at the undergraduate level within two years. Such reductions might have side benefits if the best of the displaced faculty could be swiftly accommodated by the remaining schools. Tenure commitments, however, will probably preclude this. How much better for the profession to have controlled the growth. Given the fact of over-extension, can we now devise a planned retrenchment? Should Minnesota be strengthened so that the whole North Central part of the country will have one library program? (There are now none in Montana, Idaho, North and South Dakota, Nebraska, Nevada, and Oregon.) Why three programs in North Carolina and none in Virginia?

Shifting curricula

Over the past 30 years there has been growing acceptance of the Master's degree as the minimum professional qualification. A recent proposal by the Federal Office of Personnel Management (OPM) would recognize only two-year Master's degrees as elegible for entry at the GS-9 level. Seeming to concur in this estimate of the education required for librarians is the administration of San Jose State University (mentioned earlier) and some faculty at the University of California, Berkeley. A proposal is circulating at Berkeley that calls for shifting the coursework for librarianship to the undergraduate level but retaining the program for information scientists at the graduate level. By implication, the direction at the University of Southern California's School of Library and Information Management makes the same assumption: the MSLA program is focused on training library managers, not working librarians generally. The COA, of course, does not accredit undergraduate programs at all.

Responses to Conant

If there is to be any improvement in library education it will take strong leadership, backed by both practitioners and library educators dedicated to change. A recent example of the quality of leadership in library education is the response to the Conant Report. Three deans commented on the document in the Summer/Fall 1981 Journal of Education for Librarianship. In none of these critiques were the recommendations of Ralph Conant evaluated, discussed, or even taken seriously. The three critics simply damned the Report by dissecting its methodology (which I agree was flawed), but the intellectual issues were not addressed.

Among them are: shift some coursework to the undergraduate years to allow for specialization during the first graduate year and to provide a base for more advanced courses; mandate internship programs as part of the Master's degree requirements; require faculty to renew themselves by periodic return to actual, "hands-on" experience in libraries. We need teaching libraries, analogous to teaching hospitals, where internships could be offered and where faculty in search of renewal could work.

Benefits of certification

In his landmark study 50 years ago, C.C. Williamson wanted to urge a certification program for librarians in addition to his better-known recommendations for attaching library education to universities and requiring the bachelor's degree for admission. He was discouraged from giving this the emphasis he desired because as chair of an ALA committee to study certification he had watched the proposal be voted down--for political reasons. Except for the Medical Library Association and the American Association of Law Libraries, certification has not been debated widely by librarians. It is an idea whose time, I hope, has not passed.

One problem with establishing a certification program is where to locate the granting authority. It may be too late to get states to institute certification programs, or upgrade the ones they have. If so, ALA is the logical choice for a national certifying body, although its track record, sad to say, hardly recommends it.

The basis for granting a certificate also calls for careful study. An examination, whether written, oral, or both, would be required, and would have to be carefully designed. Something doubtless could be learned from the MLA and the AALL, as well as the (British) Library Association.

The benefits of certification would be many. Library schools could be judged on the performance of their graduates. Individuals who prefer to study on their own could take the examination without the necessity of enrolling in, and paying for, library school courses. Library technicians and other support staff could move into the professional ranks with any combination of experience, course work, or individual study, so long as the requirements of certification were met. At a stroke, some of the most vexing questions of affirmative action and equal opportunity would be answered.

Practitioner problems

It would be unfair to blame library educators, COA, or ALA for all the ills now afflicting library education. Working librarians have had the opportunity to help improve library education through their personal influence, recruiting likely candidates for library schools, and teaching courses, among other things. They could have worked through their state associations, through ALA's now defunct Library Education Division, or its replacements, the Library Education Assembly and the Standing Committee on Library Education. Too few were interested to keep LED alive, and the proportion of practitioners was never large.

Unless the library community can rise to this challenge, there is little hope that the erosion can be halted. When one lists all the twigs and branches of the field that are now self-supporting (The Special Libraries Association, The Music Library Association, The Medical Library Association, The American Association of Law Libraries, The American Society for Information Science, The Association of Research Libraries) and considers the growing trend toward the fragmentation of ALA into autonomous divisions, one cannot be sanguine. Are there leaders out there? Will anyone take up this challenge?

NATIONAL LIBRARY AND INFORMATION PLANNING*

Maurice B. Line

INTRODUCTION

This paper considers the functions of a national library and information system, the requirements that need to be fulfilled to perform each function, the organizations that may be involved, the links between functions, and the desirability of planning the system as a whole. The situation in the United Kingdom, in particular the role of the British Library, is used as an example.

The need for a national library and information system is fairly obvious. As societies develop, they depend increasingly on information and its transmission. Information is needed for, and affects, all aspects of a nation's life: cultural, educational, social, economic, scientific and technological. At the one extreme, medicine very obviously depends upon information and its availability; at the other extreme, leisure also generates information needs. It should not incidentally be supposed that leisure needs have an inferior status to research needs or management needs. Technological change, in particular the electronic revolution, is reducing the amount of work that needs to be done by human beings, at the same time as means of storage and dissemination, including computers and television, are undergoing rapid development and growth, aided by huge advances in telecommunications.

The whole range of the needs of society depends in some way upon information. Without information, not only can countries not develop, but they cannot stay developed: more than one developed country is in danger of sliding backwards in terms of the average standard of living of its people. If information is interpreted in its widest sense, to embrace, for example, education and telecommunications, it is estimated that in the most developed countries over half of the work-force is now involved in some way in information and its transmission.

It must be emphasized that the needs of society are for

---
*Reprinted by permission of the author from International Library Review, 15:3 (July 1983) 227-43. Copyright © 1983 by Academic Press Inc. (London) ltd.

information, not books in themselves. Books and other media of recorded knowledge may be prized and collected in their own right as beautiful or rare objects, but the reason books were created and are still produced is to record and disseminate knowledge. If they did not, books would merely become another kind of art object, and perform a much smaller rôle in society. With the wide and increasing range of media and means of dissemination, any national library and information system based on a concept of the book as a thing in itself is now hopelessly outdated. Any system must be concerned with all media of recorded knowledge, and must always bear in mind that the system exists primarily to serve people, who want information, for which the various media are only vehicles.

All this may seem very obvious, but if its implications are spelled out and acted upon they revolutionize the concept of a national library and information system. The change in thinking and in action that is required is so great that it is not surprising that most countries have tried to meet new needs and use new technologies as they appear, without integrating them into the existing system, while existing organizations, such as national libraries, have generally been unable to adapt themselves to the changes and challenges.

FUNCTIONS OF A NATIONAL LIBRARY AND INFORMATION SYSTEM

With these preliminaries, let us look at the major functions of a national library and information system. I have identified six functions: Collection of the nation's publications, Bibliographic control of the nation's publications, Bibliographic access to the world's literature, Access to documents, Repository and exchange of publications, and Information analysis and supply.

1 Collection of the Nation's Publications

The first function of a national library and information system is a traditional one, the collection of a nation's publications. The purpose of this is to ensure comprehensive collection and preservation of the nation's heritage--cultural, scientific, historical etc.--in the form of a permanent record of the nation's information products. This function is in a sense parallel to that of national galleries or science museums, but there is the major difference that products containing recorded knowledge contain information in a way that very few other artifacts do.

It follows from what was said earlier that a collection confined to printed documents alone is very incomplete. Some national libraries confine their collections to ordinary books and journals, and even for those they are far from complete. (In fact, it can safely be said that, even when legal deposit is effective, no national library contains every book or journal published in the country; many are printed and disseminated locally, or even privately.) In addition to ordinary books and journals, a national library should aim to have a comprehensive collection of official publications, both national and local; report literature, in so far as this is publicly available (some reports issued by industrial organizations have a restricted distribution); printed music; and ephemera, that very elusive but very important category of publications that are issued to serve a particular purpose at a particular time, often within a locality, and that form a most important source of history in the future. As well as all this printed material, there should be comprehensive national collections of sound recordings--discs, cassettes, etc.--and video recordings--films, videocassettes, videodiscs, etc. In future it seems likely that much material that is at present printed will be available only in some machine-readable form, so that the distinction between printed material and cassettes and discs will begin to disappear.

For this last reason, if for no other, the national library is the obvious place to collect recorded knowledge in all kinds of media. However, in some countries specialized archives already exist for the collection of specific categories of material such as films, sound recordings, etc., and if it is difficult to transfer these to the national library, as it may well be, some national co-ordination is necessary.

The collection of a nation's publications imposes several responsibilities on the collecting institution. Obviously the material collected has to be conserved. In the case of printed material this is a major problem, since most paper produced since the early part of the nineteenth century is extremely poor, and even under good conditions is likely to decay within a few decades, often in a much shorter time than that. Deacidification and various other means of preservation can be used, but these are expensive. Alternatively, the material may be microfilmed or stored on videodisc or some other medium. This too is very expensive, and while high quality microfilm now seems to have a long life, the same is not true of other kinds of storage such as videodiscs, which may have to be renewed at intervals of less than 10 years; the renewal may be a routine process, but it still requires organization and costs money. Only in the last decade or two have libraries really woken up to the full magnitude of the problem of conservation, both in terms of the material to be conserved and the cost and problems of conserving it.

The other major responsibility imposed on the collecting institutions is to make the material available. In some cases this may conflict with conservation, since heavy use causes wear and tear. There may also be some danger of loss or damage, though this can be minimized by appropriate supervision. A much more difficult problem is that of making forms other than the printed word available for consultation. There is now a great variety of media, each of which may require a certain type of machinery for use; even when media are of the same basic type, they may be produced by different manufacturers and require different equipment. The problem is even worse than this, because the rate of change is rapid and some media and machinery may become quickly out of date. Either a collection of superseded machinery has to be kept in full working order to make it possible to consult media produced a few years ago, or the material has to be transferred to a modern medium. Either of these alternatives involves substantial costs.

Availability may extend beyond consultation. It has been accepted within the last few years as a basic responsibility of each country that it must make its own publications available by loan or photocopy to remote users, including those in other countries. The reasoning behind this is that if an individual in a particular country is to have access to all the information he may want, and if much of this information has been produced in other countries, the only way he can be sure of getting it is from the country of origin: if, for example, Britain cannot make available British publications when wanted, no other country can be expected to do so. Without the full acceptance of this responsibility, publications cannot be universally available, and a basic requirement of the concept of Universal Availability of Publications [1] cannot be fulfilled. In practice, this means that at least one extra copy of each item should be collected by the national library or the specialized archive for the purpose of supplying remotely if and as required. Even though many items can be supplied as photocopies or microfilms, constant photocopying and filming can damage the original, and so a single copy is not enough.

2 Bibliographic Control of the Nation's Publications

If a nation has a responsibility for collecting and making available its own publications, it equally has a responsibility for making and supplying records of them. The parallel programme to Universal Availability of Publications is Universal Bibliographic Control, [2] which has as its aim comprehensive bibliographic recording of all publications in the world. Without such a record, access to publications is extremely difficult if not totally impossible. Ideally, the record should be in an internationally acceptable format, and a great deal of work has been done in recent years on agreeing standard entries and formats.

Records can be made available in more than one form. The traditional one is the printed national bibliography. Many countries have computerized their national bibliographies in the last decade or two, and computerized records can be used not only for printing, updating, cumulating and indexing national bibliographies, but for the direct supply of records, whether for consultation or for use by other libraries in cataloguing their own material. Ideally, all bibliographic records should be accessible on line from anywhere in the world, as well as published in national bibliographies. While internationally standard records can be agreed, and standard classifications for worldwide subject access, alphabetical subject indexing is of course language-dependent.

While many countries may appear to have adequate national bibliographies, most of them in fact are far from complete, for much the same reasons that national libraries do not have complete collections of the nation's publications. National bibliographies usually contain records of such books as the national library acquires; they do not normally include records of report literature and many official publications, certainly not ephemera. Some categories such as printed music may have separate bibliographies, but bibliographic coverage of many kinds of material is often extremely poor. This applies with particular force to media other than the printed word: very few countries have national bibliographies of recorded sound, films, etc.

There is another major gap in the national bibliographic control of most countries. While new journal titles may be recorded in the national bibliography, the articles in those journals are not normally indexed. One reason for this is that many of them are indexed in international systems (these are considered as part of the next function, below); but a great many of them are not, and the articles in them are totally inaccessible except by browsing through the journals in question. In a country that produces a lot of journals, the magnitude of the task of comprehensive indexing is obviously enormous, but the fact remains that without it national bibliographic coverage is incomplete.

It should be without saying that bibliographic control, however extensive in coverage, loses much of its value unless it is up to date, since libraries need access to records of new publications for selection and cataloguing purposes, and readers pursuing particular topics want to know the latest publications in the field. Computerized recording should make it easier to produce up to date records and provide access to them, but not a few national bibliographies are seriously in arrears, sometimes as much as three or four years. Speedy and imperfect coverage is better than an attempt at perfection if the latter means serious delay.

The obvious location for the bibliographic control of the nation's publications is with the organization that collects them. It is clearly very difficult to ensure comprehensive recording of publications in any other way, though records produced for other purposes by publishers, often before publication, can be a very useful means whereby the national library can find out what is being produced and try to acquire it. However, ultimately, coverage is dependent on legal deposit and its effectiveness.

3 Bibliographic Access to the World's Literature

While each country has a national responsibility to collect its own publications and control them bibliographically, obviously its people want to be informed of the publications of other countries. In no field of librarianship or information science has progress been so great as in bibliographic access to the world's literature. Much of the world's scientific literature, particularly articles in journals,

is covered by huge databases, available both in printed form, such
as the familiar Chemical Abstracts, and direct by computer from
the database, whether on-line or off-line. These databases are so
familiar that they do not need to be described. It should be noted
that while their coverage of journal articles is good, even that is
by no means comprehensive--for example, a recent study showed
that Japanese scientific literature was very poorly covered in the
major databases [3]--while books and report literature are often
not covered at all. The databases produced by the US National
Technical Information Service cover most American report literature and some reports issued by other countries, but apart from
that bibliographic control of report literature is poor. There are
virtually no international databases for books, and for access to
those one normally has to go to national bibliographies. The same
applies to official publications. The situation in the social sciences
and humanities is considerably worse than in science, at least for
journal articles and report literature.

Inadequate though coverage is, it is vastly better than it was
20 or 30 years ago, and access to it is both faster and more satisfactory, since a variety of access points can be used. From the
point of view of national library and information planning, some provision is needed for access to this wealth of bibliographic material.
So far as books are concerned, this can be done only by comprehensive collections of national bibliographies and other bibliographic
tools. Since few libraries have very good collections of these, a
special responsibility should be placed upon one or two libraries
for collecting them comprehensively and giving a service from them
as required.

Access to the computerized databases is another matter.
Access to database hosts such as Lockheed is possible from any
local library or information unit with the appropriate terminals and
communication links. Since these are not always available a national backstop or backstops are necessary, in the form of a centre
or centres with on-line access to all the significant databases.

There may be specialized information centres, whether government-sponsored or commercial; or there may be a single national centre, which could be the national library, though in that case
it needs to be a very different sort of national library from most of
those that currently exist. Some countries have set up national information centres separate from the national library, but this has
the result of entrenching the national library still further in its conventional activities.

As noted above, commercial bodies may be involved in providing access to bibliographic files; this is increasingly the case in
developed countries, where government-subsidized service may be
seen as unfairly competing with commercial interests. If access is
to be comprehensive, those files to which access is not commercially profitable are either left to the government to fund or are not
accessible at all. Whatever the solution adopted by each country,

what is necessary is to ensure that provision for access to bibliographic files exists and that it is available to all, by whatever means.

4 Access to Documents

If each country should ensure that adequate bibliographic access to the world's literature is provided, it is at least as important to provide adequate access to the documents that are covered by bibliographic control. To be able to retrieve bibliographic references and not to be able to supply the documents referred to is likely to cause great frustration to users. This obvious and simple fact has received surprisingly little attention in most countries, which seem to have assumed that the supply of documents will somehow occur -- after all, this is why libraries exist. However, particularly with the huge and increasing volume and cost of publications, no library, not even the largest, can approach self-sufficiency, so that some additional provision has to be made.

Nor can it be assumed that adequate additional provision can be provided simply by the customary solution of linking libraries together by means of union catalogues. The performance of decentralized interlending systems in most countries is distinctly poor: satisfaction rates rarely exceed 70 percent, even in the best systems, and supply times rarely are less than three weeks. Such performance is simply not satisfactory: why should a user, who may need a particular document urgently, have to wait three or more weeks for it, and quite possibly never obtain it at all, because his local library does not happen to have it?

Fortunately, there are alternatives to decentralization for document supply. For example, provision can be concentrated on a limited number of libraries with subject specialisms, as happens in the Federal Republic of Germany, or even on a single centre, as happens in the United Kingdom. In general, the fewer libraries that are involved in supplying documents, the more efficient the system is. Few countries can afford comprehensive national collections, and in most countries the best solution is likely to be a combination of centralized and decentralized provision; it is known that a high proportion of demand falls on quite a limited number of journal titles, and many countries should be able to afford a central collection of, say 6000 to 7000 journal titles.

Whatever the solution adopted, there must be some central focus for planning and organization. Even totally decentralized systems can be much more effective if they are planned and rationalized. For example, many countries have a multiplicity of union catalogues; these are expensive to construct, maintain and use, and many of them are uncompleted or out of date. Not only could their numbers be reduced (preferably to one or two union catalogues), but in most countries the number of libraries included in union catalogues could be much reduced, since the holdings of smaller libraries tend to duplicate those of larger libraries; the fewer libraries that are included in union catalogues, the more manageable and efficient they are.

If there is any centralization of provision, it is obviously sensible for the same organization that is responsible for supply also to be responsible for the planning and maintenance of union catalogues. The location of the national interlending centre may be with the national library, but since this has probably been planned for conservation and reference, it may be difficult for it to adjust its procedures to give a good interlending service as well. The interlending centre could be established as a separate division of the national library, or, less satisfactorily perhaps, as a totally separate entity.

As with bibliographic access, more than one centre may be involved. For example, there may be separate interlending centres for medicine, agriculture and so on. Since there is inevitably overlap between subjects, and since some subjects will almost certainly be neglected altogether, the net result is likely to be much less economic and efficient than a single centre.

Again as with bibliographic access, commercial organizations are beginning to play a much larger part than they have in the past. This is certainly happening in the United States, and as more and more journals are stored in machine-readable form as well as published conventionally, publishers are likely to seek a much greater rôle in document supply. The solution in some countries may turn out to be a combined service of public and private organizations. Whatever the place for commercial operation in document supply, the government still has a responsibility to ensure that an adequate system exists, and this requires planning. Because bibliographic control without document access is almost useless, the more closely the two systems are linked, the better; ideally a user should be able to conduct a bibliographic search, identify relevant references, see whether they are available locally, and if not immediately translate the references into requests to a document supply centre. These linking facilities already exist in some countries, and linked bibliographic control-document supply systems are likely to be a major development area in the next few years.

One barrier to efficient document supply systems in developing countries is the lack of good and reliable postal systems. Other barriers are the inability of librarians to release their documents from the premises, unavailability of photocopying machines or supplies, inability to pay for supplying or obtaining items, and so on. While some of these obstacles are indeed formidable, the object of ensuring that publications are available to anyone who wants them when and where he wants them is so very important that they should not inhibit efforts to improve matters.

5 Repository and Exchange of Publications

When libraries in so many countries find it hard to obtain even a modest number of publications for themselves, it may seem strange to set down the permanent retention of material as a major function. Nevertheless, it should receive attention in all countries, developing as well as developed. Books can be lost, wear out through constant use, or decay because of poor paper. It is a surprising fact that in developed countries quite ordinary works published two or three decades ago are now apparently unavailable in any library in the country, because there has been no means of ensuring that at least one copy was retained and preserved for future use. Without some plan for retention, availability may actually diminish rather than increase. Since all local libraries run out of space sooner or later, a great deal of material may come to be disposed of, and much of this will duplicate material withdrawn from other libraries. As a result, there will be a large number of duplicates which are not wanted, but which other libraries might well be interested in, whether in the country itself or in foreign countries. The exchange and distribution of duplicates has become a major activity in many parts of the world.

Ensuring the retention of material can take various forms. It is possible, for example, to distribute the responsibility for retention among numerous libraries according to subject, so that material withdrawn from other libraries is sent to the appropriate library. It is also possible to concentrate responsibility on a few major libraries, again according to subject. The simplest method, and the one that most easily avoids unnecessary duplication, is for a single national centre to collect the material.

Retention without subsequent availability is of very limited value. For this reason, the retention system should be very closely linked to the interlending system. For example, in a country like the Federal Republic of Germany where a limited number of specialized subject libraries carries the major burden of interlending, it would be sensible for all withdrawn material to be distributed among those libraries. Similarly, in the United Kingdom, where most document supply is done from a single national centre, it makes sense to send withdrawn material there rather than to distribute it among other libraries, particularly as they might not have space to house it and would not be so easily able to supply it later if wanted.

It follows from the previous paragraph that the responsibility for retention and distribution policies should be as far as possible the same as, or very closely linked with, that for national document supply systems. "As far as possible," because if commercial suppliers come to play a major role in document supply, they are hardly likely to be interested in receiving and storing very large amounts of withdrawn material, and in this case the library would have to seek a different solution. Again, the need for planning must be strongly emphasised. Without planning, there may be a great deal of very worthy activity, but at high cost and to little effect.

6 Information Analysis and Supply

Since, as stressed earlier, it is basically information that is needed, and books and other media are wanted because they are purveyors of information, in every country there should be provision for the direct supply of information. Not all users have the time or motivation to search out the relevant documents, and in any case it is often more efficient for trained information personnel to supply them with information than for them to search for themselves.

Some of the information that is needed is on a day-to-day basis and may be purely local. For example, every industry needs information on the costs and effectiveness of its operations, and this may require quite a complex system of technical as well as management information. This sort of information can only be provided within the organization itself, though it may be willing to release some of it for the benefit of other organizations. Where national provision comes in is in the supply of publicly available information. This may range from a straightforward chemical formula to a highly complex package of information that has to be gathered from various sources.

The chemical formula is an example of a piece of information that can be obtained from specialized encyclopaedias or possibly advanced textbooks or journal articles. In the future, it is likely that a great deal of information of this kind will be available in computerized form, and accessible on-line; it is difficult to imagine an enterprise such as Beilstein's Handbuch der organischen Chemie being started in the future, or indeed being necessary at all. At the other extreme of the complex package of information, no single source, whether computerized, printed or in any other form, will provide what is required, and real expertise may be needed in gathering it together.

There are several levels at which information services can be offered. The first and most obvious level is the local library or information service--obvious, although many traditional libraries have not seen it as their rôle to offer this kind of service, or offer it only in a very rudimentary form. The next level may be a specialized library or information centre. Such organizations are quite common, particularly in medicine and related fields. It is possible in theory to have a national system consisting entirely of specialized subject centres, but in practice some subjects, including perhaps major ones, are almost certain to be left out, and even those that are provided for will not be served equally. Moreover, it would be impossible to avoid overlap between their coverage, and when resources are limited, as they nearly always are, overlap is to be avoided where possible. Another theoretical possibility is for commercial organizations to provide information services in certain fields where they can recover their costs, leaving other provision up to the government. Whether the government sets up services itself, fills gaps, or attempts to coordinate the whole system, some kind of national involvement and planning seems essential. This implies a national information centre of some kind. This in turn needs to be linked with national reference provision, document supply, and bibliographic control, since all of the functions are related.

LINKS BETWEEN FUNCTIONS

The functions outlined are linked, as has been pointed out more than once. Figure 1 illustrates relationships between the various functions. How in practice can adequate and effective links be ensured? If a country is in the very unusual position of being able to plan its library and information system from scratch, it can set up a single organization with various departments to fulfil the various functions. In most cases, in order to achieve an effective total system, it will be necessary either to give an existing body the responsibility of overseeing the others, or to set up an additional body to control all of the bodies involved. It has been stated several times above that for any single function to be effective, <u>planning</u> is necessary. This is equally true of the whole system. Leaving various bodies to set up their own links, or hoping that an adequate total system will somehow evolve, is not likely to produce good results. Several countries have realized this recently and have set up special committees to devise national plans, or have given a single government department an overall responsibility. A major problem in many countries is that different ministries tend to be involved; for example, one may be concerned with libraries and another with information, or one ministry may be concerned with education, one with science and technology, one with agriculture, and so on. To achieve effective co-ordination with such a distribution of responsibility can be extremely difficult.

THE SITUATION IN THE UNITED KINGDOM

The situation in the United Kingdom is the product of evolution, co-ordination of existing services, and central planning. It is not claimed that it is an ideal solution, but it provides an example of how a developed country, with well established services of different kinds, has been able to change its national library and information system in the last decade.

Until 1970, several organizations were providing parts of the national library service: the British Museum Library, with its semi-autonomous department the National Reference Library of Science and Invention; the British National Bibliography, a non-government body which produced the national bibliography and provided a cataloguing service to libraries; the National Central Library, with its very extensive national union catalogues and a

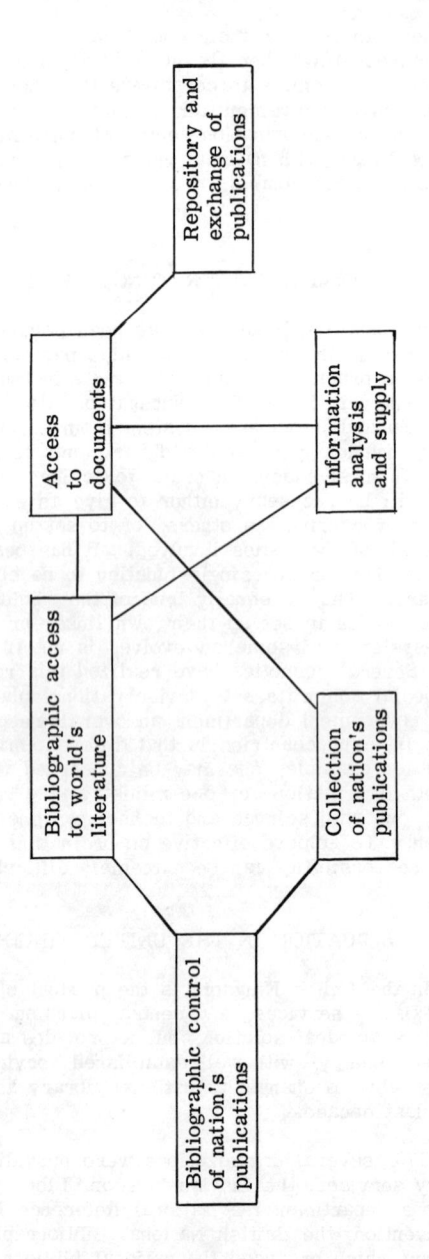

Fig. 1. Links between functions.

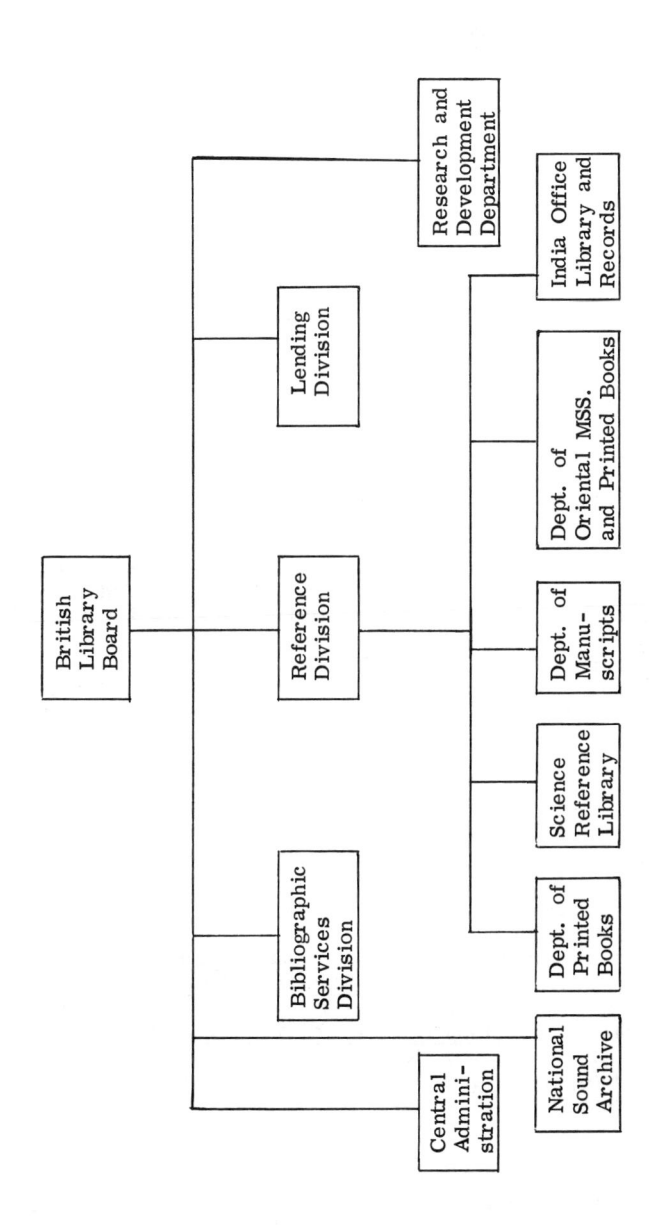

Fig. 2. Structure of the British Library.

reasonable central stock of books in the humanities and social sciences; and the National Lending Library for Science and Technology, which aimed to have a comprehensive collection of journals (except in the humanities), report literature, conference proceedings, and scientific and technical books (mainly in English and Russian). These various organizations came together in 1973 as the British Library, as a result of the National Libraries Committee,[4] which was set up by the government and which reported in 1969, and three years of subsequent detailed planning, including a major feasibility study of the application of automation to the national library system, which was in effect a total systems study of the national library system.[5] The nature and operation of the British Library, one of the world's three or four major national libraries but one with an exceptionally wide range of functions, have been described elsewhere,[6] and here an attempt is made merely to relate its operations to the functions specified above.[7] (Its structure is illustrated in Fig. 2.)

First, the British Library Reference Division aims to make a comprehensive collection of British publications in printed form. Inevitably it misses a good deal of local and ephemeral material, although its coverage is probably as good as in any country in the world. However, it does not acquire non-book materials, apart from sound recordings: the British Institute of Recorded Sound joined the British Library as the National Sound Archive in April 1983. Other bodies collect some of these, but none of them has a national mandate to do so, and the effectiveness with which it is done varies. Legal deposit does not at present extend to non-book materials, and the biggest gap in the present system of collecting British publications is the lack of any scheme for comprehensive coverage of them.

Bibliographic control of British publications is the responsibility of the Bibliographic Services Division of the British Library. This uses the intake of the Reference Division both to produce the national bibliography and to offer catalogue services to other libraries. Its comprehensiveness depends upon the effectiveness of legal deposit as well as its coverage. Books, journals and printed music are well covered, the first two by the British National Bibliography and music by the British Catalogue of Music. In addition, the Bibliographic Services Division issues from time to time a publication called the British Catalogue of Audiovisual Materials; this is not comprehensive, and does not cover the publications of a particular period, as BNB and BCM do, but contains entries for many non-book materials that are available at a particular time.

Publicly available British report literature is received more comprehensively by the Lending Division of the British Library than by the Reference Division, and the Lending Division therefore produces a current bibliography of this, included with other material in a publication called British Reports, Translations and Theses. Other kinds of material are covered wholly or partially by bibliographies that are produced by organizations other than the British

Library. Aslib's Index to Theses, for example, has a more comprehensive record of British doctoral theses than BRTT. Official publications published by Her Majesty's Stationery Office are covered by the various lists issued by HMSO. The much more numerous publications of government departments that are not published by HMSO are recorded in a new bibliography, Catalogue of British Official Publications Not Published by HMSO, issued by the commercial firm Chadwyck-Healey. There is no national bibliography of maps or commercial sound recordings.

The situation with regard to bibliographic control is therefore somewhat untidy, and it is certainly not comprehensive, but in a country that produces very large numbers of all kinds of publication the end result is not too unsatisfactory. It is difficult to see how it can be greatly improved without a more comprehensive legal deposit law.

Access to computerized databases is largely in commercial hands. Users can search them through local terminals in many libraries, academic, public and special--and national, since facilities are available in both the Reference Division and the Lending Division, together with expert assistance in searching. The Bibliographic Services Division makes available on-line its files, which contain not only records for British books but also the Library of Congress MARC records, entries for books added to the Reference Division, and for conference proceedings acquired by the Lending Division. The British Library until recently held copies of the MEDLARS and related files produced by the US National Library of Medicine, but now provides British libraries with access to the files at the NLM.

In document supply, the United Kingdom is particularly strong where most countries are particularly weak, since the main function of the Lending Division of the British Library is to support libraries in the country by acquiring and making available by loan or photocopy a comprehensive collection of books, journals, reports, official publications and printed music.[8] The only major gaps in the Lending Division's coverage of printed materials are in fiction and "lower level" books, for which demand is very slight, and foreign language books, which are published in huge numbers and for which demand is not large enough to justify comprehensive acquisition in advance of demand. Non-book materials are not acquired at all. The Lending Division can supply 85 percent of items requested from its own stock, and a further 9 percent from other sources in the United Kingdom and abroad. The Lending Division handles about three-quarters of all British interlending demand, and in addition a very large share--perhaps half--of all international loan and photocopy transactions: in all, it deals with about 2 670 000 requests a year. The nine regional library systems, which date back to the 1930s, handle about 12 percent of demand, and the remainder consists of direct library-to-library transactions. The regional systems deal with some kinds of material, such as fiction, lower level English-language books, and sound recordings, that the Lending Division does not acquire.

There is no formal national policy of retention for permanent availability, but the Lending Division serves as a de facto national repository, accepting material withdrawn by other libraries, adding it to its own stock unless it already has copies, and making the remainder available to other libraries in the United Kingdom and abroad.

Information provision, as noted above, is the responsibility of local libraries and information units, and the British Library's Reference Division acts as a backstop for information inquiries, as well as serving its own users directly. There are various other specialized bodies to which users, or libraries on behalf of users, can turn for special help.

It can be said with confidence that although there are gaps in the system, the main functions of a national library and information service are carried out in the United Kingdom. The British Library performs the major rôle in four of the functions--collection of the nation's publications, bibliographic control of the nation's publications, access to documents, and repository and exchange of publications; and it plays a significant part in the other two--bibliographic access to the world's literature and information analysis and supply.

There is however no formal national library and information plan. There are various bodies, official and unofficial, that coordinate activities; the most important of these is the Library and Information Services Council, an advisory body to the Office of Arts and Libraries, which comes under the Department of Education and Science. Whether the existing co-ordination is adequate or whether there should be some statutory body with overriding responsibility is a matter of current debate, as is the extent to which the government itself, through the Office of Arts and Libraries and other relevant departments such as the Department of Industry, should play a more positive rôle. On the whole the present system, based as it is on compromise and consensus, works quite well, largely because of the British Library's powerful rôle, but it is unlikely that the conditions that make it work would be fulfilled in other countries, and it should not be regarded as a model, unless perhaps it is proposed to establish a well-funded, national library, with a wide range of statutory functions and a will and ability to innovate.

CONCLUSION

If it is accepted that national planning for library and information services is desirable, how is planning to be initiated? Where the government takes the initiative it is for library and information associations and individuals to participate, advise and ultimately implement. But often there is no initiative from the top, and in this case it must come from librarians and information personnel, or from users (who are the sufferers from any inadequacies), or preferably from both. This requires both leadership and organization. It also requires a professional association or associations to formulate and discuss plans, and to persuade governments of their importance. It is easy for librarians to despair of improvement, but not only their livelihood but the satisfaction of users and ultimately the benefit of the country depend on it, and to believe oneself powerless is to be defeated from the start. For better or for worse, progress in most countries is largely in the hands of librarians and information personnel.

References

1. Maurice B. Line (1977). "Universal availability of publications." Unesco Bulletin for Libraries, 31(3), 142-151.
2. Dorothy Anderson (1974). Universal Bibliographic Control. Pullach/München: Verlag Dokumentation.
3. Robert W. Gibson and Barbara K. Kunkel (1980). "Japanese information network and bibliographic control: scientific and technical literature." Special Libraries 71(3), 154-162.
4. Great Britain (1969). National Libraries Committee. Report (Chairman, F.S. Dainton). London: HMSO (Cmnd. 4028).
5. Great Britain (1972). Department of Education and Science. The Scope for Automatic Data Processing in the British Library (Project head, M.B. Line). 2 pts. London: HMSO.
6. e.g. Andrea G. Polden (1980). "The British Library." International Library Review, 12(3), 269-285. See also: British Library. Annual reports, 1973/74 to date.
7. In 1981/82 its gross expenditure amounted to £48 500 000 and its staff numbered 2260.
8. Maurice B. Line (1980). "The British Library Lending Division." Journal of Information Science 2(3/4), 173-182.

Bibliography

Various aspects of national planning are dealt with thoroughly in the following reports, produced as part of the Universal Availability of Publications programme:

Maurice B. Line et al. (1980). National interlending systems: a comparative study of existing systems and possible models. Paris: Unesco (PGI/78/WS/24(Rev.)). (Summarized in: Line, Maurice B. 1979. "National interlending systems: existing systems and possible models." Interlending Review 7(2), 42-46.).
Judith Collins and Ruth Finer (1982). National Acquisition policies and systems: a comparative study of existing systems and possible models. Wetherby, W. Yorkshire: IFLA International Office for UAP, 1982. (Summarized in: Collins, Judith and Finer, Ruth (1982). "National acquisition policies and systems: an international perspective." Interlending Review 10(4), 111-118.)
Capital Planning Information. National Repository Plans and Programmes: a Comparative Study of Existing Plans and Possible

Models. Wetherby, W. Yorkshire: IFLA International Office for UAP, 1982. (Summarized in: Kennington, Don and White, Brenda (1982). "National repository plans and programmes." Interlending Review 10(1), 3-7.)

HOOPER AND THE PRIMAL TRIBE*

Karl Nyren

Autumn leaves were drifting along the gutters of Main Street, blowing past the New Mills Public Library and Spiro & Tessie's Bar & Grille, past the junkyard of Environmental Recyclers, Inc., and the candy & pot store known as The Junkyard. The library staff was waking up with the help of Spiro's coffee at a table with a sign identifying it as the Staff Room. The former staff room in the library had long been filled with densely shelved books, like every other nook and cranny of the old building, including the seven underground levels made possible by the discovery years ago of an abandoned gypsum mine under the cellar. Only the director's office had been untouched by the flood of books acquired by Hooper and his long-gone predecessor, Miss Letitia Fanshawe, whose dour visage, looking down over the main reading room, kept it as quiet as she once had in person.

"He ought to be showing up pretty soon, now," said Pelvis Katz, Maintenance Librarian. The others nodded drowsy agreement: Sylvia, the Cataloger of unbearable beauty; Mrs. Coakley, the wide Reference Librarian; Miss Axelrod, the gimlet-eyed Children's Librarian; Bert Malvolio, the Lifestyle Librarian; and watching over them all, Spiro at the coffee urn and Tessie, holding the refrigerator on one hip like a baby while she dusted under it.

"I always dread it when he goes to these library meetings," said Mrs. Coakley. "They give him the wildest notions sometimes, and it takes weeks to get his feet back on the ground again."

The door was flung open as she said these words, and Hooper drifted rather than walked in. His eyes were vague, and as he homed in on the coffee urn, they could hear him mutter, "Primal tribe ... change ... change ... change ... integration is in the eye of the vendor ... today a computer, tomorrow junk ... online ... online...."

---

*Reprinted by permission of the author and publisher from Library Journal, 108:19 (November 1, 1983) 2023-24. Published by R.R. Bowker Co. (a Xerox company). Copyright © 1983 by Xerox Corporation.

"He's still dieseling," said Miss Axelrod. "That LITA bash in Baltimore must have been really something."

Hooper drained a mug of Spiro's black coffee and his eyes came into focus. He looked fondly upon his assembled staff and said, "Baltimore was really something. Let me tell you about it."

When nine o'clock struck and they all moved across the street to open the library for the day, he was still talking. As the staff went to their posts, he flicked on the public address system at the circulation desk and his voice filled the building.

The magic names spilled forth: Ithiel de Sola Pool, Hugh Atkinson, Susan Martin, Howard Resnikoff, Connie Tiffany, Ann Lipow, Steve Salmon, Joe Matthews, Kaye Gapen, Dick Boss, Margaret Beckman, David Batty, Ken Dowlin, Barbara Markuson, Mary Ghikas: the architects of a new world. Like incantations Hooper recited the suprahuman beings of this world: OCLC, Carlyle, IAC, RLIN, Geac, ADONIS, CLSI, SOLINET....

"And it means change," he wound up grimly. "Libraries will be cut loose from the apron strings of the public purse and left to drift in the icy seas of an economy dominated by the predators of the private sector.

"It will be up to us," he shouted, his eyes flashing and the PA system booming in pain, "to seize the new weapons, the computers and their ilk, and carve out our own fiscal fates, undeterred by bureaucratic lethargy or private sector greed.

"We will become entrepreneurial ... we will cast out hierarchy and all its trappings and reform ourselves into what Hugh Atkinson, he of the gently wandering mind, called 'primal tribes.' In due time, I will come down from my office and be as one of you."

"I was wondering where we'd put the next shipment of books," said Mrs. Coakley with relief. "That great big office ought to shelve at least 5000."

Into the silence that followed, the telephone drilled an ominous hole.

"Why does that remind me of the knocking at the gate in Macbeth?" muttered Mrs. Coakley as she picked up the phone on the reference desk. "It's for you," she called across the foyer to Hooper. "The Mayor!" She made the sign of the cross reverently but despairingly. Clairvoyance was a blessing in reference work, but it left one wide open to evil tidings.

Hooper picked up the phone and greeted the Mayor in jolly fashion. "Baltimore was a very rewarding experience," he said, a little defensively. "No, I wouldn't call it a junket in any sense."

He listened for a long time then, his face growing ashen. He clutched at the circulation desk for support.

"But you can't do that," he wailed, his voice trembling. He held the phone away from him and stared at it as it went dead.

"The Mayor and the Council have cut the library off without a cent," he whispered. "It's the end."

"Well," said Pelvis Katz, "I guess we'll just have to regroup into that primal tribe and get entrepreneurial. Good thing you went to Baltimore and learned all about that stuff."

"Shut up," said Hooper. "This is real. After January 1, there just won't be any city money. All this," he waved around distractedly, "will be gone."

"Can we wear leopard skins and carry stone axes?" asked Sylvia, still caught up in visions of a primal tribe. "In spite of what the President says, I'd like to give men back their animal skins and stone axes. We could have campfires ... maybe weenie roasts?"

"How about charging admission to story hours?" said Bert Malvolio, his voice fading off as Miss Axelrod's frosty glare spiked him like a laser beam.

"Perhaps I can be of assistance," said an ancient little voice. No one had noticed the entrance of M. Ivor Bateau, Librarian Emeritus of Dijon and the world, but now resident of New Mills, his declining years made golden by access to the little-known, million-volume collection of the New Mills Public Library.

"One must be philosophical," he counseled. "Alexandria is gone with all its library treasures. The keepers of the dead sea scrolls are dust blowing in the desert. No one even knows what we lost at Mohenjodaro. Iowa City...."

"Iowa City?" They said with one voice.

"Where once there were books," said M. Bateau wanly, "there are things called 'audio visual materials.' I stopped in there some time ago on a pilgrimage to the Bancroft Library, just poked my head in for the refreshment of a sight of books--but as far as the eye could see there were machines and tapes and films and such barbaric things.

"But back to your present crisis," he said. "I think there is a way out. Can the library transform itself into an independent, nonprofit corporation?"

"Assuredly," said Spiro, who was chairman of the library board. "Without funding, no one wants us."

"Then," said M. Bateau, "all you need to do is float a loan of, say, $10 million, buy up the city's outstanding debt and perhaps also the mortgages on the home of the Mayor and Councilmen, and reopen discussions of the budget with them."

"But who would give us that kind of money?" asked Hooper.

"In the bookstacks beneath this building," said M. Bateau, "the manuscripts, Dead Sea scrolls, rare books, first editions, and other treasures are worth so much that $10 million would be peanuts. I have only to call the other surviving members of my old, old boy network of connoisseurs scattered about the globe, and Sotheby's would be happy to advance the money in the hope of putting it all on the block."

"Holy mackerel," said Hooper, "We could evolve just like OCLC and CLASS did, free of trammels like politicians and voters and going forth to do our own thing!"

"In primal groups?" asked Sylvia.

"You got it," enthused Hooper. "Now, where do we start?"

"Please sir," said a small voice. Hooper looked down to see Billy O'Reilly, a much valued library page, since he alone could fix the library's computer when it was ailing.

"If it would help," said Billy modestly, "I could arrange to have the City's credit rating reduced rather sharply. Then you could buy up its bonds really cheaply."

"No, no, Billy," said Hooper. "That might be illegal. I'll keep it in mind, however, if we ever have to get illegal to get out of this mess."

"I know something that Billy could do," said Pelvis, "Get into the computer that handles the billing for Big Nell's and her national network for franchised Gallant Guardsman outlets, and arrange for bills for her services to go to the Mayor and the Councilmen, with copies to the wives."

"We're not sadists," said Hooper stiffly. "You forget that we own Big Nell's and the franchise network with title that goes back to the Revolution. We'll just ask our liaison on Big Nell's staff, Connie Tulip Eyes, to send out the bills. Itemized. You know her--the girl who used to be a travel agent to Round the World Tours before she bettered herself and Big Nell took her on. By the time we get through with Mr. Mayor, we'll be capitalized for $10 million and we'll get back our city budget with a nice, fat increase."

Hooper squared his shoulders. The color was coming back into his face. "The corridors of power," he mused.

"Hooper," said Spiro, holding up a warning hand, "I will tell you one thing. In the corridors of power there are twice as many feet as people.

"Any time we really have to, we can go the way of OCLC and CLASS and all the others going down that primrose path. Just talk to the Mayor about Big Nell's billing plans and when he sees the light, let's just stay where we are, with a quiet little library with more books than we know what to do with. Let's enjoy it while we can. Talk to the Mayor, Hooper."

"Billy," said Hooper, suspicion clouding his features.

"Sir?" said Billy in the rising voice of juvenile guilt.

"You didn't by chance already screw up the City's credit rating and that's why the Mayor is in a panic, and cutting our budget?"

Billy scuffed his feet. "I'll fix it right up," he said hastily. "I was just fooling around. I didn't mean anything. I'll fix it."

"Don't fix it yet, Billy," said Hooper. He reached for the phone and dialed City Hall with the look of a man who had found his way in the darkness at last.

An hour later, the entire staff trooped over to Spiro's for a victory celebration. When they were all assembled, Spiro gave the counter a last wipe, replaced a sugar dispenser that had wandered from its niche, and strolled over to the juke box. "To celebrate, we must have music," he said, kicking the machine in a sensitive spot. It came alive with the sounds of the Killawatt Institute and the strains of their newest hit, one that had made the airwaves during the LITA meeting that had taken Hooper to Baltimore: "A Black, An Hispanic, Two Jews & A Cripple," a ditty almost surely destined to equal the record sales of their earlier and prophetic, "Open Season on the Bald Headed Foot Shooter."

After the champagne was finished, Hooper arose. "Well, that's that," he said briskly. "It's time we all got to work around here. I've got my weighty responsibilities and I'm sure you all have things to keep you busy. We all have our places in the scheme of things."

"You're not going to give up your office and private hi-fi and bar and executive washroom?" said Pelvis, crestfallen.

"No primal group?" quavered Sylvia, tears in her matchless eyes.

"You got it," said Hooper. "Dreams and crystal balls are all very well for dilettantes and visionaries like those people in

LITA. We're in the real world and we've got to make it work."

Mrs. Coakley winked at Miss Axelrod. "Well," she said, "we've got his feet back on the ground again. We should be safe at least till ALA Midwinter now."

LIBRARY TECHNOLOGY: THE BLACK BOX SYNDROME*

Norman Stevens

What's a black box? It is some ingenious invention designed to revolutionize the way in which we work. In recent years, there has been a widespread if not universal acceptance and use in American libraries of network systems, commercial database searching systems, and turnkey systems from commercial vendors. As those and other library uses of automation have developed and matured, we have all come to accept them as solutions to our problems.

Despite the real advantages of these systems, we need to regain some of the skepticism toward mechanical solutions to our problems expressed by Ralph R. Shaw almost thirty years ago. We should heed his admonishment to "think kindly ... of those who take pity upon our benighted state to solve all our problems with machines they have not yet thought about."[1]

The first black boxes

A true library historian could undoubtedly locate a description of some mechanical wonder designed to provide quicker access to the papyrus at the Alexandrian library. As only an amateur library historian, I have not been able to locate such an early example. The earliest example of a black box that I have been able to locate dates only from 1588.

Since 1959, the Council on Library Resources has used in its annual report a picture of a medieval scholar at his book-wheel. That picture shows the scholar seated at a large circular device that appears to hold as many as a dozen books at a time, any one of which he can bring to his line of vision by using a foot-activated pedal. This may be the earliest known example of the black box, but it is by no means the last. Our library landscape is littered with a profusion of such devices, most of which, if they are from the distant past, now appear to be somewhat quaint, if not ridiculous, although they may be fundamentally no different in their approach from the devices we now regard as our possible salvation.

---

*Reprinted by permission of the author and publisher from Wilson Library Bulletin, 57:6 (February 1983) 475-80. Copyright © 1983 by The H.W. Wilson Co.

In the mid-nineteenth century, Charles Coffin Jewett proposed the use of stereotype plates as a means of producing and distributing catalog cards prepared at a central point. At about the same time, Henry Stevens was proposing the use of what he called photobibliography, which involved the direct use of photographs of the title pages of books as a part of catalog entries. While advanced for their time, and probably for that reason never implemented, both of those ideas at least had some merit, because they did seek to address the intellectual problems of sharing cataloging information and of developing catalog entries through the aid of mechanical devices.

The late nineteenth century did see in both England and America the development of more mechanical solutions to problems that are illustrative of the black box syndrome.

The Indicator

Public libraries in England continued to operate with closed stacks during the nineteenth century, and the librarians of the time, while not yet prepared to allow readers direct access to their collections, were concerned about finding some way of indicating to patrons which books in the catalog were available for borrowing. The solution was the "indicator," a device now found only in museums, the first of which was invented in 1863. Quickly thereafter, as many as ten or a dozen various kinds of indicators became available and were put into use.

One model of the indicator, typical of the device in general, contained hundreds of small metal shelves placed in a heavy metal frame on a wooden base and covered by a sheet of glass. On each shelf was a miniature metal book representing a book in the collection. At opposite ends of the book were different colored tabs with the catalog number: one color indicated that the book was charged out, and the other color indicated that the book was available for use. After the reader had obtained the catalog number, he or she was thus able to determine the availability of the book without having to bother the library staff. This was the first public inquiry terminal. The indicator also served as the basis for the circulation system: when a book was charged out, the information about the borrower was recorded with the indicator's metal book.

For all of its seeming advantages, the indicator had one major flaw. It should be obvious that for a collection of any size the amount of space required for the indicator soon became unmanageable. A collection of about four thousand volumes might require about six to eight feet of counter space for the indicator, but a collection of thirty thousand volumes might require as much as thirty-eight feet.

It was the eventual adoption of open stacks that brought about the demise of the indicator. The real problem with the indicator, as is so often the case with black boxes, was not its advantages or disadvantages but the way in which it influenced the thinking of librarians. Writing in 1900, L. Stanley Jast, one of the most prominent British public librarians of that time, addressed "The Mechanical Appliance Craze." Building on an earlier paper by Mr. McAlister, Jast suggested that:

> The amount of time and attention that is now bestowed upon this side of library work, to the inevitable detriment of its higher and nobler sides, is astonishing and lamentable. Now there is a subtle and fell fascination about these things, which if once allowed full play becomes a positive disease....
> I have nothing to say against these things in themselves; it is a question of perspective with which I am concerned.... Let us be librarians, not mechanics. That the danger of which I speak is neither imaginary or exaggerated is shown by the strenuous efforts which some of us are making to condition the whole economy of the lending library by the indicator. Those of us who run the indicator, and find it a meritorious piece of mechanism, which serves our purposes satisfactorily, may well object when it becomes a question of the indicator running us.[2]

The card catalog

American librarians were fortunate to have escaped the black box solution of the indicator, perhaps because their libraries moved earlier to open shelves or perhaps simply by accident. The one event, more than any other, which seems to have precipitated American librarianship into the black box syndrome was the shift from the printed to the card catalog in the late nineteenth century, when it became apparent that the continuing rapid growth of library collections required a more flexible means of providing information about a library's holdings to its users. We did not miraculously adopt the card catalog as we know it today; the literature of the period seems to be replete with mechanical solutions to this problem.

The Library Journal for December 1893, for example, reports on the discussion held earlier that year at the Massachusetts Library Club on the question, "Is There an Impending Revolution in Library Cataloging?" According to that report, the discussion centered largely around mechanical issues, including a consideration of the problems encountered with the card catalog because so few users can consult it at one time. At the meeting, "Mr. Lane said that by using trays which can be taken out, this trouble is partially obviated."

In another note, appearing in The Library Journal in 1900, no less an authority than Melvil Dewey refers to such issues as the substitution of single trays for double drawers and the fact that "trays, drawers, pockets, and various devices for convenient work have multiplied with wonderful rapidity." As librarians and libraries sought the black box solution that would create the ideal card catalog, some ingenious devices were forthcoming.

On December 8, 1891, Charles N. Judson, who seems to have been an efficiency expert and a frustrated user, not a librarian, patented a card catalog drawer with the ever-popular double rod, designed "to facilitate the examination of the several cards of which the card-catalogue is composed." His solution consisted of utilizing indented cards, with the indention and the text shifting from left to right on a card-by-card basis.

As Judson carefully explained in his patent application: "In consulting card-catalogues it is necessary to separate one card from another by inserting the finger or thumb between the cards, pulling the first card away from the pack in order to consult the next, and as the cards are frequently packed in the case quite tightly and stand close to each other it is often difficult to get them apart, causing great annoyance and irritation when haste is desired. The object of my invention is to so form the cards as to enable this to be done readily and at the same time they shall be so inscribed that they can be consulted in the easiest manner possible."

The Library Journal for May 1892 contains a fascinating, if somewhat incomprehensible, description of "The New Library Drawer" designed by Frederic Badger, an assistant in the Harvard College Library. "It is not supposed," the article boldly states, "that old libraries can at once adopt it; its method effects too complete a revolution in the old ways; but it is confidently offered to new libraries and those now entering on library work. It claims to surpass all appliances heretofore used by libraries." From the description, for no copy of the actual drawer seems to have survived, it must have been very similar to the kardex units that most of us now use for our serials records.

Undoubtedly the most famous and widely promoted black box of that era was Alexander J. Rudolph's fantastic "continuous indexer," which was first announced to the world at the American Library Association's meeting in San Francisco in 1891.

Perhaps the most amazing aspect of Rudolph's invention was not the device itself but the extent to which it was promoted, with some success, as capable of solving all cataloging problems, even though it was little more than a different device for displaying catalog cards. In many respects similar to the scholar's book wheel, Rudolph's continuous indexer was simply a means for displaying a series of catalog cards on a revolving belt that could be cranked around in a cabinet until the appropriate cards appeared under a glass plate.

Just as the indicator had become, for Jast, a symbol of the black box in England, so it seems this discussion about how to display catalog cards helped set American librarianship off on its quest for mechanical solutions to its problems. Badger's library drawer, Judson's card catalog, Rudolph's continuous indexer, and other black boxes of that time seem slightly ludicrous. We would like to think that common sense ultimately prevailed and that the solution selected, as represented in our present-day card catalog, was the correct one. But was it?

Much of the discussion of such devices in the 1890s was ably summarized in an editorial in the December 1891 issue of The Library Journal. "The question recurs, of course, whether the card catalog is, after all, the final form of the library catalog, and whether, having reached the millenium of the card catalog, we shall not have to begin over again on an improved system." Far from having reached a millenium, the card catalog is now in the process of being phased out after less than one hundred years of existence.

Fascinated by technology

Having resolved, for the time being, the problem of the card catalog, American librarians were able to spend the next half-century or so purusing their fascination with machines along other avenues. Jast's warning never received much attention in this country, just as it had not in his own country.

Fortunately, or unfortunately, no major black box project captured our imagination during that period, although, to some degree, circulation systems bid fair to do so with such splendid innovations as audio-charging. Rather, our imaginations were captured by a variety of lesser problems and less dramatic mechanical solutions to those problems. The space allotted to such solutions in the professional journals, the existence of the American Library Association's Committee on Equipment and Appliances, and some of the contemporary applications of equipment are all testimony to our quest for the perfect black box that would provide for one aspect of library service or another.

Neither circulation systems nor other mechanical devices were a real challenge to American ingenuity. So, to some degree, the black box syndrome languished. But we had only to wait until the late 1930s for a new machine challenge, far greater than any seen before, to emerge in the shape of electronic data processing. All of that has led to the current fascination, vastly superior to the mid-nineteenth-century British enchantment with the indicator, that we now have with computers and other applications of contemporary technology to library problems.

By the time we were well on our way to the initial stages of today's computer craze, Ralph Blasingame reflected on our love of gadgets, echoing Jast's earlier concerns. "The common aim," he wrote in 1956, "in introducing tools or machines into almost any process is to reduce the time or energy required to perform some operation or to produce a more uniformly satisfactory result. To stick to this rule in the application of what may be referred to as 'gadgets' is sometimes difficult; many of these devices have a kind of fascination for some librarians which occasionally obscures the true economics of their application.... [Besides,] another danger of the indiscriminate use of mechanical miscellanea is that work may actually be created for them."[3] Perhaps, in this last statement, Blasingame foresaw one of the major dangers of the computer that was to come.

From the late 1930s through the early 1970s, the potential library applications of computer technology presented an unreal world of their own. Most often, as Ralph Shaw suggested in 1956, we failed to adequately distinguish between the form and the substance, or the word and the deed.[4] There were many valuable experiments, many useful developments, and even a few good operational systems. To read or recall the literature of that period, however, one would think that magnificent solutions to all of our problems had been developed.

Shaw, who was one of the few contemporary critics of library automation, was frequently chastised for his skepticism, but to read his articles on the subject and compare their contents with the developments of the time only serves to reinforce his wisdom. In reality, a large percentage of the articles, books, and reports published at that time described systems, many of which were as bizarre as the card catalog solutions of the 1890s, that never existed, had serious flaws and were abandoned, or were as widely used as Judson's catalog drawer.

"Machines that they have not yet thought about"

As bizarre as those systems may seem and as interesting as it might be to examine them in some detail, they somehow seem perfectly sensible in contrast to the visions of the library future built during that same period around the black box "machines that they have not yet thought about." It is far more interesting to examine some of those solutions, which parallel today's black boxes of tomorrow.

The advent of computers and their potential application to library services brought with it a fascination with solving the problems of library management by users knowledgeable about machines and frustrated by librarians' failure to respond adequately to the challenge of those machines. Mr. Judson, with his "great annoyance and irritation," was the forerunner of what was, for a period of time, a veritable flood of well-wishers.

The first and most famous solution was proposed by the

Libraries and Librarians 73

distinguished American scientist, Vannevar Bush, in 1945. Bush foresaw "a future device for individual use, which is a sort of mechanized private file and library. It needs a name, and, to coin one at random, 'memex' will do. A memex is a device in which an individual stores all his books, records, and communications, and which is mechanized so that it may be consulted with exceeding speed and flexibility."[5]

Bush describes in some detail the physical appearance and inner workings of a memex, which would be a kind of desk, and its construction around microfilm. "The Encyclopaedia Britannica could be reduced to the volume of a matchbox. A library of a million volumes could be compressed into one end of a desk." Fortunately, Bush did not discuss either the costs of developing a memex or the time when it might become available. Unfortunately, his approach served, in large measure, to suggest that this kind of black box solution to library problems was around the corner.

In the early 1960s, under the sponsorship of the Council on Library Resources, J.C.R. Licklider of IBM investigated what he titled Libraries of the Future. Much of his work described the size of the body of human knowledge in mathematical terms, and analysis that is not easy to comprehend. He did predict, in more manageable terms, what we might expect based on certain assumptions about the growth of random-access memory capabilities. "It would be possible," Licklider stated, "to put all of the solid literature of a subfield of science or technology into a single computer memory in 1985.... All this refers to fast, random-access digital memory. How fast? ... only an optimist would hope for access shorter than 0.1 microsecond."[6]

Project Intrex, conducted at the Massachusetts Institute of Technology in 1965 (but not, I hasten to add, within the library there), was yet another attempt to describe the library of the future, in this case in an effort to describe what the information transfer process at MIT might be like by 1975. By that time, according to calculations, a computer-based system would contain a restricted field of "about 5,000 books [at 300 pages per book] and 100 journals, the entire contents of each of which may since its inception approximate 2,500 pages of text."[7]

By 1971, John G. Kemeny, president of Dartmouth College, was proclaiming his vision of the library of the future. Reverting back to Bush's concept of microfilm, Kemeny suggested that with ultra-microfiche "1,000 miniaturized volumes can be stored in one ordinary card file a foot long," and "a million such volumes could be kept in 1,000 card drawers, with the drawers numbered and the cards numbered within the drawers." Such a simple solution, not even as ingenious as Rudolph's continuous indexer or the indicator, would provide faster access than the conventional library "but, obviously, an automated system can do much better."[8]

These are a few examples, selected not entirely at random,

of black box solutions. They foreshadow the work of those who now tout videodisc technology or who forecast a paperless information society. One of the most recent of these solutions promotes the idea that videodisc/microcomputer technology could store the entire National Union Catalog on one disc and provide an average access time of 2.5 seconds. All this at a cost, including hardware, of less than $5,000--that is, after the initial production costs for the transfer of the information to the videodisc.[9]

What went wrong?

Why have the solutions of Bush, Licklider, Project Intrex, and Kemeny failed to materialize? Why do their projections already seem as quaint, in their own fashion, as the card catalog solutions of Badger, Judson, and Rudolph? Can we really expect a videodisc of the National Union Catalog to appear in the near future, heralded by a brochure advertising all of its wonders, including the hardware, for less than $5,000? Will the paperless information society be here by the year 2000? The answers seem obvious.

For those visions of the future, suggested such a short time ago, many things have gone wrong. Technology has neither developed along the lines the visionaries suggested, nor as quickly as they thought it would. It never does. Microforms have real advantages for many library applications and serve us well, but that medium has not yet begun to, and it is never likely to, serve as a substantial substitute for the printed word.

Above all, the demand for these solutions has not been there. The planners failed to take into account all of the costs of their systems, especially in terms of how all of that information was to be transformed miraculously into some new storage medium. Those costs can be staggering and are beyond the present realm of reality for libraries, given their role in society. Project Intrex, for example, in looking at the information transfer system at MIT in 1975, proposed that it would take an annual operating budget of $15 million to provide the kinds of services it envisaged; in 1980-1981, the MIT libraries, which manage traditional library systems involving some use of automation, had a total operating budget of just over $5 million.

The best analysis of this aspect of the problem has come from Nicholas Alter of University Microfilms International. Looking at only a comparatively small body of literature, akin in many ways to what Licklider and Project Intrex examined, Alter describes some of the problems. He suggests that "to put full-text computer storage costs in perspective, consider the cost of mounting an online full-text distribution service for doctoral dissertations.... The texts of the thirty thousand new dissertations that UMI receives annually from American universities would take roughly two and a half million hours to key and proof for computer entry, at a labor cost of several million dollars--clearly not a practical option." According to Alter, the additional costs of storage and access "quickly escalate into a multimillion dollar annual investment."[10]

It is all too easy to be misled by our desire for these black boxes to think that they will somehow materialize without cost. The videodisc of The National Union Catalog will probably fall by the wayside because of the minor matter of the initial production costs for the transfer of the information to the videodisc. That is always the way. We tend to look at the glamour of such solutions and not at the practical reality of how those solutions are to be accomplished.

If there is a moral to this examination of the black box syndrome through the library ages, it is a twofold one. First, it is abundantly clear, the black box solution to our problems will always be with us. As the technological base of society increases, so can we expect the scope and vision of those solutions to increase.

Second, and this is the true moral, we need to continue to be skeptical of the claims and promises of technology.

We have come a long way since Alexandria, since the scholar's wheel, since the indicator, and since the card catalog. We have even come a long way since the first applications of computer technology to library operations and the first visions of the library of the future. Automation and technology have done much to improve library operations in the 1980s; they will do much to further improve library operations in the next two decades. But we should not expect miracles. I, for one, suspect that libraries will not be all that much different by the year 2000 from the way they are now.

Footnotes:

1. Ralph R. Shaw, "From Fright to Frankenstein," D.C. Libraries 24:10, 1953.
2. L. Stanley Jast, "Some Hindrances to Progress in Public Library work," Library Association Record 2:83-4, 1900.
3. Ralph Blasingame, "Gadgets: Miscellanea, But Not All Trivia," Library Trends 5:239, 1956.
4. Ralph R. Shaw, "The Form and the Substance," Library Journal 90:567-71, 1965.
5. Vannevar Bush, "As We May Think," The Atlantic 176:106-7, 1945.
6. J.C.R. Licklider, Libraries of the Future, Cambridge, M.I.T. Press, 1965, p. 17-18.
7. Planning Conference on Information Transfer Experiments, Woods Hole, MA, 1965. Intrex Cambridge, M.I.T. Press, 1965, p. 106.
8. John G. Kemeny, Man and the Computer, New York, Scribner's, 1972, p. 89-90.
9. R. Kent Wood and Robert D. Woolley, An Overview of Videodisc Technology and Some Potential Applications in the Library,

Information and Instructional Sciences, Syracuse, ERIC Clearinghouse on Information Resources, Syracuse University, 1980, p. 25.
10. Nicholas Alter, "UMI Looks at New Storage and Retrieval Systems," University Microfilms International Newsletter No. 14, (Winter 1981), p. 1.

COMPUTER SEARCHING:

A PRIMER FOR THE UNINFORMED SCHOLAR*

Stephen K. Stoan

The application of automation to the world of libraries has resulted in considerable improvement in the amount and type of information that can be made quickly available to the library user. The sharing of cataloging records through online consortia has not only speeded up the processing of newly acquired materials but revolutionized interlibrary loan. Online acquisitions and circulation systems, where established, function as massive inventory control records, enabling a library to determine in minutes if a title is on order, has arrived but has not been cataloged, has been checked out, has been put on hold, is on reserve, has been declared lost or missing, or is overdue.

The area of automation I wish to discuss here, however, is computer searching, more commonly known as online searching. To many scholars the term online searching is meaningless, but the potential implications for them, their teaching, and their research could well be enormous. Therefore, every researcher should become conversant with online searching, for the more ardent advocates of the technology already claim that it can substitute for traditional print tools without harming scholarly research, a point I will address later.

The earliest method of communicating with a computer, batching, was eventually replaced with the online technology we now see all around us. Computers with powerful central processing units and enormous amounts of storage capacity allow many users at once to interact with them, each user utilizing a print terminal or a cathode ray tube (CRT) terminal. Each of these terminals has a keyboard that enables the user to type in data to be sent to the computer, which then responds by typing on paper, in the case of the print terminal, or by offering a visual display on a screen, in the case of the CRT.

Almost concurrent with the rise of online technology was the

---

*Reprinted by permission of the author from Academe, (November-December 1982) 10-15. Copyright © 1982 by Stephen K. Stoan.

idea that, since vast amounts of data could be stored in magnetic
discs or other devices appended to the computer, it would be possible to store lengthy texts, like indexes of periodical literature,
for retrieval. In other words, Psychological Abstracts could be
put into machine-readable form and made available for retrieval by
someone trained in the search language designed for communicating
with the computer. It was reasoned that, since a bibliographic entry
in a database could be programmed for retrieval using many keys
other than the author or subject heading available in print indexes,
online searching could actually offer a more effective way to locate
extant periodical literature.

For a number of technical and financial reasons, the producers of indexes who have converted them to machine-readable
form do not market the computerized versions themselves. Rather,
they have made arrangements to permit vendors to do the job of
providing computers, loading the data, developing the search languages, and handling the financial aspects of the business. Thus,
each vendor may make available dozens of machine-readable indexes, each of which is generally referred to as a file or database.
The three largest vendors are DIALOG® Information Services, formerly known as Lockheed Information Systems; System Development
Corporation, or SDC, occasionally referred to as ORBIT, the name
of its search language; and Bibliographic Retrieval Services, or
BRS. Since subscribers to such services must communicate with
the computers at long range, by means of telephone lines, telecommunications networks have sprung up to provide this service. The
best known of these are Telenet and Tymshare.

A subscribing library, then, needs a terminal with an acoustic coupler, a librarian trained in the appropriate search language,
a telephone number, and a password. The search analyst, as the
searcher is sometimes called, dials either Tymshare or Telenet,
attaches the telephone receiver to the acoustic coupler on the terminal, and uses a password to log on to the desired vendor. Once
online, the searcher selects the file desired and conducts the
"search."

The bibliography retrieved will be printed by the computer
offline and put in the mail quickly. It is not uncommon to receive
the results in three days. Though searchers can, for varying reasons, choose among several formats in which to print the bibliography, they normally ask for a complete record, which will include
full bibliographic citations, the descriptors assigned to each article,
and the texts of the abstracts where available. The citations themselves will normally be arranged in reverse chronological order of
when they were entered in the database, with the most recent first.
Should the patron ask for only twenty-five citations, he or she would
receive the twenty-five most recent.

Online searching costs money. Keenly aware of the ethical
problems raised by charging patrons for a source of information,
many academic libraries tried at the outset to define online search-

ing as an essential service available to all without recourse to fees. But the economics of the situation have taken their toll, and though the complex debate over the ethical issues continues in library circles, many institutions now require that the patron pay either part or all of the direct costs of a search. These include telecommunications fees, fees for online time, and a fee for each citation printed offline. If, for example, a particular file costs $60/hour for connect time and $.15 per citation, a seven-minute search retrieving thirty citations would cost $7.00 for online time, $4.50 for offline prints, and a small additional amount for telecommunications costs. In some expensive files that may require lengthy keyboarding operations, it is not uncommon for a search to cost $50 to $100 or more. One can have the results of a search printed online, in the library, but this method costs more because of connect time, even though the terminal is printing at 30 characters per second (300 baud). The spread of terminals that print at 120 characters per second (1200 baud) is making it feasible to resort to online printing, thus retrieving the bibliography on the spot.

Many of the hundreds of files now available for searching are not bibliographic in nature; rather, they are factual or statistical. Among the purely bibliographic databases, there are now three types. The first corresponds exactly to a print index; the second incorporates a print index but includes other material; and the third has existed from the outset only online. In many cases, the online version of an index is not as deep chronologically as the print version. The online technique began at some point in the recent past, and no effort was made to load the backfiles.

Obviously, the researcher may find the latter two kinds of files advantageous, for they may turn up citations that could not be located in the standard print sources. But why pay for a computer search in a file that is fully available in print form? Part of the answer is that the computer can yield more recent citations than are available in print indexes, which lag by many months. Another part of the answer is that the computer can retrieve citations according to many criteria other than author or subject heading. And the rest of the answer is that the computer can seek out combinations of descriptors that a researcher could find with a manual search only with great difficulty. To explain these last two points in more concrete terms, let us first take a look at the common search keys, then say a few words about the Boolean logic used in online searching.

In most files, a bibliographic citation can be retrieved according to the following common keys: author, title words, journal name, year of publication, descriptors, words in the text of the abstract, language, document type (article, literature review, etc.), and a number of others. The basic search strategy involves the creation of sets which are then combined in "and," "or," or "not" relationships using Boolean logic.

Let us offer a brief example. We are looking for an article

whose exact title we cannot remember, only a title word, written
by John Doe in a journal whose name we cannot recall. The search
analyst tells the computer first to search the database and report
back on the number of articles written by Doe. The machine responds by indicating it has created a set consisting of Doe's articles
and gives the number of items in the set, let us say six. The
searcher then tells the computer to look for titles containing the
word "groupthink." The computer responds with a set containing
all such articles, let us say twenty-one. The last step is to instruct the computer to combine the two sets by selecting those articles characterized by Doe's authorship and the word "groupthink"
in the title. The machine then creates a third set which contains,
let us say, one citation.

However, although the computer can be used to great advantage in performing such acts of wizardry, its primary use in a university setting is to retrieve bibliographies on some specified subject. In other words, the majority of searches use only a few of
the search keys available. This being so, the real test of online
searching, if we compare it to manual searching, is its effectiveness
in obtaining useful bibliographical citations on a topic.

In some cases the computer has distinct advantages. It can
search out in seconds combinations of descriptors that would demand
much time of a manual searcher. If, for example, one is seeking
articles on the peasantry in eighteenth-century France, the searcher
can create three sets based on the three concepts "peasants,"
"France," and "eighteenth century," then tell the computer to combine them so as to retrieve those articles characterized by all three
ideas.

A second advantage of the computer is that it can seek out
not only descriptors, but also title words and words in the abstracts.
If descriptors have been poorly selected or assigned, the machine
can partially compensate by broadening the net to look for other evidence of potential relevance. Unfortunately, this advantage is sometimes not utilized because of the attitudes of many online searchers.
For two reasons, they have developed a fear of the "false drop,"
that is, a citation that proves to be irrelevant. The first reason is
that they feel guilty charging the patron for an irrelevant citation.
The second is that they tend to believe they have conducted a poor
search if the relevance rate is low.

For the benefit of those who may have searches run, let me
elaborate a bit more on the previous point. Basically, a searcher
can run a "clean" search, limiting the search to descriptors and
perhaps title words, or a "dirty" search, technically called a freetext search, in which the searcher tells the computer to run through
the abstracts as well. A clean search has a good chance of turning
up a bibliography with a fairly high relevance rate, e.g., twentyfive citations, twenty-two of which prove to be useful--a relevance
rate of 88 percent. A dirty search, on the other hand, because it
picks up from the abstracts concepts that may mislead as to the

major thrust of the article, will produce more false drops, though it may also generate higher recall, e.g., fifty articles, thirty of which prove to be useful--a relevance rate of only 60 percent.

For scholars who are attempting to locate every relevant citation on a topic and are accustomed to the idea that one routinely consults many books and articles that look promising but prove to be irrelevant, the dirty search is often preferable, even though it costs more. But among computer searchers, the feeling is sometimes strong that a search with a low relevance rate is a poor one. Consequently, the scholar may have a search run and get back a bibliography with a good relevance rate without realizing that, had the search been run differently, it could have yielded many more useful citations, though combined with more false drops.

Another aspect of computer searching that every patron should understand is that searches can be run in different ways with differing results, so one should never assume that an online search has indeed turned up everything in the computer that might be useful. Three searchers could be given the same topic and could retrieve three different bibliographies. This is so for several reasons. The first is that they may choose clean searches, dirty searches, or even combinations of the two. The second reason is that searchers may often choose among several files. And a third reason is that in most cases a number of different search strategies can be devised for a topic, depending on the knowledge and skill of the searcher.

Let me illustrate concretely. The scholar is looking for articles on the influence of dietary fiber in preventing cancer of the colon. Right away, the searcher may choose either Index Medicus or Biological Abstracts. The searcher then settles on a clean or a dirty search, and decides, let us say, to run the latter. The searcher must then select the appropriate terms to be used in the creation of sets for each of the three basic concepts: fiber, cancer, and colon. Now, then, the searcher may create set one by looking for "fiber" or "roughage" or "bran," set two by selecting "cancer" or "carcinogen," and set three with the single concept "colon." Now the searcher combines the three sets to obtain a final set for printing.

However, by also selecting "fibre" in set one, the searcher might have expanded retrieval significantly, for "fiber" alone misses much material published in England. Likewise, to truncate "cancer?" and "carcinogen?" might turn up a bit more, for this DIALOG command tells the computer to pick out not only the root itself but any word built up from it, such as "cancerous" or "carcinogenic." And the searcher might profitably have included "intestin?" in the final set, pulling "intestine," "intestines," and "intestinal." In short, the computer yields only what the online searcher has been skillful enough to draw out with the available search keys.

Several lessons for the patron should now be obvious. One

is that it is advisable to spend a great deal of time with the searcher explaining precisely what is desired, going over descriptors, and coming up with lists of synonymous natural language terms that the searcher might feed into the computer. Another is that the patron may wish to ask for a search aimed at high recall rather than high relevance, assuring the analyst that false drops do not matter unless the search becomes so vast as to become unreasonable. And another lesson to be learned is that it is generally preferable for the patron to be present during the search to provide the subject expertise that the searcher cannot be expected to have. Most libraries already run searches this way as a matter of course.

The probability of retrieving a high percentage of what the database has to offer varies not only according to the skill of the searcher, the accuracy of the interview, and the preparation of the search strategy, but also according to the nature of the discipline. In the sciences and engineering, where terminology is fairly precise and the titles of articles have traditionally provided excellent resumes of their contents, clean searches may often yield both high relevance and high recall. In the social sciences and humanities, where terminology is less precise and titles have often been more poetic than scientific, a search may involve keying in long lists of more or less synonymous terms for each set being constructed, with little guarantee that the recall rate will be high. Moreover, the ill-defined boundaries of these disciplines make their literatures particularly unsusceptible to control and retrieval through automated means. As a matter of fact, even the traditional print index has proven generally weak in providing coverage of the periodical literature in many disciplines, causing scholars to continue such tried-and-true techniques as following footnotes and bibliographies in articles or books pertinent to their topics. If the print tools themselves suffer major deficiencies, to put them online where a nonspecialist must then act as an intermediary is no improvement.

I do not mean to argue that computer searching does not have valuable services to perform. I believe that in most cases it can, when properly executed, provide a useful complement to the manual research technique. In the sciences and engineering, it may be able to substitute for manual searches in the same indexes. But as a person who has engaged in scholarly research himself and also done online searching, I am not sanguine about the claims being made by the more ardent proponents of computer searching. And I think that the technology, if misunderstood, poses potentially serious dangers to the world of scholarship.

I detect already among many college students a naive trust in the efficacy of the machine and a willingness to use it so as to subvert the educational experience that a term paper is meant to provide. The traditional manual search yields much valuable knowledge as a byproduct of locating relevant information. One pores over bibliographies and footnotes, reads background material, browses in the stacks, and looks through indexes. In the process, one gets a "feel" for the discipline, comes to recognize the names of many researchers, sees the same classic titles repeated in many places, skims abstracts of interesting articles on entirely unrelated topics, manipulates terminology, familiarizes oneself with the classification schemes for the literature of the discipline, and gets a sense of how interpretations have evolved.

Much of this educational benefit can now be lost on the student. He comes to the library with a poorly defined topic, explains it as best he can to a librarian who has limited knowledge of the discipline, pays money to obtain a bibliography that may or may not be a good one, reads the citations included on it, and writes up the paper. But has the cause of higher education been served?

As library finances become tighter and the costs of materials rise, it is not uncommon to hear talk of possibly dropping subscriptions to print indexes that are available online. Such an action is undesirable if not impracticable. Online searching does not have the broad educational value of the print index, even for one who can conduct a computer search himself. Ultimately, the online index cannot be browsed as the print tool can, the more so when every minute online is eating up dollars. Moreover, one sees nothing online other than the computer's response to a query, a response that consists of numbers. Also, the process involves using an intermediary who is not personally knowledgeable in the discipline. And to rely on the computer alone would certainly involve an enormous diminution in access to information, for an entire corps of online searchers could not provide the hundreds of thousands of searches a year needed to satisfy the needs of every university patron with a research project.

The dangers do not exist only at the level of the library. Some advocates of online searching are speaking of the probability that at some time in the future the production of print indexes will cease altogether. If the researcher then wishes to conduct a literature search in an index, he will be forced to resort to an intermediary, of good, bad, or indifferent skills, to do this part of his research for him. The true computer-minded visionaries even foresee a library in which patrons will conduct their own online searches. This vision, it seems to me, is even less realistic, and in any case it ignores the fact that an online index can never provide the educational experience and broad introduction to the discipline that the print tool furnishes.

The more ardent computer advocates tend, I believe, to impose on the world of knowledge, learning, and scholarly research a rationality and simplicity that it does not have. Taking their cue from the natural sciences, where "facts" can be labeled with relatively precise and unambiguous terminology, they try to project the same rationality upon the social and artistic worlds, with all their subjective perceptions, nuances, layers of meaning, and imprecise and overlapping definitions. Facts in the social and artistic worlds cannot be so easily established or labeled with a single term whose meaning is universally understood or accepted.

Computer searching, then, though it can be of supplemental value to research in any discipline, assumes an approach to research based solely on the "rational." In it, scholars and students find little or no room for browsing and serendipitous discovery that exists with the print indexes, imperfect as they are. It does not provide the broad education in the discipline that print indexes do. It assumes a precision in definition and an accuracy in assigning descriptors that often do not exist. It can be useful in tracking down citations of value, but it is only one more technique to be added to the broad array of approaches used by the research scholar. Improperly used, it could pose real dangers to the world of scholarship and teaching.

LIBRARIES AND INFORMATION SERVICES IN CHINA*

Luo Xingyun

1. History

China has lagged behind scientifically and economically since the last century, yet she had a brilliant history in ancient times, full of scientific and technical accomplishments. As the original home of paper and the art of printing, China has been noted for her great Imperial and famous family libraries. Some books on the history of libraries, however, neglect this fact when talking about the origin of the library. The existence of archives and libraries in China can be traced back as early as 3000 years ago, the period of the Chinese Shang Dynasty (1600-1100 B.C.) or even earlier than this after serious study of the bone (or tortoise shell) inscriptions discovered late in the Nineteenth Century. The earlier and cheaper materials for inscriptions which were more perishable than bones and tortoise shells could not survive to the present. An interesting fact, that a large number of bone inscriptions were found in one place recording activities concerning sacrifice, warfare, hunting, journeys, sickness, rain, and other spiritual, natural and human affairs in connection with the royal house, makes research workers think that they were no other than the royal archives or libraries. That is the only explanation, because under the conditions at that time, no one but the royal court could keep, and had need to keep, so many documents, in the form of bone and tortoise shell inscriptions, as imperial archives. Lao zi (604?-531 B.C.), a great philosopher in ancient China was, according to recorded history, the first officially appointed historian in Chinese history, charged with the upkeep of the royal archive of the early Zhou Dynasty (700-256 B.C.).

During the so-called period of Spring and Autumn and Warring States (770-221 B.C.) academic affairs were very lively. That was the time of "Contention of A Hundred Schools of Thought" in Chinese history. Every school of scholars actively expounded their ideas both in speech and writing in order to expand their influence on state affairs. Therefore, a vast amount of books representing various

---

*Reprinted by permission of the publisher from Journal of Information Science: Principles & Practice, 6:1 (March 1983) 21-31. Copyright © 1983 by North-Holland (Elsevier Science Publishers BV).

thoughts emerged at that time. Each small state had its own historian responsible for recording important events and sorting out the books and documents collected. Paper had not at that time been invented and people used to engrave inscriptions with knife on bamboo or wooden slips or write on the expensive thin, tough silk for official documents. Nevertheless, private collections by great scholars were popular.[1]

Eight years after the unification of the whole country by Qin State in 221 B.C., the First Emperor ordered the burning of all books that he thought would confuse the people's mind, with the exception of the ones on agriculture, medicine and divination, and later the burying of those scholars who dared to criticize his policy. He thought this act would thus consolidate his rule which he wished to last ten thousand generations. Contrary to his wish, his dynasty perished only 14 years after his seizure of the whole of China, and books were preserved by the people anyway.

However, most of the previous feudal emperors attached great importance to libraries and archives and appointed officials to manage them, not all because they loved books and treasured this national asset but more traditionally to show by their orthodoxy that they were qualified to be emperors. The first imperial library was established during the period of Emperor Wu (140-87 B.C.) of the Han Dynasty. These libraries, strictly speaking, did not serve the general public, but the Imperial family, ministers, high officials and noted scholars. In 77 B.C., at Imperial command, senior official Liu Xiang began to compile, and later his son Liu Xing completed, Bie Lu (The Other Register) and Qi Lue (Summary for Seven Classics). Bie Lu was the first collection of abstracts and Qi Lue was the first bibliography to be compiled in China, as far as is known. This is a very important event in the history of Chinese libraries and was the embryonic form of information work in China. Qi Lue classified books into six categories. On this basis, another scholar in the Western Jin Dynasty (265-316 A.D.), Xun Xu, produced a library catalogue called New catalogue. This work was classified into four divisions later called Four Division Classification Method. Up to the 12th Century, books were further classified into 12 divisions and in the 18th Century four divisions and 44 categories. This classification method was used until early this century.[2] The invention of paper (1st Century A.D.) and the art of printing (5th Century A.D.), especially the block printing technique (9th Century A.D.) made book production easier and books cheaper, thus promoting the wide spread of books and the development of libraries, especially the rise of private libraries. In the later period of the Qing Dynasty, for example, there were as many as 497 large private libraries. The completion of the comprehensive encyclopaedia Yong Le Da Dian (in 22877 volumes plus 60 volumes of index) in 1408 (Ming Dynasty) and the national bibliography Si Ku Quan Shu (General Catalogue of Four Treasure Libraries, in 36275 volumes) in 1782 (Qing Dynasty) demonstrated the full flourish of libraries in the feudal period of China.

Libraries in the modern sense began in the latter years of the Qing Dynasty (1644-1911). The introduction of modern science and political theory from the West into China promoted reform movement as well as library developments. In 1896, the Emperor Guang Xu issued an edict to establish libraries. The first provincial public library was founded in Wuhan in 1903, then other provinces followed suit. The adoption of the first modern classification scheme--Dewey's Decimal Classification Scheme--in 1904 and the establishment of the National Beijing Library in 1910 on the basis of the Beijing Municipal Library, marked the beginning of a new phase of Chinese library history. The former China Association of Libraries was established in 1925, and by 1930, the total number of libraries of various types amounted to 2935 in the whole country.[1]

Language translation can be traced back to the 1st century, the early days of the introduction of Buddhism, and this may be regarded as an information activity. During the period of the Western Jin Dynasty (265-316 A.D.) and the following dynasties, the translation of Buddhist sutras was encouraged by emperors though it only served religious needs. This work was carried out on a large scale especially during the Tang Dynasty (618-907 A.D.). A monk, Xuan Zhuang, who had gone on a pilgrimage to India and other Central and South Asian countries for Buddhist Scriptures, was engaged in translation for 19 years and translated Buddhist sutras in 75 divisions in 1335 volumes. During the Ming Dynasty (1368-1644 A.D.), language translation mainly served diplomatic needs. The Imperial government established a special translation agency in 1407 to translate languages of South East Asian countries. It is worth notice that just as that time a number of books of modern science dealing with geometry, surveying and hydrology from the West were translated into Chinese by the famous agriculturalist Xu Guangqi (1562-1633 A.D.) in cooperation with the Italian missionary Matteo Ricci (1552-1633 A.D.). From the viewpoint of information, it was a great event in the history of scientific and technical information of China. In the last years of the Qing Dynasty (late Nineteenth Century), owing to the needs of diplomacy and the need for learning Western science, not only did the government establish special agencies such as "Tong Wen Guan" (Language Communication House) for learning and translating Western languages, but also nongovernmental organizations began to set up "Yang Xue Guan" (Western Science School) and "Yi Shu Ju" (Book Translation House). Many Western books such as Evolution and Ethics and Other Essays by Thomas Huxley and The Origin of Species by Charles Darwin were translated into Chinese by Yan Fu, a very important person in Chinese modern history.[3] These organizations played an important role in disseminating Western advanced technology and political theory and promoting the reform movement and later revolution in China. Another event is the starting of a special bibliographical column in the Journal of Chemistry published by the former Chemical Society of China in 1934, which is regarded as a beginning of modern information work in China. However, libraries and information services could not be properly developed due to the backwardness of science and technology and the neglect of the government in old China. Things began to change only after the founding of the People's Republic of China in 1949.

2. The background to the establishment of the Chinese information network

As a result of the three-year restoration of the national economy, destroyed in the civil war, and the implementation of the first five-year plan from 1952 to 1956, science and technology developed rapidly. Many government departments carried out information work spontaneously in order to satisfy the increasing information needs of research workers. For example, four series of biological abstracts have been published by the Science Press since 1953. Information work at that time, however, was decentralized, lacking unified planning and coordination.

On the basis of the fulfillment of the first five-year plan, the Chinese government formulated the general line for socialist construction during the period of transition from new democratic society to socialism in 1956 with a goal to build China into an industrialized country. Considering that the development of science and technology was the precondition and guarantee for reaching this goal, the Chinese government attached great importance to its development, and therefore gave it leading priority in 1956. Scientific and technical information work was regarded as an important component of research in science and technology. In the long range development project in science and technology for the year 1957-1958, one of the important tasks for research in science and technology listed was the establishment of a scientific and technical information organization. In October 1956, the Chinese Academy of Sciences formally founded the Institute of Scientific and Technical information, mainly to serve the needs of its research institutes. In May 1958, the State Council approved "The Scheme Concerning the Carrying out of Scientific and Technical Information Work," decided at the first National Working Conference of Scientific and Technical Information to expand and strengthen the Institute of Information of Academy of Sciences, and changed its name to the present one: Institute of Scientific and Technical Information of China (ISTIC), thereby making it into a national scientific and technical information centre and a national coordinating organization of information work for the whole country.[4] After this conference, every Ministry and most Commissions under the State Council, and every province and autonomous region, established their own scientific and technical information institutes. In addition to that, regional information centres were established in seven big cities, and also thousands of regional and national information exchange networks were set up in the whole country. The number of information professionals amounts to some 50 000 persons or more at present.

3. Basic policy and tasks of information service

The turmoil and upheaval during the period of the Cultural Revolution from 1966-1976 caused severe damage to the production of agriculture and industry as well as to information work. While the rest of the world experienced a literature explosion, China underwent a literature contraction. Many academic journals ceased publication, international exchange and contact almost discontinued. The worst thing was the misunderstanding of the basic policy of information work, which had not been cleared up until after the National Science Conference in March 1978.

The general objective of China for the time being is to realize the four modernizations. Therefore, all the activities of scientific and technical information work should centre on this general objective. The acquisition, reporting and delivery of documents should be carried out according to the needs of the national economic plan including the key projects decided by the government. The policy of Chinese information work can be summarized in four Chinese words: guang, kuai, jing and zhun. There are no equivalent English words that can exactly cover their meanings. Broadly speaking, "guang" means that the number of people organized and mobilized should be greater, literature collected and accumulated should be comprehensive, users served should be widespread; "Kuai" means that the acquisition, processing, reporting and delivery of information and documents should be fast and timely; "Jing" means that the acquisition, processing, reporting and delivery of information and documents should be both systematic and selective so as to meet the actual needs in agriculture, industry and scientific research; "Zhun" means that the information provided to users should be exactly what the users want without mistakes. In the activities of the information service, the principles of unified planning with overall consideration, cooperation, mutual exchange of information between organizations, regions and trades are emphasized so as to share information resources. Hindering the passage of information and selfish departmentalism should be absolutely rejected.

The basic tasks of Chinese information work stipulated in the document Scheme Concerning the Carrying out of Scientific and Technical Information Work are "Reporting recent achievements and tendencies in various important areas of science and technology at home and abroad in order to enable personnel in the scientific, technical, economic, defence and educational departments to obtain necessary materials for adopting these achievements of modern science and technology, so as to save manpower and time, avoid duplication of labour and promote the development of science and technology in China." Specifically, information organizations should:

> (1) provide the authorities concerned with necessary and timely materials and data for the formulation of policies, objectives, plans and projects or production and research;

(2) quickly and comprehensively collect information and documents concerning important inventions at home and report them as quickly as possible in the form of secondary literature;

(3) systematically and selectively collect and report current scientific and technical literature of all kinds from developed countries;

(4) effect information analysis;

(5) accumulate step by step and systematically sort out information and documents for the establishment of data bases of different specialities as foundations for computer retrieval in the future.[5]

4. Elements of the information system

The Chinese information system consists of four elements. They are (see also Fig. 1):

(a) The national information centre, i.e. ISTIC and its Chongqing Branch. ISTIC is a comprehensive institution doing scientific and technical information research and analysis led by the State Commission of Science and Technology, and a centre engaged in scientific and technical undertakings for the whole country, functionally (though not administratively) the top of a hierarchy including all levels of information and documentation centres in the country. As a national centre, the major tasks are:

(1) to methodically collect scientific and technical information material at home and abroad in support of the development projects of the national economy, science and technology. Its scope of acquisition is to include related scientific and technical papers and publications, magazines, conference proceedings, research reports, patent literature, standards material, retrieval tools, catalogues and samples, films and video material, etc.;

(2) to effect comprehensive scientific and technical information analysis and study, as well as compilation, translation and reporting with attention centred on national economic construction, and the development of science and technology;

(3) to shoulder the work of compilation, translation and reporting of comprehensive information retrieval publications involved in the national systems of retrieval publications;

(4) to organize the exchange of plans on vital domestic scientific research items, intermediate scientific research results, and to participate in the compilation of domestic retrieval publications;

(5) to offer consultation, translation and retrieval services as well as services to facilitate reading and reproduction of material kept in ISTIC stack-rooms;

(6) to conduct training classes to train information staff

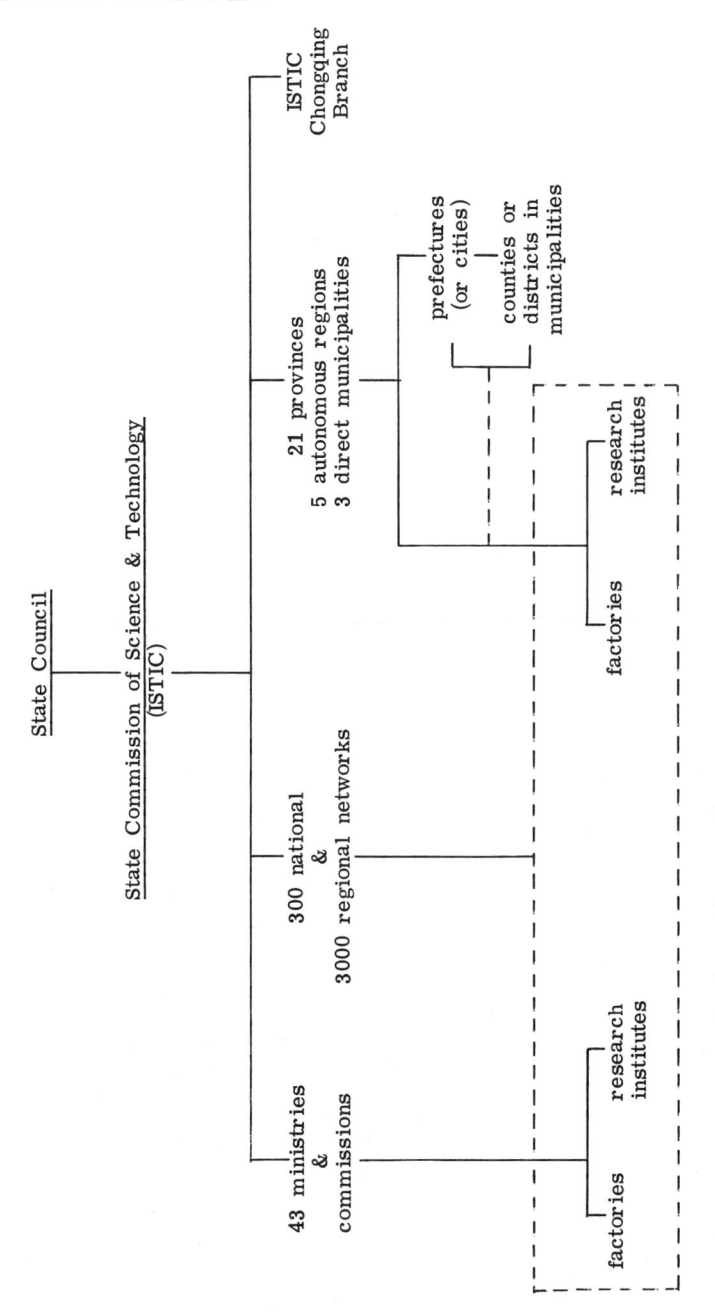

Fig. 1. The structure of information service.

of the whole country, and compile teaching texts, vocational study reference material, yearbooks and handbooks;

(7) to study the theory and method of information, and the modernization of technical means; and

(8) to develop international exchange and cooperation in information work.

ISTIC has 9 administrative and 17 vocational departments including 6 libraries with a staff of 1177 persons, and its Chongqing Branch has 5 research divisions, 1 library, 1 department and 1 printing house with a total staff of 529 persons. It is by many criteria one of the major information and documentation centres for science and technology in the world.

The total amount of accessions in ISTIC by the end of 1979 includes 12 700 foreign periodical titles accumulated since 1968, 671 000 foreign documents (chiefly research reports, conference proceedings, dissertations and theses, etc.), 6 600 000 patent specifications, 278 000 standards, 350 000 foreign product catalogues, 4000 Chinese periodical titles, 200 000 domestic documents, 1 000 000 plates and reels of micro material, 33 000 reference books, 1200 scientific and technical films. The chief means of acquisition is to subscribe and order through commercial channels. Besides this, ISTIC has established exchange agreements with 63 countries and regions as well as 71 international organizations with an exchange list of 2472 entries.

ISTIC and all related institutions as well as local information institutes are organized to form the China Scientific and Technical Edition and Translation Commission. At present it compiles, translates and publishes 379 types of publications which can be divided into three categories: indexes 137 types; translations 227 types; and research publications 15 types.[4]

The main function of ISTIC Chongqing Branch is to compile, translate and publish retrieval publications of various kinds covering most areas, which account for a large part of all the retrieval publications in the country. This Branch Institute also translates Scientific American from cover to cover and publishes it in Chinese under the title of Kexue (Science) which attracts a large public.

Before 1966, the coordination of the activities of the information system was done by the Bureau of Scientific and Technical Information of SCST, actually the same leading body of ISTIC. Now this work is done by the First Division of Planning and Operation of ISTIC and the China Society of Scientific and Technical Information with its secretariat in ISTIC. As a national centre, ISTIC is responsible for the sponsorship of the national information workshops from time to time, at which directors and information specialists from various information institutes exchange their views, make plans for future activities, discuss problems and cooperation in work. As a national information centre, ISTIC represents China in taking an active part in international and bilateral information activities, cooperating closely in staff training and facility provision in order to modernize its information work. It is already a trustee country of the Intergovernment Council of the PGI/UNESCO and one of the depository libraries of UNESCO publications.

(b) 29 provincial, autonomous regional and direct municipal information institutes with 7 regional centres. The second element of the Chinese information system includes 43 ministerial information institutes. In March last year, the Standing Committee of the National People's Congress approved a plan for restructuring the State Council so that 98 Ministries, commissions and Agencies under SC will be merged and reduced to 52. Therefore, the information institutes of these Ministries will be merged and reduced accordingly. But this information element will still exist anyway, and its functions remain the same as before. Each ministerial information institute is a documentation centre responsible for collecting and disseminating information documents within its mission and area, and offering information service to the research institutes and factories under that ministry. It is also an organizer of information work in that ministry. Almost every research institute and factory under each ministry has an information section or group depending on its size. Most of the regular users of ISTIC come from these sections and groups. They are also members of the national or regional information exchange networks of specialities. Therefore, to coordinate the activities, the exchange of information and the training of information workers for factories and research institutes within each ministry are the responsibilities of this ministerial information institute. Ministerial information institutes are also members of the China Scientific and Technical Education and Translation Commission. They either cooperate with ISTIC Chongqing Branch or themselves undertake the compilation, translation and publishing of retrieval publications relating to their areas as parts of the whole retrieval publication system and other information journals.

(c) 43 ministerial information institutes. The third element is composed of 29 provincial level information institutes and 219 prefectural level information institutes with 7 regional centres in 7 big cities in the original great administrative regions: Shanghai (East China), Wuhan (Central China): Guangzhou (South China), Chengdu (Southwest China), Sian (Northwest China), Tianjin (North China) and Shengyang (Northeast China). Provincial institutes act as documentation centres, responsible for organizing and coordinating information work in these provinces. So do the prefectural information institutes in the localities. They are administratively under the leadership of the Scientific and Technical Commissions of the local governments, but professionally guided by the ISTIC. They are the organizers of the regional information exchange networks.

(d) National and regional information exchange networks of specialities. China organizes her information work vertically, from the national level down to grassroot level as stated above and also horizontally through one region or the whole country. People of the same trade, factories producing the same products, institutes engaged in the research in the same scientific area need to exchange their views, experiences in work and the results they get in order to avoid the duplication of labour that causes waste of manpower, time and money. Therefore, people from these factories and research institutes of the same trade and same profession come together regularly to discuss their problems, exchange information and publish magazines so as to promote their work. People organized at the regional level make up the regional information exchange network, while those at the highest level constitute the national network. This is the fourth element, a very important element in the Chinese information system, because the people involved are engaged in actual research and production, and are both users and producers of information. Their activities of information exchange enable them to share information resources and research results as soon as possible. It is of vital importance to have these national and regional information exchange networks well organized. This work is done by ISTIC and the ministerial and local information institutes. But of course, the academic societies are the core, and play very active parts in these networks. At present, there are about 300 national and 3000 regional information exchange networks of various areas. Most of them were set up in a short time just after the First National Information Working Conference and most are still active now. The Shipbuilding Information Exchange Network of Guangdong and Guangsi, National Information Exchange Network of Low Voltage Electrical Equipments and Electric Transmission and the National Textile Information Exchange Network, etc. are good examples among them.

5. Structure of the library system

As in other countries, libraries in China are organized by different types [1] (see also Fig. 2):

(a) Public libraries: These include the National Library of Beijing, but in the main comprise the municipal, provincial (or autonomous regional), prefectural and county libraries, down to the district, neighbourhood and street libraries or reading rooms in municipalities, and commune (town) and brigade (now village) libraries or reading rooms in rural areas. The central authority for these is the Administrative Bureau of Library Service of the Ministry of Culture. It is emphasized, however, that in this and other cases, the libraries are not centrally controlled, but are largely self-governed and self-financed through the Bureau of Culture of the local governments at the appropriate level. At present, the total number of public libraries at county level and above is 1731 with a total collection of 190 000 000 volumes and a staff of 19 461 persons. We may compare this to 1956, with only 96 libraries, a total collection of 28 900 000 volumes and a staff of 3714 persons.

The Beijing Library founded in 1910, is a national library. Its collection is the largest in China. The total collection of books

Libraries and Librarians

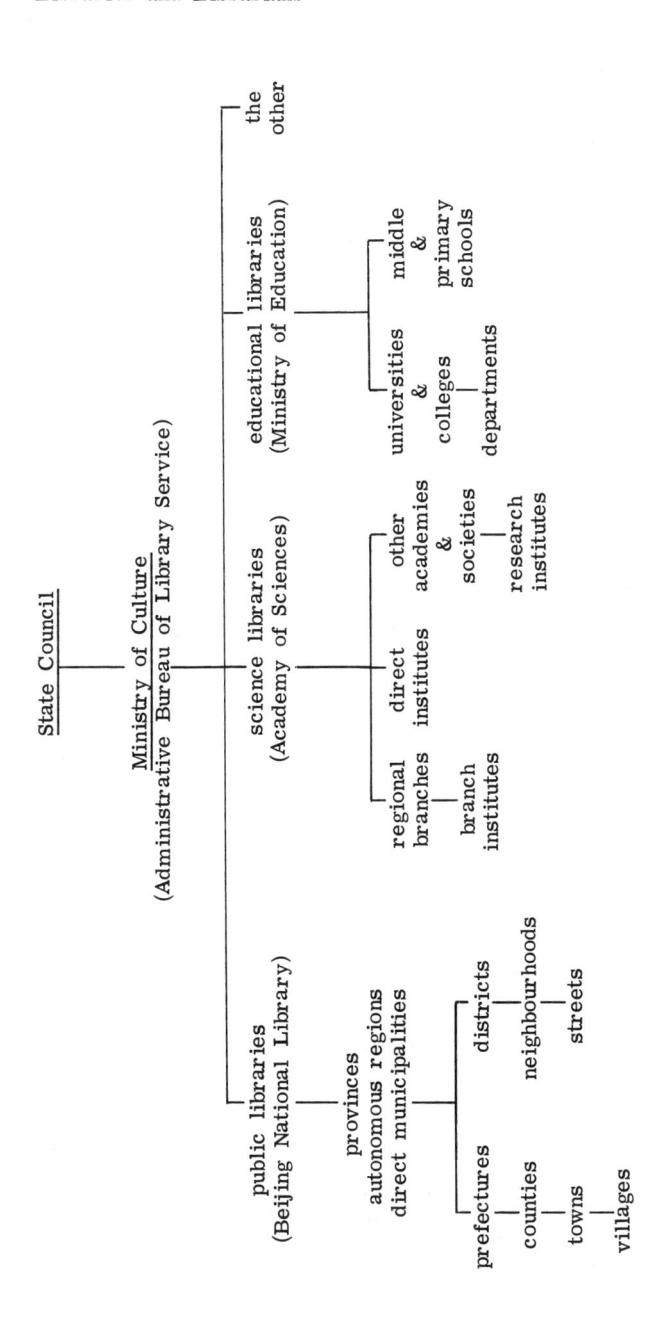

Fig. 2. The structure of library service.

- State Council
  - Ministry of Culture (Administrative Bureau of Library Service)
    - public libraries (Beijing National Library)
      - provinces, autonomous regions, direct municipalities
        - prefectures
        - counties
        - towns
        - villages
        - districts
        - neighbourhoods
        - streets
    - science libraries (Academy of Sciences)
      - regional branches
        - branch institutes
      - direct institutes
      - other academies & societies
        - research institutes
    - educational libraries (Ministry of Education)
      - universities & colleges
        - departments
      - middle & primary schools
    - the other

only is about 1 000 000 volumes published mainly from as far back as the Qing Dynasty up to recent times. It is also a depository library for all Chinese formal publications with emphasis on social sciences, includes 11 000 periodicals, of which four fifths are foreign periodicals. One third of these foreign periodicals is acquired through the channel of exchange with 2000 foreign organizations. This library includes 15 reading rooms with the facility of accommodating 7000 readers. The total staff of this library is about 860 persons. Among them, one third are university graduates, the rest having had on-the-job training in library science. Beijing Library produces the Chinese National Bibliography and catalogue cards for new Chinese books for over 2000 libraries (almost 7 million cards in 1979) as well as catalogue cards for all foreign books acquired by libraries in the Beijing area and other big libraries outside Beijing, in cooperation with the Beijing Branch of the China National Publication Import Corporation (CNPIC). Besides, Beijing Library has begun to issue a printed union catalogue of periodicals available in important libraries giving details of each holding.[6] Among other public libraries, the Shanghai Public Library is the biggest, second to the Beijing National Library.

(b) Educational libraries: These include university and college libraries, middle school libraries and primary school libraries. The central authority for these is the Ministry of Education. The funds for these libraries are received as part of the general funds of the institutions they serve.

According to the statistics of April 1981, the total collections of 670 university and college libraries amounts to 200 million copies and the total staff to 17 000 persons. But there were only 212 university and college libraries in 1956 with a total collection of only 27 280 000 copies.

The largest educational library is the Beijing University Library with 25 500 sq. m. space and 2000 seats in 31 reading rooms. The total collection is about 3 700 000 volumes. Its departmental libraries collect mainly teaching materials. This library received about 4000 foreign journals of which some 2500 are in science and technology. It establishes exchange relations with 300 foreign institutions using the journals published by the institutes of Academy of Sciences as exchange materials, and also has interlibrary loan agreements with 200 libraries in China. [6] The other large university libraries are Nanjing University Library, Wuhan University Library and Fudan University Library in Shanghai with total collections of 2 600 000, 1 900 000 and 1 600 000 volumes respectively.

The middle and primary school libraries mainly collect teaching reference materials, books related to popular sciences, literary books and children's books. Children's libraries or children's reading rooms are usually affiliated to the public libraries or children's palaces financed by the local governments.

(c) Science and research libraries: These include the libraries of the Academy of Sciences and a large number of libraries attached to research institutes throughout the country.

Within the administration of the Chinese Academy of Sciences, there are 140 institutional and 7 regional branch academy libraries. The Academy of Sciences Library in Beijing has a staff of about 360 persons. Its acquisition policy responds to the range of activities within the Academy research institutes with dominance in pure and applied sciences including the life sciences, and less emphasis on technology in a strict sense. A large number of foreign publications (including 1500 current periodicals) are received on an exchange basis since the academy publishes a number of major research journals. The Academy Library offers a plain-paper photocopy service and a microfilm service. Home loans are permitted. Apart from the Academy of Sciences Library, the major libraries covering science and technology in Beijing are libraries of the Academy of Medicine, Academy of Agriculture, Academy of Architecture, etc., offering services mainly to their own research institutes and branches inside and outside the Beijing area, actually forming service systems of their own. There is also a large number of academic society libraries covering science and technology, but of less importance in comparison with other science libraries.

(d) Trade union and factory libraries: There is a great number of factory and workshop libraries organized by the trade unions within factories, and they make extensive use of the public, educational and science libraries through group borrowing.

In addition to the above, there is also a great number of libraries or reading rooms in civil administrative organizations and army units from the central level down to the grassroot units, functionally not much different from the libraries in factories.

Different types of library are under the administration of different central authorities, but the Administrative Bureau of Library Service of the Ministry of Culture is responsible for the coordination and cooperation of different library systems in the whole country besides its direct leadership of public libraries and children's libraries. The China Society of Library Science was founded in 1979 having 28 branch societies in provinces, autonomous regions and direct municipalities with a membership of 2300 individuals.

6. Training and qualifications of staff

China has a 63 year history of library education since 1920. Formerly, only the Beijing University and Wuhan University established departments of librarianship and only 3000 students graduated from these departments from 1949 to 1968. The number is small: among the 100 000 library workers in the country, qualified graduates account for only 2 percent, not more than 5 percent even in the university and college libraries, science libraries and provincial level public libraries. Graduates majoring in information science are even fewer than those in librarianship. Altogether, not more than 100 students graduated from the Department of Information Science of the University of Science and Technology of China in 1963. This department was formerly the School of Information Science established by ISTIC in 1959 and merged into USTC in 1960 as one of its departments. It was closed down in 1963. Most of its graduates now work in ISTIC and other information institutes. Clearly, this situation cannot meet the needs for the development of library and information service, let alone serve the four modernizations of this country. Fortunately, there are already 17 universities having departments, specialities or classes of librarianship at present, with 1500 undergraduates and 1500 correspondence students.[7] There is also one speciality of information science in the Department of Librarianship of Wuhan University, the only one at present in China. Therefore, it seems imperative that a college of information science be established and information courses be offered in more universities and colleges. This is currently under consideration by the authority concerned. As an interim measure, courses of lectures on library and information science are given by the specialists from ISTIC or other libraries to undergraduates in many universities and colleges. In September 1981, the National Conference of University and College Libraries was convened in Beijing by the Ministry of Education in order to improve library service and education for librarianship in universities and colleges.

As for the training of the staff, the Beijing National Library, Academy of Sciences Library and other large libraries have established special departments responsible for the training of their staff and the staff from their affiliated organizations. ISTIC and its Chongqing Branch not only train their own staff but also those from other information institutes and organizations. The form of classes and the subjects for training are different according to different individuals. It may be on-the-job or off-the-job training, at which different courses are given such as the theory and methods of library and information science, computer technology, foreign languages or natural sciences. The principle is "study what one needs." For the non-graduates, more courses must be given in order to enrich their knowledge and be more competent in their work. Generally speaking, a qualified library and information worker must at least:

> (1) have a good knowledge of one or more special subjects, usually in the sciences;
> (2) master one foreign language;
> (3) be familiar with the theory, methods and techniques of library and information work;
> (4) possess the abilities of analysis, synthesis and interpretation;
> (5) have a good mastery of written Chinese, and familiarity with the techniques of editing and publishing.

Items 4 and 5 are emphasized for information workers.

7. Automation and prospects

For historical, political and economical reasons as well as the problem of written Chinese, the automation of library and information processes in China is far behind the Western countries. The routine work and administration in libraries and information institutes is still done manually. The effort of information automation started in the early sixties, but was discontinued during the "Cultural Revolution." The first success occurred in November 1975 when the Information Institute of the First Ministry of Machine Building completed an experiment in retrieving from 500 foreign papers on metallurgy in cooperation with the Computer Centre of this Ministry using a China-made DJS-C_4 computer. Again, in December 1977, an online retrieval experiment was conducted on the terminal in the main building of this ministry connected with the Computer Centre through telephone line. The result was satisfactory. Another example is machine translation. In cooperation with the Language Institute of the Chinese Academy of Social Sciences and the Statistics Institute of the Chinese Academy of Sciences, ISTIC has established an English-Chinese titles machine translation system using a China-made Type II computer. Satisfactory results were obtained in the pilot tests of April 1978 in translating 20 titles from English into Chinese. Research workers, encouraged by these successes, are confident in the realization of multi-language translation in the future. This system is still in trial use on a Type TK70 computer for translating papers from English into Chinese both in metallurgy and computer science. ISTIC has a TK70 and a T4100 computer with the Chinese Character information processing system imported from Japan. In order to utilise this computer in experiments to do Chinese character typesetting and retrieval, the work of programming is actively under way, and some preliminary results have been obtained. Similar experiments are also conducted in other organizations. A comprehensive Chinese thesaurus was completed in 1981 and is in trial use now. This is a very important step towards the utilization of machine retrieval.

The objective of information automation in China is, as stated by Dr. Qian Xuesen, the famous scientist of aeromechanics and deputy director of the Scientific and Technical Commission of National Defence, "to enable research personnel to search and access information and documents kept in our country at any place, in the shortest time through a network using high-density storage of the vast amount of scientific and technical information we already have; and by establishing a national information retrieval network using data bases, communication systems and terminal display facilities." To reach this objective, the following steps are to be taken according to the information automation programme formulated just after the National Science Conference:

First, take a further step to strengthen the information organizations of the whole country, making the structure more systematic, distribution more rational, and coordination and cooperation more effective so as to share the resource of information by all. Then, to enhance the acquisition, reporting and analysis of information as well as the staff training both in the information profession and information techniques in order to become prepared materially and technically for information automation. Last, to equip, in a planned way, the information institutions with computers and other advanced facilities so as to perform machine retrieval, machine translation and typesetting, and establish a computer retrieval network between important information institutes. For these reasons, the leading personnel and specialists of ISTIC have made a series of study tours to the United States, the United Kingdom, France, Japan, Yugoslavia and the Soviet Union, etc. and attended the activities and conferences of some international organizations such as UNISIST, FID, ISO, while entertaining scientific and technical information officials and experts from organizations such as UNESCO and WIPO as well as those from the countries mentioned above during their visits and tours in China and conducting academic exchange activities with them. ISTIC has also established friendly relations and cooperation with corresponding organizations such as the MIDIST of France, NTIS of the USA, GID of the FRG and the BL of the UK. For personnel training, ISTIC has sent some middle rank professionals to the USA, the UK and the FRG etc. to study information management and machine retrieval while conducting seminars and training classes in collaboration with other foreign organizations at home. For example, a training class on "Information Automation and Online Retrieval Systems" was sponsored jointly in 1980 by ISTIC, UNESCO and the National Bureau of Scientific and Technical Information of France in Beijing.

The basic conditions of libraries are almost the same as information services, but there is great awareness at the Beijing National Library of the need for computer-assisted operations. Investigation, planning and experiments are going on. To begin with (in view of the difficulties of Chinese character processing), efforts are being focused on "Western" bibliographic material, in particular for cataloguing and card production. An agreement has been reached among important libraries to use AACR II (Anglo-American Cataloging Rules, second edition) with minor changes to suit Chinese practice. Experimental runs are being performed on the Chinese Academy of Sciences (Statistics Institute) Felix 3512 computer. One short-term goal is to create a national union acquisition file. Participating institutions and libraries in the present experiment are the Beijing National Library, the People's University Library, the Chinese Academy of Sciences Library, the Beijing University Library, the Qinghua University Library and the China National Publication Import Corporation.[6] The main collections in libraries are in the Chinese language, therefore the critical problem for many important computer applications is the feasibility of Chinese character processing by the computer. Library automation cannot be realized in a short time unless the ability of computers to process Chinese characters is dramatically increased, regardless of economic constraints.

8. Conclusion

The structure of the library and information systems in China seems to be very sound, yet services and automation are backward. China is aware of her weakness in this respect and is trying to change the situation to suit her needs for the four modernizations. It must be confessed that there are several difficulties to overcome for the modernization of library and information service. But a good prospect can be expected so long as China persists in its present policies at home and strengthens friendly cooperation with other countries.

Acknowledgment

The author wishes to thank B.C. Vickery and Professor D.J. Foskett for their encouragement and guidance in writing this paper.

References

1. Introduction to library science [in Chinese], a test book compiled by Beijing University and Wuhan University, Beijing (1981).
2. Liu Guojun, "The development of the classification schemes of books in China [in Chinese]," Bulletin of China Society of Library Science 4 (1981) 46-54.
3. Li Weiqiu, "A preliminary exploration of the origin of foreign scientific and technical information work in China [in Chinese]," Information Science 2 (2) (1981) 43-47.
4. The Institute of Scientific and Technical Information of China, a brief presentation of ISTIC, Beijing (1980).
5. Teaching text for information science (in Chinese), compiled by ISTIC Chongqing Branch, Chongqing (1980).
6. M. Brawne and S. Schwarz, "Development of the Institute of Scientific and Technical Information of China," Unesco technical report RP/1979-1980/5/10.1/03.
7. Zhou Lin, "A summary report at the National Conference of University and College Libraries [in Chinese]," Bulletin of China Society of Library Science 4 (1981) 8-12.

THE NEUROCHEMICAL BASES OF LIBRARY USE...

OR, WHY WE LOVE HARLEQUINS*

James Benson and Daniel O. O'Connor

Genre Fiction, Librarians' Attitudes, and Library Collections

Librarians have long been familiar with the phenomenon of the heavy user--the library user who <u>devours</u> mysteries, science fiction, westerns, and romances. Our field's stereotypes of these readers vary from the mildly complimentary to the derogatory:

- The mystery reader may be somewhat intellectually respectable; scholars such as Jacques Barzun are known to read mysteries;
- Science fiction is often perceived as the province of weird kids who may become important scientists;
- Westerns seem to many to be the domain of the blue collar macho man;
- Romances purportedly are read by the sexually frustrated young woman and the elderly widow.

The validity of the stereotypes is highly questionable, but without doubt they have affected libraries' decisions concerning the collection of various genres and librarians' attitudes toward the readers of those works. For example, because some librarians regard mysteries and mystery readers as more respectable than romances and romance readers, more effort, more resources, and better space are allocated to mysteries than to romances.

Whatever the librarians' bias towards various categories of the reading public, the frequency of use heightens indeed the visibility of these book "addicts." Yet very few inquiries have been aimed at determining the nature or cause of this addiction. The focus remains on the genre preferred by them. On the other hand, if the motivation for compulsive reading were better understood, more fruitful approaches to satisfying these voracious needs might be explored. Could patrons be "weaned" from one genre and

---

*Reprinted by permission of the authors and publisher from <u>Collection Building,</u> 4:3 (1982) 34-41. Copyright © 1982 by Neal-Schuman Publishers.

directed to another? Does frequency of reading vary over time among different types of individuals? Can the underlying cause be reduced to a single factor or is it multiple?

We shall, in the following pages, present a theory which suggests that frequency of reading is a function of the relationships among psychopharmacological, environmental, and conventional psychological variables. It will not answer all of the above mentioned questions, but it should contribute to understanding the underlying motivation of the library habitué.

Library Use and User Studies

It appears to be a truism that circulation per capita and circulation per volume (collection turnover) increase appreciably in those public libraries that stock genre fiction in large quantities. It is assumed by librarians that certain personal characteristics (chiefly demographic) predispose certain individuals to read. These explanations, however, do not account for the routinely reported fact that a small proportion of users account for a disproportionately high percentage of use. For example, Clark [1] found 5.8 percent of the users (core borrowers) generated 28 percent of the circulation in one library.

Use and user studies, principally those of Zweizig (1973) and D'Elia (1980) have attempted to explain library use with such factors as demographics (e.g., education level, income, age), psychological traits (e.g., dogmatism), situational characteristics (e.g., distance to library), and user perceptions of library characteristics (e.g., accessibility and ease of use). Their efforts have been able to explain 33 percent to 45 percent of the variability in users' behaviors. In order to improve the level of explanation in user studies, it seems desirable to include entirely new classes of variables which might contribute to explaining the individual's use of the library.

In reviewing reading and library use studies it occurred to the authors that these behaviors may have explanations other than the current sociological, psychological, and environmental ones (Benson and O'Connor, 1979). We began to explore the possibility of biochemical and sociobiological explanations of reading and library use. This paper examines the implications of using a biological theory to explain the behaviors of heavy readers who are heavy library users.

A Biological Explanation of Compulsive Behaviors

Recent research indicates the presence of naturally occurring opiates in the human brain (Bolles and Fanselow, 1982; Wasacz, 1981; Greenberg, 1978). A portion of these opiates are called endogenous (i.e., within the body) morphines. Morphine injected from an external source would be considered an exogenous substance. The role of these endogenous morphines in human behavior is not yet entirely clear. It is known, however, that they activate the opiate receptors in the brain which allow the individual to receive the naturally present morphine. It is believed by some researchers that behaviors which are associated with the presence of endorphines (a contraction of endogenous morphines) are, in part, perceived as pleasurable because of the action of the endorphines. Others regard the action of endorphines as primarily analgesic rather than pleasure producing.[2] If endorphines are a biochemical basis for pleasure, then they may generate the reward which stimulates repetition of behaviors.

Because endorphines, chemically, are opiates, one of the important questions is whether they have addictive properties. If an individual can develop tolerance to endorphines, one may require more frequent practice and longer duration of the behaviors which generate endorphines in order to achieve the same level of pleasure. Thus, if endorphines have addictive properties, they may be the cornerstone of habitual behaviors including habitual reading. Findings about the development of tolerance to endorphines are, however, mixed (Bolles and Fanselow, 1982; Wasacz, 1981). If individuals do not develop tolerance to endorphines, the action of these opiates may still be central to the development of compulsive habitual behaviors.

Behavior, Pleasure, and Reading

Individuals, for a variety of reasons, may develop restricted sources of pleasure, a restricted ability to experience pleasure, or have limitations on their ability to recognize satiety. In such situations the person may exhibit compulsive habitual behaviors, even if addictive tolerance is not developed. Westermeyer reports on this process:

> Investigators working with the perception of pleasure in human beings have so far restricted their studies to olfaction, taste, and thermal sensation. If their theories can be extrapolated from the visceral realms to a spectrum of human experience (including emotionality and social existence), then experiences capable of relieving loneliness, anxiety, feelings of unimportance or meaninglessness may provide pleasure depending upon the individual's need state --just as food is more pleasurable when the organism is hungry.[3]

It is our belief that pleasure-reading habits are affected by the action of endorphines and in particular that, in order to explain the behavior of heavy readers, the interaction of endorphines and behavior must be better understood.

Westermeyer suggests a general model of the linkages among neurochemical events, perceptions, and social behavior:

1. Pleasurable experiences are perceived in the brain.

One of the mechanisms for this involves a morphine-like compound--probably a neurotransmitter--that produces sensations described as analgesic, pleasurable, rewarding or perhaps even 'addicting.'
2. The pleasurable experience generalizes to events associated with it.[4]

Viscerally pleasurable experiences might accompany reading and other information-attending events. Thus the reader associates this behavior with pleasure and eventually these behaviors independently generate pleasure. This process may be important in the development of a reading habit in young children. If a mother reads to a child on her lap, the holding of the child may cause the release of pleasurable endorphines. The child may then associate pleasure with the mother and with the process of reading. The mother acts as a conditioned stimulus who provides touching and holding which are unconditioned stimuli and these in turn are indirectly related to reading behavior. Later, when the child is too big to be held, the indirect stimulus of reading may still produce the release of pleasurable endorphines. At the extremes, there may be individuals with over-production of these endorphines which may make them likely candidates to be compulsive readers. This could have implications for the design of children's services where libraries tap into the release of endorphines which then help to shape individuals into being heavy users of libraries over their entire lifetimes.

To this point it has been argued that reading is connected with pleasurable experiences involving contact with other individuals. The contact between mother and child is one form of human bonding. Westermeyer's model goes on to address these phenomena which may or may not lead to such bonding:

3. Pleasurable experiences usually accompany human bonding. The fully comfortable, fully satiated individual may not be in a state as conducive to new human-bonding experiences as is the unsatiated, uncomfortable, or dysphoric individual.
4. Dysphoria or pleasure need not necessarily lead to human bonding. For example, uncomfortable or noxious experiences may continue indefinitely without relief. Or pleasure would not lead to human bonding if human contact did not accompany the pleasurable experience (e.g. eating alone or masturbation). Or the pleasurable experience can occur in the company of a great number of different individuals such that no one or a few individuals are ever associated with the pleasurable activity (e.g. eating alone in different restaurants, or sexual intercourse with constantly changing partners).[5]

It is our premise that reading, especially habitual reading, can reinforce prior experience of human bonding and may even act as a substitute for them. If sitting on your mother's lap while she reads produces an endorphine "high," then later habitual reading as an adult might be used to avoid pain. This is analogous to the use of heroin (an exogenous substance). The reading addict initially gets a "high" from reading but this eventually reaches a level where a similar quantity of reading is needed to avoid pain. If this need is not met, then irritability and other "withdrawal" symptoms may be evident in the reading addict. Libraries which fail to supply materials which can be easily read for pleasure may force this dedicated user group to seek out new outlets for reading matter. In turn, if a relatively small number of addicts abandon a particular library, then this may have a significant impact on circulation statistics. Extrapolating from Clark's data, as few as 600 individuals might account for 28,000 circulations.

Reading and Depression

If heavy reading is not explained by the addiction paradigm, then it is possibly a compulsive behavior associated with restricted sources of pleasure or a restricted ability to experience pleasure.

The person with a situation and/or environment which limits pleasure sources (e.g., an elderly widow whose friends have died or an isolated forest ranger), will turn to the remaining sources with greater intensity and frequency. If reading has become a pleasure source through earlier conditioning, then a higher frequency of reading will result when circumstances become otherwise limiting. When circumstances again change, the person may not always be able to return to a more varied range of pleasures.

Depressed persons do not appear to be able to _fully_ experience current pleasure, to anticipate future pleasure, or to reminisce about past pleasure. Such individuals turn to activities which allow them to experience the limited pleasures which they can still achieve. Again, if they were conditioned to reading as a pleasurable activity, they may turn to it heavily, because it is a low-anxiety, low-threat, socially acceptable behavior, which does not involve much human contact. In large doses, reading may still be capable of generating a pleasurable response. For example, the depressed Harlequin reader has the benefit of vicariously experiencing the normal emotions and intimate relationships of others without the burden of a reality perceived as empty. Extreme depression may result in no perception of pleasure and thus cause a cessation of all reading.

The work of Goldstein (1980) about the emotional response to music tends to support the concept that endorphines are important in the experience of pleasure as a response to stimuli of a non-physical nature. In order to verify that endorphines are associated with the pleasurable response to music, some subjects were injected with a saline solution while others were injected with naloxone (an opiate receptor antagonist or blocking agent) prior to listening to music. Naloxone lessened the emotional response to music. The findings, while based on a small group of individuals, were statistically significant. Such evidence supports the underlying theory of the propositions which we have advanced.

Hypotheses on Library Use and Neurochemical Factors

A relationship between neurochemical factors and library use has been proposed. One specific library use behavior, reading, has been discussed in terms of this relationship. A model outlining a series of general propositions based upon the foregoing ideas follows:

1. Through association of the use of formal information sources with physically pleasurable events (where pleasure is produced by the action of endorphines), information use can become a stimulus for the release of endorphines in the human brain.
2. Not all individuals develop this response.
3. Those individuals who do develop this response will typically become pleasure-information users (e.g., pleasure readers with moderate frequency).
4. A variety of situational, environmental, and emotional circumstances may arise which will cause the conditioned information user to engage in heavy information use. In some instances, it may become a disordered behavior.
5. Some few individuals may be exposed so strongly to the pleasure stimuli/information use association that they are imprinted with the information-use behavior. For example, reading may actually become a fetishlike behavior.
6. "Habituated" information users may find the free public library to be the most economically feasible source for the gratification of their needs, but are unlikely to restrict themselves to this provider of information sources. It is quite likely that heavy users exhaust the relevant portions of any collection with some rapidity (McClellan, 1973).
7. Individuals with other "habits" of a similar nature (based on a pleasure response) and intensity are unlikely to become consistent library users.
8. The genesis of information use for pleasure and purposive information use may be entirely different. The factors which predispose individuals to use the library may differ depending on which type of information use (purposive or pleasure seeking) is being pursued.

The first research priority to confirm the reasonableness of the above propositions is to study the effect of opiate antagonists (e.g., the drug naloxone) upon the emotional response to various forms of information use, such as reading, viewing, and listening. If emotional response to information use can be attenuated by opiate blockers such as naloxone, then the role of endorphines in such behaviors as pleasure reading will be supported. The use of such drugs to reduce the pleasure of reading will raise ethical questions.

Librarians must begin to differentiate the habitual reader from other readers and temper their application of stereotypes. Disdain of the genre fiction reader, whether habitual or not, is an inappropriate response to legitimate needs. The habitual reader of genre fiction may be a significant contributor to overall library use. When that habit is excessive because of situational, biological, or emotional circumstances, the librarian can respond with understanding and concern rather than with contempt. In general, we believe that libraries' collections and services reflect librarians' attitudes toward the various genres because of the effect of derogatory and frequently vicious stereotypes of the genres' readers. In part, the reactions to genre fiction stem from several factors: (1) the concern of librarians with who reads what; (2) the human tendency to over-generalize; and (3) hostility toward young adults and less educated women (Benson and Boyd, 1980; Harris and Sodt, 1981). If the theory presented in this paper is correct, then we as a profession must reexamine our attitudes toward the habitual or compulsive reader of materials which do not suit our own tastes. A biologically determined behavior must be viewed differently than a volitional behavior. It should not be beyond librarians to exhibit professionalism and humanity rather than petty judgmentalism.

References

1. Philip Maize Clark. "The Individual Library Patron as the Unit of Research Analysis: The Development of a Methodology of Public Library Use." Ph.D. Dissertation. (New Brunswick, N.J.: Rutgers University, 1982): 59.
2. Robert C. Bolles and Michael S. Fanselow. "Endorphins and Behavior." Annual Review of Psychology. (Stanford, Calif.: Annual Reviews, 1982): 96.
3. Joseph Westermeyer, Janet Bush and Ronald Wintrob. "A Review of the Relationship Between Dysphoria, Pleasure, and Human Bonding." Journal of Clinical Psychiatry 39 (1978): 415.
4. Ibid., 416.
5. Ibid.
6. Ibid., 418.

Bibliography

Benson, James and Boyd. Alex. A Study of Library Delivery Systems with an Emphasis on Bookmobiles vs. Books-by-Mail. Tuscaloosa, Alabama: University of Alabama (Graduate School of Library Service), 1980.

Benson, James and O'Connor, Daniel O. "Speculations on the Relationship Between Endogenous Morphines (Endorphines) and Library Use and Reading." Paper presented at the Information Exchange Suite, Library Research Round Table, Dallas, Texas, June 25, 1979.

Bolles, Robert C. and Fanselow, Michael S. "Endorphins and Behavior." In: Annual Review of Psychology. Stanford, California: Annual Reviews, 1982, pp. 87-101.

Clark, Philip Maize. "The Individual Library Patron as the Unit of Research Analysis: the Development of a Methodology of Public Library Use." Ph.D. Dissertation, Rutgers University, 1982.

D'Elia, George. "The Development and Testing of a Conceptual Model of Public Library User Behavior." Library Quarterly 50 (1980): 410-30.

Greenberg, Joel. "Memory Research: an Era of 'Good Feeling.'" Science News 114 (1978): 364-65.

Goldstein, Avram. "Thrills in Response to Music and Other Stimuli." Physiological Psychology 8 (1980): 126-29.

Harris, Michael H. and Sodt, James. "Libraries, Users, and Librarians: Continuing Efforts to Define the Nature and Extent of Public Library Use." In: Harris, Michael H. (ed.). Advances in Librarianship. New York: Academic Press, 1981, pp. 109-33.

McClellan, A.W. The Reader, the Library and the Book. London: Clive Bingley, 1973.

Wasacz, John. "Natural and Synthetic Narcotic Drugs." American Scientist 69 (1981): 318-24.

Westermeyer, Joseph; Bush, Janet; and Wintrob, Ronald. "A Review of the Relationship Between Dysphoria, Pleasure, and Human Bonding." Journal of Clinical Psychiatry 39 (1978): 415-24.

Zweizig, Douglas. "Predicting Amount of Library Use: an Empirical Study of the Role of the Public Library in the Life of the Adult Public." Ph.D. Dissertation, Syracuse University, 1973.

Part II

COMMUNICATION AND EDUCATION

PUBLIC LIBRARY REFERENCE SERVICE: MYTH AND REALITY*

Mary Lee Bundy, Amy Bridgman, Laura Keltie

<u>What is the current status of legislation bearing on military registration? What hearings are pending?</u>

These questions and others asked of nine libraries between April 7 and 21, 1980 were part of an inquiry into public library responsiveness to requests for information bearing on controversial issues.

The findings of this study, analyzed here, offer insight into public library reference performance. They ask, the writers believe, for serious professional consideration, for they suggest that too frequently there may be a wide discrepancy between the ideal of reference service and actual practice.

Libraries should, of course, always be concerned with the quality of their services. Today in the face of severe budget cuts and rising costs, the caliber of their performance is even more crucial.

Librarians talk about changing the image of public libraries from that of a passive storehouse of books, used most often for entertainment or not used at all, to that of a dynamic information institution, responding to community needs. But do they respond? The library profession's proudest ethic is intellectual freedom. The ethic is a stirring one, linked to essential democratic freedoms. How is it lived up to in the real world of practice?

This article was prepared to support this serious reflection on reference practice in public libraries at a time when their economic future is in question.

<u>The Study</u>

The original intent of the research was to find out whether public libraries carry and will give out information of an "anti-establishment"

---

*Reprinted by permission of the authors and publisher from <u>Public Library Quarterly,</u> 3:3 (Fall 1982) 11-22. Copyright © 1982 by The Haworth Press, Inc. All rights reserved.

character, that is, information which challenges government policy or which goes against prevailing public sentiment and opinion.

The military draft was selected as the issue for case study, since it was currently in the public limelight and arousing considerable opposition due to pending draft registration invoked by President Carter. Organized opposition included a national anti-draft rally in Washington, along with smaller rallies around the country.

As with the earlier studies of Crowley and Childers, and more recently the study by Marcia Myers of telephone reference in academic libraries, questions were asked of a sample of libraries. Using unobtrusive measures, researchers posed the questions as coming from actual patrons, and then recorded and analyzed the results. They telephoned the main library or largest branch in the library systems studied to ask their questions and also went in person to this library. Here they searched its resources for materials related to the draft, and asked the librarian on duty for assistance. Thus, they undertook the same activity an inquirer would be likely to pursue in a real life situation.

The study design had another dimension. To determine whether libraries in the study carry anti-establishment literature, the researchers used a core listing of peace literature, checking the holdings of each library to see if they had the books, pamphlets and films on the list. The Washington Peace Center because of its expertise was turned to for this listing.

The central concern of this study was with how open libraries are to information which challenges the status quo. But because of the nature of the questions asked, the study unexpectedly raised another issue. With the exception of a question about availability of a meeting room and one other question, these were questions of a factual character, that is, they could be answered rather readily by reference to print sources and/or by referral to an appropriate government agency or private organization.

The nature of the queries may be the reason the library staff did not fully or reliably answer the questions asked or provide the guidance sought on the library visits. Some of the staff may have deliberately chosen to give less than usual in the way of service.

However, the researchers believe that this was not the case. They believe that the study did reveal bias in some respects due to the issue. But that for the most part, they got treated in the way these libraries customarily treat people who call or come to them seeking information. What was at stake, then, was the very quality of reference service.

The Telephone Questions

The questions asked by telephone were chosen to represent the kinds

Communication and Education

of questions various community elements have with regard to a public issue. These elements were identified as <u>Affected People</u>--in this case, potential draftees and their families; <u>Concerned Citizens</u> --people wanting to learn more about the issue and who might want to get involved; <u>Activist Groups</u>--groups involved and active around this issue and <u>Other Groups</u>--other groups who become interested in the issue.

The following questions were asked:

1. Can you tell me under what conditions a person can be exempted from the draft? Do you know of any groups that would have information on exemptions from the draft?
2. I'm concerned about what the military registration is going to lead to--what it means. Are we going to have a draft? Does this mean war? Are there other solutions?
3. How can a group get a license to hold a demonstration in front of the White House?
4. What is the current status of legislation bearing on military registration? What hearings are pending?
5. I am a member of a group that is organizing to oppose draft registration, and we are looking for a place to hold some meetings. Do you have a meeting room that we might be able to use? [Responses to this question were for the most part affirmative. Since the question did not call for a reference response, it was not used in the later analysis.]
6. Where can I go to get a speaker on the draft?
7. I need information. I'm becoming more and more opposed to the draft or registration, Carter's proposals and would like to get in touch with some anti-draft activist groups. Could you give me some names of groups?

These, then, are the questions each of the nine libraries was asked by telephone in April, 1980.

Libraries in the Study

The libraries studied include metropolitan, suburban and rural library systems, the smallest serving a population just over 10,000 and the largest serving a population of over 850,000. Taken together, these libraries serve a population of $4\frac{1}{2}$ million people.

Viewed in income figures, four libraries had incomes of $7 million or over in 1978-79, two, incomes of approximately $6 million, and another library $3 million. The two smallest libraries had incomes of $300,000 and $500,000.

Limitations

The small number of libraries in the study and the small number of questions asked, the difficulties in saying readily whether many of the answers given were satisfactory, the problems of categorizing library holdings--these made the researchers cautious about drawing conclusions of a quantitative nature. Because the analysis dealt with aspects not built into the study design, it is difficult on some points to detail what happened in more than a general way. Nevertheless, the researchers tried to accurately represent what happened as did the writers here in this further presentation and analysis.

How Well Did They Do?

The major conclusions drawn by the investigators were:

> The majority of public libraries studied here do not give callers information of an anti-establishment nature concerning current issues, even when such information is clearly desired. And when people seek this information in person, they are able to find very little.... But with regard to information available from standard sources and/or agencies, the record is little better. At least half fall down here, too....

What happened to make the researchers draw these largely negative conclusions? The treatment given their questions and the holdings of these libraries on draft related subjects raise, it would seem, virtually every question about best practice in reference as well as the question of balance in collection building.

Again, we cannot say with certitude that the behavior of these libraries, in response to these few questions, characterizes their behavior generally. And the researchers' conclusions were, in part, subjective. But there is certainly enough evidence so as to call into question important aspects of reference and selection practice, particularly when in other studies (Crowley,[1] Childers,[2] Myers [3]) almost half the questions asked were not answered correctly.

What Went Wrong--The Telephone Answers

With regard to the telephone answers, several times the information supplied callers did not answer the question. For instance, three libraries gave information about pending legislation which was either dated or while current, did not provide the answer. One library in answer to the draft exemption question simply told the caller that they had no materials in the library related to the question.

These responses were not surprising. What was surprising was the number of times that a wrong answer was given. Four libraries told the caller that there were no exemptions to the draft in force since no draft was in effect. This is misleading and would do a disservice to a potential draftee who might want to prepare to register as a conscientious objector should there be an actual draft. The Military Selective Service Act which is the law, standing as

Communication and Education

part of the United States Code, spells out the exemptions. The law has not been revoked so the exemptions apply until changed by act of Congress. A proclamation by President Ford halted registration but could not nullify laws. Inactive laws are still laws and should be so reported by responsible reference services.

With regard to bills pending in Congress on military registration, two libraries wrongly said that no bills had been introduced. In answer to the question about how a group could get a license to hold a demonstration in front of the White House, three gave out incorrect information. One told the caller that a permit is not needed. One said that whether or not a permit is needed depends on the size of the group, and one told the caller that the District of Columbia issues the permits. (Permits are given by the U.S. National Park Service.)

Incorrect Referrals

Referrals made in answer to questions which called for the name of an organization or agency and referrals made in answer to other questions were sometimes dubious, being very vague, only indirectly helpful, or wrong.

One library when asked for a source for a speaker on the draft said they did not know of any groups. For an anti-draft group one library merely referred the caller to the Readers' Guide. One referral made in answer to the question about bills pending was so vague as to constitute no answer, the caller being referred simply to "Congress."

Some referrals did not point directly to the organization or the information asked for, but eventually led one to it. For instance, with regard to bills in Congress, the suggestion to call the Library of Congress did lead to the appropriate Senate committee where the information was given. And recommendations to call the American Friends Service Committee for information on draft exemptions led to a referral by AFSC to the Washington Peace Center which does supply this information.

But some referrals must be labeled as essentially incorrect. Five libraries referred people wanting a speaker on the draft to the National Guard, to "recruiting offices" and to various college speakers bureaus, sources which later calls established do not provide speakers on this subject. And four libraries when asked for anti-draft groups, referred the caller to the National Council to Repeal the Draft, an organization which was found to be defunct. Five referrals given in answer to how to get a White House demonstration permit were to one or another department in D.C. government.

In answer to the less concrete query, "I'm concerned about what the military registration is going to lead to--what it means. Are we going to have a draft? Does this mean war? Are there other solutions?," these libraries, probably rightly so, told the caller to come in to use library resources.

But surely more help could have been offered than proved to be the case. Three libraries merely told the caller to come in to use magazines or newspapers, failing to say what type of material or how they could be accessed. While others did suggest tools to use, only one made a check of holdings before telling the caller to come in and only two libraries, despite the vagueness of the question, made any attempt to find out more specifically what was wanted. None of them offered more help if the caller should come to the library.

The analyzer summed up these particular calls:

> All of the libraries gave at least a modicum of useful information in response to this question. However, none of the responses could be considered adequate.... In general, responses to this question seemed to indicate both a lack of interest in the subject and a lack of concern with respect to the inquirer's information need.

Yet it was not surprising to find some unwillingness to take on this telephone question or even others or that some library staff proved uninterested and were essentially unhelpful. <u>The unexpected finding was the number of times that "misinformation" was given out.</u>

Assistance Given in Person

These were inadequacies in information service provided by telephone. The performance of reference staff when approached in person by researchers requesting information on the draft was slightly better.

A stock response, telling the researchers to check the <u>Readers' Guide</u> and the vertical file, was evident. Four libraries mentioned one or the other of those two sources, and four other libraries mentioned both. The majority, six, also suggested other sources including <u>Editorial Research Report, Congressional Quarterly, Congressional Digest, Microfilm Periodicals Index, Editorials on File, Facts on File,</u> the <u>Washington Post Index,</u> and <u>Magazine Index.</u>

In answer to the specific request for names of organizations involved in the issue, only one library gave names of more than one active peace group. Librarians themselves seem aware of only one group, The American Friends Service Committee.

The extent of helpfulness of the staff varied. The most extreme case was one in which the researcher was met with no more than a finger hastily pointed toward the <u>Readers' Guide.</u> In other cases, the researchers reported more friendly, but still hurried service from an obviously busy staff. One researcher summarized the experience as a "quick and dirty" approach to reference--saying something quickly rather than taking the time for thoughtful consideration and a real effort to utilize the full resources of the library. Another described what must have been a negative experience: "The walk-in visit did not reassure one, since neither the library atmosphere nor the personnel seemed especially service oriented." In yet another library the opposite situation prevailed. The staff was warm and attempted to be helpful, but the library was lacking in resources and failed to give on-target reference service.

Deviations from Best Reference Practice

Apart from the quality of the answers themselves, there is yet another criterion to employ in assessing the quality of the reference service provided to telephone and walk-in users--that is, the degree to which staff behavior conforms to standards of best practice.

Deviation from standards included: failure to ask questions of the patron to find out exactly what was wanted; failure to check sources for answers (reliance on memory only) with wrong answers the result; failure to cite sources to patrons; failure to check or use sources on hand in the library; misuse of standard reference tools so that wrong answers were given to the inquirer or incorrect referrals made; and failure to spend sufficient time with the patron.

Apparently it is customary practice in these libraries to give information without citing the source. It also unfortunately appears that these libraries by telephone and in person do not as a matter of practice question inquirers to determine what they want. Only a few staff asked anything at all.

As for relying on memory, the researchers recorded eight times that a wrong answer was given because the staff member relied on memory. We cannot say with certainty what tools these libraries could have checked and didn't. Indicative of this failure, three of the libraries were found to have the book Washington Five: A Comprehensive Directory of the Nation's Capital, which lists 13 anti-draft and anti-war groups, yet they failed to use it.

A conspicuous misuse of a standard tool occurred when libraries used Gale's Encyclopedia of Associations, to find the names of antidraft groups. They referred the caller to the National Council to Repeal the Draft, although Gale's specifically states the NCRD is currently inactive.

Whether sufficient time was spent with the patron has to be a subjective judgment. Certainly in not one instance did the staff on the library visit follow through to see if the requestor was satisfied. And the picture which emerges is one of telephone reference being a hurried affair, no questions asked, sources used not given to the inquirer, and limited time spent by the staff. Using tools wrongly and depending on memory also fit the hurried pattern. Viewed most dismally, the point is to give an answer rather than to see that inquirers get the information they need.

Access to Anti-Establishment Information

When an American turns to a public library for information that challenges the system or reflects unorthodox or unpopular beliefs, can she/he get it? Going by this study, the answer is--no.

As discussed foregoing, in regard to library visits, library staff did not refer people to anti-draft literature and their knowledge of anti-draft groups is limited to the Quakers.

When confronted with telephone inquirers, they refer an individual obviously wanting to look at alternatives to the draft to such sources as Congressional Quarterly Weekly Report and the Department of State Bulletin. The majority advise people to contact the National Guard, university speakers' bureaus and recruiting offices for speakers on the draft. These libraries gave only a limited number of anti-draft organization referrals and were found not to carry literature of the groups they did refer people to.

Public librarians, as evidenced in this study, do not apparently know of or search out anti-establishment literature and sources in reference work. Similarly, they apparently fail to do so in selection.

The holdings of these libraries of literature on the core listing supplied by the Washington Peace Center were slim. Two films were named. No library held them. Four pamphlets were listed. No library had any of them. Of the four newsletters named, only two libraries had one. One library had apparently actually subscribed to Reporter for Conscience Sake and another library system had been given a gift subscription to the Washington Peace Center Newsletter.

The libraries did somewhat better when it came to books, with one library system carrying five out of the six titles listed. Two libraries listed four out of the six books in their catalog though four libraries listed only one or none. Listing in the catalog did not mean that the books were available for browsing immediately for in several instances, these were large library systems with 15 or so branches. A book at one branch would have to be requested and transported to the others.

Libraries may of course have other literature of an anti-draft nature, even if they do not have those on the core listing. Dishearteningly, the search of the vertical file and catalogs of these libraries revealed very little. Only one large library with a considerable collection on the subject (about 70 titles) had any number of anti-draft books. The researcher estimated that possibly one-fourth were of this nature.

Pamphlets kept in vertical files under the headings military draft or military conscription ranged from none to 29. This largest collection had approximately 10 pamphlets of an anti-draft leaning. Only a few pamphlets could be thus characterized in any of the other libraries.

In conclusion, these libraries do not avail themselves of the considerable literature bearing on the draft issue available from nontraditional sources. Some further check into selection policies and practices suggests that public libraries collect very little literature from non-commercial sources. Dependent on publishers lists and book reviews that extend largely to commercially produced literature and with selection committees that fail to represent the nontraditional consumer, few libraries have in place systems that will alert them to literature that is current and out of the main stream of establishment information. They may not choose consciously to exclude it; the question simply does not come up.

These, then, were the sobering findings of one of the few studies to ask whether public libraries respond to politically related questions without a censoring influence. They seem to cry out for professional attention.

Comments

In seeking understanding of the findings, the writers circulated the initial report to a number of people working in public libraries and to library school students. Although the comments varied, there was considerable consensus.

Only a few felt that callers were given less than usual service because the questions were of a controversial character. One public library staff member said, "They told them anything just to get rid of them." And another said that since the subject was so "esoteric," libraries may have given scant help. Another reader commented sadly on the apparent unwillingness of public libraries to acquire and utilize alternative information sources. One perceptive student suggested that until the public is educated to expect more, the situation probably will not change for the better.

But some students felt that the researchers' expectations were much too high. Given all that librarians have to do and the limited time they can spend with library inquirers, little more could be expected of them. And some of these students obviously felt that the library's main functions are to build and circulate a collection of books, reference being more icing on the cake, than an essential function. Through these comments threaded an acceptance of the status quo in reference.

Several people working in public libraries said that the quality of reference service given depends entirely on who answers the telephone and that in their system the variation is great. One pointed out the difficulty of supervising the handling of reference inquiries. Staff at least in some systems are trying to answer telephone questions while on the reference desk. Commentators observed that in many libraries reference staff are very overloaded, "telephones are ringing constantly." Deviations from best practice, they feel, are very understandable.

These comments are helpful in understanding the reference situation. They suggest the very real constraints on reference practice in public libraries. They also suggest that reference standards have been adjusted to meet bureaucratic necessities and priorities.

The important need at this point in time is not, however, to merely analyze current practice. Rather, it is to stand back and consider the consequences of long term "less than adequate" reference service.

There are, it seems to these writers, three grave implications which public librarians must not be too sanguine, or too busy to ignore.

If misinformation is being given out by public libraries frequently, the very credibility of the institution and its profession is being put in jeopardy. If libraries, for whatever reason, are frequently essentially unhelpful to people who seek their help, the reference function will not develop to the point that communities will see it as an asset. And, equally crucial, if people wanting controversial information cannot get it from most public libraries, then librarianship's effort to protect intellectual freedom is all for naught.

The original study was conducted by members of Dr. Bundy's Research Methods class in Spring, 1980 under her guidance and presented in a report entitled, <u>Public Libraries Dodge the Draft; A Case Inquiry into Public Library Response on Current Controversial Issues</u>, by Hetty Barthel, Amy Bridgman, Laura Keltie, David LaPenotiere, Carol Legarreta and Daniel Mlagisi.

References

1. Crowley, Terrence. "The Effectiveness of Information Service in Medium Size Public Libraries" in Terrence Crowley and Thomas Childers, <u>Information Service in Public Libraries: Two Studies</u> (Metuchen, N.J.: Scarecrow Press, 1971).
2. Childers, Thomas. "Telephone Information Service in Public Libraries" in Terrence Crowley and Thomas Childers, <u>Information Service in Public Libraries: Two Studies</u> (Metuchen, N.J.: Scarecrow Press, 1971).

3. Myers, Marcia J. The Effectiveness of Telephone Reference/Information Services in Academic Libraries in the Southeast (Florida State University, 1980). [Published by Scarecrow Press, 1983, under the title: The Accuracy of Telephone Reference/Information Service in Academic Libraries: Two Studies.]

YOUNG ADULT REFERENCE SERVICES IN THE PUBLIC LIBRARY*

Mary K. Chelton

Reference services to young adults should be delivered within the dual philosophical framework of the Library Bill of Rights [1] and RASD's "A Commitment to Information Services: Developmental Guidelines, 1979" [2] and this chapter makes no attempt to repeat or enlarge upon arguments defending those service philosophies readily available elsewhere.[3] Young adults do, however, have special problems in the reference services area which are crucial to the success of the service. Not the least of these problems is the separate historical development of reference and young adult services in public libraries.

Historically, young adult services have attempted to offer adolescents a non-school-related option in their lives, whereas most of the factual information seeking which brings young adults into public libraries today is related to school assignments. Public libraries themselves were begun to enlighten and enrich those who had completed formal schooling,[4] so ambivalence on school-related needs is just part of a larger service history.

It is ironic that the first viable [5] young adult program in public libraries in the United States was begun in the New York Public Library by Mabel Williams under the title, Superintendent of Work with Schools. In 1929, ten years after creating a department separate from children's work, Miss Williams had this to say about schools in her preface to the first "Books for Young People" list (later to become Books for the Teenage):

> This list is primarily for use in the adult sections of the Library, to suggest books to boys and girls when they are first transferred from the Children's Rooms. It is not expected to replace any of the lists now used by the schools. High School lists are naturally affected by curriculum and the desire to give pupils an opportunity of knowing all forms of literature before leaving school. Furthermore, their use is dependent not only on inclination

---

*Reprinted by permission of the author and publisher from Reference Librarian, No. 7/8 (1983). Copyright © 1983 by Mary K. Chelton. All rights reserved.

but also on compulsion, because of the various checking-up methods used in the schools. This list, on the other hand, includes only those books which boys and girls are known to have enjoyed either through their own discovery or the suggestion of a friend, a teacher, a librarian, or through the impetus received from book talks or reading clubs.[6]

This is not to imply that Williams, or any of her successors, totally ignored school needs, because they did not. Much of Williams' early career was devoted to persuading adult departments to pay attention to young adult needs and to hire staff suited to that task.

The fact remains, however, that young adult services emphasized reading guidance and out-of-school group programs, rather than factual, didactic, curriculum-related information. This philosophical orientation persisted even after public school curricula started to emphasize the use of materials beyond textbooks. Schools were seen only as a means to reach the mass audience of adolescents, ever increasingly confined in them through child welfare and compulsory education legislation. No one expressed this better than Margaret Edwards, who was obviously ready to quit her beloved Enoch Pratt Free Library job in frustration over her lack of access to Baltimore high schools:

> The Baltimore high schools in the thirties were closed to visits from the public library. The superintendent of public instruction had told Dr. Wheeler that he did not intend for broom salesmen or any other outsiders to take up time in the schools. Nevertheless, I was determined to attempt a gradual infiltration of the high schools. I cultivated individual teachers and school librarians and found an influential Pratt co-worker to say a good word for me to a supervisor. Despite all this, after ten years I was making only about ten classroom and assembly talks a year. Then out of the blue I was offered a position in a Western city where I would be in charge of all young-adult work in both the public-library and the public-school system ... I wrote a letter of resignation.[7]

Another historical aspect of young adult services which contributes to current misunderstandings of the YA/reference function is that services to young adults evolved out of the movement to have separate services, equal to those for adults, for children in public libraries. Public libraries were initially "adults only" libraries until a conglomeration of philanthropists, visionaries, and resulting chaos in libraries opened to children without adequate provision for them led to the establishment of separate children's services.[8] There was no real attempt to integrate services to adults and children, and the assumption of separateness, in combination with an emphasis on readers advising and programming, excluded youth services from the development of reference services, increasingly seen as being synonymous with services to adults. These divisions and assumptions were then institutionalized in public library staffing and budgeting. As a result, no one felt a special responsibility for YA student reference service at the same time that the school experience came to dominate adolescence, except for school libraries which were often inadequate.[9]

A New Age

While the passing of the post-World War II baby boom into adulthood and a slower birth rate have eased the problem in terms of sheer numbers of students, declining budgets and the assumptions of the past continue to inhibit reference services to young adults in many libraries. Many young adult librarians, while providing student reference service in practice, fear the absorption of their primary functions of reading guidance and programming by the school-related reference function. Many adult/reference librarians find student young adult patrons irksome and reading guidance less important than "information." Young adult patrons are obviously the losers in this either-or philosophical battle over what is most important--information or enrichment.

The truth, as usual, lies somewhere in between the two extremes, and if we still believe that books contain ideas, then it follows that they are ideal vehicles for conveying information. Hopefully they will help young patrons learn how to think, a process absolutely necessary in human development and one which flounders badly in an information climate rich in facts but not reflection and discussion. Knowledge is internalized, processed information, and reference services to all ages would be greatly enhanced by pulling the either-or views of information or enrichment together into an holistic philosophy which promotes knowledge.

Young adult patrons specifically do not always appear in libraries in neat either-or functional packages. In contemporary secondary school curricula, many popular titles are required reading, and many assignments require the use of the entire adult and juvenile circulating collection. Some book report assignments easily overlap the arbitrary information-enrichment categories. Take, for example, a student who is required to read a story set in the U.S. from 1860 to 1900. It takes a librarian with a person-centered (as opposed to function-centered) approach to recommend a title set in or about the period which is of interest and at the reading level of the YA patron. Many young adults, especially early adolescents, approach traditional reference desks reluctantly because, first, they resent the compulsory nature of the assignment, and secondly, they know that their reading needs will not be considered by the librarian providing them with the book. If user satisfaction is to become one way of measuring reference service, then the artificiality of either reading enrichment or information must be broken down once and for all.

The use of the entire, as opposed to just the reference,

collection is especially important if person-centered approach to service is achieved. Reference librarians must realize that juvenile publishing editors deliberately include topical materials on simpler reading levels for school assignments on their lists, and ignorance of the juvenile collection is a major barrier in providing good reference service to YA's, especially to the junior high students.

If the library is divided into adult and juvenile departments, the YA/reference librarian must be tactful in the way in which juvenile materials are used with young adults, especially those who may look, but no longer consider themselves juvenile. A tactful acknowledgement of developmental feelings is possible in several ways, depending on the architecture, budget, and policies of the particular library. The easiest way is to purchase duplicate copies of juvenile books on frequently requested school topics for the adult/YA collection. In smaller libraries, some have found it useful to interfile the entire nonfiction collections. Interfiling, however, does have several problems which have to be anticipated. One is the juxtaposition of very juvenile and very adult materials on sexuality; the other is that popular reading stories which happen to be true may get "lost" unless there is both space and an inclination on the part of the librarian to display or promote them separately from time to time. Interfiling can also be a problem when different cataloging codes and subject headings are used for the adult and juvenile collections.

Dichotomy

If the collections remain separate, and there is little money for duplication, the YA/reference librarian should feel perfectly comfortable accompanying the young patron back to the children's department, and vice versa. If scheduling and architecture make accompanying the patron a problem, the YA/reference librarian should explain briefly the differences in publishing and why the desired book/information is in the other department. It is important to make young adolescents understand that they are not just being shunted back to childhood at the very time they are beginning to feel adult.

One attempt to overcome the adult-juvenile dichotomy of library departmentalization was the creation of separate young adult rooms which provided both reference and readers advisory services. These rooms, which came into favor in the forties and fifties, featured trained staff and materials chosen from adult and juvenile publishing lists. While the idea of separate areas for young adults continues in many ways, these larger rooms fell into disuse and were disbanded. Besides their expense, which was enormous because of the duplication of titles involved, these rooms often perverted their intended purpose of better service to young adults by becoming just one more barrier to the total use of the library collection. At their worst, such rooms were developmentally unsound because they contributed to the age-segregation of young adults so prevalent in our larger society, and so problematic for them. It is difficult to figure out what kind of adult you might like to be when no institution provides conditions under which you might interact with many different kinds of adults. Age-integration is a major program goal of all YA services.

Some libraries have attempted to fill school assignment needs of young adults by creating reserve shelves in the public library's reference department. A school assignment reserve shelf in a public library has little philosophical defense except the alleviation of student frustration if the materials on the shelf are exclusively of student interest. If the materials are of interest to the larger library user population, I feel that such a reserve shelf is totally unjustifiable, and that duplicate copies and/or a frank discussion with school authorities are called for. Some other methods should be tried beyond making the public library either a pseudo-school library in a community setting or a place of failure for students in their school assignment needs.

School Assignments

School assignment reference services are unfortunately complicated by a variety of factors originating outside the control of the public library. Teachers inevitably assign the same titles or subjects to masses of students regardless of home, library, or bookstore resources in the area, because such assignments make life easier, and classroom discussions better for the teacher, or so the teacher thinks. Such assignments often carry the implicit assumption that by completing the assignment, the student is learning the process of library research, so little prior instruction is given by the teacher. Furthermore, to avoid student plagiarism and inertia, many teachers prohibit the use of encyclopedias, or assign a minimum number of required pages or formats on a particular topic. All of these requirements, prohibitions, and assignments may seem sensible to teachers familiar with college and university and large public library resources, but they are guaranteed to drive the average YA /reference librarian in small and medium sized public libraries-- and the students--crazy!

Such assignments also drive school librarians mad, too, although the local school librarian can usually be the public librarian's best ally in combatting the worst of these. A timely call to the school librarian can often get the teacher to adjust the assignment so that it will meet teaching objectives without creating needless student frustration. Unfortunately, the mass assignment problem will probably always be with us, despite attempts to stop the process. An annual attempt at faculty meetings should be made, however, to remind teachers that such assignments increase student resentment, inhibit the learning process and make libraries continual places of failure for students. One simple way to alleviate the problem is to ask teachers to alert librarians when such

```
┌─────────────────────────────────────────────────────────────┐
│                    ASSIGNMENT ALERT                          │
│  If the _____ Library is to have material    │
│  for ALL your students on a particular assignment, it is im- │
│  portant that you fill out and mail this card ten days prior │
│  to giving out the assignment.  Thank you.                   │
│                                                              │
│  Assignment: _____ │
│                                                              │
│  ─────────────────────────────────────────────────────────── │
│  Grade: _____   Section: _____         │
│  Teacher: _____   No. of Students: ____         │
│  School: _____                                 │
│  Date to be given: _____  Date due: _____         │
│  Send to: _____         │
│  ─────────────────────────────────────────────────────────── │
│  Other instructions to students/librarian: _____ │
│                                                              │
└─────────────────────────────────────────────────────────────┘
```

Figure 1.

assignments are imminent through the use of an assignment alert form such as the one shown in Figure 1.

Getting teachers to agree to the use of encyclopedias and to the selection of alternate titles/topics at the discretion of the librarian would be another major achievement. In lieu of that, the student patron who sincerely attempts to complete an impossible assignment should be protected from both teacher and parental retaliation, if possible, by the use of some sort of notification form. An example is given in Figure 2. Unfortunately, such a form is the only possible communication with some teachers.

Mass Assignments

One method of getting around mass assignments which falls somewhere between the reserve shelf idea and anarchy is the creation of reference pathfinders on frequently requested topics. A pathfinder is a one or two-page guide to the literature on a topic. It includes a definition of the topic, and the various subject headings and cross references found in standard tools such as encyclopedias, the Readers' Guide, the vertical file, and the library's own classification system. Some prominent names associated with the topic may also be given. Essentially, a pathfinder is a shortcut which relieves the YA/reference librarian of repeated individualized user instruction on the same topic for masses of students. Pathfinders, do, however, raise the question of just how much work librarians should do for students, especially when so many assignments seem to intend to teach the process of library research. The answer is not always simple.

```
┌─────────────────────────────────────────────────────────────┐
│             PARENT/TEACHER NOTIFICATION FORM                │
│   Library _____ Date _____     │
│                                                             │
│   Dear Parent/Teacher:                                      │
│                                                             │
│   _____ came to the library today.  We re-  │
│   gret that we are unable to fill the request for _____   │
│   _____ │
│   because                                                   │
│                                                             │
│   1___ All material on the subject is in use.               │
│   2___ Reasonable search failed to supply suitable material.│
│   3___ There are too many restrictions on the types of      │
│        materials students may use.                          │
│   4___ All material on the subject must be used in the      │
│        library.                                             │
│   5___ Further clarification of the question is needed.     │
│   6___ We are unable to provide so much on one subject to   │
│        so many students at one time.                        │
│   7___ Material on this subject is in heavy demand by       │
│        other library patrons not in this class.             │
│   8___ The assignment deadline does not allow time for      │
│        interlibrary loan of materials.                      │
│   9___ Other _____   │
│        _____    │
│                                                             │
│   May we request that you give us advance notice of assign- │
│   ments so that we may better serve the students?  We would │
│   welcome a call or visit from you.                         │
│                                                             │
│   Librarian _____ Phone _____  │
│   Library _____ │
│   _____ │
└─────────────────────────────────────────────────────────────┘

                          Figure 2.

        Even with library process assignments some work is neces-
sary on the part of the librarian, whether it is done by way of a
pathfinder or one-to-one interviewing or instruction to a succession
of single patrons, or in groups.  Library geography and procedures
are not easily mastered.  Indexes are not totally similar or con-
sistent or all inclusive.  The library may not own everything in-
dexed.  People feel strange and insecure in strange places, etc.

        Frankly I think pathfinders are useful tools.  If by creating
them, the YA/reference librarian deserves an "A" on a resulting
paper as much as a student, so be it.  Some balance must be
achieved between the knowledge and procedural objectives of library
process assignments.  If the process obscures or frustrates the
acquisition of knowledge then the librarian not only has the right,
```

but should, make the process less inhibiting. An arbitrary rule about how much help will be given with homework assignments is useless. The amount of help will vary according to the self-sufficiency of the patron, regardless of age. With so many adults returning to school, a library making strict homework rules for secondary students is being blatantly discriminatory. YA/reference librarians should also keep in perspective the fact that only they find endless fascination in library use. To most patrons, the library is simply a means to an end. To students, the "end" is a completed paper and a passing grade, and the amount of help given by the librarian should be adjusted to this reality without prejudice toward YA patrons. User instruction is a service, a means toward getting information to the young adult patron. A pathfinder is simply an efficient means of such instruction.

One means of personalizing user instruction for students and avoiding the use of pathfinders is the creative one-to-one use of trained volunteers or "Homework Helpers."[10] Whether the helpers are adults from a local service organization, or, more ideally, young adults themselves, they can relieve the YA/reference librarian of time-consuming, repetitive instruction, and free that person for collection and staff development, in-depth research assistance, and related professional duties.

Helping the Young Adult

Another aspect of the discussion over how much work should be done for young adult students concerns reference service given over the telephone. Some libraries demand that students come in person and offer only the most perfunctory telephone reference service as soon as they learn that the caller is requesting information in connection with a school assignment. Such a telephone policy is unfair in several ways. It assumes that the student needs are of low priority when they may be of paramount importance to the callers; it ignores the realities of nonexistent, unescorted transportation for young people; it places a value judgment on the motives of the caller; and it assumes that all school assignments are intended to teach library research when that is not the case. With mainstreaming of the disabled a reality in schools, such a policy may also be legally as well as philosophically discriminatory.

Either telephone reference is more than a title location location service and it is available to everyone equally, or it is not. If it is, then the same kind of nonjudgmental service given in person should be offered over the phone, preferably by someone doing telephone service exclusively for scheduled periods of time. Telephone reference service should not be measured by the amount of time one talks on the phone, with an assumption that assignment service takes more time, nor should priorities automatically be set to favor non-homework requests. After careful interviewing and mutual agreement, the librarian may be justified in asking the caller to come in person, but such a determination should be both individually determined, and mutually acceptable, not based on the myth of a lesser class of users who should automatically come in person and be self-sufficient. If anything, someone who phones first should be rewarded for being better organized and for having more foresight, whether or not that person is a young adult student.

One aggravation of young adult reference service is the problem of parents who do their kids' homework. The librarian generally feels annoyed at the mythical adolescent paragon of scholastic achievement who is too busy to come in person, and at the parent who is oblivious to the fact that doing all the student's work will not help him to learn anything, except possibly how to manipulate parents and librarians.

While annoyance is understandable, there is absolutely no point in trying to break up a family pattern years in the making. What is even more difficult is when the parent and young adult come in together. If there is a discreet way of separating them so that the librarian can talk directly to the young person, this is by far the most preferable way to deal with the situation. It also may not be possible. The librarian may have to resign him or herself to dealing primarily with the parent with a silent, apathetic, or resentful adolescent in tow. What is so painful about this situation is that the librarian is made a visible accomplice in a destructive dynamic, but I see no way around it except polite, nonjudgmental service. Embarrassing the young adult or insulting the parent will only add more misery to an already bad situation.

Some parents will immediately request help for their son or daughter and be totally vague about the scope of what it is they are asking for. In that case, a telephone call to the young adult can elicit the information, or the parent might be persuaded to send the adolescent in person. Each parent "problem" is unique and the librarian should use judgment and tact in each individual case.

Some public libraries make deposit classroom collections available to teachers for the length of a specific assignment. This practice, dating from the days when public libraries provided all school library service, can still be useful, but only under certain conditions, --if the teacher formally assumes lost book responsibility in writing; if school library services are inadequate; if duplicate copies remain available to other library users; and if there is only one local school to contend with. In a state-mandated curriculum, all public schools in the state may study certain topics simultaneously. To favor one at the expense of others is bad politics and bad practice, especially if it is precedent-setting. Once a precedent is established, it is extremely difficult to stop the practice.

Assess Strengths

Before undertaking the practice of classroom collections in schools, the public library needs to assess school library strengths. Many teachers totally bypass their own school librarians in requesting such collection service, or they mistakenly assume that their school resources are inadequate. In areas where school librarians are not legally mandated, requests for classroom collections from the public library may well be a deliberate tactic to keep them from becoming mandated. On the other hand, some local schools and public libraries do not have contiguous boundaries, and deposit collections might be the only way to give the students who live within the larger school district boundary, but outside the public library boundary, access to supplementary materials. Private school requests raise the issue of how to set up spending and service priorities for public money.

Policies on classroom collections should be based on local political realities, available resources, and traditions of cooperation. Such policies should also be formalized in writing and by library board approval. Whatever is available through such a policy should be available to all.

Interlibrary loan services are often problematic for YA reference service because of the eternal YA tendency to ignore homework deadlines until the last minute; however, they should be offered routinely if a requested title/topic cannot be filled locally. Unless ALL the cooperating libraries in an interlibrary loan (ILL) network agree that school-related requests are a local-level library responsibility, it would seem unethical not to offer ILL services to YA students. Unfortunately, many networks include academic and special libraries who refuse to interloan materials to minors in a class. Such policies are discriminatory not only to YA patrons but to public libraries in the network, since public libraries rarely make such overt age distinctions of their own volition.

Most ILL networks assume a hierarchy of needs and responses which prevent overutilization of the service, especially by the smaller libraries in the network. The hierarchy is enforced in several ways, usually by reimbursement formulas which assess borrowing libraries and favor lending libraries, by policies on the types of materials which may be borrowed (e.g., excluding reference books, recent fiction, juveniles and/or mass market paperbacks), and also by a sifting process built into ILL procedures at the local library reference desk.

The most obvious and legitimate sifting process is whether the patron will get the materials in time for them to be useful. Most YA students will be eliminated from using ILL services on the basis of short assignment deadlines and their own procrastination. The problem will be worse with young adolescents because many of them still lack the ability to speculate on the future, including future homework deadlines.

A less legitimate sifting process is the determination of a serious (versus frivolous?) need for the ILL material. Arriving at a determination of "serious" is like trying to define pornography--

it is often in the eye of the beholder. Unless the YA/reference librarian can prove that a YA patron is consistently requesting and ignoring ILL materials, "seriousness" is much better left to the determination of the patron, regardless of age. YA student requests are not frivolous as a class, as some ILL policies would have us believe.

ILL Services

An even less legitimate sifting process, from the public library perspective, is determining the "status" of the borrower. This process is based on the value system of service in large academic libraries where faculty status is higher than graduate student status, which is higher than undergraduate student status, etc. In such a status ranking of preferential service, it is easy to see that secondary school student status is close to nonexistent. Such nonexistent status may result in total lack of access to ILL services for young adults, unless public libraries resist the inappropriate use of status determinations in ILL codes. It might be argued that ILL policies and procedures based on status are in violation of the Library Bill of Rights.

Access to ILL services for all ages is best protected by a written agreement, with built-in evaluation procedures, among library participants in an ILL network on which materials/requests will be filled locally, and which will be borrowed from central or larger libraries. Access is not provided by making potentially discriminatory value judgments on the needs or status of patrons, inevitably minors, at the local reference desk.

The mythical user hierarchy and fears of overutilization become even more pronounced when YA access to expensive computerized database search services is discussed. Again, the public library must determine a policy which is equitable for all ages. A strict user fee-based policy is almost always discriminatory against minors as a class of users, because they are excluded by society as a class from the means of earning the money to pay for the service. The larger ethical questions of fee-for-service practices and preferential users in public libraries are still being debated.[11] YA/reference librarians should monitor and contribute to the debate on behalf of YA patrons.

One other continual problem in the area of reference services to young adults is the abysmal record keeping of such service in public libraries and in state library reporting systems. Most statistical reporting systems divide reference questions answered into a numerical count of adult and juvenile, with the YA-related statistics lost between the two. Worse still is the lack of qualitative reporting of what was requested with what frequency. Some libraries do not even keep the qualitative information internally, which makes collection and service evaluations almost impossible.

The developmental realities of young adults themselves contribute to the problem. A visual assessment of a fully clothed teenager can be meaningless for an adult attempting to guess the person's chronological age. The most tactful way around the problem might be to ask young-looking patrons what school or grade they are in at the time service is given, with an explanation of why the information is requested. A sampling procedure by day of the week and time of day might be less intrusive than demanding grade/school information routinely. Whatever data-gathering mechanism is decided upon should be used at ALL public service desks where reference service is given--adult, YA, juvenile, and circulation. It is only through improving YA reference service record keeping that actual service patterns will be discovered and evaluated.

Since common definitions of readers advisory and reference services break down when serving young adults, some serious attempt at operational service and client definitions must be made before state reporting is shaped up. Reporting undefined services is as useless as present practice. This may mean that YA readers advisory work will finally be seen for the information service it is, and also that an holistic view of service will prevail. To that end, I offer the most eloquent comment I have read on information services to the young:

> The word INFORMATION has become a loaded one for those concerned with library service to children. In this respect, also, we have shrunk back rather than moved forward, as our goals might have us do. Because the provision of information services, data banks, referrals, etc., have tended to make libraries seem lopsidedly but resolutely committed to the presentation of facts rather than the encouragement of pleasure or even the development of culture, we have reacted by eschewing the idea of information as an important product of the public library. As I have said before, I believe the more reasonable approach is to stress that, for children, the provision of pleasure, encouragement of reading, enlargement of vocabulary, and development of a sense of fantasy or even of a sense of humor are informational services which the public library can provide in a unique, nonthreatening environment. We ought to take every opportunity to say this to the information-mongers who need to be reminded that personal development is the most significant kind of information process.[12]

References

1. Library Bill of Rights. ALA, 1980.
2. "Commitment to Information Services." RQ 15: 327-30, Summer, 1976; and 18: 275-9, Spring, 1979.
3. Berninghausen, David K. Flight from Reason. ALA, 1975; Katz, William, Introduction to Reference Work. McGraw-Hill, 1978; RQ. ALA, quarterly.

4. Shera, Jesse. *Foundations of the Public Library.* University of Chicago Press, 1949.
5. Johnson, Sister Marie Inez. "Development of Separate Service for Young People in Public Libraries of the United States and its Implications for Library Schools." Enoch Pratt Free Library, 1940. Thesis: M.A. Columbia University, 1940. Mimeographed.
6. New York Public Library. *Branch Library Book News* 6:8 (October, 1929), p. 114.
7. Edwards, Margaret. *Fair Garden and the Swarm of Beasts.* rev. ed. Hawthorn, 1974, pp. 40-41.
8. Gross, Elizabeth. *Public Library Service to Children.* Dobbs Ferry, NY, Oceana, 1967.
9. Martin, Lowell. *Students and the Pratt Library: Challenge and Opportunity.* (Deiches Study NO. 1). Enoch Pratt Free Library, 1963, and Coleman, James, ed. *Youth, Transition to Adulthood.* University of Chicago Press.
10. *New Jersey Libraries* XII:5 (September, 1979), pp. 16-17.
11. Blake, F.M. and Perlmutter, E.L. "Rush to User Fees: Alternate Proposals," *Library Journal* 102: 2005-8. October, 1977. Many articles have continued to appear since then, and they are cited in *Library Literature.*
12. Sullivan, Peggy, "Goals of Public Library Service for Children" in *Children's Services of Public Libraries* (Allerton Park Institute 23rd, 1977), ed. by Selma K. Richardson, University of Illinois, 1978, p. 7.

TOO MANY BOOKS?

PUBLISHERS' PROBLEMS AND COLLECTION BUILDING*

Audrey Eaglen

Given the astonishing number of new book titles and new editions of older books published each year in the United States, one could assume that collection building (and maintenance) would be a virtual snap, made difficult only by the problem of what to finally choose for purchase from such an embarrassment of riches. According to Publishers Weekly in its "Statistical Report on Domestic Title Output" (October 1, 1982) a total of "at least 48,793 book titles were published in the U.S. in 1981"--41,434 brand-new titles and 7,359 new editions, a staggering total on the face of it. (The words "at least" are used because many published books are not counted in the PW totals: government publications, many professional law book publications, subscription reference sets, book club editions, irregular serials and annuals, books sold only to schools, books of fewer than 49 pages, etc.) And if further proof is needed that an awful lot of books are available for librarians to purchase for library collections, Bowker's advertisement for the new edition of Books in Print notes that the 1982-83 edition has increased to six volumes, from two in the 1960s and four in the 1970s. The ad further states that the newest edition lists more than 600,000 titles in print and includes more than 80,000 new titles and editions than did last year's.

How does it happen, then, given the fact that tens of thousands of new books are published each year and hundreds of thousands are in print at any given time, that libraries find that anywhere from 20 to 40 percent or more of the titles they order are cancelled by the publisher, and what implications does this have for collection building?

As a case in point, the Cuyahoga County Public Library system in Cleveland, Ohio, recently opened its 27th and newest branch library in an affluent suburb of the city, Beachwood. Residents of Beachwood are generally highly educated, and felt the need for a

---
*Reprinted by permission of the author and publisher from Collection Building, 5 (Spring 1983) 40-42. Copyright © 1983 by Neal-Schuman Publishers.

well-stocked, good-sized library in their community. That need was translated into passage of a $2.5 million bond issue to construct a building, with the capacity to eventually house 100,000 volumes. From the time the decision was made two and one-half years ago to go ahead with the building of Beachwood Library, the branch manager, Nancy Fisher, has been ordering materials for the collection. Today, the collection consists of approximately 25,000 volumes, with 75,000 yet to go. Ms. Fisher has found that "instant" collection building is nearly impossible because an extraordinarily high percentage of books ordered are canclled as out-of-stock (OS) or, even worse, out-of-print (OP), the latter, often while the books are still being reported as available in the latest edition of Books in Print.

In one case alone, Ms. Fisher told me, she ordered some $13,000 worth of books; $10,000 worth were cancelled as OS or OP, and every title ordered had been verified in BIP. She mentioned a series which is a basic collection item in nearly every school and public library in the U.S., and which is used constantly by library patrons, This Fabulous Century, an 8-volume set published by Time-Life Books. Knowing how much use these books would get, Fisher ordered 5 copies of each volume after verifying their availability in the 1981-82 BIP (the most recent edition available at the time). In spite of this, the orders were cancelled by the publisher as out-of-print.

As a result, Beachwood patrons are learning that their spanking new library is simply unable to provide many of the books they need when they need them, and that they must wait, often for weeks or months, to borrow them through interloan. The collection suffers, but more importantly the library user suffers when the books needed are impossible to obtain.

And why are so many thousands of titles impossible to obtain because they have been allowed to go out-of-print? Publishers answer that it is because of, not in spite of, the fact that so many titles are being published each year--that the market is so glutted that the odds against any title surviving for even a year have become astronomically high.

Leonard Shatzkin, a publishing professional for more than 35 years, predicts in his recent book In Cold Type: Overcoming the Book Crisis (Houghton Mifflin, 1982), that the American trade book publishing industry is facing problems "of a magnitude unparalleled in its 342 years of existence," and "unless urgent and far-reaching reforms are undertaken," "one should expect to see a number of respected publishing houses quietly exit the scene." He also notes that publishers are already generally reducing staff and publications lists--which means, for those who are building collections or even just trying to maintain them, that fewer of the books they must have in order to build will be available, and most will become unavailable even sooner than they have in the past. Shatzkin gives some startling examples of what is happening to those tens of thousands of new titles that are being published for the library and bookstore market each year.

Example 1: Ninety to ninety-five percent of the trade books published in the United States each year are "stone cold dead by the end of their first year of life"--in other words, out-of-print.

What this means for collection building, of course, is that if a library does not purchase a new title while it is still very new, it will be highly unlikely to ever purchase it--and libraries are notoriously slow to order books.

Example 2: One out of every three trade books sold is sold to a library. Of the remaining two-thirds which are sold to book wholesalers and retailers, one out of every three will be returned to the publisher unsold for full credit.

In other words, those books will be going out-of-print just as quickly as the publisher can find a way to dump them. The publisher simply cannot afford to warehouse unsold merchandise indefinitely any more than any other producer of goods can. The recent Supreme Court decision in the Thor case, which in simplest terms prohibits publishers from claiming certain tax benefits on unsold stock, has made it even more unlikely that a publisher will be willing or able to hold on to large numbers of unsold books. In some extreme cases, a few publishers have come close to ruin because of wholesalers who, after buying large quantities of books found they could not sell them to their customers, and ended up returning them. One can only imagine what happens to the profit and loss statement when this occurs.

Example 3: In the case of mass market publishing, the rate of return is approaching fifty percent; in other words, one out of every two mass market paperback books in the U.S. will be returned to the publisher.

At a recent Association of American Publishers meeting, Ron Busch, president of Pocket Books, stated that his company lost $1 million on one title alone, John Irving's The Hotel New Hampshire. Millions of copies were printed, and millions of copies just didn't sell. Further, he predicted that in the next six months "at least one [mass market publisher] and possibly three will be gone." Libraries, which purchase more and more paperbacks as budgets shrink, will either buy these almost as fast as they are available, or they will simply be unable to obtain them.

Example 4: For every copy of a trade book sold in the U.S., another is "remaindered" as publishers' overstock.

On the face of it, these remainders, selling as they do for about 20 percent of their original cost, should be a boon to libraries faced with shrinking book budgets and inflationary pressures. The catch, however, is that remaindered books are, for all intents and purposes, out-of-print and no longer listed in the standard in-print sources such as BIP. It can be difficult for a librarian to try to tell a patron that the library cannot obtain a book because it's out-of-print when the patron has just seen it on a remainder table at B. Dalton or Waldenbooks!

All of these examples tend to support what publishers believe is the reason that so many books have such short lives, which is simply that too many books are published each year. And this is borne out by Books in Print, which in the 1982-83 edition, dropped "more than 40,000 titles that [were] declared out-of-print since last year's edition...." (italics mine). But is the problem as simple as it appears?

Shatzkin thinks not, and quotes some UNESCO figures to back him up, namely that although in 1978 the U.S. published one title per 2,324 inhabitants, Israel published one for every 1,671 inhabitants, and France, Germany, and Great Britain published one title, respectively, for every 1,680, 1,258, and 1,542 inhabitants. He then mentions other figures which would indicate that U.S. trade publishers sell each U.S. inhabitant only about one book each year, and that each of the 220,000 trade titles available therefore only sells an average of about 1,200 copies per year.*

Shatzkin believes that the number of books published each year in the U.S. is not the real problem at all. It is instead, a combination of several other factors, the most important and destructive of which are the publishing industry's antiquated and unbelievably inefficient methods of marketing and distributing their books, which, combined with the rise and expansion of the major bookselling chains, make retail bookselling marginally profitable at best, and thus endangers the publishing business itself.

But what does this have to do with libraries? Why should we be concerned about book retailers and their problems? The answer is a simple one. Most publishers have sold and, if they survive, always will sell most of their books to booksellers, either wholesalers or retailers. Of the entire book industry's total sales of $6 billion annually, only about $2 billion worth of books are sold to libraries. In other words, the library market simply cannot pay for the broad range of publishing we see today, so it is axiomatic that if the greatest part of the market for books does not survive, many publishers will also fail and the library's options will be severely restricted. At the same time, it is largely the retail market which in effect determines which books will and which will

---

*Shatzkin makes an interesting though not necessarily valid point, that from the point of view of the authors who write the books, not nearly enough books are published. A survey of published authors done for the Authors Guild revealed that only a tiny fraction of published writers have high incomes and that "writing income places most authors below the poverty line."

not stay in print, because of the ridiculous returns and remainders policies embraced by almost all publishers who sell to retail and wholesale booksellers.

Publishers themselves recognize the inadequacies of the distribution system, so much so that in 1981, the Book Industry Study Group, whose members represent all types of entities within the industry, commissioned Arthur Andersen & Co. to do a major study of the distribution quagmire. The study was reported on in 1982 in that company's Book Distribution in the United States: Issues and Perceptions.

Because of its importance to libraries, who depend so greatly on the publishing industry and thus have a vested interest in this industry problem, the subject of this column in the next issue of Collection Building will be an analysis of the Andersen report (and also because of the report's cost--some $160 per copy!).

THE ELUSIVE LIST PRICE AND THE FPT FACTOR*

Connie C. Epstein

The hottest, most controversial topic in bookselling and buying just now may possibly be a new system of pricing called "freight pass-through." Although the eyes of the uninitiated glaze over at its mention, those who have mastered the intricacies of FPT hold many strong opinions about it, ranging from outrage to approval. How freight pass-through came to be, what it is, and questions raised by it shed a great deal of light on the health of the present-day book distribution system and the competitive relationships among publishers, wholesalers, retailers, and libraries.

  The concept of freight pass-through first surfaced at a PEN meeting on December 3, 1980, when Joan Ripley, owner of The Second Story, a Chappaqua (N.Y.) bookstore (then president of ABA, the American Booksellers Assocation), described a two-tier pricing plan being discussed by booksellers and publishers. This plan was intended to help retailers meet the problems of rising freight charges that, in the words of G. Roysce Smith, executive director of the ABA, were becoming "the difference between profit and no profit" for many small bookstores. In the decade from 1970 to 1980, the rate for shipping a two-pound book had increased from 18¢ to 81¢, and the additional cost had become a major blow to independent booksellers. According to the ABA, the book business was the only one in which the customer did not pay freight costs. Many felt the time had come to find a remedy, and freight pass-through was the remedy hit upon.

  The FPT idea was worked out, more or less simultaneously, by Ripley, Smith, and Ivor Whitson, president of E. P. Dutton. Dutton became the first publisher to adopt the new pricing policy, and announced that it would be put into effect with their spring 1981 list; backlist titles would be brought into the plan as they came up for reprint. Other publishers who followed this plan or used variants of it were: Harper & Row; William Morrow; Random House; Holt, Rinehart & Winston; Farrar, Straus & Giroux. By midsummer 1982, six publishers with their associated imprints were using freight pass-through pricing; now the count is up to eighteen.

---

*Reprinted by permission of the author and publisher from School Library Journal, 29 (April 1983) 23-26. Published by R.R. Bowker Co. (a Xerox company). Copyright © 1983 by Xerox Corporation.

Communication and Education

    Because of its two-tier structure, freight pass-through pricing is more complicated than the old or former system. This may be one of its biggest problems. Those who don't have adequate information or the necessary time to understand it are apt to become impatient and consider it a gimmick or, even worse, a fraud. But a case can certainly be made for FPT. In essence, the publisher using this pricing method gives each title two prices. The lower price appears in the company catalog and on invoices to purchasers --it is called either a "catalog" or "invoice" price. The higher one appears on the book jacket, sometimes as a number code, sometimes designated FPT--it is called the "freight pass-through" price.

    Companies using FPT base discounts to commercial purchasers and royalties to authors on the lower, invoice price. Originally all channels of distribution--wholesalers as well as publishers-- were envisioned as using the invoice price for their dealings until the books reached retail stores. There retailers were to charge the higher FPT prices and retain the increment, or surcharge, and thus recover some of the higher freight costs. If the retailers did not sell the books and returned them to the publishers they would not gain the increment, and they would still pay freight charges.

Variations in FPT

The basic idea of each publisher's freight pass-through plan was much the same, but the details sometimes differed. Two major variants have emerged. The first figures the freight increment as a percentage (either 3 percent or 4 percent) of the retail price. For example, Dutton set it at 3 percent, so that a book with an invoice price of $9.95 would have a freight pass-through price of $10.25. In this way, the amount of the increment could be adjusted to the price and indirectly to the weight of the book, but the drawback was that odd prices causing customer resistance could result, a factor that all involved wished to avoid.

    In the second variant, the freight increment was set at a fixed amount, such as 50¢. Morrow adopted this approach; it announced that a book with a $15 catalog price, for example, would carry a FPT price of $15.50 on the jacket. In line with its intention to keep prices as simple to work with as possible, Morrow began to round off its catalog prices to the nearest dollar; thus, the $15 book became the equivalent of one formerly priced at $14.95.

    FPT plans also differed in another respect; this is the styling of the price designation on book jackets. As another aid to the retailer, some publishers using the percentage plan worked out a code stating the double price information for the bookseller in a way such that most customers would not understand it, and therefore not object to it. A Dutton jacket, for example, might read: 01258-370 $12.95. Decoded, this means that the title carries an invoice price of $12.58, a surcharge of 37¢, and a freight pass-through price of $12.95. The Harper code also includes month and year of publication, so one of its jackets might offer the numbers 02134182 with a price of $13.95. Decoded, this says that the book was published in February of 1982 with an invoice price of $13.41 and an FPT price of $13.95. Publishers using the fixed amount plan were not faced with the problem of explaining the specific increment for each title. They could simply print FPT $15.50 on the jacket and assume that retailers would remember the invoice price was originally $15.

Another variation in the FPT plans involved the type of book to be included. Some companies applied FPT pricing to all titles published; some excluded children's books in library bindings that carried suggested net prices in catalogs, and others such as Farrar, Strauss & Giroux excluded children's titles altogether.

To Roysce Smith, freight pass-through pricing was the "only logical answer" to the sharply rising freight costs of small retailers, who were usually inhibited by the price printed on the book jacket from raising the price of their product, as had happened in other industries. Publishers, on the other hand, were reluctant to add the freight charges to the publishing costs (as rising costs are traditionally dealt with), because the retail price would then become so high it might encounter customer resistance. As one example, Smith cites what would happen to a $10 book if its price was raised in the usual way and then increased by the FPT method, using the publisher's rule of thumb that the list price is roughly five times that of production costs, in this case $2.00. If 50¢ is added to these costs, they become $2.50, and the list price to the customer, at five times that figure, becomes $12.50. However, a retailer, who may be buying at a discount of 40 percent, also pays more for the book, in this case $7.50. Instead, if the 50¢ is added at the end of the buying chain, FPT style, the list price to the customer is $10.50, a retailer buys at a discount price of 40 percent off $10, or $6, and it seems as if everyone saves.

Recent Actions & Reactions

Initially one group of interested parties--the writers--were suspicious and felt that the savings might be coming from their earnings. Their reaction to the plan, when Joan Ripley first described it at the 1980 PEN meeting, was hostile. But when the Authors Guild looked into the matter for its membership in the summer of 1981, it decided to recommend cooperation with FPT pricing as long as two safeguards were obtained. The first was that the author's contract include a clause that limited the freight increment to a maximum amount, such as 50¢ or 4 percent of invoice price, so that the difference between invoice price and FPT price would be kept close to the actual freight charges. The second was that the invoice price be defined as the price charged to the bookstores before the application of the booksellers' discount, not afterward.

Irwin Karp, legal counsel for the Guild, says that "if FPT pricing helps the store at all, it is to the author's good." He points out that authors' royalties have never been based on price changes made in the bookstore. If retailers sell the book at a lower discount price, the author's royalty does not drop, so logically, if booksellers retail it at a higher price, the royalty should not rise. As of last fall, the Guild's position was still the same, that is, in Karp's words, "we are not ardent supporters, but we are willing to accept FPT pricing on a continuing trial basis as long as the two safeguards are observed."

To make the necessary contractual adjustments with authors on books already published, publishers have had their writers sign letters of agreement approving the plan; most seem to have done so. A few noteworthy holdouts have been reported, such as Harper's Shel Silverstein and Dutton's Richard Leakey, but to date they are the rare exceptions.

Authors seem to be holding off making a final decision until they have a chance to see whether sales volume has increased sufficiently by the help to the store to offset whatever price resistance might be encountered from customers. Still, Vincent Agnifilo, manager of library sales for the wholesaler, Bookazine, feels that authors may well have the deciding vote. "Whether FPT lasts, he says, "will depend on the final attitude of the really big authors like Michener."

One reason why the effectiveness of FPT pricing remains uncertain is the question of the role that the book wholesaler is playing in the process. One wholesaler (who asked that he not be identified) wonders whether publishers had considered how FPT would affect the <u>entire</u> distribution system. Judging from Royce Smith's explanation of how the plan began, the answer seems to be they had not. "Our concern was with the small retailer, who was the one living from hand to mouth," he says, "we didn't even think about the effect it would have on libraries and retailers buying from wholesalers." This effect was slow to be perceived, but now that the plan has been in operation for almost two years it is becoming apparent.

FPT Pricing & Libraries

Now a battle seems to be shaping up between wholesalers and libraries over the issue of FPT pricing. For one thing, most wholesalers are not doing business on the basis of the lower, invoice price as the original announcements assumed that they would. In the case of retailers buying from wholesalers, this development is not as upsetting as it is to librarians, because whatever added cost the FPT price brings to them, they are able to recover from their customers. Libraries, however, were not well-informed about FPT pricing practices, and they have no customers to repay them for the added cost. In the vacuum created by librarians' lack of knowledge of FPT, some suspect that they are being billed unfairly, possibly in violation of their contracts. The accusation has been made

in the Unabashed Librarian that "Libraries are the only commercial
book buyers who are being charged this high FPT price."

From an informal survey of the FPT policies of five major
wholesalers, this accusation does not appear to be true. But wholesalers are following different procedures, which is confusing--
clearly the question of the legal definition of list price as cited in
a contract remains to be settled.

One explanation for not discounting to library customers on
the lower, invoice price is that wholesalers have also been hit by
rising freight costs and need help with the pricing structure. Some
feel that the FPT price might work better for wholesalers than retailers since they don't have the problem of competing against discount outlets. From this point of view, the publishers' original
FPT plan was ineffectual because the retail marketplace is so competitive that the increment offered appears too little to do the retailers any good. If wholesalers decreased their discounts to customers to make up for added freight costs, libraries would also be
paying more. FPT pricing will be effective, said one wholesaler
"as long as the distribution channels hold the line. Otherwise, it
won't be worth a damn!"

Recent Changes in FPT

Just before ALA's 1983 Midwinter Meeting last January, the country's largest book wholesaler, Baker & Taylor, whose business is
both retail and institutional, broke that line when it announced that
it would no longer impose FPT charges on library customers.

At Ingram, a different policy has evolved. It also discounts
to customers on the higher, FPT price, whenever it is offered by
a publisher. However, maximum-order customers, buying fifty or
more assorted titles at a list price of $2.95 or more, then receive
an additional discount of 2 percent, raising it to 42 percent from
40 percent. Freight costs are usually an additional charge. Vicki
Barnes, who handles library sales for the company, says that this
policy holds for all customers, whether library or retail, and that
both are given the same discount schedule. Uniformity of treatment
is the core of Ingram's philosophy, according to Barnes, and the
company feels that whether a customer sells in turn to somebody
else or lends to someone should make no difference. Barnes says
the Ingram policy is not complicated to apply and that librarians
are happy with it because it offers the possibility of a higher discount, which is especially important to them these days. In effect,
the practical Ingram policy seems to be a way of dividing the extra
freight pass-through money between the wholesaler and the customer;
Ingram takes the 3 percent or 4 percent increment and gives back
2 percent. Less-than-maximum-order customers, of course, do not
get any share at all.

Yet a third policy is followed by the Follett Library Book

Company, whose business is entirely with schools and libraries.
Head of the purchasing department Gary Chmielewski says that the
company discounts to its customers on the invoice price and also
pays all freight charges. In any case, he estimates that FPT
prices would not apply to almost half of the inventory they carry as
library bindings are usually excluded. A typical shipment received
by Follett is apt to be three or four skids in contrast to the one or
two cartons that go to a retail store, and Chmielewski points out that
when freight charges are prorated over such large volume, the unit
cost may be less than the FPT increment, therefore the company
does not feel the need to use the higher price.

Bookazine's business is approximately half institutional and
half retail, and discount schedules are different for both categories.
President Bill Epstein says that the reason for the difference is that
the cost of doing business with libraries and bookstores is not the
same. Bookazine pays all freight charges to the libraries while
charging up to a maximum of $3.75 to retailers. Furthermore,
sales are virtually guaranteed to libraries since there are so few
returns; thus, business with libraries holds almost no risk. Accordingly, Bookazine is discounting orders to libraries on the lower, invoice price, although Epstein says that "the company is still
thinking through its retail policy, which is complicated by more difficult freight problems." His reason for not using the FPT price
with library accounts "even though we need it" is his concern that
it will not be legally upheld as the list price specified in his company's library contracts. "If someone would define what list price
is now, that would be half the battle," he says. Meanwhile, Epstein doesn't want to take a chance and is passing up possible gains
by FPT pricing to protect Bookazine's profit margins.

Bookazine isn't surprised that librarians are now voicing
strong objections to FPT pricing. "If I were a librarian," says
Epstein, "I would try to find out what definition of list price my
contract called for." Undoubtedly because they do not feel free to
use FPT pricing with libraries, Bookazine's people don't like the
system and would like to see it done away with. In their opinion,
"it has created a tremendous amount of additional work, a lot of
animosity, and we are still paying the freight." Even in the case
of retail business, where they do feel legally able to use FPT
prices, Bookazine is disenchanted. Instead of the new method helping small retailers, as the ABA intended, they say that it has become a great boon to chain operations.

New York City retailer Deirdre Adler of the Canterbury
Bookshop says that FPT pricing is an "absolute gimmick that is
not helping anyone," and she doesn't expect it to last. However,
as she is quick to admit, she does not have the freight problems
of a Colorado retailer, so her prediction may be flawed.

Unfair Competition

That the bookstore chains should be the prime beneficiaries of the new system is ironic, but this development seems clear. With their large volume of sales and opportunity for centralizing orders, these chains are able to buy directly from publishers, which is a sure way to be billed on the invoice price.

Smith says that although bookseller response to the FPT plan was mixed at first, "the chains ate it up--they knew what it meant to them right away." Bookazine's Epstein is concerned that chains are now buying directly from the publisher with the result that wholesalers are losing what chain sales they had since they cannot compete with the publishers.

Libraries, too, have the option of buying directly from the publisher to avoid FPT prices, but in most cases they do not view this alternative as a practical one because of the enormous increase in paperwork it would entail. Also, those public libraries that are members of large systems have their buying done for them, so they are one step removed from the center of a purchasing policy. For example, the suburban public library of Port Washington, Long Island, is a member of the Nassau Library System, which uses Baker and Taylor and Bookazine as suppliers. Library Director Edward de Sciora says, "We are aware of the issue and have raised the question of what can be done about it with the purchasing agent of the system."

But finding out what price their supplier is discounting on is not easy for the staff as their invoices show only list price, discount, and discounted price, so they are also asking, "What is list price?" One method of identifying it is to check against the publisher's catalog, which gives the lower, invoice price; the process may be laborious, but does provide a double-check. Still, this confusion is causing suspicion. As Port Washington PL's Assistant Director Virginia Parker comments, "From a public relations standpoint, the way the information about FPT pricing has been disseminated seems unfortunate."

Since wholesalers are following different FPT practices, libraries have the second alternative of placing their business with the wholesaler whose policy they prefer. Frequently, however, this decision is complicated because they must weigh services offered, such as cataloging and range of inventory, against the list price used, discount, and freight policy. Some centralized library purchasing departments, reluctant to lose services, are considering still a third option: using the leverage of their large-volume orders to negotiate the definition of list price.

In the meantime, many librarians are up in arms over FPT, for their ordering procedures have been complicated, and they see no gain to themselves. Yet the reason does not seem to be conspiracy, but rather one of those instances in which the interests of the commercial book distribution system collide with those of the nonprofit system.

What is list price? Today that question has become a tough one to answer. For now, FPT pricing is such a new development that libraries will need to learn about as quickly as possible so they can settle on the distribution channel most suited to their needs. There _are_ alternatives, and if a library is not happy with the prices it is charged, those prices can be changed.

THE GOLDEN AGE OF SCIENCE FICTION IS 12*

David G. Hartwell

Twelve-year-olds who read science fiction understand it perfectly and learn from it. Millions of readers over the years have found it great fun (it is supposed to be fun) in spite of the fact that most educated readers, including librarians, would spurn science fiction without knowing anything about it except what "everyone knows": it is not generally serious literature, and since the word science occurs in the name, you probably wouldn't be interested or able to understand it if you did try to read it--so why try?

Science fiction was essential to me at age twelve and remained important to me and a lot of my friends throughout my teenage years. I read every sf book in the Lock Haven, Pennsylvania, city and college libraries and then moved to Massachusetts and read everything in the Reading Public Library, every paperback I could afford or borrow. I read a book a day, at least. When I taught a college course in the mid-1970s on sf, I asked the students for guesses on how many sf books they had read and the numbers ranged from one or two hundred to two or three thousand by age twenty or twenty one.

From my present vantage point as head of Timescape Books, I must say that the situation remains very much the same with today's sf audience. I stopped trying to convert people to sf years ago, but I still know that more sympathetic understanding of the science fiction phenomenon is necessary for its continued growth. Thus the following introduction to science fiction, through a consideration of sf people, how and why they read the way they do.

As Thomas Pynchon so amusingly posited in his eccentric little classic novel, The Crying of Lot 49, if you begin to look beneath the surface of everyday life, almost everyone is involved in some sort of underground or underground activity. This kind of activity is so much a part of what everyone does (without ever seeing the big picture) that if you pull back and look at it all, the real world seems very different. That is (in a very real sense) what this essay is about. I have adopted an informal style and an ironic

---

*Reprinted by permission of the author and the American Library Association from Top of the News, 39:1 (Fall 1982) 39-53. Copyright © 1982 by David G. Hartwell.

tone to emphasize that I am not trying to win converts with inflated literary claims but to investigate and represent an extraliterary phenomenon.

How to Tell an SF Fan

When you spot a science fiction devotee on a bus, in a library, or on lunch break in the cafeteria, she or he is identifiable only by a display of some kind: she is reading a flashy paperback that says "Science Fiction" on the cover; he is wearing a "Star Trek Lives!" T-shirt over his bathing trunks at the beach; she is quietly asking the newsstand dealer if there is a copy of Women of Wonder in the store; he is arguing loudly with a friend that Star Wars is much better than Close Encounters (which is not truly sf) while munching a sandwich and sipping Coke.

Otherwise there are no reliable outward signs, unless you happen to stop over at a hotel or motel anywhere in the U.S. where one of the at least weekly science fiction conventions is being held; after one look, you switch accommodations, because the whole place is filled with people in costumes, bacchanalian howls, teenagers in capes with swords, normally dressed adults wearing garish name tags that identify them as Gork or Kalinga Joe or Conan or David G. Hartwell or Beardsley Trunion. Your immediate perception of this social situation is either "Feh!" or "Let me back off and view these weirdos from a safe distance, say at the end of tomorrow's newscast!"

The science fiction person, you see, always lives in the sf world, but under cover of normality most of the time--except while attending a gathering of like minds such as the convention given in understated flashes above. The science fiction reader may be your attorney, your dentist, your child's schoolteacher, the film projectionist at your local theater, your wife or husband or child, happily living in two worlds at once: the real world of science fiction and the dubious reality of everyday life.

If you have lived with or worked with a science fiction person, you will have noticed how intensely she seems to be involved in science fiction, how much she reads it, watches it, recommends to those around her that they try it, because it is her special kind of fun. And if you examine her behavior in everyday life, you may well notice an impatience with the way things are, an ironic, sometimes sarcastic attitude toward everyday things (particularly imposed tasks of a wearisome nature), a desire for change. This complex of attitudes is closely congruent to the complex of attitudes found in the normal human teenager. In fact, a majority of all science fiction readers are under the age of twenty-one. The question is not how they got that way but why it should surprise anyone that they are.

Teenagers are not fully integrated into the tedium of adult

life and tend to view such life with healthy suspicion. Quite logical. The science fiction reader preserves this attitude as long in life as his association with science fiction continues, more often these days into full maturity. It makes him act strange sometimes. But mostly, he feeds his head with more science fiction and continues to get the job done, whatever it is.

Nearly a thousand readers of Locus, the newspaper of the science fiction field (a semiprofessional monthly published by California fan Charles N. Brown), responded to a survey which indicated that the median age of Locus readers is twenty-two but that the initial involvement in science fiction of almost every respondent happened between the ages of ten and fourteen. This lends a great deal of substance to the tradition in the science fiction world that active involvement starts early and lasts at least until the early twenties. Science fiction is an addiction (or habit) so reasonable in any teenager who can read (and many who can't very well, in this age of Star Trek and Star Wars) that it is superficially curious that it doesn't always last. But it doesn't, and most of us do end up well adjusted (more or less), resigned to life as it is known to be, heading toward 1984.

The science fiction drug is available everywhere to kids, in superhero comics, on TV, in the movies, in books and magazines. It is impossible to avoid exposure, to avoid the least hint of excitement at Marvel Comics superheroes and "Star Trek" reruns and Star Wars, to not become habituated to the language, clichés, or basic concepts of science fiction even before kindergarten. Children's culture in the contemporary U.S. is a supersaturated sf environment. By the time a kid can read comic books and attend a movie unaccompanied by an adult, early in grade school, her mind is a fertile environment for the harder stuff. Even the cardboard monsters of TV reruns feed the excitement. The science fiction habit is established early.

Omnivores

In some cases, accompanied by the hosannas of proud parents, a kid focuses his excitement on the science and goes on to construct winning exhibits in school science fairs, obtain scholarships, and support proud parents in their old age with his honorable gains as a career corporate technologist. Most often, a kid freezes at the gosh-wow TV/comics/movies stage and carries an infatuation with fantastic and absurd adventures into later life. But sometimes, usually by the age of twelve, a kid has progressed to reading science fiction in paperback, in magazines, book club editions--wherever she can find it, because written sf offers more concentrated excitement. This is the beginning of addiction; she buys, borrows, even steals all the science fiction she can get her hands on and reads omnivorously for months or even years, sometimes until the end of high school years, sometimes a book or more a day. But the classical symptom is intense immersion in written sf for at least six months around age twelve.

Publishers adore this phenomenon, which is akin to the addiction to mystery and detective fiction that flourished in the decades prior to the mid-sixties. One major publisher of sf has been heard to remark that his books are supported by twelve-year-olds of all ages. Every professional writer, editor, and publisher in the science fiction field knows that the structure of science fiction is founded on the large teenage audience, which guarantees a minimally acceptable market for almost every book published: it requires extreme ignorance and professional incompetence, determination akin to constipating oneself by an act of will, to be unsuccessful when selling science fiction to the omnivorous teenage audience.

What happens to science fiction omnivores? Well, obviously, sooner or later most of them discover the compulsive excitement of the opposite (or same) sex, and stop reading much of anything for pleasure, most of them permanently. However, once an omnivore, your life has been permanently altered, if only in minor ways. Years later, you may experience an irrational desire to watch "Battlestar Galactica" on TV, even though you know it's dumb stuff. You tend not to forbid your kids or kid your friends if they want a little toke of science fiction from time to time. A news report on solar-energy possibilities in the near future doesn't seem like total balderdash, just, perhaps, a bit optimistic in the short run; a front-page newspaper article on the U.S. space probe to Jupiter doesn't read like Sanskrit or form associations with guff like spirit-rapping. Surprise!--your life has been altered and you didn't even notice.

Discovering sex (or competitive sports or evangelical Christianity or demon rum) is not always a total diversion, though. And there are further discoveries open to the fan in the omnivorous stage: hundreds, often thousands of fans gather at conventions every weekend throughout Western civilization (the World Science Fiction Convention of 1979 was in Brighton, England) to act strange together. To a teenage omnivore, such a weekend of license to be maladjusted in the company of and in harmony with the covertly alienated of all ages can be golden. No one much notices how you dress or act as long as you do not injure yourself or others. Swords and capes (Ah, romance!) are particularly favored among the fat and pimply population, male and female. One wag counted seventy-two (!) Princess Leias at the World SF Convention of 1978 in Phoenix. Or you can hang out in your everyday slacks and jacket or jeans and T-shirt with like minds. And right there among the crowd are all the big-name professionals, from Asimov to Selazny, by tradition, and in fact approachable for conversation and frivolity. Just being there makes you a potentially permanent member of the sf family.

It's a clique, you see. Just like the ones you are cut out of in the local junior high or whatever, only now you are automatically a member until you do something beyond the pale. Even if you are so shy as to be tongue-tied for your first ten conventions, still, if you walk into a room you can sit on the floor and listen to Isaac Asimov sing Gilbert & Sullivan and join in if you like, then go home and tell your friends that you spent time with Asimov last weekend. And just so you don't feel lonely in the arid stretches between conventions you can afford to attend, there are approximately four thousand individual fan magazines produced by individuals and written by themselves and/or other fans to keep you in communication with the sf world day-to-day.

Chronic SF Fans

As you might have gathered, the great family aspect of sf is only for the most ardent in the long run, maybe ten thousand active fans in the U.S. at any time. After all, there is a lot of time-consuming silliness that comes with the territory. And, most often, you mature socially enough to adjust to your home environment and just read the stuff off and on, attending, perhaps, a world convention every year or two to keep contact with a few friends. This is the chronic stage of addiction, following the active phase. It can last for life.

Let me stress at this point that a whole lot of science fiction is read by occasional readers, people who never quite get caught up in the sf world or kids who leave the omnivore stage and go directly into some other compulsive enthusiasm, readers who do not see themselves as sf readers at all. Sometimes they only read one or two sf books a year, books someone recommends or books they see friends reading; the sf world reaches out to them and affects them, and they are potential members of the sf community. But most of them remain latent for life, remain part of the mainstream of contemporary culture. The occasional reader is immensely important in big mass-market sales and a significant factor in library patronage.

If you grew up in isolation from movies, TV, and comics, and have never read a work of science fiction (or tried one, once, and found it dumb, incomprehensible, or both), you might ask at this point, Why the fuss? The answer is that even if you have kept yourself in pristine separation from the material, you are interacting daily with people who have progressed to at least a stage-one involvement in science fiction and who have altered your environment because of it. More about this after a short investigation of the thing itself.

Science Fiction Today

Science fiction as written and published during the last twenty years is so diverse in every aspect that no reader, except at the height of the omnivorous stage, can expect to be attracted to all of it. And more science fiction has been published in the 1970s than ever before, twenty or thirty new paperbacks every month, several magazines, even a number of hardbounds--too much for even the most dedicated omnivore to read. The quality of the individual book or story varies from advanced literary craftsmanship to "hack trash," from precise and intellectual visions of the future to ignorant swordsmen hacking their way through to beautiful damsels (less than one-quarter clad) across an absurd environment. There are enough varieties of science fiction and fantasy to confuse anybody. But most of the time you can tell what you are getting from the cover.

If you look at a wide spectrum of covers in your local sf paperback section, you can begin to notice a lot of subdivision into categories of science fiction. How do the advanced omnivores and chronics select what to read? By this very process of looking at covers. As in every other kind of book, you can tell the importance of the author of a science fiction book by the size of the author's name on the cover. Another reliable gauge of importance, or at least popularity, is: how many copies of an individual title by an author does the store have and how many of the author's titles are on the shelf? But popularity and importance aside, how do you identify whether this is the kind of sf you are looking for? By the complex symbology of the cover.

Not always, of course, for the paperback industry (never mind hardcover publishers, who tend to be indeterminate) is guilty of lack of confidence or ignorance, which leads to mispackaging fairly regularly; but in the huge majority of cases, science fiction is quite precisely marketed and packaged.

The images on science fiction covers range from futuristic mechanical devices (which connote a story heavily into sf ideas, or perhaps just science fictional clichés) to covers featuring humans against a futuristic setting, with or without machines (which connote adventure sf), to covers with humans carrying swords or other anachronistic weapons (which connote fantasy or fantastic adventure against a cardboard or clichéd sf background), to hypermuscled males with clinging hyperzaftig females (both scantily clad) against a threateningly monstrous background, male carrying a big sword (which connote sword-and-sorcery or heroic-fantasy adventures, with perhaps some sf elements), to covers representing several varieties of pure fantasy (from rich, romantic flowery quests to freaky supernatural horror). Every sf omnivore has sampled all the varieties of sf, from Lovecraftian supernatural horror to the swashbuckling adventure tales of Poul Anderson to the technical and literary conundrums of Samuel R. Delany. Chronic readers usually center their interests on one limited area and read everything packaged to their taste.

The net effect is that there are a rather large number of sf audiences in terms of focused interests, all of which interlock and overlap to form the inchoate sf reading audience. Most individual books reach their targeted audience and prosper from overlap into other related audiences. Occasionally, a sf work exists which satisfies several of these overlapping audiences at once (e.g., Dune by Frank Herbert) and reaches what the publishing industry calls the mass audience (i.e., a truly humongous number of readers)--and then extends for a decade or more in sales into that audience which consists of normal people who decide to try the stuff and have heard three or four big names (like Robert A. Heinlein's Stranger in a Strange Land, which paid most of the light bills in the period 1961-78 for its publisher and allows Mr. and Mrs. Heinlein to visit opera festivals in Europe on whim).

The situation is exceedingly complex; some say that the whole sf audience is composed of teenagers, for all practical purposes, and turns over almost completely every three to five years. This theory (the omnivore theory) eliminates all chronic readers from consideration. It has the virtue of practicality from the publishing point of view, though it means you can recycle individual books endlessly and can publish practically anything, no matter how crippled, and reach a basic, dependable, profitable (though small) audience. The combined theory (omnivore/chronic), which is the basis, unarticulated, behind most sf publishing, would sound something like a classier version of the omnivore theory: keep the good books in print for omnivores who pass into the chronic state and for the non-sf reader who wishes to sample the field through books or authors he has heard of, and scatter the rest of your publishing program among the three spectra (fantasy/science fantasy/science fiction) in hopes of discovering chronic sellers--works that everyone who reads sf must sooner or later hear about and read. At its best, this philosophy (if we may so dignify a marketing strategy) leads to the publishing of vaulting works of the speculative imagination--but mostly it leads to carefully marketed crap. Yet even that is okay. Both omnivores and chronics are patient and have long memories, they are willing to wade through a fair amount of swamp to find islands of rationality and the real thing--wonderful sf.

It's a kind of quixotic quest, you see, admirable in its way. The sf reader is willing to keep trying, reading through rather large amounts of half-cooked ideas, clichés, and cardboard characters and settings in search of the truly original and exciting and good. How many of us outside the sf field could be so determined? This essay is about the fun the sf reader has along the way, which is not often visible to outsiders.

The true sf reader sneers in scorn at fake sf, artificially produced film tie-in novels and stories, most sf films, most TV sf. This he calls sci-fi (or "skiffy")--junk no right-thinking omnivore or chronic should read, watch, or support. But with beatific inconsistency he will pursue his own quest through endless hours of "Space: 1999," "Battlestar Galactica," "Mork and Mindy," "My Favorite Martian," and some truly horrendous paperbacks and magazines in search of something as good as he remembers finding during his initial omnivore excitement. And this quest through the rubble is not without its rewards.

Communication and Education

SF Conventions

Consider: the aforementioned conventions are broken down into discrete areas of programming and many conventions have a general or even quite limited theme. Aside from the World Science Fiction Convention, which is a general gathering of the clans, there is a World Fantasy Convention, numerous Star Trek conventions, a pulp-magazine convention (Pulpcon), Ambercon (devoted to the Amber novels of Roger Zelazny), an sf-film convention, numerous "relaxicons" (at which there is no programming--chronics and omnivores gather to party with like minds for a weekend), and literally dozens of local area conventions, with the number of attendees ranging from hundreds to thousands (Boskons--Boston; Lunacon--New York; Westercon--West Coast; V-con--Vancouver; Kubla Khan Klave--Nashville; Philcon--Philadelphia; Balticon--Baltimore; Disclave--Washington, D.C.). The list is extensive, each "con" having a guest of honor, films, panels, speeches, a roomful of booksellers, an art show, many special events, often including a masquerade, and continual parties, pretty dependably for twenty-four hours a day. Aside from their general air of saturnalia, these conventions build audience for name authors (guests of honor and other featured guests) and reflect audience fascination with discrete kinds of sf.

The World Science Fiction Convention, a six-day bash, has nearly five continuous days of programming. Iguanacon (Worldcon '78), named after a favorite fan animal (T. Williams, <u>Night of the Iguana</u>: "Women are fine, Sheep are divine, but the Iguana is el numero uno"), had attendees who came specifically for the Edgar Rice Burroughs Dum-Dum (famed great ape party); feminists and those interested in women writers came for the several Women in Science Fiction items; film fans came for the twenty-four-hour-a-day film program (a bargain); Georgette Heyer fans came for the Regency Dress Tea (yes, at a science fiction convention); some came to see and hear their favorite big-name authors: heroic-fantasy readers to see Fritz Leiber and L. Sprague De Camp, Darkover fans to see Marion Zimmer Bradley, Amber fans to see Roger Zelazny; L-5 fans came to proselytize for industrial space colonies.

Among the more than five thousand who attended, a large number of complex audiences were represented, often identifiable by the individual package. Aside from the general run of be-jeaned teenagers and suited publishing types, the Star Trek fans often wore costumes from the show (or at least Spock ears), the Regency fans dressed Regency, the heroic-fantasy fans sported swords and capes, the medieval fans and Society for Creative Anachronism members dressed in a variety of medieval costumes, the women rapped in the special women-space room (the year before there was a "Happy Gays Are Here Again" party), Princess Leia costumes abounded, and David Gerrold, well-known <u>Star Trek</u> author, handed out David Gerrold Fan Club cards and buttons. These people filled more than four hotels. Each reader discovers his or her special fun at conventions.

Kinds of SF, Including Fantasy

Omnivores tend to form preferences early on in their reading spree and chronics are usually fixed for life. This is a quick rundown of the main possibilities that an omnivore might fix on: classic fantasy (ghost stories, legends, tales); supernatural horror (two categories: classic, from LeFanu, Blackwood, and Machen to Stephen King and Rosemary's Baby; and Lovecraftian, the school of H.P. Lovecraft and his followers); Tolkienesque fantasy (in the manner of Lord of the Rings--a carefully constructed fantasy world as setting for a heroic quest); heroic fantasy (barely repressed macho sex fantasy in which muscular, sword-bearing male beats monsters, magicians, racial inferiors, and effete snobs by brute force, then services every willing woman in sight [and they are all willing]); Burroughsian science fantasy (adventure on another planet or a thinly rationalized sf setting in which fantasy and anachronisms [sword fighting among the stars] are essentials); space opera (the western in space); hard science fiction (the sf idea is the center of attention, usually involving the sciences of chemistry or physics or astronomy); soft science fiction (two alternate types: first, in which character is more important than the sf idea; second, sf focusing on any science other than physics/chemistry); experimental science fiction (stylistically, that is); fine writing (may include a work from any of the above categories, hard though that may be to accept); single author (reads all published stories of H.P. Lovecraft, his nonfiction, the five volumes of collected letters, the volumes of posthumous collaborations, all pastiches, etc., etc.--archetypal fan behavior). You can begin to see the enormous variety available.

SF and "Mainstream Writing"

The most significant development of the last decade for the future of sf is that by about the middle 1960s enough fine writing had been done in the sf field so that a chronic might fixate on that aspect of sf without running out of reading matter before running out of patience. There has always been excellent writing in the sf field, but now there is an actual audience looking for it; before the 1960s, literate prose was fine when it occurred, a real treat, but generally irrelevant to the sf endeavor for all omnivores and most chronics.

The increased volume of fine writing has had its effect on outsiders' evaluations of the medium. In the 1970s, the academic appraisal of sf moved from "It's trash" to "It's interesting trash" to "Some of it is important and worth attention, even study." Oh, sigh. Already there are dissertations written by Ph.D.'s on science fiction. But sf is alive and growing still, it has not become literary history, and most of the Ph.D. work is a waste of good dissertation paper (universities tend to require expensive paper in return for sheepskins) because (1) many advanced omnivores have read more sf than almost all of the Ph.D.'s and (2) given the categories presented above that represent the varieties of sf, no one has yet been able to define sf well enough so that non-sf readers can figure it out. Science fiction readers know it when they see it, and can distinguish what is real from what is sci-fi (which has come to denote, among the chronics, that it is probably admissible as sf but extremely bad--able to fool some of the people some of the time). The question of that large mass of books from Brave New World to 1984 to The Andromeda Strain, which are real science fiction but are never published with the sf label, is a separate discussion. Let it suffice for now that the people who inhabit the sf world know what is really sf and what is "mundane."

The SF Fan

Science fiction people know, for instance, that Superman is real sf --Sam Moskowitz tells the story of the teenage fans associated with the creation of the character and its early publication in Action Comics, 1938, in Seekers of Tomorrow--and if the first generation of science fiction people had produced nothing more than Superman and Buck Rogers, still the effect of science fiction on American culture would have been profound. Because to the science fiction devotee, sf is naturally carried over into every area of everyday life. She tends to solve problems at work with science fictional solutions or by using the creative methodology learned through reading sf. He tends to see visions of alternate futures that can be influenced by the right actions in the present. She tends to be good at extrapolating trends, and especially good at puncturing the inflated predictions of others by pointing out complexities and alternatives. He tends to be optimistic about ecology through technology, has no fear of machines, and tends to be a loner. The science fiction person never agrees with anybody else in conversation just to be friendly. Ideas are too important to be betrayed. Science fiction people, among their own kind, are almost always contentious (after all, a favorite subject of discussion is to point to an unlabeled work that may be considered sf and argue about whether or not it is, really, sf).

Science fiction is what holds the world together for the science fiction person. It is important, exciting, and gives the science fiction person a basis for feeling superior to the rest of humanity, those who don't know. The early fans, the generation of the thirties, many of whom (Ackerman, Bradbury, Asimov, Pohl, Wollheim, and a host of others) are among the major writers and publishers and editors today, evolved a theory to justify the superiority of science fiction people, then a persecuted, mainly teenage, minority. At the Third Annual World Science Fiction Convention (Denver, Colorado, 1941), Robert A. Heinlein (then, as now, the most respected author in the field) gave a speech intended to define the science fiction field for its readers and authors, the theme of which was change: it examined the concept and problem of "future shock" nearly thirty years before Alvin Toffler wrote his famous book.

"I think," said Heinlein, "that science fiction, even the

corniest of it, even the most outlandish of it, no matter how badly it's written, has a distinct therapeutic value because all of it has as its primary postulate that the world does change." He then went on to tell the fascinated audience (this is a legendary speech in the sf field, even after four decades) that he believed them to be way above average in intelligence and sensitivity, a special group. "Science fiction fans," said Heinlein, "differ from most of the rest of the race by thinking in terms of racial magnitude--not even centuries but thousands of years.... Most human beings--and those who laugh at us for reading science fiction--time-bind, make their plans, make their predictions, only within the limits of their immediate personal affairs.... In fact, most people, as compared with science fiction fans, have no conception whatsoever of the fact that the culture they live in does change; that it can change."

We can only imagine the impact of such a coherent articulation of alienation and superiority on a bunch of mostly late-adolescent men at the end of the Great Depression. Though the inferior mass of humanity laughs at us, we are the ones who know, we are the wave of the future, the next evolutionary step in the human race. If only our pimples would clear up, we could get on with changing the world. Fans are Slans! (Slan, a novel by A.E. Van Vogt, serialized in Astounding Science Fiction, about a superior race living in secret among normal humans, was an instant classic in 1941.)

Adults ignore lousy technique when they are being deceived (in literature or elsewhere) if the deception supports the view of normal reality they have chosen to embrace. They have a sense of security to cling to and something to lose if they don't. Teenagers (and other groups of people described above) have no sense of security, as a rule; they are searching for something: change, a future; and unconvincing, mundane reality does not satisfy. Oddly, then, the assumptions made in a science fiction story, which are transparently assumptions and which the young social reject (of any age) can share as an intellectual exercise, are more acceptable to him than the everyday assumptions made in a "serious" work of fiction about "real" (mundane adult) life in which he cannot or does not wish to participate.

Thus the science fiction novel or story is generally aimed at the person who has not embraced a particular set of assumptions about the way things are; which helps to explain both its appeal to the young and its seeming shallowness to most "mature" readers. Science fiction is most often shallow in its presentation of adult human relations, and this is the sole concern of most other literature; but it is profound in the opportunities it offers the reader to question his most basic assumptions. And you still have to ignore lousy technique a lot of the time to participate in the illusion. This is easy for the omnivore and chronic reader; in fact, the minute you overcome the suspension-of-disbelief problem (admittedly much easier in early teenage than in later life), you tend to enter your omnivore stage. Make no mistake: you don't lose your critical ability or good judgment or literary education when you begin to read science fiction. You just have to learn the trick of putting <u>all</u> your preconceptions aside every time you sit down to read. Hah! You were right, this is just another piece of hackwork. But the next one, or the story after that, may be the real thing, innovative, well written, surprising, exciting.

<u>The Function of SF</u>

Throughout the past decade, there has been a growing number of adults who have discovered science fiction as a tool without discovering the thing itself. There are now many new uses for sf in the mundane world: it can be used to combat future shock, to teach religion, political science, physics, and astronomy, to promote ecology, to support the U.S. space program, to provide an index to pop-culture attitudes toward science, and to advance academic careers and make profits for publishers, film producers, even toy makers. But the business of science fiction, the thing itself, is to provide escape from the mundane world, to get at what is real by denying all of the assumptions that enforce quotidian reality for the duration of the work.

This is reflected in what really goes on at science fiction conventions. Beneath the surface frivolity, cliquishness, and costumery, beneath the libertarian or just plain licentious anarchism of the all-night carousing, beyond the author worship, the serious panel discussions, and the family of hail-fellow-fan-well-met, the true core of being a science fiction person is that the convention is abnormal and alienated from daily life. Not just separated in time and space, but different! There is no parallel more apt than the life-style/artwork of the underground movements of the last two hundred years in Western civilization: the Romantic group in England, Baudelaire and his circle in France, the Modernists, the Beats. (Note to literary historians: there is a significant study in this.) The difference is that to an outsider, it looks like just fun and games, because these people go home after a convention, go back to work, school, housewifery, unemployment, mundane reality, or so it seems.

While they are spending time in the science fiction world, though, things are really different. How different? Let's circle around this for a moment. For instance, you can almost certainly talk to people there who, in normal life, are removed from you by taboos or social barriers. No matter how obnoxious you are, people will talk to you unless you insult them directly, and the chances are excellent that you can find one or more persons willing to engage in serious extended conversation, knowledgeable conversation, about some of the things that interest you most, whether it is the stock market or macramé, clothing design or conservative politics, science or literature or rock 'n' roll. Science fiction people tend not to be well-rounded but rather multiple specialists; the only thing that holds them and the whole sf world together is science fiction.

Actually you spend a minority of your time at a convention talking about science fiction, but the reality of science fiction underlies the whole experience and is its basis. For the duration of the science fiction experience, you agree to set aside the assumptions and preconceptions that rule your ordinary behavior and live free. A science fiction convention, like a work of science fiction, is an escape into an alternate possibility that you can test, when it is over, against mundane reality. And even the bad ones provide this context.

Fantasy and SF

Harlan Ellison, writer and science fiction personality, has spoken of his first encounter with science fiction as a kid in a dentist's office. He discovered there a copy of a science fiction magazine, on the cover of which Captain Future was battling Krag the robot for possession of a scantily clad woman, a picture that filled his young mind with awe and wonder and excitement. His life was changed. He wanted more of this.

The reason science fiction creates such chronic addicts as Harlan Ellison is that once you admit the possibility that reality is not as solid and fixed as it used to seem, you feel the need for repeated doses of science fictional reality. Of course, sometimes what you discover in science fiction that attracts you is not the thing itself but one of its relatives. As cataloged above, the chronic often fixates on a limited area, sometimes quite far from center. And a chronic reader may actually read almost entirely classical fantasy and Lovecraftian supernatural horror, and a writer such as Fritz Leiber may spend a career writing in every variety of fantasy and science fiction across the whole spectrum of possibilities and always be "in the field." There is an interesting investigation to be done someday on why the classical fantasy, a main tradition of Western literature for several millennia, is now part of the science fiction field, but it is. In the latter half of the twentieth century, with certain best-selling exceptions, fantasy is produced by writers of science fiction and fantasy, edited by editors of science fiction, illustrated by sf and fantasy artists, and read by the omnivore fantasy and sf addicts who support the market.

Science fiction, since the 1930s, has provided an umbrella under which any kind of estrangement from mundane reality is welcome (though some works, such as John Norman's Gor series, sadomasochistic sex fantasies in a Burroughsian sf setting, are admitted but generally despised and generally believed to sell mostly to an audience outside of any other sf audience). To present the broad, general context of the sf field, let us consider the main areas and relationships as they have evolved over the past several decades.

The general question of fantasy has been dealt with frequently, from Freud's well-known essay on the uncanny through recent structuralist works such as Todorov's The Fantastic, and is not

central to our concern with science fiction. There are several
things that need to be said, however, about fantasy literature before we move on to varieties of science fiction. Fantasy, through
its close association with sf since the 1920s in America, has developed a complex interaction with science fiction that has changed
much of what is written as fantasy today. H. P. Lovecraft, the
greatest writer of supernatural horror of the century, a literary
theoretician and mentor (through correspondence and personal contact) to Frank Belknap Long, Robert E. Howard, Robert Bloch,
Fritz Leiber, Clark Ashton Smith, August Derleth, Donald and
Howard Wandrei, and a number of others, was an agnostic, a ra-
tionalist, and a believer in science. His work was published both
in Weird Tales, the great fantasy magazine that flourished between
the twenties and the early fifties, and in Astounding Stories, the
great science fiction magazine of its day. Most all of his acolytes
followed the same pattern, of commercial and literary ties to both
areas. In 1939, after the greatest sf editor of modern times, John
W. Campbell, took the helm at Astounding, he proceeded to found
the second great fantasy magazine, Unknown, encouraging all his
newly discovered writing talents (Heinlein, Sturgeon, L. Sprague
DeCamp, L. Ron Hubbard, Anthony Boucher, Alfred Bester, H. L.
Gold, Frederic Brown, and Eric Frank Russell as well as Henry
Kuttner, Jack Williamson, C. L. Moore, and Fritz Leiber) to create a new kind of fantasy, with modern settings and contemporary
atmosphere, highly rationalized and as consistent as the science
fiction he wanted them to write for Astounding. Thus through Lovecraft and Campbell a strong link was forged not only commercially
but also aesthetically between fantasy and science fiction. Today,
and for the last two decades, the most distinguished and consistently
brilliant publication in the field has been the Magazine of Fantasy
and Science Fiction, required reading for all who wish to discover
the field at its best and broadest--but also never the most popular
magazine in the field commercially, always surpassed in circulation
by more-focused magazines that zero in on a more limited definition.

   The third towering figure in fantasy thus far in the twentieth
century is J. R. R. Tolkien, whose trilogy is both a classic of contemporary literature and an example of the dominant position of the
science fiction field as stated above. Tolkien's works were acquisi-
tioned by sf editors, popularized in paperback through sf publishers,
and have spawned an entire marketing substructure to support works
of world-building fantasy in the Tolkien tradition. More books appear every month featuring the quest of a single heroic figure across
a detailed and rationalized fantasy world accompanied by a group of
major and minor subsidiary fantasy characters involving a final confrontation between Good and Evil, in which Good always wins.

   And the fourth towering figure is a posthumous collaboration
between an artist and an author: Frank Frazetta, formerly a comic
illustrator, and Robert E. Howard, pulp fantasy adventure hack,
who committed suicide in 1936 on the day his mother died and who
created a number of fantastic heroes, but principally Conan the
Barbarian. Howard's works had been mostly out of print since his

death, except for several small-press editions and a few paperbacks, until the early 1960s. Then L. Sprague DeCamp obtained the rights from Howard's estate to arrange and anthologize the whole Conan series for the first time in paperback and to write additions and sequels himself or with others. Through a stroke of genius, comic artist Frazetta was hired to illustrate the paperback covers, which seized the imagination of the audience enough to sell Conan books in the millions of copies, established the Howard name, and made Frazetta wealthy and famous. Howard now has nearly fifty books in print in the fifth decade following his death, and the sword-swinging barbarian hero brutishly adventuring across a fantastic/ historic landscape (inside a book with a cover by Frazetta or a near imitation) is the principal reading focus of a large number of chronic sf readers. This category, which was formerly called sword-and-sorcery fiction, is now referred to more accurately as heroic fantasy. If Mickey Spillane wrote sf, it would be heroic fantasy. In fact, a hundred years from now sf may have acquired Spillane's works under this rubric.

There are only two areas of fantasy that have not been annexed under the sf umbrella, perhaps because these two areas have never fallen into popular disrepute; Arthurian romances and the occult horror best-seller. There are indications that these two areas may remain separate and independent; both types tend to be written by authors who have no desire to associate themselves and their works with low-class, nonliterary, low-paying (until recently) stuff.

The only science in all the areas of fantasy is either strawman science (which cannot cope) or black science (used by the evil sorcerer). Amoral science is a recent addition to some heroic fantasy (especially noticeable in the works of Michael Moorcock), as is the idea of magic as a scientific discipline (a contribution of the Campbell era). And we can generalize without fear of contradiction and say that except in a tiny minority of cases technology is associated with evil in fantasy literature. So it is particularly curious that the element of estrangement from everyday reality can yoke by itself the two separates, fantasy and science fiction.

Final Thoughts

The moment Hugo Gernsback invented modern science fiction in April 1926, it was heterogeneous. Gernsback was an eccentric immigrant and technological visionary. He knew what he meant by scientifiction (as he named it) and assumed it would be evident to others--all that stuff that Wells and Verne and Poe wrote ("charming romance intermingled with scientific fact and prophetic vision," as Gernsback says in his editorial in the first issue of the first magazine, Amazing Stories). In addition to this confusion, Gernsback was tone deaf to the English language, printing barely literate stories about new inventions and the promise of a wondrous technological future cheek-by-jowl with H.G. Wells, Poe, Edgar Rice Burroughs (!), and a growing number of professional pulp writers who wanted to break into the new market. Thus in embryo and at birth, the new thing was amorphous, formed and reformed over the decades by major editors and major writers, and by all the chronic readers into the diversity that is science fiction today.

It is a source of both amusement and frustration to science fiction people that public consciousness of science fiction has almost never penetrated beyond the first decade of the field's development. Sure, *Star Wars* is wonderful, but in precisely the same way and at the same level of consciousness and sophistication that sf from the late 1920s and early 1930s was--fast, almost-plotless stories of zipping through the ether in spaceships, meeting aliens, using futuristic devices, and fighting the bad guys (and winning).

Today science fiction has flowered into a rich blossoming of interbred strains, which divide into two large areas: science fantasy and science fiction. All of it is sf, a repository of diverse fulfillments for sf people.

And by now it should be obvious that we are dealing with not a limited thing but a whole reality. The science fiction world exists here and now, coexistent with but not congruent to mundane reality. More than an alternate literary form and an alternate life-style, science fiction is coequal reality, informing the lives of thousands and affecting the lives of millions, a fact of life more intimate than inflation, whose influence is so all-pervasive that it is traceable daily in every home, through the artifacts and ideas that represent the presence of all possible futures, and all possible change, in the present.

DOIN' DA MISSIN' BOOKS BOOGIE:

THOUGHTS ON AXIOMS, FLEXIBILITY, AND ATTILA THE HUN*

Carole Marie Hastings

Authoritative sources assert that the single most requested item in the library is the most likely to grow legs and walk away. (See Hastings. Diary entry: September 19, 1974. Toledo, Ohio. "The Guinness Book of World Records is el gonno!") The formula for computing the percent of probability of the book doing the boogie is: $X\% = 100(\frac{N}{T})$ where N is the number of requests for the book that week and T is the total number of reference requests that week. (This does NOT include requests for the bathroom pass.)

This stupendous problem, a previously unnamed corollary to Murphy's Law, is multiplied when the age of the patrons is restricted to the second decade. Hence, the formula for the HASTINGS BOOGIE AXIOM is: $X\% = 100(\frac{2N}{T})$.

As you see, as the number of requests for the Rand McNally Road Atlas increases so does the probability of its being stolen. If the library is in a high school, you can safely double that figure.

Do not panic!

There is also a parallel probability that while you were tabulating reference statistics and computing percentages one of the kids hid the French-English dictionary behind the globe.

If you search frantically, you will NOT locate it. However, tomorrow, after he finishes his homework, he may leave it lying on a table. If you had a policy allowing liberal overnight checkouts, this might not have been necessary.

---

*Reprinted by permission of the author and publisher from Reference Librarian, No. 7/8 (1983). Copyright © 1982 by The Haworth Press, Inc. All rights reserved.

Ask a Teenager

Teenagers, when asked (Have you asked lately?), will demand strict security measures for the protection of reference materials. ("Lock it up!") Administrators, when consulted (Have you asked lately?), will suggest harsh punishments as a deterrent to theft. ("Lock them up!") Try to soothe both groups and then ignore their advice. With the exception of 17th-century hand-drawn, one-of-a-kind, leather-bound treatises (What's that doing in a high school anyway?), lend everything. You can restrict it to overnight; you can require that they see you and only you for check out; but make sure that they know that these books can be borrowed. This reduces the amount of fun involved in surreptitiously taking the book. Be prepared, however, to spend a good portion of time signing checkout cards. Look at the kid. Be a tape recorder and repeat to each child, "Don't forget that this is due back tomorrow." And record a picture of his face in your brain in case you have to run him down in homeroom two weeks later. ("Hi there! Didja forget something? Uh huh. Yeah. We need that directory for other students. OK?) It's okay to mutter violent threats under your breath. It adds muscle tone to your smile.

Lock up as few books as possible, but keep careful track of those and be honest when explaining. When a student asks why the book is in the glass cage, tell her: "It's very expensive and we couldn't afford to replace it if someone adopted it permanently." OR "It's very old and frail and exposure to acne medicine would destroy it." OR "It's so very popular that some creep would steal it and then no one could use it." Don't try to con the kids. They know a stash when they see one. Allow checkouts for the restricted books, too, but preface each one with a lecture on not 1) stuffing it into a jammed locker, 2) laying it on a lunchroom table, 3) leaving it on a locker room bench while showering, etc.

Lectures

Actually, I am both pro- and anti- lecturing. Usually I oppose lecturing individuals. Try to de-emphasize the problem. Point out that some cruddy, selfish baboon type has prevented you from answering the question at hand and deprived all future generations of students of their right to information. Then prove your flexibility by finding the answer elsewhere. (Always have at least three sources in mind when you begin a search.)

When you need to lecture, speak to whole groups. Try to deal with a negative subject in a positive manner. Emphasize sharing. Let them know that the books are for students to use, not the teachers and not you. Recall one or two instances where an innocent student was hurt by the unavailability of a missing book. Pick true horror stories like the time John needed ten extra credit points to save a "D" in Senior Civics but didn't get them because the Guide to Congress, the only book listing Senator Tootle's middle name, had been stolen.

Don't linger on the subject. If budding punks get the idea that you care a lot, they'll sharpen their claws on your nerves and leave your collection in shreds. Stay cool. Do NOT put hysterical announcements on the P. A. ("A $150.00 literary biography volume is missing from the library. Anyone caught with it in his possession will be prosecuted for MAJOR FELONY THEFT AND FLOGGED!!!!!") You come off sounding like Boss Hogg in "The Dukes of Hazard [sic]."

And remember the saying, "The best defense is a good offense." Make Reference enjoyable. In class introductions, choose gaudy or absurd examples to illustrate the kind of information found in each book: things like Attila the Hun, the most eggs eaten in sixty seconds, a famous person's ridiculous middle name, what happened on one student's birthdate. This keeps them awake and helps them remember. ("Hey, book lady, where's the Hun book?") With individual students, never NEVER refuse to help. If you can't assist at the moment, offer to find the answer and deliver it later. And keep your promise. The better you are at reference service, the better library users the kids will become. Only after seeing you (miraculously!) find a needed answer to a question will they believe that it's even possible. Being adolescents, some will still be skeptical and try you again. Help them as long as they ask. Some will never stop asking and that's okay, too. Sure, you prefer to teach them to become independent researchers, but a dependent asker is better than a library hater.

And besides, if they could all find their own sources, you'd miss questions like, "If we want to have twins, do we have to do it twice?"

NOT YET, GUTENBERG!*

Estelle Jussim

The question is "How will we talk to one another tomorrow?"--a gloss on the larger topic, The New Communications Technologies. How, indeed!

The astonishing proliferation of new electronic and computer-based communications technology is almost beyond comprehension. Hurtling through interplanetary space, communications satellites jabber to us about the moons of Jupiter, the braided rings of Saturn, the torrid infernos of Venus. Whizzing around our own turbulent planet, like so many miniature starships, a vast army of increasingly articulate communications satellites crackle, gibber, beep, click, tick, and ping.

Back on earth we are surrounded by the instrumentation for our next overseas telephone call, our stock transactions with Japan, medical emergencies, Time-Life teleprinting its regional magazines from on high, educational programs buzzing down to the plains of Kansas, and the ominous codes of military surveillance.

The serious and the absurd, the urgent and the trivial, the profit-making and the profitless, all manner of human discourse can now circle the globe in what Shakespeare's lovely Ariel called "a twinkling of an eye." All would be well if Ariel were our only courier, but alas, lurching, stupid Caliban has also learned that expertise.

What is so wonderful and so terrifying about the new communications technology is that it is nearly instantaneous. That's wonderful if the red telephone instantaneously stops a nuclear missile from being ejected obscenely from its silo, wonderful if a teleconference brings together the opinions and compromises of peacemakers, wonderful if viewtext saves the life of even a single child. The problem is no longer how will we talk to one another tomorrow --for the technologists and technocrats are rapidly inventing what

---

*Reprinted by permission of the author and publisher from Library Journal, 108:12 (June 15, 1983) 1203-06. Published by R.R. Bowker Co. (a Xerox company). Copyright © 1983 by Xerox Corporation.

we need--but much more important, what is it that we will be saying to whom and for what purposes.

Who are "we"?

Before we assume incorrectly that "we" are all doing the same things and will be talking about the same things tomorrow, consider even a small sample of the total array of the information professions: medical librarians, archivists at historical societies, data managers, cable television programmers, public and academic librarians, research and consultation experts, film librarians, rare books and special collections personnel, children's librarians, information scientists, school librarians, and unified media specialists, slide librarians, art librarians, law librarians, photographic archivists, conservators, business librarians, oral history archivists, instructional media producers, records managers, indexers and abstracters, public relations experts (or to use the more acceptable term, public information specialists), personnel managers, young adult librarians, regional systems specialists, book and film reviewers, computer experts and programmers, and all the special science and technology librarians. The list is inexhaustible.

The point is that "we" are many, and varied, not few and single-minded. As "information professionals" (a term forced on us by the new technologies), we are joined together in an enterprise founded upon the human need to communicate across space and time. Communication is our essential unifying art, whether in real time across space or in connecting to recorded time. Our professions have been devoted primarily to the management of access to what we call "recorded knowledge." We will continue to be devoted to managing recorded knowledge in whatever form. The necessity for speed of communication will force us to become more involved with electronics. In that process we may not understand that we will not be transformed magically and robotically into adjuncts of machines. We will always be devoted to the traditional functions of libraries: the selection, acquisition, organization, storage and retrieval, and dissemination of the world's fund of wit, wisdom, knowledge, and information.

Manipulating dissemination

Dissemination, always our weakest service, is now on the verge of radical transformation. Now the foolish arguments about media have finally paled into appropriate insignificance. Now we have begun to recognize that we are all communicators and that we must be exceedingly good ones in order to remain relevant and to survive. Now we must look at the social, political, and economic implications of the new communications technologies.

Within the past two years, a book and a television program called Goodbye, Gutenberg! (Anthony Smith, Goodbye Gutenberg:

Communication and Education

The Newspaper Revolution of the 1980's, Oxford Univ. Pr., 1980) offered a variety of insights into the communications revolutions. One sinister bit of reportage revealed the manipulation of one of our more traditional methods of communicating, the post office. In mounting campaigns and in propaganda efforts to dislodge liberal representatives and senators, political organizations have been using the computer's astonishing ability to juggle data to communicate to specialized groups by individualizing campaign letters. Thanks to the computer, Washington offices can be inundated by mail for or against political, economic, and social proposals. Relatively small political groups have been successfully marketing their ideologies. This ominous development breaks no laws, subverts no Bill of Rights, but it is nevertheless characteristic of the new abuse of information. By using a new distribution mechanism, computer-individualized mailings coupling members of congress with influential lobbyers, shrewd politicos are moving us far away from the idea that an informed citizenry is the bulwark of democracy. It is one more example of the vital communications hypothesis: Control of communication is control of individual consciousness and social structure.[1]

The print library, with its books, newspapers, and magazines was considered to be a marketplace of ideas. It offered free access to considered opinions, entertainment, and the means to conduct business and scientific research. Goodbye, Gutenberg! insists that print is dead. Its essential hypothesis is that the new communications technologies are precipitating a revolution comparable to and superseding that made by that renaissance entrepreneur, Johann Gutenberg. According to this British perspective on the invention of movable metal type, printing as we knew it is now dead, therefore the book is dead, and, therefore, by implication, the library as we have known it is dead.

Print communication

The printed book was quite clearly conceived as a superior distribution mechanism. That was really all that Gutenberg had in mind. He busied himself (and bankrupted himself) inventing a systematic way to produce exactly repeatable statements using interchangeable parts corresponding to our alphabet. Gutenberg relied upon the channels of greasy ink, metal types, and damp paper, not because he was a starry-eyed altruist, not because he magically foresaw the tremendous benefits that would accrue to education, the sciences, the arts, literature, or the activities of polemicists and propagandists. Gutenberg simply wanted to make a profit from the swift and accurate manufacture of Bibles. Bibles were just a commodity to Gutenberg. He could never have foreseen the effects of his invention on logic, rationality, nationalism, academicism, monopolies of literacy, the democratization of knowledge, the permanent dislocation of religious homogeneity, the exponentially expanding propagation of scientific data, and the ultimate cause of his invention's purported downfall: the chaos of the information explosion. Nor could Gutenberg have foreseen the struggles to control and own his invention, the patents royal, the courts of censorship, the centralization and monopolization of the printing industries in, for example, Paris, London, or New York.

Pressured by a multitude of forces, from the proliferation of books made possible by Gutenberg's invention to the paralysis of physical movement to and from those books, our professions have welcomed the advent of communications technologies which seem to have the potential for solving some of our problems, especially by bringing information to people rather than bringing people to information.

Technologies, unfortunately, have a way of altering societies in totally unforeseen ways. They can centralize or decentralize industries and populations, enhance or diminish the humanitarian uses of human beings, increase or decrease productivity, rigidify or loosen political structures (including the politics of sex and gender), or isolate the young and old from the mainstream of rewarding labor, and provide a surfeit or a scarcity of entertainment and leisure.

Are the new technologies of communication, including computers, simply offering us faster, increasingly ubiquitous distribution of certain types of knowledge and entertainment? Can we foresee the consequences?

Quantitative seduction

On the good side, John E. Sawyer, President of the Andrew Mellon Foundation, recently observed: "The new information technologies take us beyond quantities of information to some of the processes of human intelligence. Techniques of microprocessing have been used to measure and improve perception, logic, conceptualization, and languages." On the bad side, he incisively remarked that if humanists were to learn how to cope with the information explosion, "we share a responsibility to avoid being 'seduced by scientific mannerisms,' or smothered or captured by analytic methods that are blind to allusion and allegory, or the complexities of historical and aesthetic judgments. There is real danger that quantitative techniques and fascination with mathematical modelling will shape the course of inquiry, as it has in some of the social sciences. Not all problems have quantitative solutions, and computers cannot decide for us what is important. Microprocessors have little tolerance for ambiguity or capacity for awareness of context, metaphor, or perception of the question not yet posed."[2]

To make knowledge more accessible, more generally available--these are two praiseworthy, but very old goals of the information professions. They are goals that tend to be easily translated into improving the machinery of distribution. After all, Gutenberg was only trying to improve the codex form, which had been with us through the dark ages as a very beautiful, but tediously slow and terrifically expensive way of distributing ideas.

Junk food for the mind

The fact that it speeded the distribution of ideas did not mean that Gutengerg's invention guaranteed virtue or good taste despite its early applications to theology and philosophy. He could not have foreseen the positive influences of the book. On the other hand, neither could he have predicted the mountains of tripe, junk, trash, gibberish, pomposity, dehumanizing pornography, and mind-rotting drivel that have littered bookshelves and libraries in ever increasing numbers since literacy became a behavioral attribute of the bourgeoisie and an adjunct to material well-being in the late 18th century. As a distribution mechanism, the book has delivered almost as much junk food for the mind as television.

There are no inherently pure, reliably virtuous, or perpetually honest media. All have the ability to transmit and distribute stupidity, venality, or straightforward viciousness.

The need for the document

Ben Bagdikian summed it up, when he discussed television: "Print is neither dead nor dying. It is being forced to make a place in the family of human communication for a new way of transferring information and emotion, the electronic reproduction of scenes and sensation. The new medium is disrupting and even revolutionary, but it leaves the alphabet and document still indispensable to the efficient use of eye and brain and to the demands of human rationality."[3] These remarks can be applied to all media.

Despite our ability to exchange business, medical, or military information across continents and oceans instantaneously, we are essentially exchanging ephemeral and constantly changing bits of data. On the fundamental level we still need the document, in whatever form, to keep us from having to memorize ponderous amounts of information. The document is our external memory.

On a more complex level, we need the document in its larger forms, like the book, to help us to comprehend, study, and analyze large conceptual structures at leisure. We need the document to study a new approach to dynamics of small groups or a revision of Albert Einstein's general theory of relativity. Whether or not we reformat that document into machine-readable bits, whether or not our documents are in the shape of motion pictures transmitted over cables or via satellites, whether or not we store a billion images on videodiscs, or inundate our living rooms with cable television's promiscuous plenitudes, we will always need a format that will permit us to study, think, analyze at leisure. Whether or not the words are spewed out in the twinkling of an eye by some rampaging computer makes a difference only if it is truly urgent that we have in hand the print-out of some distantly conceived and written idea. Remember, the book was also conceived as a mechanism to distribute human ideas over space and time.

What is the question?

How will we talk to one another tomorrow? Through the agency of machines, machines guided by computers. A sentence in a recent Time magazine essay about computer whiz-kids raises the fundamental issues: "The only difference between a machine and us is that a machine is an answer and we are a question."[4] If a machine is an answer, what is the question? An answer to what? A question about what?

When asked if a computer could ever resolve an issue concerning values, my Simmons colleague, Candy Schwartz said, "You can ask a computer questions concerning probability because it will make judgments entirely on probability. You can never get through to belief.[5] This is the heart of the problem inherent in the new communications technology. It was, alas, the problem inherent in the older technology of the book. How do you adjudicate between value systems? On what basis do you choose a course of action? On what religious or philosophical underpinnings do we base human relationships or social priorities? A computer can tell us how many different kinds of poor people there are in Boston, but it cannot yet tell us whether or not it is virtuous to make them less poor.

You would have to explain to the dumb machine, for example, that it should not pay attention to the Bible's badly misquoted, "The poor you shall always have with you," because that statement has to be judged in the context of the rest of the compassionate sayings and commandments of the Good Book. Economists may argue about whether or not the trickle-down theory will work ultimately to the benefit of the very poor. It is a set of beliefs about the intrinsic merit of each human being, beliefs not shared by everyone, that encourages anyone to believe that the poor are as deserving as the rich. In view of the extreme diversity of the information professions, we must remember that not all of us are directly concerned with either the poor or the Third World. We are not yet unified as a group. All of us are not attentive to the threat to the poor and to the Third World posed by the increasing concentration of the tools of communication in the hands of large corporations, as Unesco's Kenneth Roberts has reminded us. We do not yet know how to persuade the prejudiced, the despots, the petty tyrants, the rigid militarists, or the religious fanatics to mend their ways. Not by means of a computer. Not yet.

The mighty computer has its limitations. It may help us organize and provide access to opinions, beliefs, and value systems, and in that process aid our communication. The computer cannot yet respond with a direct answer to a direct question about the values upon which we should rely. Jean Paul Sartre, who spent a lifetime on the problem, ultimately could do no better than to extrapolate from the Golden Rule. In essence Sartre said: "Don't do anything that you wouldn't want everyone else to be doing in terms of the survival of the human race."

Communication and Education   175

The question & the machine

To what is the machine an answer? Why are we so easily infatuated with machines? An obvious answer is that we operate on the principle of least effort, and machines help us. Most of us normally act on what might be called humanitarian impulses, and machines can help us improve the lot of the sick and helpless. We want to improve education and certain machines do marvels to individualize instruction, though they risk making the manipulation of discrete items of information seem to be the goal of all education. We want instantaneous solutions to problems, and machines have the aura of the instant magical solution. We want distraction from the disturbing intractability of serious social problems, and machines encourage us to tinker and play. As human beings, we want to rest, to be recreated and entertained. These issues bring us back to the questions that cable television was supposed to answer:

• How can we vastly enlarge the number of channels which a television monitor can receive so that we can diversify the levels of aesthetic pleasure, social awareness, and political action for a diversified and varied population?

• How can we reduce the monopolization and centralization necessarily created by the major broadcasting networks because the massive capital outlay needed is beyond the means of any individual and probably beyond the means of the major cities of the world?

• How can we guarantee access to the means of production of communication to the ordinary person who is not a communications expert but who simply wants to have his or her say about the state of affairs?

Community access television, as it was once called, was supposed to answer all these human questions. According to a recent issue of Information Hotline, satellite and cable networks are about to perform that presumably desirable miracle of bringing the doom of the national TV networks, making it possible and viable for programmers to reach smaller audiences. According to that report more than half the country's households will subscribe to cable by the end of the decade. Advertisers, therefore, will abandon the networks, and as they have with specialized magazines, aim for specific markets. (The report upon which these comments are based costs a mere $1,285, but in the enchanting phraseology of the knowledge industries, it contains an overview of the fast growing "satcable" market.)

Lessons from video

No one is surprised that cable television is big business, but some will be surprised to know that cable will make most of its money offering what is euphemistically called "adult entertainment." Nothing should surprise us. Cable is merely a distribution mechanism. It is not a new and virtuous program for a new and virtuous society. Cable is not alone in seeking reward for titillation.

How we welcomed videodisc! Those of us interested in access to pictorial information were thankful, until we discovered that what videodisc companies are selling (about 80 percent of all their sales) is that same kind of "adult entertainment." What a marvelous distribution mechanism: 54,000 images on each side of what looks like a shiny long-playing record. It is interactive, too, if you are hooked up to a computer. What a boon to museums, photographic archives, film distributors, manufacturers of industrial parts. As I said, that distribution mechanism called "the book" delivers awesomely fabricated and distinctly monotonous pornographies. We can hardly complain about cable or videodisc because they are prostituting their capabilities with the same vigor as any other contemporary medium!

Yet we should protest about what has happened to cable because we know there is more to watching television than being titillated or bored. There is the very act of watching, that indulgence in "the plug-in drug," that addiction to having one's alpha waves endlessly and purposelessly stimulated, that narcotizing of any will to resist the entertainment industry's travesties of creativity and imagination. When 1984 comes and our walls are room-size video screens, and our ears are grown over with acoustical earmuffs which cannot be removed, while a procession of merchandise sold and ordered via television spills in through the mechanical doorports, what will we have achieved beyond much convenience in shopping, and the loss of our inclination to do much more?

Consider the naive and innocent fantasies about local origination of programming, especially in the traditional library. Would we kill the human contact so necessary for the stimulating effects of the children's story hour? We pretend that it does not take talent, practice, and commitment to produce even a ten-minute videotape of any quality. We pretend that anybody can do it, as though it didn't take talent, production crews, and large capital outlays to make it possible for Mickey Rooney to say to Judy Garland, "I know! We'll put on a show!"

Training for creativity

In the attempt to make libraries seem more relevant, to make them more adaptable to contemporary needs, what priority shall we give to training creative staff for locally originated programming? The word is creative. If the machine, including cable television, is simply a distribution mechanism, then we must consider that ripely disgusting word, "software." (That term conjures up images of tapioca pudding, custard pies, and oozing gelatinously melting chocolates.) "Software" is what you are communicating via your distribution mechanism. It is amazing how little our professions understand software, how easy we think it is to produce. Consider how mightily we talk about criteria for book selection while we simultaneously demand the ability to turn out a first-rate narrative structure of superbly experiential value of library media personnel. What do most of us know about communications research?

The machine is an answer but we have to know what question to put to it. For something more than simple entertainment or simple instruction, we must learn the limitations of ourselves and the machines. We must know the ultimate effects of our commitment to a specific type of machine, a specific distribution mechanism. We need to know how to interpret research. A new report by the National Institute of Mental Health, <u>Television and Behavior: Ten Years of Scientific Progress and Implications for the Eighties,</u> reveals overwhelming evidence that "expressive" violence on television causes aggressive behavior in children. (Why has it taken so long?!) Don't we all know that fundamental characteristic of human behavior, "Monkey see, monkey do?" We talk constantly about role models, but we fail to recognize that we model ourselves continually on the behavior of others. If all the models exhibit endless, mindless, cruel violence, why do we expect our streets to be anything but relentless warfare styled precisely after certain TV shows? If rape is constantly implied if not always directly shown, or if the good guys are constantly being beaten or delivering beatings, what else can we expect?

The panacea of machines

When cogent, humane communication and genuine political action seem beyond our reach isn't it a characteristic of our various and interrelated professions to seek the panacea of machines? How will we talk to one another tomorrow? Is that really the question? The program <u>Goodbye, Gutenberg!</u> talked of the development of an international language. It suggested that peace and prosperity would inevitably arise from the fact that satellite business systems deliver everything from electronic mail to endless, so-called "news," to almost anything we might want by way of instantaneous transmission of ephemera. In a recent class I discussed the possibility of a return to cottage industry through telecommunications. One bright student who has two grown children and is returning to a career, exploded: "I'm going back to school because I want to get out of the house! I don't <u>want</u> to work at home! I want to get out there where the people are!"

Ten years ago, when I was asked to talk about Marshall McLuhan, I talked about the history and theory of media. Today my vocabulary has shifted. I now use terms that identify <u>distribution mechanisms.</u> This is not a minor shift. All types of libraries, information centers (a sub-species of those libraries with their 7000-year history), whatever you call them, they are all <u>distribution mechanisms.</u> They and we are embedded in the complexity of modern communication. Communications technologies, whether books or satellites, constantly alter the roles, functions, and services of our professions. With courage, strength, humility, patience, compassion, dedication to continually re-educating ourselves, and the commitment to political action when necessary, we can put these new technologies at the service of humane endeavor.

References

1. See the works of George Gerbner (Mass Media Policies in Changing Cultures, Wiley, 1977; The Analysis of Communication Content: Developments in Scientific Theories & Computer Techniques, with Holsti and Krippendorff, Krieger, 1978) for extended discussions of these basic communications hypotheses.
2. John E. Sawyer, quoted in the CAA Newsletter (College Art Association), Spring 1982, p. 4.
3. Bagdikian, Ben. The Information Machines: Their Impact on Men and the Media. Harper, 1971, p. 205.
4. Rosenblatt, Roger. "The Mind in the Machine," Time, May 3, 1982, p. 59.
5. Professor Schwartz later supplied a reference to Jaime G. Carbonell's Subjective Understanding: Computer Models of Belief Systems (Univ. Microfilms, 1981), ed. by Harold S. Stone. It does not reassure me that computers can ever believe for us, or make value judgments about our beliefs. The millenium has not arrived yet.

SUBLIMITY VERSUS CIRCULATION:

FOR A CRITICAL METHOD OF POETRY SELECTION*

J. B. Miller

Ever since Callimachus opened the doors of the Alexandrian Library, poets have been trying to crawl out of their studies and onto that dusty shelf called posterity. While Callimachus, the poet-librarian, could assert that "I drink not from the fountain and I loathe everything popular," the contemporary American librarian appears handicapped by democracy. The inclination seems to be to avoid a critical or discriminating approach to poetry selection by casually shifting the concern from sublimity to circulation. Thus, community standards, statistics on the makeup of local populations, and shrinking budgets become the primary concerns for today's generation of underpaid librarians.

While it may be vital for the smooth and effective maintenance of libraries to focus on pragmatic variables, I will indulge in a merely cursory treatment of them, and concentrate specifically on the more critical standards that have been or may be used by the librarian.

Libraries attached to academic institutions are generally large enough to hire, for better or worse, the critically indoctrinated English Lit. graduate. The Library of Congress hires a poet every one or two years to serve as its "Poetry Consultant." But most libraries are too small or too poorly funded to hire a specialist for each section of their collection, leaving their librarians unrealistically expected to serve as all-purpose specialists. Such librarians, as victims of the economy, have access to few resources for pursuing poetry selection critically.

From the moment the first Neanderthal began grunting in meter, there have no doubt been poets to dispute the criteria of "good verse." Rather than acknowledging inherent distinctions in form, poets have traditionally attacked one another, reducing the

---

*Reprinted by permission of the author and publisher from Library Journal, 107:22 (December 15, 1982) 2309-14. Published by R.R. Bowker Co. (a Xerox company). Copyright © 1982 by J. B. Miller.

precise art of criticism to a blur of internal dissent. While such tactics may be useful in perpetuating the stereotypically preposterous notion of poets, this dissension does little, if anything, to aid lay people in the appreciation of verse or librarians in maintaining a critical circulation of same.

Although the average American (if such exists) could easily distinguish, within a few notes, a disco piece from a classical composition, he or she appears reticent to make similar fundamental distinctions when confronted with the medium of poetry. While a popular afternoon game show such as Name That Tune may exist and prosper under the Nielsen ratings, it is dubious that a show such as Name That Poem could survive in America. But, in fact, shouldn't a few syllables be just as suggestive as a few notes to the critical listener?

The serious student of aesthetic theory may respond at this point by distinguishing the so-called sensual arts from those which are said to be of a more intellectual orientation. There may even be ground for such distinction, but this strays from the point. Lay people must fight the instinct to be intimidated by syllables, and accept them at face value initially, as they would notes in a piece of music.

Attenuated variables such as library circulation history, community statistics, obscure reviews (invariably written by a comrade of the poet), or Nobel awards (often based on the politics of publishers) cannot be relied on exclusively.

Circulation history

Ginsberg's place in the world of letters may have been hailed over two decades ago with the publication of "Howl," but this must not be relied on as any indication of the merit of his present work. His continued notoriety is undeserved and, yet, this could hardly be gleaned from a glance at the library circulation history of his earlier publications. The later works of both Wordsworth and Frost are embarrassments to the overall contributions of both poets. History offers similar examples from each generation. Because a poet has succeeded in putting out one good book does not guarantee that all of his future work will be of consistent quality.

More troublesome and less clear is the case of those poets whose successes and failures may not be easily divided by their various publications. Both Lowell and Walcott, two fine modern poets, have at times put out inconsistent publications. With poets such as these, though, the successes are such that we must allow the failures as we look for the exceptions. Lowell is no longer with us, but Walcott most definitely is, and each poem in The Star-Apple Kingdom, for example, is excellent. Further, the alternative to frequent but occasionally inconsistent publications appears even less desirable. Joseph Brodsky, one of the greatest poets living today, has been more consistent in the quality of his publications, but he has rationed out only two books with a gap of a decade between publications, leaving his public in the dark for too long. One might forgive this poet, partially, given the additional burden of the necessity of translating his poems from his native Russian, but the same idea may be applied to poets writing in English.

Community statistics

Another suggested method for selecting poetry is to base it on the characteristics of the community and so insure circulation. This method assumes that the aesthetic appetite is exclusively dictated by cultural vanity. If statistics reveal, for example, a large black population in the area, librarians must select black poets. Critical or qualitative anaysis is subordinated. While such a system may be reasonable for special interest areas of the library, it has no place in the poetry section. Given a high Jewish population in the community served, it makes sense to build a Judaica collection. For a community of blacks, a collection geared toward black history is quite reasonable. Culture may be preserved and respected, without confining art by categorization. A method for selecting poetry by such categorizing is simultaneously insulting to both the audience and the poet.

For a few years before the death of Robert Hayden and immediately after he had served as Poetry Consultant to the Library of Congress, I had the privilege of enjoying his friendship. I remember one day when he was praised in the New York Times. Rather than noting the praise with satisfaction, he focused, with great dissatisfaction and almost sadness, on the fact that he had once again been categorized as a "black poet." The Times did not recall that he had been a student of W.H. Auden's or suggest the variety of aesthetic modes he had explored. He was merely labeled. Hayden's work definitely should be in libraries, not because he was black, but precisely because he was a good poet. If this method of categorizing the poet and generalizing from community statistics were applied as a blanket over all poetry, we would lose access to such important figures as W.B. Yeats, unless we happened to live in an area with a large Irish population. The better poets merely use their background or starting point as a launch pad for a flight into the universal. One does not have to be black to read Robert Hayden any more than one must be Irish to appreciate Yeats.

Reviews

One need only recall Whitman's notorious use of reviews to suggest a certain vulnerability. Whitman, having allied himself to the New York journalistic circle of his day, was able to not only solicit several favorable reviews, but have three that he had written himself printed beneath someone else's byline. One of his own reviews began modestly, "AN AMERICAN BARD AT LAST!" While one is grateful for Whitman's deviousness (especially when considering that he was virtually unknown at this time), the point remains. Librarians and lay people who have no fundamental familiarity with verse should not rely blindly on reviews.

Nobel awards

Czeslaw Milosz was just as remarkable a poet in 1979 as he was in 1980. However, when he received the Nobel Prize in 1980, his circulation doubled. Can librarians rely on awards to gauge a recognition factor? Many critics speculate that the Nobel (which Milosz unquestionably deserved years earlier) is frequently based on ancillary variables. In 1980 the political climate in Poland attracted the sympathies of the West. What if the situation had been different and the prize had not been awarded to Milosz? The poet would remain neither more nor less than the great poet he is recognized to be today. Would libraries still contain his work today? Would libraries still be encouraging the circulation of his work by carefully following and selecting each of his publications?

Even if nobody else is, librarians should be reading poetry--not just reviews, criticism, or statistics--but poetry. Magical formulas used for deducing mass appeal will not sustain poetry. However, the subjective perception, disregarding the common concerns of circulation, just might.

"The application of democratic principles in the sphere of knowledge leads to equating wisdom with idiocy," as Joseph Brodsky recently stated. In the sphere of poetics a critical approach must be applied. The best poetry excels because it provides an addition to the craft of verbal expression, despite either the absence or presence of a potential market for the so-called "product." The focus should be shifted toward the identification of contributions to art, and away from projections of market response.

I do not pretend to know of a clear and precise alternative formula or method that will help the librarian discover such poets as Milosz, prior to their receiving the Nobel. The need for attempting to maneuver the librarian into just such a critical position appears indisputable. The most obvious, first, and crucial step toward such a transition for the librarian must, at the very least, involve a fundamental familiarization with poetry itself. I do not believe that librarians must be reduced to the role of mere administrators. They are faced with the dual duty of serving the public and serving posterity. There need not be a dramatic dichotomy in the exercise of these tasks, if one is working toward the establishment of reliable critical standards.

Familiarization

Dismissing questions of deontology, reading poetry requires more concentration than reading a menu or the TV Guide. But as the rewards reaped from an appreciation of verse generally exceed the transient distraction provided by a meal or a TV show, the slightly greater investment of concentration satisfies itself well beyond the initial returns.

While it has been noted that a civilization was founded on Homer, it is difficult to cite a meal or a TV show that has had a comparable impact.

Poetry, to be more fully appreciated, must be read over and over again. The reader must develop his ear until verse is no longer <u>heard,</u> but simply <u>overheard,</u> as if the poet's voice has been inadvertently carried from one room to another.

Reading and technique

Just as the habitual listener of music may sense when a musician performs with a tremendous respect for his instrument or when a composer writes with a great respect for the notes that are to be played, poets who are dedicated to language may be identified in a similar manner. Many avid listeners, who are enriched on a daily basis by their passion for music, are entirely oblivious to such basic technical concerns as the key signature or time signature of the pieces they admire most. But this could not be said to invalidate their appreciation of the form. Similarly, readers of poetry must not be initially intimidated by an ignorance of such basic structural concerns as meter and rhyme. When such devices are employed most effectively they should, by their very nature, be subtle and difficult to discern. What should initially impress the reader is an instinctive connection with the musical or lyrical qualities of the verse--the effect--and not the technical foundation--the cause.

The poet has failed if one leaves a reading dominated by a distracting impression of the skeleton that lies beneath the surface of the poem. Technique, displayed in its full and blatant pomp, is an embarrassment to the potential of language. Only when it is employed discreetly, enhancing the work while remaining quietly in the background, is technique being utilized properly.

At first do not be easily distracted by technique, and if you find that you are, perhaps you should be reading another poet.

Only after one has developed and refined one's ability to <u>overhear</u> poetry is it useful to work toward an understanding (beyond mere identification) of the underlying technical devices which often trigger the verse. Eventually, it will be of substantial interest to the reader that, for example, first-rate verse frequently mirrors the semantics in the structure. However, at first one must concentrate on the overall effect of the work before embarking into the seemingly swampy mathematics of poetry. Only after the reader has applied time and compression to the charcoal of poetic structure may a diamond be revealed.

The test drive

On purchasing a car, the concerned consumer will not query into the nature of its grisly history from plant production to showroom; instead, the prospective buyer will concentrate on its potential to be utilized as a vehicle for transportation.

It has been suggested that one rationale for the reading of poetry is its ability to promote travel or provide vivid pictures of areas which may be entirely foreign to the reader. A citizen of the U.S.S.R. may surreptitiously read a battered edition of Robert Frost's verse in Leningrad while dreaming of New England. The better poets (of course, this includes Frost) also promote a type of travel which is not dependent on the limited geographical regions of our planet. This generally comes down to the scope of exploration advocated by the individual poet in each instance. As with the identification of a poet's devotion to language, the recognition of the depth or density of verse which explores existence beyond the simplicity of certain limited levels requires a patient and unintimidated development of the critical facilities. A beginning point, as with the car analogy suggested above, is to initially accept poetry at face value and take it out for a test drive. Here one must focus on the "effect" of the verse, prior to inquiring into the "cause," and see how far the poetry takes one, what is the potential for travel.

The principal reason for initially taking this general approach to verse, besides avoiding intimidation, is that it is far too easy for verse to fall victim to individual projections of personal feelings or ideas when, ultimately, one should be attempting to isolate what the poet feels or thinks. While it is quite common to assist one's understanding by contrasting one's own experience against the experience of the poet, a fine line must be drawn between the two. If one wishes to be true to the poet or the language, one must search the poem for the poet's statement, not one's own.

Dostoyevsky was right in noting that "all respectable men will talk most readily about themselves." Everyone knows, however, that readers of poetry are rarely "respectable," so this does not provide an excuse for self-indulgent projections.

Categories

While most poetry being written today may be immediately vulnerable to categorization ("street poetry," "the poetry of the vernacular," "public, popular poetry," or "poetry which confronts political and social issues"), the most powerful poetry cannot be isolated by its subject matter or technique to one limited level. The best verse strategically sails in and out of categories, defying assault by movement, yet simultaneously embracing the "human" concerns without being confined in the transient illusiveness of a "cause."

<u>In this sense, if a poet's work can be cornered into a category, it should perhaps be best left to the corner, rather than elevated to a shelf in the midst of an otherwise reasonable collection.</u>

With this treatment of categorical analysis, one might begin by making a fundamental division between two distinct classes of poetry. In the first class reside those poems in which the intent of the poet is immediately recognizable and all that remains for the reader is a determination as to the fulfillment or inability of the poet to fulfill that intent. In the second, or more serious, class reside those poems in which the ambition is of such a level or crafted in such a way that any inquiry as to its achievement is clearly subordinated and the ambition itself captures the reader almost entirely. Having made this division, the reader will most often find that those poems of the first class are quite frequently vulnerable to categorization, while those poems in the latter class may not be so easily limited by a casual labeling. For example, of all living poets writing in English today, Derek Walcott's poems perhaps best exemplify the virtues and power of the latter class:

> The last leaves fell like notes from a piano
> and left their ovals echoing in the ear;
> with gawky music stands, the winter forest
> looks like an empty orchestra, its lines
> ruled on these scattered manuscripts of snow.
>
> ....
>
> there is no harder prison than writing
> verse
> what's poetry, if it is worth its salt,
> but a phrase men can pass from hand to mouth?
>
> From hand to mouth, across the centuries,
> the bread that lasts when systems have decayed,
> when, in his forest of barbed-wire branches,
> a prisoner circles, chewing the one phrase
> whose music will last longer than the leaves, ...
> --excerpted from "Forest of Europe" [1]

<u>Nuance</u>

Ezra Pound suggested that great poetry is "language energized with Nuance to the utmost degree." Returning to our hypothetical car for a moment, just as gasoline is required to fuel the automobile, nuance is required to propel poetry. While the consumer pays for the gasoline and reaps the benefit of the physical mobility it provides, the reader must pay for nuance with the concentration required to recognize it in order to reap the benefit of the emotional and intellectual mobility it may provide.

To recognize nuance the reader may begin by concentrating on the refinement of emotions and thoughts that are provoked by the poem. This focus, as implied earlier, may be aided by an assessment of the poet's devotion to or respect for language. As in the brief treatment of poetry as a vehicle for travel above, one must look to the multi-level nature of the work. Just as a successful poem avoids confinement in a category, the language must avoid lingering too long on merely one level. Nuances may frequently be observed in the varying levels of inquiry suggested by the poem. Frost was not fond of the woods, contrary to popular belief. His seemingly simple glimpses of the woods merely present us with the first and most obvious level. The nuances may be observed upon proceeding several levels further and noting that concealed beneath the idyllic New England landscape are woods that may provoke terror and a correlation between these woods and the life that appears to proceed outside of them.

In looking to nuances, however, the reader must carefully distinguish the statement within the poem from the means or method by which that statement is provoked. Before leaping to a rash judgement that the subtleties have successfully aspired to the status of the "new and unusual," one must recall the warning of Koheles (Solomon):

מַה־שֶּׁהָיָה הוּא שֶׁיִּהְיֶה וּמַה־
שֶּׁנַּעֲשָׂה הוּא שֶׁיֵּעָשֶׂה וְאֵין כָּל־חָדָשׁ
תַּחַת הַשָּׁמֶשׁ: יֵשׁ דָּבָר שֶׁיֹּאמַר רְאֵה־זֶה
חָדָשׁ הוּא כְּבָר הָיָה לְעֹלָמִים אֲשֶׁר הָיָה
מִלְּפָנֵנוּ:

> *Whatever has been done is what will be done. There is nothing new beneath the sun! Sometimes there is something of which one says: "Look, this is new!"—But it has already existed in the ages before us.*

Of course, there is nothing "new" to be said, yet this does not exclude the potential for injecting "nuance" via the means or method of provoking a derivative perception. In this sense, Frost is working from the identical premise with which Dante commenced the <u>Comedia</u>, i.e., "Nel mezzo del cummin di nostra vita/ mi retrovai per una selva oscura, / che la diritta via era smarrita." ("In the middle of the journey of our life I came to myself in a dark wood where the straight way was lost."). Indeed, whether consciously or not, his work may be seen as a response to the implicit challenge within Dante's next verse, i.e., "Ahi quanto a dir qual era e cosa dura / questa selva selvaggia ed aspra e forte," ("Ah! how hard a thing it is to tell what a wild, and rough, and stubborn wood this was.").

In short, Koheles was right: the rules of the game don't change, only the dimensions of the playing field. A mere single murder may no longer be enough to chill the modern conscience, but genocide definitely does. The proportions of the phenomena that must be confronted by the poet change, while the underlying sense of guilt or terror remains constant.

<u>Therefore, the librarian must simultaneously develop a sensitivity to nuance, while turning a cold shoulder to that poetry of today which suffers by asserting the pretense that it contains something "new."</u>

What individual institutions advocate has a greater effect on direction than what might generally be considered foreseeable. For example, the University of Michigan's English department annually sponsors a poetry contest in which the prize is awarded to that poem which "best aspires to the direction of the new and unusual." Such institutional support for the so-called "new and unusual" only succeeds in perpetuating this absurd and asinine myth. This is but one example that may serve to suggest why libraries, along with so many other institutions, must exercise extreme care in the selection of the policies or directions they wish to support and encourage. Given the pretense of the certain Constitutionally protected freedoms in America, and the excessive censorship under which so many other nations operate, the American librarian is faced with a greater moral burden. We must encourage and protect such freedoms and, at the same time, develop greater critical facilities to ensure that complacency and apathy do not diminish the potential literary wealth that may come from under the wing of such freedoms.

While an article of this length could never be exhaustive, I hope that this brief treatment of the subject will be of some use to the reader. There is an almost infinite variety of suggestions which might be inserted instead of the above; however, these suggestions are merely starting points. Just as I have warned the reader not to blindly accept reviews, the same may be said of criticism, and this piece is no exception. I strongly recommend testing these suggestions against individual reading. Once again, ultimately, one must return to the subjective test.

This article was written with the intent of exploring ideals, and a wealth of realistic, pragmatic considerations wait in the wings to pounce on the suggestions I have made. Whether the ideal of a critical method can survive the attack must rest with the librarian. In the words of Alexander Blok: "Life is worth living only if you place exorbitant demands upon it--... believe not in what does not exist in the world but in what should exist in the world."

<u>Reference</u>

1. From <u>The Star-Apple Kingdom</u>. Copyright © 1979 by Derek Walcott. By permission of Farrar, Straus & Giroux.

THE NONESUCH PRESS*

Ashley Montagu

It was in the autumn, I think, of 1923 that I almost visited the Nonesuch Press, then newly founded; at least, I stood on the floor above the basement the Press had rented as its office. The occasion was my introduction to the bookshop run by Francis Birrell and David Garnett at 30 Gerrard Street, off Shaftesbury Avenue, in what was then, as now, known as Soho. Birrell and Garnett sold rare books, mainly in English literature. It was a lovely shop, stocked with enticing items.

Gerrard Street was famous for being the habitation of ladies of leisure who plied their trade there, for it was an ill-lit street as became its ill-fame, though it was perfectly safe at all times of the day. Number 43 Gerrard Street was the home of the "43" Club, a dark, damp basement, where one could drink and dance, under the auspices of Mrs. Kate Meyrick and her four daughters, all of whom married into the nobility--for the club was frequented by the "best" people, and it was raided by the police, as I seem to recall, about once a month. Another much respected feature of Gerrard Street was that it was the home of the 1917 Club, founded in the first flush of liberal enthusiasm to celebrate the October 1917 Russian revolution. It was a delightful place, affording all the amenities of a civilized company, where one could dine, and talk, and even play Ping-Pong, or bridge, which was then the rage. So that was the circumambiency in which the Nonesuch Press had its first home. The Press clearly rose to the challenge it presented.

The friend who introduced me to Birrell and Garnett's bookshop was Edward Evans-Pritchard, my fellow student, under Malinowski, Seligman, and Westermarck, at the London School of Economics, and later professor of anthropology at Oxford University. Evans-Pritchard had probably known Birrell or Garnett or both during his undergraduate years at Oxford, though I do not recall that Evans-Pritchard had any interest in the kind of antique books that Birrell and Garnett sold.

---

*Reprinted by permission of the author and publisher from The Princeton University Library Chronicle, 44:2 (Winter 1982) 127-34. Copyright © 1982 by Friends of the Princeton University Library.

Communication and Education 189

During our visit Birrell acted as host in the absence of his partner. No mention was made of the Nonesuch Press. Had there been, it would not have meant anything to me, for the Press had only just begun to publish. It was not until half a dozen years later that I first saw a Nonesuch book. In 1929 I was staying with a friend in his villa in Fiesole, when one bright morning I saw the postman trudging up the hill heavily laden with several large parcels. I received them from him and took them to my host. With my friend I beheld, and savored, the unveiling--for that is the proper term for such a ritual occasion--of several of the most beautifully designed books I had ever laid eyes on. One was La Divina Commedia, and the other was the four-volume Complete Works of Sir John Vanbrugh. The two works could not have been more unlike in design, but what struck me at once was the perfect appropriateness of the design to each book. From the full orange vellum binding to the splendid typography of the Italian on one side and the Cary English translation on the other, the Divina Commedia, with its 42 illustrations after drawings by Botticelli, is a magnificent work of art. The four Vanbrugh volumes keep splendid company with Congreve, Wycherley, Otway, Farquhar, and Rochester. Textually all these works remain the best we have; their design beautifully retains the flavor of Restoration title pages, and the text, printed in Monotype Caslon, delightfully extends the promise of the title pages. The immediate enchantment I experienced in 1929 has remained throughout my collecting of and pleasure in Nonesuch books. I am still collecting everything I can lay hands on relating to the Nonesuch Press. I am wanting in some items. As a Nonesuchophile I remain devotedly hopeful. When I was young, and knew no better, I gave away some of the very items I now lack. What I most lament are the books I could easily have acquired but failed to do so because of a certain innate stupidity. For a bookman this is the most poignant of all regrets.

In the course of the years I corresponded with Francis Meynell, first writing him a fan letter saying how much I admired his books. At the time I did not know that he wrote poetry in a minor vein, but I do recall writing him that while his mother, Alice Meynell, put her poetry into words, he put his poetry into the creation of beautiful books, for they were, indeed, nonpareil. In his autobiography, Meynell later wrote, "Nonesuch was a craft, a trade, a happy synthesis of my two fervours--poetry and print."[1]

When at long last I made the acquaintance of that wonderful holiday maker's vade mecum, The Week-End Book, the Nonesuch Press's best seller, I learned that Meynell was fond of limericks, so I sent him one of mine. He liked it so much that he wrote me that even if I brought an action against him in the courts, nothing would stop him from publishing the limerick in the next edition of The Week-End Book, which he promptly did, in the 1939 edition.

It was early in July 1939 that I at last met Meynell and his charming wife Alix, at dinner, at their flat in London. We had great fun, until I introduced the somber subject of the war with Hitler. I made things worse by commenting on Britain's unpreparedness, but rescued myself by blaming it all on the "Cliveden Set," the arch-appeasers headed by the Virginian Lady Astor, and her cronies, Garvin of the Observer, Dawson of the Times, Lord Halifax, Neville Chamberlain, Stanley Baldwin, Lord Lothian, and others. The Observer was a paper to which I had subscribed for years, for it was the most literary of English newspapers. I recall referring to an editorial by Garvin as having been built on the southern slopes of impending disaster, a remark that prepared us for an adjournment to that most delicious of nightclubs, the Players Theatre or "Joys." This was situated in an elaborate loft in Covent Garden. It was frequented mostly by intellectually-minded people and their friends. The performers were delightful, and very funny. I particularly remember a rabbinical skit by Leonard Sachs (who also served as chairman), and a marvelously amusing monologue, in a heavy Russian accent, parodying the theme of so many Russian plays, which had become popular in England in the translations of Mrs. Constance Garnett. All that I remember of the Russian performance was that the monologist looked his part perfectly, with sandy yellow hair parted down the middle, with pince-nez, and wearing a frock coat, seated at a small round table, and opening with the unforgettable words, "I was seeting by River Stench."

In his autobiography Meynell tells how in the changed days and management at the Pelican Press, he began to hanker after more independence, personal and professional.

> Now I wanted to devote myself to books rather than to miscellaneous printing; so I made inquiries of several publishers. Would they allow me to print for them this, that and the other English classic which really lacked any "really nice" edition? My somewhat arch formula was to point out that if they chanced to be wrecked on the conventional desert island and made the conventional choice of only two books to accompany them, the Bible and Shakespeare, they would not find a current edition of either fit for a tasteful shipwreck. The response was no more than a frown or a smile. So I myself set out to be a new kind of publisher-designer, an architect of books rather than a builder, seeking the realisation of my designs by marshalling the services--often mechanical services--of the best printing houses, papermakers, binders. We were lucky in our hour: we were the first to cater for a large, growing and unsatisfied interest in "fine books" at less than the fine prices required by the great "private presses."[2]

It was in this way that Nonesuch came into being in 1923. During its existence Nonesuch had many distinguished competitors, the Cresset Press, the Golden Cockerel Press, the Shakespeare Head Press, the Greygnog Press, the Fortune Press, the Blackmore Press, Haslewood Books, the Fanfrolico Press, and several others. Not one of these, alas, is any longer in existence, but their books will live as long as works of art are appreciated.

All these presses produced distinguished books, many worthy to rank with the best ever created, but what distinguished Nonesuch from them all is that it was the first press created to prove that beautifully designed books could be produced at a cost not significantly greater than commercially produced books, and far below the prices of the great "private presses." In this intention Meynell so well succeeded that the small editions of 1,500 copies or so of each of his books were soon oversubscribed and exhausted. The prices of Nonesuch books were incredibly low for the value given, and even as they were being published were commanding three or four times the list price.

I well remember going in search of one of the compendious Nonesuch volumes, complete editions of the works of such writers as Milton, Donne, Swift, Shelley, Hazlitt, Coleridge, and others-- even Pushkin. It was the Shelley I needed to make my collection complete, but I found that all the booksellers I tried had sold their copies, so as a last resort I tried the Nonesuch office in St. James Street, off Theobalds Road, where I was successful in obtaining a copy, which with all my other Nonesuch treasures still brilliantly graces my shelves. Interestingly enough, a photochemical trick of the sun has caused Shelley's name to materialize from the lettering on the blue dust jacket onto the blue binding beneath--which I take to be a celestial tribute to the genius of the poet.

Sir Rupert Hart-Davis, the distinguished publisher and author, told me, over lunch at the Garrick Club (I think it was in 1955), that the compendious series he published following the Second World War as part of his list, a list that set new standards for the publishing world, drew from Meynell a letter berating him for imitating the Nonesuch compendious series. Hart-Davis was both astonished and amused by this piece of folly, for he was the first freely to acknowledge, and with unqualified admiration, that his own series was based on the model set by Meynell. The truth is that Hart-Davis's series both complemented and constituted an advance upon Meynell's. Hart-Davis felt that no greater compliment could be paid an innovator like Meynell than to learn from him and take his influence a step or so further. Hart-Davis's Ben Jonson, Goldsmith, Wordsworth, Macaulay, Tennyson, Newman, Arnold, Carlyle, and others complement the Nonesuch compendia, and improve upon them, as do the wonderful duodecimo Muses' Library volumes, with such authors as Drayton, Ralegh, Lovell, Beddoes, Diaper [sic], Marvell, and others.

Anyone familiar with the English publishing scene over the last half-century, who is at all interested in the appearance of books, will know what a great influence Meynell has been upon book design, not only in England but also in America. In America, Random House for many years published Nonesuch books, as did the Limited Editions Club. In the course of this transatlantic communication the design of their own books was perceptibly influenced.

Another innovation for which Meynell was responsible was the Press's beautifully designed announcements of forthcoming publications. These took a great variety of shape and form, and remain invariably fascinating, not only for the books listed and described but also for the news of the Press, its present and future plans. The prospectuses and retrospectuses were sometimes quite elaborate. In one case they took the form of a single volume, bound in blue cloth, with essays by Arthur Waugh and Thomas Hatton, and a good deal else. It is a delightful volume entitled <u>Nonesuch Dickensia</u>, announcing the forthcoming publication of 877 sets of the complete Dickens in 23 volumes plus an original copperplate for 48 guineas, or, from the Limited Editions Club of New York, for $252. Today one would be lucky to find a set at $3,000. <u>Nonesuch Dickensia</u>, which was given away to anyone who asked for it, is even more difficult to lay hands on than the Nonesuch Dickens (1937).

The Nonesuch prospectuses and retrospectuses have long been sought after by Nonesuch enthusiasts. I consider myself most favored, for when I visited the Meynells at their home in Lavenham, Suffolk (sometime in the early seventies), Meynell and his wife Alix presented me with an almost complete set of these rarities. My wife and I had enjoyed a lovely tea with our hosts in the delightful garden of their home, Grey House, opposite the very establishment in which Constable had gone to school and where he had been mercilessly beaten by the usher, in common with the other boys. Meynell had recently celebrated his 80th birthday, and I remember him several times remarking "Eighty-teighty--it's a good age." He appeared to me at this time rather frail; he died four years later in July 1975 at the age of 84.

It is sad to recall that at no time was it easy going for Nonesuch; indeed, from the beginning the Press led a precarious existence. Sales were good, but Meynell was always hopeful that the public would respond in greater numbers. They did--to one book, <u>The Week-End Book</u>, not because it was well designed, which it was, but because it appealed to weekenders and to stay-at-home would-be weekenders, because it was (and still is) great fun, and because there was nothing else like it. Launched in 1924, <u>The Week-End Book</u> had sold by 1955 more than half a million copies. It captured the peculiar atmosphere of the twenties. "The true message of the Twenties," as Cyril Connolly wrote, "was hope, gaiety and sophistication, with an attempt to combine personal relationships and eroticism." Beneath the whimsy and ingenious frivolity of <u>The Week-End Book</u> Connolly perceived the influence of Bloomsbury, "a solid core of good taste and wide reading."[3]

When, after years of valiant effort Meynell was forced to enlist the cooperation of American publishers, an editorial in the <u>Times Literary Supplement</u> bemoaned the loss of Nonesuch as a national institution. Meynell replied (11 October 1938) in a spirited letter gratefully acknowledging the generosity of the Americans who came to the rescue when the Press was languishing for lack of support. In a letter Meynell wrote me at the time, he expressed himself rather more bitterly on the lack of support he had received from English sources.

The truth is that it is rare for a private press to enjoy a long life, even a press that has been supported by the wealth of its founders. Unless there is enough public support for it, it soon becomes a most expensive hobby. The Cresset Press was supported by its founder Denis Cohen, a man of considerable private means, great charm, and exquisite taste. Such qualities are reflected in his books, perhaps the most outstanding of which is Gulliver's Travels, illustrated by Rex Whistler. With the Nonesuch Herodotus and the Golden Cockerel Four Gospels, Gulliver's Travels stands in a very special class. Cresset books were slightly more expensive than Nonesuch, and very much worth the slight difference in price, for each book was a gem.

Meynell was finally reduced to taking a job, which brought him a steady income, but with less free time he operated the Press as a hobby rather than a business, although the business of Nonesuch had, in fact, always been his hobby. In this postwar period there were no more lavish formats. There was the Coronation Shakespeare, the postwar Bible, a series of Cygnets, and a compendious Blake.

In the design of books Meynell set out to make the machine the ally of art. That he succeeded so well was owing to a fine esthetic sensibility and a happy invincibility, which led to an elegant synthesis of poetry, paper, print, and binding, a general refinement that made a Nonesuch book immediately distinguishable from all others. Fundamental to all this, of course, was Meynell's interest in the text coupled with a sympathetic understanding of the reader's needs. Added to this was a sound knowledge of printing and printing types. Bruce Rogers had rightly said that the first requirement for a good book designer was that he be a book lover. Meynell, who idolized Rogers, was all of that. Meynell's purpose was to fit the book appropriately to the text, "allusive or sensitive design," as he called it. This required attention to every detail of the book, down to the calligraphy of the number of each volume or set.

I do not wish to give the impression that Nonesuch was a one-man show--it was not. Meynell was always asking friends for advice and submitting samples of what he proposed for their criticism. Meynell's second wife, Vera, was indispensable for many of the Nonesuch early projects. Meynell was such a perfectionist that he was not beyond destroying a whole edition if it failed to live up to his expectations. This he did with Kisses by Johannes Secundus, a book that he denounced to its subscribers and begged them to return. I own a copy and find it a pretty little book, of which any designer, other than Meynell, would be proud.

As a collector of private press as well as other rare books, I firmly believe that Meynell's achievement is unequaled, and other collectors of my acquaintance share my opinion. Geoffrey Keynes, who was closely associated with the Press from its beginning, in his introduction to John Dreyfus's A History of the Nonesuch Press, described Meynell as "the most successful general book designer England has known."[4] Meynell was the supreme architect of the technically beautiful book, and no other press has produced a range of beautiful books so rich in variety of format, typeface, paper, illustrations, and binding.

References

1. My Lives (London: Bodley Head, 1971), p. 155.
2. Ibid.
3. The Sunday Times, 6 November 1955.
4. John Dreyfus, A History of the Nonesuch Press. Introduction by Geoffrey Keynes. Descriptive catalogue by David McKitterick, Simon Rendell, and John Dreyfus. Edition limited to 950 numbered copies. Printed and bound at the University Press, Cambridge, for the Nonesuch Press, and distributed by the Bodley Head in England, and by John Howell Books, San Francisco, in the United States. Pages xv + 320, 1981.

A PORTRAIT OF WORKING WOMEN

IN FEDERAL GOVERNMENT PERIODICALS*

Joe Morehead

Introduction

The Equal Rights Amendment expired on June 30, 1982, as opponents like Phyllis Schlafly celebrated its demise and proponents like the National Organization for Women mourned its defeat. However, the indomitable backers saw to it that ERA was reintroduced in the Congress in July, 1982, and the long and arduous struggle for ratification was again set in motion.

During the ERA's ten-year struggle, the federal establishment published a large quantity of literature dealing with the several issues espoused by the feminist groups and decried by the Schlafly organization. The purpose of this essay is to indicate some of the concerns in the area of working women reflected in the publications of federal agencies, particularly in their serial issuances. For despite the Reagan administration's opposition to ERA, previous administrations left a legacy of statutes and regulations which oblige at least the appearance of compliance on the part of the bureaucracy. In the review of federal documentation that follows, keep in mind that some of the facts and statistics may not reveal the underlying reality. However, one must also remember that publications issued by federal entities do not necessarily reflect the hidden or overt agenda of the government in power at the time.

For an overview the researcher might begin with Subject Bibliography (SB)-111, entitled Women. Revised periodically, this current awareness source lists over 120 monographs, series, and serials issued by various agencies on a variety of topics concerning women. SB-111 is available free from the Superintendent of Documents, and is sent to depository libraries (GP 3.22/2; item 552-A).

Whereas SB-111 lists only those publications sold by the

---

*Reprinted by permission of the author and publisher from The Serials Librarian, 7:4 (Summer 1983) 47-56. Copyright © 1983 by The Haworth Press, Inc. All rights reserved.

Superintendent of Documents, wider coverage is found in the Monthly Catalog of United States Government Publications. The results of the 1980 census provide comprehensive data on women, and these are announced in Census Bureau lists like Monthly Product Announcement and Data User News. All federal statistics concerning women may be accessed through the commercial abstracting service American Statistics Index.

The annual Serials Supplement to the Monthly Catalog shows the provenance of periodicals like Women & Work and Women in Action. The best source for articles about women's issues is Index to U.S. Government Periodicals, a commercial service issued quarterly with an annual cumulation. A partial list of federal periodicals that contain statistical or descriptive information on subjects relating to women includes Monthly Labor Review, Perspectives: The Civil Rights Quarterly, American Education, Army Reserve Magazine, Energy Consumer, Employment and Earnings, Agenda, Occupational Outlook Quarterly, Black News Digest, Management, State (formerly Department of State Newsletter), Airman, Trends, Postal Life, Family Economics Review, United States Army Aviation Digest, NOAA Magazine, etc. In the narrative that follows, I have relied upon all of these sources of information. The accounts of women in the labor force that appear in federal government periodicals contain both good news and bad news. According to an old saw, an optimist sees an opportunity in every calamity while a pessimist sees a calamity in every opportunity. I fear that the public record on this topic proclaims more calamities than opportunities.

Apprenticeship Programs

Over the last decade there has been an increase in the number of women participating in apprenticeship programs nationwide. To meet the affirmative action goals promulgated by the Equal Employment Opportunity Commission (EEOC), an independent agency created by Title VII of the Civil Rights Act of 1964, apprenticeship program sponsors are obliged to use separate or "dual" eligibility lists in the selection of women and men applicants for training. In June, 1979, the Associate Solicitor of Labor issued Circular 79-19 clarifying the special circumstances under which these methods of meeting affirmative action objectives are permissible. Dual eligibility lists may be used to remedy the present effects of past discrimination or to redress the adverse impact on selection of women by "unvalidated" testing procedures.[1]

Indeed, 1980 Department of Labor statistics showed that women were gaining in participation as apprentices in the skilled trades and crafts. There were 8,950 women in registered apprenticeship programs at the end of 1978, an increase of 52 percent over the previous year. According to the administrator of the Labor Department's Bureau of Apprenticeship and Training, over 4 percent of all new registrants in apprenticeships during 1978 were women, "a significant jump from 1973, when women registrants represented

Communication and Education   197

only seven-tenths of a percent." Nevertheless, this figure is still
small. "Women represented 3.1 percent of the total number of registered apprentices at the end of 1978." Officials declared that the
"Labor Department is certainly not satisfied nor pleased with the
present small percentage ... but we have been showing steady progress over the past five years in bringing more and more women
into the skilled trades."[2]

      Examples of apprenticeship programs involving women in-
clude those sponsored by the AFL-CIO's carpenters' union,[3] on-
the-job training in the textile industry,[4] training to help low-
income, unemployed "displaced homemakers" who need work because of separation, divorce, or loss of the primary wage earner
due to disability or death,[5] and the Woman Offender Apprenticeship Program, jointly administered by the Women's Bureau, the
Bureau of Apprenticeship and Training, and the Federal Prison
System.[6] But many programs like these were funded under Title
III of the Comprehensive Employment and Training Act (CETA), a
social program terminated by a feckless Congress during Ronald
Reagan's first year in office.

      Despite these very modest gains, a national longitudinal
study of over 5,000 families revealed that white men generally receive more apprenticeship training than white women, black men,
or black women. The author of the study, a professor of economics at the University of Delaware at Newark, noted that "on-the-job
training is an important determinant of individual earnings and especially of the growth of earnings over the life cycle."[7] The
above data show how difficult it is to determine real improvement
through the interpretation of statistical surveys. It is not difficult,
however, to realize that federal retrenchment policies jeopardize
apprenticeship programs; the states have displayed little enthusiasm
for obligating monies when the federal well runs dry.

The Earnings Gap

A study published in 1980 showed that the wage differential between
working men and women is widening. In 1955 the median income
of full-time working women was $2,734, while that of their male
counterparts was $4,246. "In short, for every dollar earned by
men, women made only 64.3 cents." In 1978, the ratio came to
$16,062 for men and $9,641 for women. Thus, for every dollar
earned by men, women earned 60.0 cents. But this income disparity does not apply only to entry-level, "pink collar" workers; it
extends to the academic world, the professions (engineering, law,
medicine, banking, etc.), and female employment in the federal
government. The inequalities of the General Schedules (GS) ladder
for men and women working in federal agencies are such that "it
would take 83 years for women to reach parity with men at the GS
16 level and above; 109 years at the 14-15 level; 125 years at the
13-15 levels; and 36 years at the 9-12 levels."[8]

Speaking at a conference, the Director of the Women's Bureau noted that in the 1980s the "persistent earnings gap between women and men must be a target for action." Women have to work 9 days to gross the same amount of money men gross in 5 days. Women workers who have graduated from high school have less income on average than men who have less than an 8th grade education. Women with 5 or more years of college earn less than men who have completed no more than high school. These discrepancies, the Director stated, "must be reckoned with in this decade if we are to address the problem of wage determination as a consequence of the undervaluation of women's work."[9]

One theory of the earnings gap suggests that most employers simply prefer things this way, even though they may lose money owing to their bias. Another theory holds that male dominance of the best jobs is the most profitable arrangement for employers. Still another theory calls attention to the fact that hiring for a good job is a gamble, and employers minimize their risk by placing their bets on males.[10] While the experts, as usual, disagree, a 1981 Bureau of Labor Statistics (BLS) survey determined that whereas weekly earnings of women employed full-time in wage and salary jobs increased more rapidly than those of men (9.9 versus 8.0 percent), women continued to earn substantially less than men ($211 versus $335).[11] Statistics on the earnings gap are incontrovertible; and, as the Director of the Women's Bureau observed, the "challenges in the 80s will center around how women participate in the work force instead of why."[12]

Employment Opportunities

According to a number of reports in government periodicals, employment opportunities for highly educated women in certain fields are improving. Here the literature is largely confined to the chances of gaining employment, not the inequity in wages outlined above. A National Research Council study showed that between the years 1974 and 1978, the number of women scientists and engineers hired by the federal government grew by 50 percent while the total employment of scientists and engineers over the same period increased by only 16 percent. But men scientists in federal service are better paid and enjoy higher rank.[13] The Department of State reports evidence of the need for more senior women in overseas missions. This need was deemed desirable for three reasons: 1) women in senior posts are accepted and respected even in countries with strongly male-dominated societies; 2) women symbolize the way the United States makes use of a valuable resource [parenthetically I must remark that this bit of flummery reminds one of the "token black" syndrome]; and 3) their visibility encourages women in macho countries to train for and seek similar levels of responsibility in their own governments or in diplomatic service.[14]

In the private sector high technology careers are increasingly available to women. These jobs are defined as "skilled workers

who assist engineers, architects, doctors and other professionals--
a computer technician, for example." Working with complicated
equipment, "technicians typically require 1 to 2 years of specialized
training at a postsecondary school."[15] Women who are graduates
of engineering schools "have made a wise career choice," according
to the American Society of Civil Engineers. "Since 1971, female
enrollment in engineering schools has increased 300 percent. Women now constitute from 10 percent to 25 percent of the engineering
students currently in school, and fewer women are transferring out
of engineering than in the past years." But despite the more aggressive efforts at recruiting, women engineers constitute only 2.7
percent of the engineering profession. And there are few women
above middle-management levels in engineering firms. Indeed, women perceive that companies "are still loath to give [them] supervisory powers over males."[16] And women with other specialized
skills are finding employment opportunities significantly improved.
The American Geophysical Union, for example, reports that more
and more women are sought for seagoing scientific careers. Women
with brains and brawn hold positions as chief scientists on vessels,
oceanographers who operate winches and cranes in sun and weather.[17]

Up to 1981 the federal government through grants encouraged
employers to train and place women in various male-dominated industries such as transportation, construction, coal mining, and architectural services.[18] But funds for this purpose have been severely curtailed by Reagan's commitment "to reduce the level of
Government spending and thereby restore the vitality of the nation's
economy."[19] Thus the gains won by women in the marketplace
are threatened by what Vice-President George Bush called "voodoo
economics" during the 1980 Republican presidential primary.

Women in the Armed Services

Relative to private sector and federal civilian opportunities, the
picture for women serving in the military is bright. The Army,
Navy, Air Force, Marines, and Coast Guard are fully integrated.
Although current law precludes women from serving in combat positions, Defense Department policies have resulted in making possible the assignment of women to almost all other career fields.
Appropriations for military women's programs have shown a steady
increase since fiscal year 1973. Career progression is roughly
comparable to that for male personnel. Women are now routinely
assigned to overseas locations formerly closed to female personnel.
And admission of women to the service academies began in the fall
of 1976, furthering the goal of increased numbers of women officers.

Military periodicals make every effort to highlight the achievements of women in the uniformed services (and why not?). In 1980
the first all-woman flight crew was aboard a C-9A Nightingale carrying a normal patient load for the Military Airlift Command's 37th
Aeromedical Airlift Wing, Scott Air Force Base, Illinois. Aboard

the aircraft were the aircraft commander, medical crew director, two pilots, a flight nurse, two aeromedical technicians, and a flight mechanic--all women.[20] In 1979 Second Lieutenant Marcella A. Hayes became the first black woman to receive aviator wings in the United States armed forces when she completed Army helicopter flight training at the Army Aviation Center, Fort Rucker, Alabama. Hayes, who is also a qualified paratrooper, became the 55th woman to be graduated by the Aviation School.[21] As the number of women in law schools increases, recruiting and retention of women in the Army's Judge Advocate General Corps have become high priority items. Various factors account for a low application rate of women for a legal career in the military: salaries are not competitive with the civilian opportunities open to the best women law graduates; many women in law schools today are older, married to men with established civilian careers, and unwilling to relocate; the Army has an "image problem" for women law students; and Judge Advocate General Corps field recruiters have been men, many of whom never worked with a female attorney. But the Army is making great efforts to change its overall recruiting program, and its sincere desire to recruit women lawyers cannot be impugned.[22]

But while the armed services have provided genuine leadership in opportunities for women, the situation for the wives of military males is not as sanguine. A study published in the February, 1981, issue of Monthly Labor Review entitled "The Employment Situation for Military Wives" shows that the increase in labor force participation of military wives has followed that of all women, and describes some of the factors that inhibit employment. Among these are the frequent separations from husbands, which place the burden of family responsibilities on the wife, and the frequent moving and long-standing customs for women to do volunteer work in the military community. Moreover, the occupational distribution of military wives also mirrors that of their civilian counterparts with a high proportion in clerical jobs and large numbers in technical and service positions. Generally, military wives are more likely to be unemployed than civilian wives, due to factors associated with the location of military bases and the frequent moves that characterize the military life.[23]

Summary

Federal government serials and series provide a wealth of quantifiable data for analysis of labor force patterns of working women. Unprecedented numbers of women entered the job market during the 1970s, and this phenomenon has kept the assiduous bureaucrats of the Bureau of Labor Statistics busy. The following developments obliged the BLS to create a number of new data series, remodel others, refine and redefine basic terms, and issue new reports.

Single women workers (those defined as never married) sixteen years and over represent a growing portion of the total labor force. During the 1970s, the number of single women in the workplace increased from about 6.4 to 10.2 million. In part this increase was due to the rise in the proportion of women in their twenties who postponed marriage or chose to remain single.

The dramatic development is that of married women in the female labor force. They have overtaken single women as the dominant group and have accounted for nearly one-half (48.9 percent) of the increase in the labor force during the last decade. In general, the gain in the women's labor force during the 1970s was large among women under 35 years of age. Quite simply, the post-World War II baby boom children reached labor force age.[24]

By the end of the previous decade, about 16.1 million women in the marketplace had children under age 18 and, of these, about 5.8 million had children under age 6. A significant number work simply because they or their families need the extra income. Some social scientists argue that the women's liberation movement has increased women's awareness of work opportunities. Other researchers contend that the new labor force role of women may itself have stimulated a strong reaction.

As in past decades, most working women are employed full-time, defined as 35 hours or more per week. If unemployed, most are looking for full-time jobs. As women have become a larger proportion of the labor force, they also have become a larger proportion of the unemployed.

The greatest percentage increase in women's labor force participation rates occurred for those with preschoolers, and the number of women who were the mainstay of their own family--very often a family with young children--rose in the 1970s to the highest level ever recorded in the nation's history.[25]

These and other developments have necessitated changes in some basic definitions. For example, the "average American family" had long been defined by government statisticians as a husband who worked, a wife who stayed home, and two children. Yet in 1978, only seven percent of married-couple families fit that definition, while 58 percent of these families had two or more earners. Moreover, standard Census Bureau procedures had for two centuries automatically designated the husband as the "head" of every married-couple household. So significant has the household relationship become as a consequence of women in the workplace that the 1980 census questionnaire was revised to replace the "head of household" category with a format using a reference person.[26]

But while statistics are necessary and important, they must be combined with a sense of justice, an awareness of stereotypic thinking among employers, and other elements affecting employment and earnings, characteristics which are not so easy to quantify. How does one counter the attitudes about women (held by men and by many women, too) exemplified in the following exchange between the Honorable Patricia Schroeder (D-Colorado) and a male constituent?

Schroeder was asked, "What makes you think you can be a woman and a politician too?" Her answer: "Because I have a uterus and a brain and they both work."

Anthropologist Marvin Harris speculates that the women's movement "did not create the working woman; rather, the working woman--especially the working housewife--created women's liberation.... The timing of the feminist outburst at the end of the 1960s marks the moment of collective realization that women, married or not, would have to continue to work as a consequence of inflation. By the early 1960s the baby-boom parents were finding it increasingly difficult to achieve or hold on to middle-class standards of consumption for themselves and their children, and the wife's job had begun to play a crucial role in family finances. As their children approached college age, the burden of medical care, schooling, clothing, and housing for the average family increased far faster than the male breadwinner's salary. Because a growing number of men could no longer support a household on their own, women realized that unless they rebelled they would continue to get the worst of all possible worlds: a dull, boring, dead-end job at work, and cooking, cleaning, child care, and a chauvinist male at home. At the end of the 1960s, women were being drawn through a pneumatic tube. At one end of the tube there was inflation squeezing them out of the home and into the job market; at the other end there was the expanding service-job market, sucking them into a niche specifically designed for literate but inexpensive and docile workers who would accept 60 percent or less of what a man would want for the same job."[27]

Whether Harris' analysis has merit, or whether other theories more capably explain the tremendous increase in the number of working women, the reality of these numbers is neither reversible nor transitory. I am convinced that the ERA initiative was and continues to be a logical response to the inequities women find in the workplace, injustices based upon deep-seated perceptions and prejudices. Feminists of both genders are united in their conviction that only an amendment to the Constitution of the United States will bring about equality of job opportunity and wages in the public and private sectors. The need for protection under the nation's basic document was made manifest when, in 1980, the Republican Party platform abandoned its 40-year-long endorsement of the ERA and adopted the following desiccated statement: "We acknowledge the legitimate efforts of those who support or oppose ratification of the equal rights amendment."[28] And when the amendment was reintroduced in July, 1982, it bore the same language of the March, 1972, resolution: "Equality of rights under the law shall not be denied or abridged by the United States or by any State on account of sex."

I have deliberately excluded from this account the ubiquitous issue of sexual harassment. This pernicious form of misconduct permeates all facets of women in the labor force and will be the subject of my essay in The Serials Librarian, Volume 8, Number 2.

References

1. Women & Work (December 1979), p. 4.
2. Women & Work (February 1980), p. 3.
3. Women & Work (September 1980), p. 3.
4. Women & Work (November 1980), p. 3.
5. Women & Work (February 1980), p. 5.
6. Women & Work (May 1980), p. 1.
7. Black News Digest (July 20, 1981), pp. 1-2.
8. Philippa Strum, "Pink Collar Blues: For Women Who Work, It Still Doesn't Add Up," Perspectives: The Civil Rights Quarterly 12: 33-34 (Summer 1980).
9. Women & Work (March 1980), pp. 1-2.
10. Monthly Labor Review 104: 47 (April 1981).
11. Women & Work (April 1981), p. 1.
12. Supra, note 9, p. 2.
13. Women in Action 10:1 (July/August 1980).
14. Department of State Newsletter (June 1980), p. 24.
15. Occupational Outlook Quarterly 25: 26-27 (Summer 1981).
16. Occupational Outlook Quarterly 24: 14, 16 (Summer 1980).
17. NOAA Magazine 10: 32 (November/December 1980).
18. Family Economics Review (Winter 1981), p. 47.
19. Women in Action 11: 1 (July/August 1981). Women in Action, Spotlight, and La Mesa Redonda merged in October 1981 to form one consolidated newsletter entitled Spotlight On Affirmative Employment Programs.
20. Translog 11: 20 (August 1980).
21. United States Army Aviation Digest 26: 49 (January 1980).
22. The Army Lawyer (July 1980), p. 7. [DA Pam 27-50-91]
23. Women & Work (April 1981), p. 2.
24. Supra, note 18, p. 45.
25. Supra, note 9.
26. See David E. Silver and Jean E. Foster, "The 1980 Census Questionnaire," Statistical Reporter (July 1979), p. 261.
27. Marvin Harris, "Why It's Not the Same Old America," Psychology Today 15: 29-30, 36 (August 1981).
28. The World Almanac & Book of Facts, 1981 (New York: Newspaper Enterprise Association, Inc.), p. 276.

BIBLIOGRAPHIC CONTROL OF

LIBRARY AND INFORMATION SCIENCE LITERATURE*

Guy A. Marco

For a body of literature to be under "bibliographic control," it is necessary for the writings contained in it to be listed in generally available public sources. In other words, there must be one or more sources which answer the question: what has been written? These sources include bibliographies, indexes, abstract services, library catalogs and reviews of the literature. In the field of library and information science, the sources which give us control over the professional literature are very numerous and often extremely complex to use. A search for everything which has been written up to the present time about librarianship would require many hundreds of separate bibliographies and indexes in dozens of languages. Indeed, much of what has been written could not be traced at all, since it was never listed in any public source.

    Whoever might wish to examine all the bibliographic control sources--those bibliographies and indexes which give us a measure of access to library literature--would face an immediate obstacle. The problem is that we lack a guide to those sources of bibliographic control. In this paper the basis for such a guide is offered. Attention is restricted to control sources in European languages, including English.

    Some introductions and background writings about control sources are of interest, although they do not attempt to give comprehensive guidance. The <u>Drexel Library Quarterly</u> issues of January and July 1979 presented a number of useful studies, of which the contribution by Tegler on indexing and abstracting services may be most relevant to the concerns of the present paper.[69a] Heidtmann's practical overview of search tools [35a] offers selective descriptions of major information sources in librarianship, including bibliographies, abstracts and indexes, with a chapter on periodicals.

    Publication in library and information science (LIS hereafter)

---

*Reprinted by permission of the author from <u>Libri</u>, 33:1 (March 1983) 45-60. Copyright © 1983 by Munksgaard, Copenhagen.

is extensive and growing rapidly. The aggregate monographic literature probably exceeds 50,000 titles in European languages. In 1971 it was estimated that there were about 1,000 new books each year [68]; by now it would be reasonable to estimate that number between 1,500 and 2,000. Since there are now about 1,000 active periodicals,[31] the number of articles published annually must exceed 15,000. It appears that there has been a rapid increase in the number of articles per year: in 1972 Coblans offered the figure 5-10,000,[18a] and Dansey, in 1973, suggested about 6,000 as the annual total.[22a] There is no single source which can lead to more than a third of all those documents. Most of the bibliographic control sources deal with small categories of the literature, such as the output of one country, or the writings on a subtopic; furthermore there is a high level of duplicate coverage among the control sources.

The arrangement of entries utilized in the present paper offers one approach to the structure of the control literature. It begins with a discussion of the most comprehensive universal lists of writings, then goes on to selective retrospective lists--universal, regional or national. There follows a description of annual and periodic lists of current publications. Then there are brief sections on indexes to composite works, dissertations and works in progress. Some familiar works are given only brief notices. Details about them are at hand in Walford's Guide to Reference Materials,[72] and Sheehy's Guide to Reference Books.[66] In the bibliography at the end of this paper, items described in Walford or Sheehy are appropriately identified.

Comprehensive Universal Lists: Library Catalogs

In this category there are several important works. None are truly comprehensive, but they include a significant portion of the total LIS literature. Two are catalogs of specialized libraries. The Columbia University (New York) School of Library Service issued a printed form of its card catalog in 1962, with a 1976 supplement [19]; the entire set reproduces nearly 200,000 cards for authors, titles and subjects. However, much of the collection is outside LIS; probably not more than 20,000-25,000 writings would fall into the specific LIS field. From Great Britain we have a comparable inventory, the catalog of the Library Association library.[46] After a basic edition in 1958, covering about 19,000 books, pamphlets and periodicals, there have been supplements in the Library Association Record, and in the Library and Information Bulletin.

Aside from specialized libraries, the catalogs of major national and university libraries may provide useful access to LIS literature. They are useful only if they have subject arrangement or subject indexing; otherwise the basic question--what has been written in LIS?--cannot be efficiently answered. The Library of Congress (Washington) Subject Catalog [70] shows, under relevant topics, all books cataloged by the Library since 1950. The 1970-74 cumulation of this catalog listed about 3,000 monographs under "Library Science" and related headings. Another huge collection, that of the British Library (London), is accessible by subject through a published series,[13] but the subject heading structure is inadequate. In 1964 there appeared a 129-volume set of photolithographed card entries, representing the author-title-subject cards in the University of California at Los Angeles (UCLA); LIS topics are scattered among the 2,700,000 entries.[71]

Although there are several printed catalogs for other great libraries, such as the Bibliothèque Nationale in Paris, the lack of subject indexing places them outside the scope of the present survey.

Bibliographies and Indexes

The only universal bibliography of LIS with any claim to comprehensiveness is the Internationale Bibliographie des Buch- und Bibliothekswesens, published in, or in conjunction with, the Zentralblatt für Bibliothekswesens in Leipzig.[42] This exhaustive work covers European and American writings from 1904; it is however difficult to use because subject headings are very broad and there is no cumulation of indexing.

Selective Retrospective Lists: Universal Scope

In this category there are several works which are based on a subjective appraisal of what has been written in the past. They present what the authors consider to be the most significant literature, without regard to the country of origin. Of these the most useful is Die Fachliteratur zum Buch- und Bibliothekswesen, a compilation of some 5,250 monographs and periodical articles.[30] There are no abstracts or annotations, and citations are inconsistent at times in terms of bibliographic data provided. While selection policy is not clarified, there is an emphasis on very recent materials. In contrast there is the historical orientation of the references in the venerable Handbuch der Bibliothekswissenschaft.[52] This is the principal scholarly encyclopedia of LIS, originally edited by Fritz Milkau, later by Georg Leyh. The authors have prepared learned essays on many aspects of librarianship (rather than information science), and also bibliographic footnotes which provide valuable guidance to all that had been previously written. The limitations of the Handbuch as a guide to the literature are its traditional, humanistic emphasis, and the fact that the footnote references are not cumulated into a systematic bibliography.

The other important encyclopedia in the field, the Encyclopedia of Library and Information Science,[28] still in progress of publication, has some useful bibliographies connected to certain articles, but in many cases the bibliographies are very weak. The editors of the Encyclopedia have not announced any plan to cumulate the article bibliographies into a single listing.

One other selective work may be mentioned: An International Bibliography of Non-Periodical Literature on Documentation and Information, by Hans Zell and Robert Machesney.[73] It emphasizes newer topics within LIS, and is biased toward British and American authors while omitting material in the Russian language entirely. It extends only to 1964.

Selective Retrospective Lists: National or Regional Scope

One of the classic reference works in library science is the Bibliography of Library Economy by Cannons,[17] an extensive subject list of journal articles which appeared in the English language from 1876-1920. There is also a useful list of early books, mostly British and American but with some titles from continental Europe.[15] A more recent compilation of English-language writings is found in two books by Gertrude Schutze [65]; the author takes the limited perspective of practical and administrative aspects, excluding theoretical and historical materials.

A number of surveys have been prepared of the LIS in Latin America; only two are noted here, Emma Linares compiled more than 3,000 items--books and articles--in a 1960 bibliography.[49] And Judith Castañeda gathered 1,603 references for her 1968 bibliography.[18] Much of the Latin American research and writing in LIS has centered in the country of Colombia, home of the Inter-American Library School. There is a good inventory of writings by Colombians, and about Colombian libraries, extending up to 1960.[34]

For India there is a bibliography of library literature for the period 1955-71; it includes 3,550 books and articles, with some annotations.[55] A good portion of the literature produced in Spain was covered by a 1958 publication.[63] For Soviet research there is a good bibliography in German, covering the years 1945-72; it includes 1,819 entires, without annotations.[44]

An interesting new guide presents a selection of important titles in computer science, in English only.[52a] About 800 books published since 1970 are listed by subject, with a list of 450 journals, 100 technical reports, and titles in several other categories.

There are other selective retrospective lists for individual countries, but they are limited to short periods of time, or have other restrictions which limit their usefulness as bibliographic control sources. Of course all such lists would have to be consulted to carry out a comprehensive search of the LIS literature.

Another source of guidance for various LIS topics is the scholarly periodical, through bibliographies appended to the articles. An easy one to use for the purpose of surveying the literature is Library Trends.[48] Each issue of this quarterly journal, which started in 1952, concerns one specific subject; the bibliographic references are therefore clustered, and give a good summary of the principal writings. Other scholarly journal articles are frequently good sources of bibliographies. Anyone looking for bibliographies which are parts of articles in journals will be assisted by the Bibliographic Index,[8] which offers a subject arrangement of bibliographies which are being published in current books and journals of Europe and North America. A comparable work, covering German-language bibliographies which have appeared as parts of books or periodical articles, is also available.[9a]

Still another type of publication with strong selective bibliographies is the annual review of progress. Three fine examples are Advances in Librarianship,[1] Annual Review of Information Science and Technology,[3a] and Five Years' Work in Librarianship.[33]

Annual and Periodic Lists of Current Publications

This is the largest category of the bibliographic control literature. It covers a wide range of types, which will be discussed in this sequence: international indexes and abstract services, national and regional indexes, national bibliographies, and general periodical indexes. Only publications which appear to have the widest interest and utility have been included. Items of more local interest can be located through Sheehy, Walford, or Bibliographical Services Throughout the World.[9]

International Indexes and Abstract Services

About half of the world's LIS journals are indexed in Fachbibliographischer Dienst: Bibliothekswesen [29]; this seems to be the most comprehensive of the current indexes. One recent volume contained about 5,700 entries, for books as well as periodical articles, which would approximate 40 percent of the estimated writings in the field. There are no abstracts.

A very thorough universal coverage of current LIS output is given by Referativnyi zhurnal: informatika, published in Moscow since 1971.[59] It presents nearly 5,000 abstracts per year (in Russian), from journals, books, and conference proceedings. A parallel English-language edition is available.

Another prominent abstract service is the Bulletin signalétique, from Paris. In its section 101, Information scientifique et technique,[35] it gives about 3,000 abstracts per year, drawn from more than a hundred journals, plus books. About 75 percent of the entries are from Great Britain and the United States. This source is available in computer-readable format as well as in print.

About 150 journals in 15 languages are examined by the editors of Informationsdienst Bibliothekswesen, which offers more than 2,500 abstracts each years. Most of the entries come from continental Europe.[39a]

Several key sources for the control of new literature come from Britain and America; these will now be discussed as a group. Library and Information Science Abstracts (LISA) [45] is perhaps the most useful of these. It has been published in London since 1969, as a continuation and expansion of the earlier Library Science Abstracts. LISA presents summaries of articles from about 300 LIS journals, plus a number of book abstracts. The editor of LISA once noted that there were 2,873 abstracts published in one recent year; he observed an emphasis on articles and a relative neglect of monographs and other reports.[27] A source which is often compared to LISA is the bimonthly index Library Literature (LL),[47] one of the series of indexes issued by the H.W. Wilson Company in New York. LL began as a continuation of the Bibliography of Library Economy, already cited [17]; its coverage of journal articles dates from 1921, of books from the 1930's. In comparison with LISA, LL is more comprehensive--with three times as many entries per year--and is stronger is attention to North American periodicals, while LISA is better for European coverage. LL does index about 80 journals from outside the United States, plus 140 American journals. It includes the category of library school student writings, which LISA does not approach. But LISA has abstracts, which LL does not have (though it did give summaries of certain materials until 1957). Edwards found 89 journal titles indexed in common by both LISA and LL, suggesting that either service would suffice for awareness of the so-called core journals in LIS.[27]

Information Science Abstracts [38] is another American service of importance, covering some 400 journals and producing some 4,000 abstracts annually. Its scope of interest is not as limited as the title suggests; there is some coverage of traditional library topics as well. A more restricted scope is found in Computer Abstracts,[20] and in Computer and Control Abstracts,[21] both from London. The technical and mathematical aspects of computer science are emphasized in these services, but librarians will find useful attention to information storage and retrieval topics. The range of Computer and Control Abstracts is very impressive: the 1980 volumes included about 40,000 abstracts.

Unfortunately there is much overlapping and duplication of effort among the international abstract services and indexes. It is disturbing to think of all the abstractors, working independently in so many cities, summarizing the same monographs and articles. The situation resembles the wasteful practice of original cataloging in every library, which prevailed until the emergence of shared cataloging systems. One result of duplication is that a considerable number of less popular journals are not covered by any index. The British and American control sources just cited probably miss as many as half of the world's English-language journals. While many of the unindexed periodicals may justly be regarded as ephemeral, they would contribute unique facts to the literature, and would have research value in appropriate historical or regional contexts.

The same phenomenon, duplication of journals examined, is found among several continental European indexes. Soviet journals covered by Referativnyi zhurnal, already cited,[59] are also indexed by Novaia sovetskaia i inostrannaia literatura.[54] The last-named work also indexes about 50 non-Soviet periodicals, all of which are already covered by several European control sources. In the German Democratic Republic there are three major control sources, of which two have been cited: the Internationale Bibliographie des Buch- und Bibliothekswesens [42] and the Informationsdienst Bibliothekswesen.[39a] The third source is Information und Dokumentation: annotierte Titelliste.[39] A high level of duplication is found among these three works; for example the approximately 100 journals covered by the Titelliste are all included also in the Internationale Bibliographie. The Titelliste does have abstracts, however, while the other does not.

In the Federal Republic of Germany, there is duplication between Fachbibliographischer Dienst, already cited,[29] and the literature reviews in Nachrichten für Dokumentation.[53] Nachrichten encompasses about 100 German-language journals. Some of those journals are Austrian, and thus are also indexed in the Austrian journal Biblos.[11]

A major abstract journal from Poland covers domestic and foreign literature in LIS; it produces about 3,000 abstracts annually.[56] A Czechoslovak service has comparable scope and approximately the same number of abstracts.[7] Of course the Polish and Czech works are of limited value outside their own countries, since their languages are not well known elsewhere. And their coverage appears to duplicate for the most part the coverage of the abstract services already mentioned.

Romania publishes a useful index of modest scope: the Buletin de informare ein bibliologie.[14] It examines about 20 journals, all but three of them from Europe, and gives about 1,800 citations per year. Since 1973 the British periodical Aslib Information has included international lists of LIS publications, numbering about 1,500 each year.[4]

A different sort of guide should be mentioned. IREBI; Indices de revistas de bibliotecologia has been published in Madrid since 1973.[43] Instead of indexing or abstracting the LIS literature, IREBI simply photocopies the contents pages of about 250 journals, allowing the reader to scan quickly the titles of articles which have appeared around the world. A similar publication, covering periodical titles as they are received in the library, has been issued by the College of Librarianship Wales since 1972.[18b] For several years a comparable guide was issued in the United States.[16]

Various topical specializations within LIS have their own literature control sources; a few examples will be cited. The world writings on classification and related subjects are abstracted in the German periodical International Classification.[40] Publications concerning archives are thoroughly indexed in issues of the Boletín de la Dirección General de Archivos, [12] of Madrid. There is an Annual Bibliography of the History of the Printed Book and Libraries, [3] published in the Hague. It presented 3,205 entries in one recent year.

Some important services are generated by the United States Educational Research Information Center (ERIC), publisher of Resources in Education [33] and Current Index to Journals in Education. [12] Both of these ERIC productions have coverage of library matters which are related to primary, secondary or higher education. The citations are available in the ERIC data base, [26] and may be accessed interactively by computer.

A computerized format is also available for LISA, [45] through the DIALOG and ORBIT data networks.

A good yearly review of new American books in LIS appears as a chapter in the American Reference Books Annual (ARBA). [2] In one recent ARBA there were descriptions with critical comments for about 148 new monographs on many library topics.

To close this section a unique and valuable work will be mentioned. It is SPEL, Selected Publications in European Languages, issued by the College of Librarianship Wales. [67] This is a very selective review of certain continental writings, with background information on the countries and topics, and with full abstracts in English.

National and Regional Indexes

Many countries have produced, at least for a time, indexes of their own LIS output. Only a few of the prominent examples are noted here, in alphabetical order by country.

Argentina: Bibliografia bibliotecológica Argentina, 1968/69- [6]
Austria: Biblos, "Bibliographie," 1952- [11]
Brazil: Bibliografia brasileira de documentação, 1960- [62]
Bulgaria: Bibliotekoznanie, bibliografiia, knigoznanie nauchna informatsiia, 1968- [10]
Hungary: Magyar könyvtári szakirodalom bibliográfiája, 1973- [51]
Hungary: Hungarian Library and Information Science Abstracts, 1972- [36]
India: Indian Library Science Abstracts, 1967- [37]
Poland: Bibliografia bibliografii i nauki o ksiazce, 1947- [5]

LIS in the Scandinavian countries is indexed by Nordisk BDI-indeks, issued since 1979 as a cooperative venture by the library schools and information centers of Denmark, Finland, Norway and Sweden. [39a]

National Bibliographies

It is not possible to discuss, in the confines of this paper, the coverage of library and information science literature in the various national bibliographies. However, it may be observed that when national bibliographies have adequate subject indexing they become valuable components of the control literature. In some countries--for example in the Republics of the Soviet Union, in Bulgaria and in Czechoslovakia--sections of the national bibliography are devoted to lists of university dissertations and to indexing of articles in periodicals. In the developing countries, it is often the case that the only notice of a book or document in LIS will be found in the national bibliography.

General Periodical Indexes

National and international indexes to periodical articles are a major source in locating specialized materials, of which the LIS literature is one example. There are at least three reasons for taking note of these indexes. One is that their total time span is likely to be much longer than that of specialized LIS indexes. Another reason is that some of them are more timely in current publication than the LIS counterparts. And--perhaps most important--they will present a facet of the LIS literature which may not be found in the specialized control sources. That facet is the body of material about libraries or information which appears in periodicals of general interest, such as the news magazines and literary magazines. The two oldest ongoing indexes are the German IBZ,[41] dating from 1896, and the American Readers' Guide to Periodical Literature,[58] dating from 1901. Another old and valued work is the Dansk tidsskrift-indeks, [23] recently expanded to cover indexing of newspaper items, under the name Dansk artikel indeks. Sheehy or Walford can offer other possibilities in this genre.

Indexes to Composite Works

Only one title stands out in this category: J. Periam Danton's Index to Festschriften in Librarianship, with its supplement.[24] The first volume included about 3,300 essays, from 283 collected volumes published from 1864 to 1966. It drew from 22 countries and 16 languages. In the 1979 supplement, another 1,500 essays from 143 composite works were added, taking the coverage up to 1975; 23 countries and 19 languages are represented. To judge from the account given by Danton, in the preface to the 1979 supplement, his work has superseded all other compilations of its kind.

Dissertations and Theses

There are in each country various guides to academic writings, on all subjects, of which perhaps the best known and most useful is the American compilation Dissertation Abstracts International.[25] Doctoral dissertations, in LIS and in other fields, are summarized and ordering information for microfilm copies is given. Comparable bibliographies for other countries are too numerous for identification here; they are noted in Sheehy and Walford. As already suggested, such inventories are sometimes published as parts of national bibliographies.

Specialized lists of dissertations in LIS are not so numerous. For American universities there is a comprehensive bibliography by Davis,[24a] and an extensive annotated list by Schlacter and Thomison which covers 1925 to 1972.[64] At the master's degree level, there are lists of theses from American library schools, including the category of master's "papers," in Library Literature,[47] and also in two cumulations by Shirley Magnotti.[50] Peter J. Taylor has compiled a list of academic theses in LIS written in the United Kingdom and Ireland, from 1950-1974.[69] Current annual lists for the U.K. are published by Aslib.[3b]

Research in Progress

The International Federation for Documentation (FID) has gathered and disseminated information about research and development projects since 1971.[32] This service would be more effective if greater cooperation from researchers and organizations could be obtained. Research being done in the United Kingdom, and by British nationals abroad, is recorded in the semi-annual RADIALS Bulletin, issued by the Library Association.[57] Current projects in the Federal Republic of Germany are listed in the annual Forschungs- und Entwicklungsprojekte in Informationswissenschaft und -praxis [34a]; these are classified, indexed lists with summaries.

Concluding Observations

Taken as a group, the 80 sources of bibliographic control identified in this paper give satisfactory access to the "core" literature of LIS. They are particularly effective in coverage of periodicals, with the exception of local journals and others of an ephemeral nature. Monographs are less adequately controlled. There is a great deal of duplication and overlapping among the world's control sources.

But one type of LIS writing--which may well belong to the "core"--is scarcely controlled at all. This is the conference paper (unless the conference proceedings are published). There is no list of presentations made at meetings of the American Library Association, for example, nor at meetings of most national and local associations in the United States. Until recently, the situation regarding IFLA conference papers was equally dismal, but a new publication by the Royal School of Librarianship in Copenhagen has provided both a retrospective index from 1968-1978, and current coverage.[9b] This invaluable contribution to bibliographic control is to be issued in a computer-readable format in the future. Yet the world-wide picture of conference papers still suggests that much of important exchange of information which takes place at library and information meetings is lost to bibliographic control, and thus to the profession at large.

Abstracts, as well as title lists, are needed for conference papers. One may envision a distinct new publication which would endeavor to gather such papers and summarize them. But the vision could well have a grander dimension: why should we not visualize a comprehensive international registry of LIS writing, including what is at present covered in LISA and other control works, and adding those categories which are now outside the net of control? Local journals, book reviews, academic writing, conference papers, government documents, consultant reports--all these could be and ought to be made intellectually accessible to the profession which specializes in information. For a model outside our field, we may cite the outstanding bibliographical achievement which serves the world of musical scholarship: the Répertoire international de littérature musicale (RILM Abstracts),[60] which has since 1968 cumulated and abstracted material on music from the global community. Forty-two national committees, and some 25 volunteer editors for special topics, cooperate in discovering and summarizing a range of material which would otherwise be lost.

We are practitioners in a young discipline. The emergence of a significant scholarly literature about libraries and information is a phenomenon of the past half century. We have done rather well in bringing much of the vital literature under bibliographic control. But there is much more to be done: and as information and bibliographic experts, we ought to be prepared for the challenge.

Bibliography (with Citations to Sheehy and Walford)

1. Advances in Librarianship. New York: Academic Press, 1970- (annual). Walford, p. 56.
2. American Reference Books Annual; ARBA. Littleton, Colorado: Libraries Unlimited, 1970- (annual). Sheehy AA380, Walford p. 96.
3. Annual Bibliography of the History of the Printed Book and Libraries, 1970- The Hague: Nijhoff, 1973- (annual). Sheehy AA268.
3a. Annual Review of Information Science and Technology. Washington: American Society for Information Science, 1966- (annual) Sheehy supplement p. 246.
3b. Aslib. Index to Theses Accepted for Higher Degrees in the Universities of Great Britain and Ireland, 1950/51--London: Aslib, 1953- (annual) Sheehy AH44. Classified, with subject and author indexes.
4. Aslib Information. London: Aslib, 1973- (monthly).

5. Bibliografia bibliografii i nauki o ksiazce. Bibliographia poloniae bibliographica. Warsaw: Biblioteka Narodowa, 1947- (annual).
6. Bibliografia bibliotecológica Argentina, 1968/69- Since 1970 published as part of the journal Documentación bibliotecológica. Bahia Blanca: Centro de Documentación Bibliotecológica, 1970- (annual).
7. Bibliografické prehledy z oblasti technickeho knihovnictvi a vedeckotechnickych informací. Prague: UVTEI, 1969- (bimonthly).
8. Bibliographic Index; a Cumulative Bibliography of Bibliographies, 1937- New York: H. W. Wilson, 1938- (quarterly; annual and other cumulations). Sheehy AA15, Walford p. 10.
9. Bibliographical Services Throughout the World, 1970-74, by Marcelle Beaudiquez. Paris: Unesco, 1977. Earlier volumes in this series covered 1950-59, 1960-64, and 1965-69. Sheehy AA16, Walford, pp. 10-11.
9a. Bibliographie der deutschen Bibliographien. Leipzig: Deutsche Bücherei, 1954- (monthly).
9b. A Bibliography of IFLA Conference Papers 1968-1978. Copenhagen: IFLA Clearinghouse, Royal School of Librarianship, 1979. Annual supplements.
10. Bibliotekoznanie, bibliografiia, knigoznanie nauchna informatsiia, 1968- Sofia: Narodna Biblioteka, 1970- (annual).
11. Biblos. Vienna: Gesellschaft der Freunde der Österreichischen Nationalbibliothek, 1952- .
12. Boletín de la dirección general de archivos y bibliotecas. Madrid: Ministerio de Educación y Ciencia, 1952- (bimonthly).
13. British Museum. Department of Printed Books. Subject Index of the Modern Works Added to the Library, 1881-1900; ed. G. K. Fortescue. London: British Museum, 1902-1903. 3v. Continued by five-year supplements, which are enumerated in Sheehy AA101 and Walford p. 44.
14. Buletin de informare in bibliologie. Bucharest: Biblioteca Centrala, 1960- (2 per year).
15. Burton, M.; Vosburgh, M. E. A Bibliography of Librarianship; Classifed and Annotated Guide to the Library Literature of the World (Excluding Slavonic and Oriental Languages). London: Library Association, 1934. Reprinted--New York: Franklin, 1970. Walford p. 52.
16. CALL: Current Awareness--Library Literature. Framingham, Massachusetts: Goldstein Associates, 1972-75. Walford p. 53.
17. Cannons, Harry G. T. Bibliography of Library Economy; a Classified Index to the Professional Periodical Literature in the English Language ... from 1876 to 1920. Chicago: American Library Association, 1927. Reprinted--New York: Franklin, 1970. Sheehy AB1, Walford p. 53. Note also: Anne Harwell Jordan and Melbourne Jordan, Cannons' Bibliography of Library Economy, 1876-1920: an Author Index with Citations (Metuchen, New Jersey: Scarecrow Press, 1976).

18. Castañeda, Judith. Bibliografía bibliotecológica latinoamericano, Parte II: Analítica de publicaciones periódicas. Medellín: Escuela Interamericana de Bibliotecología, 1968.
18a. Coblans, Herbert. "Progress in Documentation: The Literature of Librarianship and Documentation: the Periodicals and Their Bibliographic Control." Journal of Documentation, 28-1 (March 1972): 56-66.
18b. College of Librarianship Wales. Current Contents. Aberystwyth: CLW, 1972- (weekly).
19. Columbia University. School of Library Service. Dictionary Catalog of the Library. Boston: G.K. Hall, 1962. 7v. Supplement, 1976. 4v. The supplement covers materials added 1962-1975. Walford p. 52.
20. Computer Abstracts. London: Technical Information Company, 1957- (monthly). Sheehy EJ200a.
21. Computer and Control Abstracts. Science Abstracts, Section C. (Title varies) London: Institute of Electrical Engineers, 1966- (monthly). Sheehy EJ164.
22. Current Index to Journals in Education, 1969- New York: CCM Information Sciences, 1969- (monthly; semiannual and annual cumulative indexes). A companion publication to number 61, below. Both are parts of the ERIC program. Sheehy CB81.
22a. Dansey, P. "A Bibliometric Survey of Primary and Secondary Information Science Literature." Aslib Proceedings, 25 (July 1973): 252-63.
23. Dansk tidsskrift-indeks. Copenhagen: Dansk Bibliografisk Kontor, 1916-- (annual) Sheehy AE202. Superseded by Dansk artikel indeks.
24. Danton, J. Periam. Index to Festschriften in Librarianship. New York: Bowker, 1970. Sheehy AB2, Walford p. 52. The supplement is Index to Festschriften in Librarianship, 1967-75, by J. Periam Danton and Jane F. Pulis (Munich: K.G. Saur, 1979).
24a. Davis, Charles H. Doctoral Dissertations in Library Science, 1930-1980. Ann Arbor, Michigan: University Microfilms, 1980.
25. Dissertation Abstracts International. Ann Arbor, Michigan: University Microfilms, 1938- (monthly; annual indexes; retrospective index). An important adjunct is the retrospective Comprehensive Dissertation Index, 1861-1972, and its supplements. Title and coverage vary. Sheehy AH14, Walford p. 127.
26. Educational Resources Information Center (ERIC). A program of the U.S. Office of Education, which includes a computerized data base of materials related to education, and various printed indexes and bibliographies. See numbers 22 and 61. Sheehy CB80-CB81.
27. Edwards. T.E. A Comparative Analysis of the Major Abstracting and Indexing Services for Library and Information Science ... Paris: Unesco, 1975. Walford p. 53.
28. Encyclopedia of Library and Information Science. New York & London: Dekker, 1968- (in progress; volume 30, "Taiwan

Communication and Education

29. Fachbibliographischer Dienst: Bibliothekswesen. Berlin: Deutscher Bibliotheksverband, 1965- (annual). Walford p. 52.
30. Die Fachliteratur zum Buch- und Bibliothekswesen. 9. Ausg. Munich: Verlag Dokumentation, 1970. Walford p. 9. A shortened version: Bibliographie des Bibliothekswesens; Bibliography of Library Science. 3. Ausg. Munich & Detroit: Verlag Dokumentation & Gale Research, 1970.
31. Fédération Internationale de Documentation (FID). Library, Documentation and Archives Serials. 4th ed. The Hague: FID, 1975. Sheehy AB18, Walford p. 56.
32. ———. R&D Projects in Documentation and Librarianship. The Hague: FID, 1971- (bimonthly).
33. Five Years' Work in Librarianship, 1961-65. London: Library Association, 1968. Earlier five-year volumes 1951-55, 1956-60; continuing the Year's Work in Librarianship, issued 1928-1950. Succeeded by British Librarianship and Information Science, 1966-1970. Sheehy AB13-AB15, Walford p. 56.
34. Florén Lozano, Luis. Bibliografía bibliotecológica colombiana publicada hasta 1960. Medellín: Editorial Universidad de Antioquia, 1964.
34a. Forschungs- und Entwicklungsprojekte in Informationswissenschaft und -praxis 1977- . Frankfurt am Main: Gesellschaft für Information und Dokumentation MBH (GID), 1977- (annual).
35. France. Centre National de la Recherche Scientifique. Bulletin signalétique. Section 101. Information scientifique et technique. Paris, 1970- (monthly). Sheehy BA91, Walford p. 523.
35a. Heidtmann, Frank. Wie finde ich bibliothekarische Literatur. Berlin: Berlin Verlag, 1976.
36. Hungarian Library and Information Science Abstracts. Budapest: Centre for Library Science and Methodology, 1972- (2 per year).
37. Indian Library Science Abstracts. Calcutta: Indian Association of Special Libraries and Information Centres, 1967- (quarterly).
38. Information Science Abstracts. Philadelphia: Documentation Abstracts, Inc., 1969- (quarterly). Title and sponsoring body vary. Sheehy AB13, Walford p. 1.
39. Information und Dokumentation: annotierte Titelliste. Berlin: Zentralinstitut für Information und Dokumentation der D.D.R., 1966- (monthly). Former titles: Schnellinformation; Informationsdienst Information.
39a. Informationsdienst Bibliothekswesen. Leipzig: Deutsche Bücherei, 1971- (six per year).
40. International Classification. Munich: Verlag Dokumentation, 1974- (2 per year).
41. Internationale Bibliographie der Zeitschriftenliteratur (IBZ). Osnabrück: Felix Dietrich, 1965- (2 per year). A continuation of two earlier indexes published by Dietrich: Bibliographie der deutschen Zeitschriftenliteratur, 1897-1964; and

Bibliographie der fremdsprachigen Zeitschriftenliteratur, 1911-1964. Sheehy AE162, AE163, AE205, Walford p. 151.
42. Internationale Bibliographie des Buch- und Bibliothekswesens. Leipzig: Harrassowitz, 1923-41. Preceded by annual supplements to Zentralblatt für Bibliothekswesens covering 1904-12, 1922-25; and continued by supplements in the same journal. Sheehy AA25, Walford p. 9.
43. IREBI; Indices de revistas de bibliotecología. Madrid: Oficina de Educación Iberoamericano, 1973- (quarterly).
44. Krause, Friedhilde. Sowjtisches Bibliotheks- und Buchwesen: Bibliographie 1945-1972. Berlin: Deutsche Staatsbibliothek, 1975.
45. Library and Information Science Abstracts (LISA). London: Library Association, 1969- (bimonthly). An expanded continuation of Library Science Abstracts, 1950-1968. Sheehy AB12, Walford p. 53.
46. Library Association (London). Catalogue of the Library. London: The Association, 1953. Walford p. 53.
47. Library Literature, 1921/32- New York: H.W. Wilson, 1934- (quarterly through 1968, then bimonthly; annual cumulations). Subtitle and publisher vary. Sheehy AB10, Walford p. 53.
48. Library Trends. Urbana, Illinois: University of Illinois, Graduate School of Library Science, 1952- (quarterly). Walford p. 57.
49. Linares, Emma. Bibliografía bibliotecológica. Washington: Pan American Union, 1960. Sheehy AB7.
50. Magnotti, Shirley. Master's Theses in Library Science, 1960-1969. Troy, New York: Whitston, 1975.
51. Magyar könyvtári szakirodalom bibliográfiája. Budapest: Könyvtártudományi és Módszertani Központ, 1973- (quarterly).
52. Milkau, Fritz, ed. Handbuch der Bibliothekswissenschaft. 2d ed., ed. Georg Leyh. Wiesbaden: Harrassowitz, 1950-65. 3v. in 4. (1st ed. 1931-42). Sheehy AB26.
52a. Myers, Darlene. Computer Science Resources: a Guide to Professional Literature. White Plains, New York: Knowledge Industry Publications, 1981.
53. Nachrichten für Dokumentation. Frankfurt: Deutsche Gesellschaft für Dokumentation, 1950- (bimonthly).
53a. Nordisk BDI-indeks. Pohjoismainen KDI-indeksi. Copenhagen (etc.), 1979- (semi-annual).
54. Novaia sovetskaia i inostrannaia literatura po kul'ture i iskusstvu. Bibliotekovedenu i bibliografovedevie: [1] Sovetskaia literatura, [2] inostrannaia literatura. Moscow: Lenin Library, 1974- (Title varies).
55. Prasher, Ram Gopal. Indian Library Literature: an Annotated Bibliography. New Delhi: Today & Tomorrow's Printers and Publishers, 1971. Sheehy AA715, Walford p. 53.
56. Przeglad pismiennictwa zagadnien informacji. Warzaw: Institut Informacii Naukowei, Techniczei i Ekonomicznej, 1962- (monthly).
57. RADIALS Bulletin: Research and Development--Information and Library Science. London: Library Association, 1974- (semiannual).

58. Readers' Guide to Periodical Literature. New York: H. W. Wilson, 1901- Frequency and cumulations vary. Sheehy AE169, Walford p. 157.
59. Referativnyi zhurnal. Informatika. Moscow: All-Union Institute of Scientific and Technical Information, 1963- (monthly). English edition: Informatics Abstracts.
60. Répertoire international de littérature musicale. RILM Abstracts of Music Literature, 1967- . New York: International RILM Center, 1967- . A publication of the International Musicological Society, International Association of Music Libraries, and American Council of Learned Societies. Sheehy BH58, Walford, p. 402.
61. Resources in Education. Washington: U.S. Department of Health, Education and Welfare, 1966- (monthly; semiannual and annual cumulated indexes). A companion publication to number 22; part of the program of ERIC, number 26.
62. Rio de Janeiro. Instituto Brasileiro de Bibliografia e Documentaçao. Bibliografia brasileira de documentaçao. Rio de Janeiro: El Instituto, 1960-
63. Ruiz Cabriada, Agustín, Bio-bibliografía del cuerpo facultativo de archiveros, bibliotecarios y arqueólogos, 1858-1958. Madrid: El Cuerpo, 1958. Sheehy AB92.
64. Schlachter, G. A.; Thomison, D. Library Science Dissertations, 1925-1972; an Annotated Bibliography. Littleton, Colorado: Libraries Unlimited, 1974. Walford p. 56.
65. Schutze, Gertrude. Documentation Source Book. New York: Scarecrow Press, 1965. Supplemented by: Information and Library Science Source Book (Metuchen, New Jersey: Scarecrow Press, 1972). More than 2,000 summaries of articles, books and reports. Sheehy AB185, Walford p. 98.
66. Sheehy, Eugene. Guide to Reference Books. 9th ed. Chicago: American Library Association, 1976. Supplement, 1980. Second Supplement, 1982.
67. SPEL; Selected Publications in European Languages. Aberystwyth: College of Librarianship Wales, 1973-
68. Taylor, L. "Library Science Literature." ASLIB Proceedings, 23-9 (September 1971): 474-485.
69. Taylor, Peter J. Library and Information Studies in the United Kingdom and Ireland, 1950-1974; an Index to Theses. London: Aslib, 1976.
69a. Tegler, Patricia. "The Indexes and Abstracts of Library and Information Science." Drexel Library Quarterly, 15-3 (July 1979): 2-23.
70. United States. Library of Congress. Subject Catalog. Washington: Library of Congress, 1950- (quarterly; annual and five-year cumulations). Title varies. Sheehy AA99, Walford p. 46.
71. University of California, Los Angeles. Library. Dictionary Catalog. Boston: G.K. Hall, 1963. 129v. Walford p. 45.
72. Walford, A.J. Guide to Reference Materials, Vol. 3: Generalities, Languages, the Arts and Literature. 3d ed. London: Library Association, 1977. Sheehy AA404.
73. Zell, Hans; Machesney, Robert. An International Bibliography

of Non-periodical Literature on Documentation and Information. Oxford: Maxwell, 1965. Sheehy AB191.

This is a revised version of a paper presented at the 47th General Conference of IFLA (Leipzig, 1981). It incorporates the material of an earlier paper which was presented at the 46th General Conference of IFLA (Manila, 1980). Grateful acknowledgment is offered to Leif Kajberg, Danmarks Biblioteksskole, for providing valuable suggestions and information.

THE MUSE IN THE STACKS:

A SURVEY OF POETRY IN PUBLIC LIBRARIES*

Darby Penney

The bulk of modern poetry is published by little magazines or by small presses in book form. Few public libraries make an effort to collect small press materials widely, nor can they realistically be expected to, given the vast number and sometimes unpredictable publication schedules of these materials. Even the more sophisticated little magazines, those usually published under the auspices of a university and having a more professional appearance than the more common basement-mimeographed little magazine, are seldom found in any but major metropolitan public libraries. Given the budgetary limitations under which most public libraries operate, as well as staff and space restrictions, it is unrealistic to expect public libraries to acquire many of these publications, desirable as they may be.

In addition to limitations of money, staff and space, the fact that small press publications are not widely reviewed in the journals used in the selection process, creates a barrier to their inclusion in the collection.[2] Few public librarians have the time or inclination to search out and order obscure small press materials. The small press books and little magazines are not widely indexed, [3] which might tend to make librarians see them as of limited value. For these practical reasons, and because many of the publications are politically or socially radical, they are not favored by many public librarians. This is unfortunate as new developments in modern poetry are unveiled here, and the public library user is denied access to these avant garde works. Because these publications are not widely available in public libraries, library users are therefore exposed to an unrepresentative sample of modern American poetry.

Some poetry is published in mass circulation magazines, but far less than a generation ago. Publications such as The New Yorker, Harper's and Ms. publish poetry, but they are necessarily selective, as they can print only a small amount of poetry. These

---

*Reprinted by permission of the author and publisher from Public Library Quarterly, 3:3 (Fall 1982) 33-39. Copyright © 1982 by The Haworth Press, Inc. All rights reserved.

magazines are generally available in public libraries, and poetry-loving patrons can turn to them. Here again, though, the user will encounter the work of major or established poets rather than work from all parts of the poetry spectrum. When one considers the number of books printed each year, the major New York presses publish very little poetry. Only major poets, those whose works are studied in colleges and universities, can hope to have their manuscripts published by the large houses.

In order to discover whether the plight of poetry in public libraries has improved in the intervening years, the modern American poetry collections in five New York State public libraries were recently evaluated. It was a challenge to devise a checklist of modern American poetry that would accurately gauge the quality of collections in public libraries, given the limited number of available volumes of published poetry. Twenty titles published since 1970 of a sufficient variety to serve as a useful evaluation tool were selected. Hard to find titles, books published by small presses, and works by little-known poets were deliberately not included. The works selected were published by major New York houses or by university presses (with the exception of Allen Ginsberg's The Fall of America, published by City Lights). Most had won a recent award; a Pulitzer Prize, a National Book Award, a National Book Critic's Circle Award, or the Yale Series of Younger Poets Award. Those few titles not award winners were selected from The Reader's Advisor (12th edition) or recent Public Library Catalog Supplements. Of the twenty volumes selected, seventeen were works by individual poets and three were anthologies. Of the individual works, three were the collected works of that poet. These books were chosen specifically because they were the works of major poets.

After compiling the checklist, five public libraries were visited and the list checked against the card catalogs of each. The findings are summarized in Tables 1 and 2. The public libraries visited represent libraries serving both urban and rural populations. Because of the small size of the sample, no claims can be made about the applicability of the findings to public libraries in general. In addition to checking the libraries' collections, the twenty titles were searched through Book Review Index and statistics compiled on the number of reviews each one received in five important library review journals. These findings are summarized in Tables 3 and 4.

The five libraries surveyed included Library A, with a total of 275,829 volumes, serving an urban population of 114,000. It is the central reference collection for a library system.

Library B, an association library serving a small town and the surrounding rural area (total population 35,000), has a collection of 55,268 volumes.

Library C, the central reference collection for a system in a largely rural county and with an urban population of 64,500, has 159,770 volumes.

Table 1: Selected Modern American Poetry Titles Found in Five Public Libraries

	Lib A	Lib B	Lib C	Lib D	Lib E	Total
1. Ashbery, John. *Self Portrait in a Convex Mirror* (Viking, 1975)	x			x		2
2. Bishop, Elizabeth. *Geography III* (Farrar, Straus & Giroux, 1976)	x	x	x	x		4
3. Broumas, Olga. *Beginning With 0* (Yale University Press, 1977)				x		1
4. Eberhart, Richard. *Collected Poems* (Oxford University Press, 1976)	x	x	x	x		4
5. Forché, Carolyn. *Gathering the Tribes* (Yale University Press, 1976)	x		x			2
6. Ginsberg, Allen. *The Fall of America* (City Lights, 1976)		x				1
7. Hacker, Marilyn. *Presentation Piece* (Penguin, 1974)	x		x	x	x	4
8. Hewitt, Geoff, ed. *Quickly Aging Here* (Anchor, 1969)			x	x		2
9. Kumin, Maxine. *House, Bridge, Fountain, Gate* (Viking, 1975)	x			x		2
10. Lowell, Robert. *Dolphin* (Farrar, Straus & Giroux, 1973)				x		1
11. Merrill, James. *Divine Comedies* (Atheneum, 1976)	x		x	x		3
12. Monaco, R., ed. *New American Poetry* (McGraw-Hill, 1973)			x	x		2
13. Nemerov, Howard. *Collected Poems* (U. of Chicago Press, 1977)	x			x		2
14. Rukeyser, Muriel. *Breaking Open* (Random House, 1973)	x		x	x		3
15. Ryan, Michael. *Threats Instead of Trees* (Yale University Press, 1974)						0
16. Sarton, May. *Collected Poems* (Norton, 1974)			x	x		2
17. Sexton, Anne. *That Awful Rowing Towards God* (Houghton-Mifflin, 1975)	x	x	x	x		4
18. Snyder, Gary. *Turtle Island* (New Directions, 1974)	x		x	x		3
19. Stanton, Maura. *Snow on Snow* (Yale University Press, 1975)				x		1
20. Waldman, Anne, ed. *Another World* (Bobbs Merrill, 1971)	x		x	x		3

Table 2: Total Volumes of 20 in Each Library's Collection

Lib A	Lib B	Lib C	Lib D	Lib E
12	3	13	17	1

Table 3: Reviews Received Among Five Major Review Journals

Ashbery	1	Merrill	0
Bishop	2	Monaco	1
Broumas	3	Nemerov	2
Eberhart	1	Rukeyser	2
Forché	5	Ryan	1
Ginsberg	1	Sarton	1
Hacker	1	Sexton	5
Hewitt	2	Snyder	1
Kumin	5	Stanton	1
Lowell	1	Waldman	2

Table 4: Titles Reviewed Per Journal

Booklist	5
Choice	8
Kirkus	5
Library Journal	10
New York Times Book Review	11

Library D holds 316,961 volumes and is the central reference library for a system. As a county library, it serves a population of 161,078 which is both urban and rural.

Library E holds 107,526 volumes and serves a city of 62,900.[4]

The three libraries which are central reference collections for systems owned more of the titles than did the other libraries. Library D owned seventeen of the twenty books, while Libraries A and C had twelve and thirteen respectively. Library D's rating is respectable, library A and C's scores are low but adequate. These findings tend to indicate that these libraries, and the systems to which they belong, are making an effort to develop sound collections of modern American poetry. The other libraries made altogether dismal showings. Library B had three of the titles, Library E only one.

Two reasons for this dismal showing are possible. Both are small libraries with small staffs and small budgets and their limited resources are more immediately necessary for more practical matters than poetry collection development. Another explanation for the lack of modern poetry in these collections is the availability of such material through the library systems. One librarian interviewed indicated that one reason the systems were formed was to supply patrons of small libraries with books otherwise unavailable to them. While this system is certainly preferable to a lack of access to these materials, it still deprives the library user of the delight of happening upon a new poet while browsing in the stacks. People familiar with interlibrary loan services and with poetry can and will request what they cannot find. Other users, not familiar with poetry and with procedures in the library, may not be as fortunate. Despite the budgetary restrictions these libraries face, and the possibility of access to materials through their library systems, the findings seem to show an attitude of indifference and even neglect toward poetry on the part of these libraries.

Library B's poor showing was surprising, as the poetry section takes up a disproportionate amount of the library's scarce shelf space. The poetry section was examined more closely. A random sample of fifty volumes was selected off the shelf, and all but one of them had a publication date beyond 1950 and 1965. One can surmise that a former librarian was fond of poetry and paid special attention to developing that area of the collection. Apparently successors do not share that dedication to poetry for not only have they neglected to develop the collection properly, they have neglected a weeding that is long overdue.

In Katz's 1968 report, he suggested that one reason for public libraries' poor poetry collections might be the dearth of reviews in the journals most often used as selection tools in public libraries.[1] He found that a number of the titles on the checklist in his survey did not even have an entry in Book Review Digest. In this area, at least, there has been some improvement. All the titles on the checklist were reviewed widely, most of them in at least a dozen sources. Most of these reviews, however, appeared in little magazines, publications not usually used by public librarians as selection tools. None of the five reviewing publications surveyed (Booklist, Choice, Kirkus, Library Journal and the New York Times Book Review) was well represented in the number of titles from the survey which they reviewed. The New York Times Book Review had the highest rating (eleven) followed closely by Library Journal (ten). None of these were obscure titles but were major works which merited reviews. The findings here suggest a lack of serious commitment on the part of these journals to reviewing poetry.

In order to investigate a possible connection between the number of reviews received and the number of libraries in which a particular volume was held, statistics were also tabulated on the number of reviews each book received among the five journals.

These appear in Table 3. The figures fail to show a connection between the number of reviews received and the number of copies owned by the libraries. Some books were selected even though they received few or no reviews. Still others were heavily reviewed but were not selected by the libraries.

Based on the results of the survey, several conclusions were reached which can take the form of recommendations for improving poetry collections.

It is recommended that libraries purchase additional poetry titles, the works of major modern poets in particular. It is also suggested that their poetry collections be weeded. Since libraries have space problems, they might wish to concentrate on developing solid collections of the major modern poets and to discard older, extraneous works. By concentrating on major poets, librarians could rely on their library systems to provide them with access to older or more obscure works.

It is also suggested that, in addition to relying on the standard review media for poetry selection, that the larger libraries use the reviews that appear in Poetry, The Small Press Review and other little magazines that review poetry. Besides serving as selection aids, these magazines will enrich the libraries' periodical collections.

Of most importance, I would urge each library to add a poetry-loving librarian to its staff.

References

1. Katz, Bill. "Statistical Wailing Wall: A Nationwide Survey" Library Journal, June 1, 1968, p. 2203-2208.
2. Booklist has initiated a "Small Press Poetry" review column which appears quarterly, and Library Journal runs an annual round-up of small press book reviews.
3. One exception is Sander W. Zulauf and E. M. Ciffelli's Index to American Periodical Verse, (Metuchen, N.J.: Scarecrow Press, 1975 to date), an annual index which covers a number of little magazines.
4. Information from American Library Directory (31st ed.), New York: R.R. Bowker, 1978.

INFORMATION TECHNOLOGY AND THE MYTH OF ABUNDANCE*

Anthony Smith

> Inevitably, the culture within which we live shapes and limits our imaginations, and by permitting us to do and think and feel in certain ways makes it increasingly unlikely or impossible that we should do or think or feel in ways that are contradictory or tangential to it.
>
> --Margaret Mead
> Male and Female [1]

What really is a technological revolution? And who are the revolutionaries? What are the criteria for a historical process to be so described? Where do we look for the results? I cannot claim that this essay will answer these questions, nor even that they are precisely enough formulated for useful answers to be provided. But it might be possible to construct a new kind of mental picture of the phenomenon of technological transformation, of its driving motivations and cultural consequences, by looking at certain aspects of current developments in information technology within a historical setting. The advent of printing had obviously "a great deal to do" with the rise of the nation-state, and Elizabeth Eisenstein's researches and narrative,[2] as well as those of Martin and Febre,[3] have helped to fill out the picture of a late Renaissance "information revolution." An age in which a new transforming technology is taking hold must, almost self-evidently, express its most profound social, economic, and political changes in terms of that technology --so closely and complicatedly, that historians inevitably try, but fail, to disentangle the resulting skeins of cause and effect. Was there a drive for empire that altered the technologies of European navigation in the fifteenth and sixteenth centuries? Was imperialism a result of technology-push or economic-pull? Do the processes of "take-up" of innovation relate to the dominant creative, emotional, and intellectual mindset of an age, so that the tracks may be found again through later research?

Such questions are the permanent concern of social history,

---

*Reprinted by permission of the author and publisher from Daedalus, 111:4 (Fall 1982) 1-16. The Journal of the American Academy of Arts and Sciences, Cambridge, MA.

but need to be asked also in the present, while the transforming
process is underway. The intention of this essay is to suggest that
there exists a great unifying social and cultural urge behind a technological revolution, particularly one that relates to information.
The search for the emotional satisfactions of the vernacular and the
evolution of the feeling of nationhood were indeed tied to the technology of "moving letters." The Victorian bourgeois' obsession
with the perfect mechanical reproduction of images in movement,
sound, and hue had some psychic link with the evolution of the representational technologies of film, phonograph, telegraph, and the
wireless. Today, a surging belief in the perfect development of the
individual as consumer is somehow discovering its own confirmation
in the development of technologies of information abundance; but that
individualism is tied also to a new imperialism or transnationalism
in the growth of the phenomenon of cultural dependence of the South
upon the North. The new information technology is reconfirming
the world vision of the developed world, reestablishing its confidence as the primary subject of culture, as the developing nations
fall victim to the cultural pressures of external data flow. Thus,
if this argument works, information technology leads toward the displacement of nationhood, of national cultures.

I

We have all become modishly aware that the information environment, so to speak, of the late twentieth century individual is in the
course of being transformed. News columns with titles that play
neatly on the words _revolution, age, galaxy, shock,_ appear monthly.
But we remain prisoners still of an essentially Victorian idea of the
requisite constituents of social change, in the sense that we tend to
predicate the transformation upon the technology. We relate and
chart development according to a measure of machinery, alongside
the evolution of inventions. So numerous are the gadgets of the
computer age (there goes an example of what is being criticized!)
that the designated historic turning points--the number of "revolutions" per decade--are too numerous to absorb, their effects too
shrilly predicted for easy listening. We are paralyzed by the dimensions of the transformation, partly because we have internalized
a kind of Whiggian principle, by which machines "produce" social
effects of a measurable or, at least, observable variety. The
trouble is that technological and social history cannot be related in
this way, since the extrapolated trends shoot off the graph every
time. Consider the influence of the photocopier, the coaxial cable,
television news, teleconferencing, and so on. There are no anchors
to cast in each voyage of speculation; every trip rushes straight
toward infinity.

   We would be greatly helped in the present epoch of speculation if we had available some improved metaphors for social change,
something less traumatic and less overworked than "revolution,"
something more intermingling of cause and effect, something that
suggested less emphasis on technology and placed more pressure on

social need as the starting point of technology. New technologies close gaps, resolve tensions, register the temporary shelving of problems, as well as automate jobs out of existence and fill the home with new junk. Above all, in order to reduce the current bewildering hyping of technical history, we need some explanatory models of the inventing process that demonstrate the collective, though concealed, social dialogue that almost invariably precedes the advent of a new device.

The apparatus of the modern media of information has been accumulating steadily through the century; the modern home may possess a telephone and a typewriter, a camera, a record player, a pocket calculator, a pile of disks or cassettes, probably by now a couple of television receivers, possibly a cable TV link, an 8mm. film camera and projector, a device for playing video games, for receiving pay TV, for decoding teletext or videotext signals, perhaps even a video camera, and a home computer. Few people, however, are as yet aware of the linkages that exist--or that can exist--between all of these gadgets; the information revolution of the late twentieth century consists very largely of the increased propensity for these text and moving image machines to converge and to interact. That propensity has been latent since Victorian times. Thomas Edison invented the phonograph as a repeating device to aid the telephone, thinking that a central office such as the telegraph bureau would record messages sent down the telephone lines and deliver the disks to the homes and businesses of nonsubscribers.[4] It was not a fallacy so much as a prophecy, for we are witnessing today that intermixture of telecommunications with information storage that he envisaged. What happened in the late 1970s was a sudden increase in the potency of telecommunications and in the computing capacity of society that has made it possible for us to reap a whole series of benefits that were impossible when the same technical possibilities existed on a smaller scale. The present "revolution," if such it is, is one of investment rather than technical innovation, of transformation of scale more than of technological horizon.

All of the devices that have emerged as discrete physical media of information and entertainment have their own industrial housing, so to speak. The century has witnessed the growth of a music industry around the phonograph and radio, a TV industry, a film industry, and telecommunications, computing, and book publishing industries. These great blocks of investment and industrial activity are currently undergoing a transformation, and in every society in which they flourish (surprisingly few, in fact, since most societies are becoming highly import-dependent in respect of media software), there is currently a reconsideration of the regulatory environment in which they operate. In some societies, the process is being labeled "deregulation," where it is perceived as a process of removing legal constraints against intercorporate competition. In other societies, the same process is envisaged rather as one of making new and appropriate regulations to stimulate similar releases of enterprise, often accompanied by moves to protect indigenous culture. The new devices of cassettes and disks and the new paid broadcast services entail an extremely complicated regearing of all the established industries that hitherto have been device-specific. In other words, it has to be possible for a set of rights and obligations that have been acquired in respect of a given artifact (say, a film made for theatrical release) to be transferred to a wider range of distribution systems (cassettes, cable television). The changing situation is bringing about a gradual alteration in the way we think about the property element in information and entertainment, and about the cultural demarcations between genres. At one level, the change consists in a series of publishing devices and promotional arrangements; at deeper levels, it must alter our ideas about what constitutes a "book," what separates an "academic work" from a popular one, indeed what body of data should properly be considered a book or an "author."

Let us consider a not unusual career for a modern work of fiction. It may begin as a novel about which an individual writer has pondered for years, or it may originate as a commission conceived by an agent or a publisher and fostered upon a writer of recognized skill. If it seems likely to sustain the investment, the finished work may be promoted, and through dextrous manipulation of the apparatus of literary review and public discussion, forced through a series of different kinds of text distribution. It will come out in hardcover and paperback, in serial fiction and digest form, and then as an even cheaper paperback. But it may also be transmuted into a set of moving images, where its basic authorship will be further dehydrated and industrialized in complex ways. A film designated for cinema distribution may in fact be shown, in widescreen format, only for further promotional purposes; the 70mm. image will be seen only by a small fraction of the emerging audience, as the work passes into 35mm. and 16mm. gauges for distribution in various specialist systems (such as the film society network or the college circuit). It will appear in cassette form (all the framing of the original lost in the transformation to the smaller screen) and videodisk, on cable and pay TV, ending up on "free" over-the-air television, public or commercial. At later stages in its career, the work may return to one or more of its earlier phases, but it will remain in public consciousness with greater permanency than that bulk of Victorian fiction which failed to become one of the tiny band of classics.

The new work of today faces a wider variety of audiences and enjoys a more finely calculated career. It is commensurately more heavily dependent upon promotion, and, indeed, more and more different kinds of entrepreneurs will speculate upon its possibilities during the course of its complicated life. There is a rush of newcomers to the marketplace, but inevitably, a wave of cartelization will ensue as soon as this market is rationalized. Thus in this period of convergence of devices, a new division of cultural labor is growing up among them. At the same time, there is a search for new and appropriate forms of material, not dissimilar to that which took place when the telephone and cinematography were evolving, when perception of social role preceded each of a multitude of technical offshoots. The social impact of television and telecommunications has been much subtler and more far-reaching than that of other devices of the same era. Both telephone and cinematography were very slow, however, in gathering around them the aura of transformationism that today envelopes the offshoots of the computer and the television receiver.

In the 1880s it seemed possible that the telephone would become a medium of entertainment. In London and Paris, experimenters were to set up connections between the principal theaters and the central operator, so that subscribers could listen to plays and to the songs of the music hall. Others thought that the new medium would be a useful supplier of general information, supplementing that of the newspaper. As a person-to-person instrument, it suffered from obvious limitations: there were few people with whom one could speak, the costs were high, and established systems of social discourse inhibited subscribers from incorporating the machine into their lives. The telephone was neither intimate nor reliably private. It was often confined to small professional groups, such as the lawyers and doctors of Glasgow, who enjoyed their own separate and mutually incompatible exchanges. As an instrument of business, the telephone suffered from other limitations: it was more expensive than using messenger boys; it created tension within the national telegraph administrations (one of which actually proposed charging for the telephone according to the number of words spoken along the line). It came into use at first through a series of specialist groups: the construction teams on early skyscrapers, the police, doctors, lawyers, and so on. It grew within the interstices of society, later coming to occupy a more general public role.[5] The influence of the telephone on the development of social structures and the physical layout of societies is extremely hard to calculate and has tended to be overlooked.

Road and rail systems are more visible, and the great feats of engineering that made them possible have seized the attention of social historians more tenaciously than the invisible forces of telegraph, telephone, and radio. But the areas of influence of the communication devices are themselves different: while transportation facilitated suburbanization in the present century, communications has had a great deal to do with the changing "images" of the different parts of a city, the constantly shifting areas of respectability and trend. Suburbanites have not been migrants on the whole; they have desired to retain the advantages of metropolitan life and to remain in constant touch with the centers of the society, while shunning the geographical core. Communication systems have thus helped with the light-and-shade of social evolution, and have provided a wider range of matters over which social nuance can be expressed. However, each device developed in the Victorian era (and later) began life in an aura of a certain vagueness as to its destined purpose. Was the telephone destined for entertainment purposes, or did it fulfill a special role in preserving social order or in providing general information? Did it facilitate person-to-person or group-to-group communication? The purposes have constantly shifted, although each device eventually acquired its own clear purposes, its own "culture." Now, all is in doubt again, all the boundaries are moving.

Each fresh wave of new devices has registered and expressed a new stage in the evolution of city structure, in neighborhood development, and in the structure of the family. Cinemas in the twenties and thirties released people from their homes; television in the fifties recemented the home as focus of the family, until in the sixties, a new politics of the family seemed to break up that tight postwar grouping. Today, the new multiple devices slice up the family and reindividualize it, permitting and encouraging a new microconsumerism, the pursuit of a fresh, but (temporarily) satisfying, illusion of individual gratification through endless freedom and "choice."

II

The communication and representation devices of the late Victorians were manifestations of a vast, unarticulated urge; they were an act of ideology expressed again and again, in different versions, of a machine for the perfect reproduction of the lifelike. It is worth dissecting the "invention" of film in some detail and comparing its tortuous progress, via a complex of interactions between technique and social aspiration, with the phenomenon of today, when it is still difficult to express, in one similarly neat phrase, the nature of the parallel contemporary aspiration. There appears today to exist a latent collectivist, egalitarian consumerist urge, a prompting to break through economic and institutional constraints, toward an abundance of messages, from which a mass of individuals can draw material according to their "personal" choice. Choice is the chimera of the age, the hypothesis of a new adulthood arising from the opportunity to "perfect" the self as the basic mechanism of consumption. The Victorians, however, were pursuing, through their technologies of illusionism, an ideal mode in which their desire for a kind of artificial immortality could be assuaged.

The moving image was a substitute for--an extension of--the cemetery. The mass suppliers of early film cameras blatantly exploited this deep need of the age: the retention of the perfect images, in motion, of one's loved ones. One of the newspapers that reported the first public screening by Louis Lumière of his films said: "When these cameras become available to the public, when all are able to photograph their dear ones, no longer merely in immobile form but in movement, in action, with their familiar gestures, with speech on their lips, death will no longer be final."[6] The representation and extension through time of the human body was one aspect of the great bourgeois aspiration, but the techniques have their roots in the Renaissance, with the development of anatomical study and the growing importance of perspective as the enabling science that made it possible for the new knowledge to be recorded and imparted.

Marey's discovery of the persistence of vision in the nineteenth century played a similar role in the development of machines to capture, record, and dissect the nature of movement.[7] But Marey was not in pursuit of moving pictures as illusions; indeed, he rejected the machines that enabled movement to be synthesized in favor of another line of invention (which included his own chronophotograph--the first camera to employ celluloid strip) that captured movement on a still frame through strobic effects. Marey and his follower Londe were both attempting to overcome deficiencies in human perception rather than create an illusion of reproduced movement that deceived human perception. They wanted to depict reality in a form that slowed down or speeded up true movement. In a sense, Edward Muybridge's notions lay along the same line of thought; his Zoepraxiscope succeeded in reanimating a series of still photographs taken in succession by different cameras of a horse in motion. The purpose was scientific--to dissect a natural phenomenon and to reconstitute the movement, in order to prove the correctness of the analysis. Muybridge's images were generally taken to be aesthetically unpleasing. They were to influence painting in due course, but only after delivering a shock to those artists of the traditional schools who thought that the real world corresponded to the idealized images that had been taught academically.

Earlier in the century, a flow of devices demonstrated the other half of the Victorian inspiration--illusionism. Daguerre's invention was a natural development of his skill in trompe l'oeil. At the Great Exhibition of 1851, the stereoscope had drawn fascinated crowds, since it seemed to add a dimension to still photography by supplementing a gap in the pure representation of nature. Baudelaire mocked the hungry eyes "bending over the peepholes of the stereoscope, as though they were the attic windows of the infinite." At the same time, the demand for the perfect illusion was being fed through nonphotographic devices for creating the sensation of movement or of three-dimensional images, such as the Thaumatrope and the Praxinoscope, which depended on a disk with images that appeared to combine in motion through rapid rotation. These were representational toys dismissed by the more scientific school of Marey, since they demonstrated, but did not analyze, scientific phenomena.[8] Thus the pursuit of the Victorian aspiration for representing an image of life in its perfection veered from one line of development, in which its various manifestations were deemed to be recreational and at best educational, to another line, in which the quest was not to substitute for painting but to serve science.

It was the Lumière moving-picture show that captured the contemporary imagination in the mid-1890s. Writers as far spread as Gorky, Kipling, and Henry James witnessed the show as it traveled between Spain and Moscow, Austria and America. They were presented with one-minute scenes of real-life events, unstaged but nonetheless contrived, through choice of camera angle, location, and timing. The train arriving at a station, the workers leaving the factory, the gardener turning the hose upon himself--all became familiar metaphors that impressed upon those pioneer audiences the first collectively experienced moving images that inaugurated the great store of shared allusion which has subsequently accumulated. At the same moment, Edison's laboratory and its breakaway group, the American Mutoscope and Biograph Company, were feeding the same popular drive toward perfect representation with a series of inventions that offered short travel or anecdotal films projected in a machine into which the viewer had to peer. Edison was working to a much grander design that led him to overlook the importance of his own silent camera and projecting device; he wanted to link his own phonograph invention with a film and recording technique, with stereoscopic effects added for good measure. Edison wanted to perfect a total system of representation that would perceive, record, and transmit across space, and he thus employed, in a spectacular series of electrical and mechanical inventions, the whole range of sciences that were to be worked on in the course of the following eighty years.[9] All of the experimenters alluded to, and many others, were technicians primarily, but with a keen eye either on the audience of science or on the audience of contemporary showmanship, sometimes a little of both. The first decade of the twentieth century saw a further group of experimenters who were primarily artists, such as Georges Méliès and Edwin Porter, though both had some technical background. Both saw the possibilities of developing narrative forms by means of the new moving cameras. Méliès had started as a conjuror, and he drew from a line of nonrealist illusionism for his film ideas, of which he developed hundreds. His stock--transformations of human beings into animals, the appearance of strange apparitions, a Jules Verne-type space journey--was the culmination of the aspirations of a Victorian conjuror. Porter, however, drew upon a realist line of narrative, breaking away from the theatre rather than from popular showmanship. He is famous for having developed the pacing techniques that laid the foundations of modern narrative cinema--the cutting, linking, and transposition of shots, and the suggestion of simultaneity through building-up a chase scene by intercutting events taking place in different locations.[10]

Behind these different lines of artistic and technical development, all of which proved ultimately interactive and intensely creative of technology, was a growing institution, cinema. Behind each movement forward--and many that proved to be cul-de-sacs--there lay a shared phenomenon that grew by accretion, based upon an audience whose perception and expectations were being progressively intermingled; each mechanical device depended upon a range of artistic conventions that had to be accepted and internalized by a rapidly growing audience if the institution of cinema was to develop. That institution itself was obliged to follow the contours of contemporary taste, to search for the city locations, the distribution systems, the pricing mechanisms, the patent and copyright devices that would sustain the new medium. The technology that emerged registers a series of interim readings of the relationships that between them constituted, as they still do, the institution of cinema.

Of course, it is impossible to produce a perfect record of

the evolution of a technology by concentrating on the interactions and dependencies--social, artistic, technical, and intellectual--since to do so would entail an analysis of an entire society. Marconi's work on radio was taking place at exactly the same moment as the work of Lumière; Zworykin was working on the basic principles of television in the same decade as the main work of Méliès. Regulatory systems for the telegraph and the telephone were being simultaneously created, and these were greatly to influence the early and continuing institutions of radio and television. And of course, contemporary developments in all of the other sciences--from biochemistry to metallurgy, optics to engineering--played their part in the evolution of the communicating technologies. Nonetheless, those lines of development that led to film, television, and radio entailed clusterings of technique that derived their impetus from the same animating aspiration, that of creating a perfect and enduring representation of the perceptual world.

III

It is rather harder to discern the central drive that united the various new communication media that have been developed in the last and current decades from that earlier aspiration. Certainly, there no longer exists an unsatisfied craving for the mere illusionist representation of reality; perhaps a reverse principle might today be at work, whereby the techniques for suggesting reality are being pushed toward a realm of perfect fantasy in the new potential for, say, computer imaging. But there is some more general demand or perceived demand that is being stimulated and satisfied by the new media--demand for an abundance of supply and an image of the consumer as individual, arising above an ocean of materials. There is the image of a new leisure, a worklife without toil, a textured, variegated career structure. Many of the new devices are concerned with text storage and distribution as much as with still or moving images, with data processing as much as with storage. Some of the new devices appear, in the present stage of their development, to be concerned with supplying a new multiplicity of channels (cable systems, videodisks, satellite broadcasting, cassettes), while others have more to do with adding to the conveniences of the home or reducing information overload (home box office for first-run movies, videotext), or both. The suppliers of new services are breaking down, unconsciously for the most part, old traditional genres, such as the newspaper or magazine, by offering the chance to dial directly a specialist line of information; they are also providing a chance to evade the many constraints of over-the-air broadcasting with its "paternalistic" overtones of prescribed, preselected patterns of material. The new specialist cable channels are on the whole reworkings of the public broadcasting service model, and offer the chance for a new kind of self-definition on the part of the subscriber into a class or subculture type, rather as the newspaper industry did in the era when newspapers of every conceivable stripe flourished.

All of the new services have broken into preexisting monopolies of some kind, but all are searching for new monopolies of their own in order to survive--monopolies of first-run movies, monopolies of travel or business information, monopolies of high culture material, monopolies over certain geographical zones or certain social groups. With the advent, a decade or so from now, of direct broadcasting by satellite, a wholly new complication will arise, since the satellite, unlike any other transmission system devised hitherto, is capable of equal address across a whole society or group of societies.

Yet these services are, in the main, systems of supply quite separate from the industry providing material to a variety of systems reaching different layers of the audience. Thus a cable offering a cultural channel acquires its content from a multinational industry, programs that have been created to serve a primary market elsewhere (though with an eye to further sales). The market for software is becoming many-layered, even though various homogenizing market forces have already set in. The previous forms of distribution for much of this visual material continue to exist and tend still to be the primary sources of funding--the major national television networks and their independent suppliers. There are half a dozen annual markets and festivals at which the main lines of dealing and the main relationships are built up: Milan, Monte Carlo, Cannes, Berlin, New York, Los Angeles. Film festivals have created video offshoots, with new video markets in Europe and the East being established. But the dealing on individual projects continues throughout the year by means of bilateral arrangements between banks and production houses, television channels and cable organizations, Hollywood majors and publishing houses. Inevitable rearrangements of capital within the media conglomerates are taking place. A new world industry of moving-image products is emerging, highly diverse, but still dominated by the companies that established their grip over the heartland of the audience in the days of the old national television monopoly. The material today is beginning to pass through a complex mesh of distribution systems, each one technology-specific, each with a different pricing mechanism and in a different stage of development. A European publishing house owned by an American bank, for example, will initiate a project designed as a series of films and an international book. It will presell the films to a London-based television company for a price that covers a large proportion of the basic production costs. To cover the rest, it will presell the same series to a U.S. public television station or one of the New York cable stations, the London TV company retaining a percentage. The publishing house will then proceed to organize translations that will sell well, on the reputation of the British and American television transmission. The profit to the original publishing house, however, will tend to come from vastly enhanced book sales, since the whole scope of the market for the books has been transformed by the broadcasting operation. Gradually, the materials will flow into other cable and box office systems, while selling in cassette form in the education market. The product will retain strong national overtones; it is owned ultimately by the American bank, but its makers are British, and its accent will tend to be also. The same thing is happening in Paris, Frankfurt, Tokyo, and Amsterdam, but five geographical locations in the developed world are coming to play an ever greater role in the world supply of moving images and, indeed, of text materials also.

The five locations are New York, California, London, Frankfurt/Munich, and Tokyo,[11] places where there exist strong and sophisticated national audiences for the first-generation television materials, plus the necessary access to capital and the habit of working together on the part of a critical mass of relevant skills and institutions. It is likely that these five centers will remain at the heart of the world market for software in the entertainment and information fields. (Computer translation might eventually enable the Japanese to break also into the world text-information software market, already dominated by Japanese hardware). There was a similar concentration in the world of book publishing a hundred years after the development of moving type, but the evolution of the newspaper, with its polycentered culture, was quite different. Quite different, too, was cinema, which, though it rapidly became a narrow market, began with a wide variety of supply centers. The developing world contains a number of major centers for film-making (India, the Philippines, Hong Kong), but these have remained largely national in the 1970s. Today, one or more of them could break into the wider world market, but probably only through major investment from the existing centers, since they are "hampered" by the different musical and literary traditions of the East.

It is clear that two quite distinct developments are taking place. There is a new range of physical artifacts on which are inscribed images and text--cassettes and disks--and these are distributed in roughly the same manner as books and gramophone records. These are, however, to some extent different from their forerunners, in that the material they offer is already familiar to the potential buyer, through the promotion and marketing of a film, of which the cassette or disk constitutes an extended line of supply. The other new media are all services rather than artifacts, although the recipient may, legally or illegally, make a physical copy of the text or image in the home. Thus the new videotext systems are publishing devices, where payment is made through the telephone company for "pages" of material that have been received on a domestic television receiver. Some of the cable systems are paid for overall by the subscriber, as European public broadcasting systems have always been, while other cable systems or scrambled signal systems oblige the viewer to pay for each selected program; these leave the recipient without a physical artifact, unless a domestic personal recording has been made. Policing the uses made by individuals of private recordings is, for the rights-holders, something of a nightmare, and pricing mechanisms are having to adjust for the practical impossibility of retaining rights long-term after the distribution of a new product. The owner of those rights has to consider the timing of the whole package of new media outlets, relying on industry-wide organization for the policing of the multitude of new networks that are springing up.

It is still far too soon to see which technologies will prevail for specific purposes, to discern whether an optic fibre network set up nationwide would eventually take over and swamp all other systems of cables, microwaves, direct satellites, and broadcasting channels, in the establishment of a universal broadband domestic system, a kind of general information ring-main, like the electricity ring-main, linking every individual to the entire national and international system. It does appear, however, that Western societies are on the verge of the development of a system, or collection of systems, that, in their net effect, will tend to negate the basic principles by which information has traveled through society since the Renaissance. Even though the cassette and the videodisk operate in the same mode as books, distributed on the basis of single copy purchase by each user or group of users, the pressure of the non-artifact services is such as to suggest that the artifacts may play a diminished role in the longer term. The Gutenbergian principle is so firmly rooted in our culture that it is hard to imagine a society in which it has been abolished (and, indeed, no one is suggesting that anything like abolition is likely to occur). Rather, we are liable to witness a rapid erosion of the settled notion that information is naturally multiplied in physical copies until the number of copies approximates the number of those wishing to receive it. The Gutenbergian principle has already ceased to function in the case of broadcast material, where the opposite--or what one might call the Alexandrian principle--operates. There, a single copy exists in the originating tape or live performance, which then reaches its audience in nonmaterial form; a physical tape can be generated by the individual recipient, but the mass multiplication of physical materials, as in the newspaper and in publishing, is absent.

One uses the image of Alexandria, because it suggests a great store of material that is deemed to be fully authentic, but available only to those who come to it to choose. A modern data base is, in a sense, an electronic version of the principle where material is added to a central store according to fixed and accepted methods, and is then available to all who have the means and skills to unlock it. In the field of moving images, the world is today steadily building such a store of accredited materials, which have, most of them, been through the authenticating procedures of network transmission before becoming available through the newer systems of distribution. Unlike the materials of a great library or a computerized data base, these materials have still to be laid out as a program by a cable company or satellite distribution company before they can be chosen; but as broadband systems develop, we are veering slowly toward some new condition in which an individual can choose electronic dissemination of a single item that was itself chosen from a vast or total store of video products. In the field of data, this condition is rather closer, if anything, as the various videotext systems slowly agree on international technical standards and interconnections. One further aspect of the steadily dissolving

Gutenbergian principle is the part that distance has always played in fixing the cost of communication of any kind: this has applied equally in the case of the telephone and telegraph and the printed book. As the electronic systems emerge, it is becoming increasingly clear that distance is a rapidly diminishing factor in costs, both of collecting information and of redistributing it.

We are witnessing, therefore, a subtle transformation of the underlying principle that has sustained the information systems of human society since the Renaissance. The shift is coming about as a result of a vast number of quite separate responses of corporations to perceived demand, responses of technology to science and of science to imagination. There is no central machine generating this change, no great corporation or conspiracy of corporations. There does indeed exist a powerful, almost total dependence of the whole structure of change upon a number of giant corporations, but they are tending to grope toward the trend while trying to influence it. Their corporate needs greatly influence the pace of change, and while they often choose specific private directions for a period of time, the central pulse reestablishes its rhythm.

Despite the atmosphere of feverish change that has always beset the information media, the basic technologies and context forms have changed very slowly indeed. One may take, for example, the novel and the newspaper as direct emanations of the printing press, and note how each has changed fundamentally in form not more than, say, once in a century. Despite the enormous number of attempted means for creating moving pictures in Victorian times, the celluloid strip, which established itself in about 1897, has remained on the same gauge until today. The development of celluloid only took place at the end of the 1880s, and the earliest cameras for shooting a succession of images on a moving strip of celluloid hardly left their experimental stage before 1895. And yet a piece of Victorian film can be taken in 1982 to any city on earth and screened. A newspaper printed in any language since roughly the same date will be clearly perceived to be a newspaper in any part of the globe, and many of its chief contents --puzzles, news, editorials, share prices, reviews--apprehended as such in scores of cultures where the language itself may not be known. Radio and television have developed more rapidly, but even with these, each new development--from the valve to the cathode ray tube, from color signals and transistors to cables--has required about fifteen years to become established within the market. Forms remain stable because the market keeps them so; the public's expectations of any particular device or genre take years to develop, and these expectations, transmuted into listener, viewer, or reader habits, are the capital assets of the publishers and companies that have discovered or nurtured them.

Yet behind the kinds of material and the hardware, important trends do make themselves apparent. Two that have been at work since the beginning of the century are worth emphasizing in any attempt to size up the changing information environment. One characteristic of the nineteenth-century systems and devices--from the popular reading room to the peepshow--was that the audience was expected to make no investment in the system itself; revenue was derived either from the purchase of an artifact, such as a newspaper, or from the sale of a right, such as admission to a hall or tent. Indeed, the quest of the age had been so to multiply the product that the mass audience could have access at the lowest coin available. Thus arrived the half-penny newspaper, created as a result of expensive and diligent development of the mass press, mass distribution system, and the mass transportation system. As the century developed, however, the audience has been expected to indulge in an ever higher proportion of the total investment. Today, most of the investment necessary in maintaining a national television channel is held by the viewer rather than the supplier of the system --compare this with the theatre, or cinema, or the church.

In all of the new media, the audience's share of the investment has gone even higher, and the equipment companies have unsurprisingly been among the chief impresarios of development. The audience has to buy or rent the receiver and the recorder, the cable decoder, the videotex black box and so on. In fact, most of the new media are dependent upon there being several television receivers in a majority of homes; otherwise, there would be little hope of splitting the family as a viewing unit and thereby exploiting the potential for individual choice of material. With the arrival of direct broadcasting by satellite, the cost of each unit audience will rise substantially, since the engineering mechanisms required for switching from satellite to satellite, and thereby obtaining a wider choice, are fairly expensive. The whole expansion of the information sector thus hinges on the general expansion of the consumer economy, on the expansion at a steady rate of the consumer's propensity to invest in new entertainment systems. In the changeover from the old to the new systems, we are thus watching a very considerable switch in total investment in the resources of social communication from the manufacturer and the supplier to the audience at home.

The other important overall trend is for the gradual growth of local monopoly in any system. Information is historically torn between the condition of competition and its condition as a natural monopoly. One may cite the newspaper as a good example. Competition within the market for newspapers seemed natural, inevitable, and desirable in all democratic countries--as it still seems so today in places--so long as political circumstances made this desirable, and so long as the advertising done by mass consumer manufacturers required large slabs of display material. Gradually, television has become the channel for political material and the preeminent disseminator of national and regional manufacturer-to-consumer advertising. This has occurred on both sides of the Atlantic, although there are still a few European societies in which television advertising is illegal or minimal. Newspaper circulation has fallen a little in many countries, but seldom dramatically; where the total circulation has in fact fallen, the explanation often lies in the erosion of the habit of purchasing more than one newspaper as papers have become more comprehensive overall. The markets for advertising have, however, significantly altered throughout the economies of the West. The major area of growth has been in classified advertising, especially in recession-sensitive advertising such as that for jobs and contracts. The market has therefore become more volatile, while television advertising--dependent more upon manufacturers and sellers of commercial services--has tended to be much more resilient to temporary economic trends. There is a natural tendency for a newspaper to be most attractive as a source of advertising (and of news) where it is believed to be most comprehensive in its content, and this tendency, in the context of the changes mentioned, has greatly accelerated the development of natural local monopolies among the printed press. In the United States, this tendency has occurred alongside a growth of chains and of cross-media ownership at the corporate, if not the local, level. The newspaper has thus been coaxed by stages into becoming typically a local monopoly. Only a very few countries, such as Britain and Japan, have retained thoroughgoing newspaper competition, and in those cases, the reason has been the institution of national distribution, which has produced monopolization of another kind--within social strands rather than geographical location. Even in Britain, however, with its highly competitive journalism, the same phenomena have occurred with local newspapers as in Germany, the United States, France, and elsewhere.

The processes of monopoly have not set in as far as the electronic media are concerned, where cartelization is restrained through regulation. It would not be surprising, however, if a certain clarification did not begin--in those markets with a very large number of television outlets as the new media, with their far greater promise of abundant choice--to reach the middle and lower levels of the market. The same tendency toward a single outlet has occurred in the case of cinema, though mitigated by the habit of tripling or quadrupling movie theaters--not to create wider choice, but to provide finer tuning of the audiences for the existing repertoire as they grow and shrink during the run of a given film.

I have deliberately refrained from stressing national differences of trend or of magnitude throughout this paper, in order to bring out the shared phenomena of Western economics. We are witnessing a cultural shift, or set of shifts, that are more subtle and far-reaching than the physical devices, the products of modern electronics, themselves suggest, but that are more deeply rooted in the continuing and the slowly evolving than is often believed. After all, abundance of choice does not in itself constitute a transformation, since an individual will make conditioned choices and will probably not greatly increase the total hours of his exposure. But the role of text in our civilization and the development of the various skills of text are indeed in all probability today in the course of fundamental change. The management and use of a data base require quite new skills, and will emphasize different aptitudes from those required traditionally in primary education. The computerization of text suggests that we may absorb smaller quantities

of text into our lives, but it will be text that is better ordered and
more appropriately selected. The term book will probably come to
cover a narrower range of products than it now does, and the technical aids to research will, in the late 1980s, enable a wider range
of disciplines to benefit from the boon of the computer.

One might take, as an extreme example of the kind of "book"
that is becoming outmoded, the telephone directory, where the form
is used, in full Gutenbergian trappings of binding and single copy
mass distribution, as the housing for a collection of data, only a
tiny fraction of which is required by any individual reader. The
time taken to collect the information and to reproduce it is so great
that a high proportion of the material required by any individual
reader is invalid by the time the finished product reaches him. As
the total number of telephone subscribers rises, the proportion
whose addresses change more frequently also rises. The directory
is an essential body of data in urgent need of an appropriate mode
in which to present itself to its readers. Clearly, the format of
the traditional book is inappropriate, or will become so as soon as
an alternative technology becomes as easily accessible, or where
the level of accessibility of the alternative outweighs the disadvantages built into the existing mode. It is thus that the book will
"die," not through sudden technological redundance, but through the
prudent choices of those who actually require the information it
carries. As the newspaper passes through its own crises of form,
many of its traditional elements will probably be lost to the new
electronic mode. The pursuit of information "abundance" in this
case is in reality the pursuit of a manageable modicum of relevant
information.

But for the most part, the contemporary drive for abundance
of choice is a besetting ideology much more than a practical need.
It is more like the Victorian illusion of mechanized immortality,
providing evidence for the psychic tension of the moment rather
than for a social or economic need. The pursuit of plenty in the
sphere of information is a psychological analogy to its pursuit in
the sphere of nourishment in the developed world, where the use
of food has more to do with marketing, fashion, and general culture than with biological need. Information abundance has likewise
much to do with cultural identity in the late twentieth century, and
little to do with need. Nonetheless, it is a motive force and a
justification for an industrial evolution with revolutionary repercussions. As a recent OECD report observes:

> The production, transmission and processing of the most
> varied information will be at the heart of economic activity and social life ... through its links with data processing and telecommunications, the electronics complex during the next quarter of a century will be the main pole
> around which the productive structures of the advanced
> industrial societies will be reorganized.[12]

There are plenty of documents in circulation that outline the growing disparity in the provision of information, and especially the communications technology, between the countries of the North and those of the developing South. Eighty-five percent of existing data bases are in the North; 70 percent are in the United States. One company, IBM, is responsible for manufacturing two thirds of the world's computers. The abundance both of hardware and software is the privilege of a tiny group of societies, who are themselves enjoying a continuingly increasing disparity. Information grows by what it feeds upon.

Studies of the flows of data from computer to computer reveal its increasing internationalization. The growth of international networks is growing in the wake of the establishment of effective national networks: EURONET is establishing itself after the American TELENET and TYMNET systems. Even the countries of the socialist camp are now becoming connected to Western economics through the flows of international data. There is a strong tendency for all data flow to be concentrated on capital cities, however, because that is where the main data users are located. But there is also a tendency for data to flow from the less developed to the more developed, where processing facilities are more plentiful and more efficient. In the three least advanced countries of Europe, for example, over a quarter of their national data flow is toward other countries. The revenues from computer services in the United States have more than quadrupled in the last decade ($2 to $8 + billion), the international element tripling ($300 to $900 million).[13] The newly emerging techniques of remote sensing and satellite distribution of data are bringing about further exponential growth and further tiltings in the international flow of data from developing to developed worlds. The cultural implications are self-evident, and the political implications, easy to deduce. Behind the emblem of information foison there exists a growing phenomenon of global cultural domination, produced not by powerful armies, but by powerful international companies. The greater the stock of expertise in a society, the greater is its ability to make use of the information technology and benefit from its software. The educated society is the one best suited to prosper in the new age, and everything conspires against the society that has a deficit in its national balance of educated talent. The profusion of data through which the Western industrialized consumer indulges his or her choice, and expresses the nuances of a carefully refined and nurtured life-style, is the same oversupply that is drawn from the international data flow and jeopardizes the nationhood of developing societies. We may expect in the next decades the lines of international tension to shadow the contours of data abundance.

References

1. London, Gollancz, 1949.
2. Elizabeth Eisenstein, The Printing Press as an Agent of Change, 2 volumes (Cambridge University Press, 1979); "The Advent of

Printing and the Problem of the Renaissance," *Past and Present*, no. 45 (1969): 19-89.
3. Henri-Jean Martin and Lucien Febre, *The Coming of the Book: 1450-1800*, translated by David Gerard (London: New Left Books, 1976).
4. Ithiel de Sola Pool et al.: "Foresight and Hindsight: The Case of the Telephone," in *The Social Impact of the Telephone*, edited by Ithiel de Sola Pool (Cambridge, Mass.: MIT Press, 1977), pp. 127-57.
5. See the above volume, *passim*, but, in particular, Ronald Abler, "The Telephone and the Evolution of the American Metropolitan System," pp. 318-41.
6. This passage draws considerably on several essays in *Afterimage 8/9*, Spring 1981, in particular on Noël Burch, "Charles Baudelaire v. Dr. Frankenstein," pp. 4-24.
7. E.J. Marey, *Movement* (London: 1895. Listed in *Afterimage* above.)
8. C.W. Ceram, *The Archaeology of the Cinema* (London: Thames and Hudson, 1965).
9. Matthew Josephson, *Edison* (London: Eyre & Spottiswoode, 1959).
10. D.J. Wenden, *The Birth of the Movies* (London: MacDonald, 1975), pp. 19-22.
11. I am indebted for the train of thought in this section to conversation with Mr. Stephen Hearst of the BBC in London.
12. OECD: Interfutures. *Facing the Future, Mastering the Probable and Managing the Unpredictable.* (Paris: 1979).
13. See "Transnational Corporations Dominate International Data Flow," *Intermedia* (London) 10(3) (May 1982).

THE COMMUNITY OF THE BOOK*

Samuel S. Vaughan

The community of the book, it seems safe to assume, consists of those for whom the written word, especially as expressed in printed and bound volumes, is of the first importance. Little else may be safely assumed, including the question of whether it is, in fact, a community.

Those who constitute the community, its ethnics, are authors; editors and publishers; booksellers, librarians, and wholesalers; literary agents and literary critics; book reviewers and book journalists; book designers and artists; translators; educators; and--not least, though often omitted from full citizenship--readers. Other groups are functionally, economically, or spiritually involved, though in less obvious ways. These include newspaper and magazine people, papermakers and printers, binders, bankers, television talk show hosts, motion picture story editors, foundation administrators, prize-givers. They are the community's uncles, aunts, and cousins.

I propose in this paper to offer observations on issues confronting, supporting, or undermining the community of the book, as well as several reassessments, reconsiderations, and possibilities for future work. These notes necessarily focus on only a few sectors, neighborhoods, rather than the entire landscape. One objective is to challenge some of our favorite assertions.

Book publishing, for example, tends to be spoken of as if it were largely general or "trade" books. (Trade as applied to books further contributes to the confusion. Trade magazines are meant for specialized audiences. Trade books in the main are for general audiences, designed to be sold through the book trade, i.e., booksellers.) Instead, general books constitute one of the smaller sectors of book publishing, an industry that, by any conventional measure, is itself small,[1] though insistent arguments stress its "bigness." And the confusion is widespread. Recently, Curtis Benjamin, retired chairman of McGraw-Hill, told an otherwise able reporter who had been covering publishing for the New York Times

---

*Reprinted by permission of the author and publisher from Daedalus, 112:1 (Winter 1983) 85-115. The Journal of the American Academy of Arts and Sciences, Cambridge, MA.

that his paper's reports on the "publishing industry's" deep recession were in part inaccurate. Benjamin's point was that, yes, a number of general book publishers and mass market paperback houses were in difficulty, but that professional, scientific, and technical publishers, textbook publishers, and other significant segments of the industry, were not. Indeed, some were having their best years. The reporter replied that his beat was to cover trade publishing, not the whole industry, and it did not seem necessary to him to make this distinction in his reports. To Benjamin, it seemed less than likely that one tenth of the Times' readership understood this difference in stories about the health of the "book publishing industry."

Do such differences of opinion matter? Yes. Slipshod reporting affects the motivation and morale of authors and of those in publishing, the opinions of bankers and other backers, of industry suppliers--printers, papermakers--contemplating expansions of capacity (or otherwise), and politicians, academics, reviewers, and teachers whose judgments have a bearing on books.

Chronic misrepresentations about the nature, makeup, process, and profitability of publishing plague the community of the book. Those who care about books also care deeply about what goes with them: reading, writing, rewards, literacy, freedom, prestige. But we must also learn to care more for facts. There are, admittedly, too few facts available, but one is that our curious community is rife with rumor, riddled and rattled by speculation and assertion passed off as truth, and oversupplied with false issues that make all but impossible real confrontation with genuine ideas.

Misunderstandings are causing malfunctions. If a good general-assignment reporter approaches a story about Big Steel or the Department of Defense, he is apt to dig thoroughly, because he knows he is not a specialist in the steel industry or in military matters. If a reporter approaches a story about book publishing, it is usually with the conviction that he knows the answers before he asks the questions. He is, after all, a writer, sometimes with published books to his credit. If a steel company executive or an army officer makes a public statement, he is apt to do so with a measure of sensitivity about his community. When a publishing executive pops off, it is often straight from the hip, shooting out the lights.

When it comes to books about business, writers and publishers believe themselves to be tough-minded and hard-digging. About ourselves, we are soft-minded and lazy. Our too few facts are too often misunderstood, misapplied, or garbled. Much of our industry's "data" is unreliably obtained, casually examined, and delivered as gospel. The rumor mills of America are the only ones operating at capacity.

From all corners come the cries and claims: publishers

are pillars of greed, grasping, inept, insensitive, unethical, powerful. Librarians are timid, ultraconservative, unconcerned about protecting the rights of writers, readers, or publishers. Teachers are inept and indifferent, incapable of maintaining order, increasing knowledge, or simply teaching people to read. Big bookstore chains swallow up big books and small bookstores, and they are, of course, grasping, greedy, insensitive to sensitive books. They attempt to dictate publishing practices. The small bookseller is besieged, beleaguered, a frail reed. The American reader is disappearing--or never existed in the first place. Our children don't read anymore; television is sapping their will and preempting their time. There are no good book reviews.

With each argument, new alignments form. Authors and publishers condemn librarians; booksellers and authors rail against publishers; the small bookseller joins the "small" author to inveigh against the big bookstores. Publishers mutter that authors demand too much. Wholesalers complain that publishers do not give them a sufficient discount. Librarians say books are too cheaply made. Publishing employees protest that the pay scale is absurdly low. Authors accuse publishers of not spending enough money on advertising. So do the newspapers.

I have become an injustice collector. My thick file of what otherwise responsible people have said about publishing is an amusing dossier of damnation, but its long-term consequences are damaging, and not just to the well-being of publishers.

The community is full of those who would police it. We need constant vigilance--but do we need vigilantes constantly? Some would stamp out certain practices; others, certain kinds of books or authors. (The latter groups are not only self-elected censors but, in certain instances, authors themselves.) Some of this carping is traditional, merely part of the cultural static. But individual issues deserve comment. For example:

CHARGE: <u>Big publishers dominate the industry, imperiling the small publisher and the small bookseller alike. Small is Beautiful. Subtitle: Big is Ugly</u>.

Not so. One industry specialist, Paul D. Doebler, wrote recently: "Small publishing is exhibiting robust health."[2] And it is growing. <u>Publishers Weekly</u> reports that "the world of smaller publishers is numerically huge and getting bigger all the time. According to R.R. Bowker, 12,845 publishers have books in print and most of these are, by any definition, small publishers. Perhaps 200 firms can be considered large, well-known companies with sales in the millions."[3] And these smaller organizations are not, by any means, all literary publishers. Richard Morris, who edits the COSMEP (Committee of Small Magazines/Press Editors and Publishers) newsletter, estimates that their current membership is roughly 40 percent "literary publishers, 30 percent self-publishers, and 30 percent commercially oriented." And, says Morris, "the number of people not primarily literary in orientation has been increasing."[4]

How are they doing? Very well, it appears. In its annual survey, Huenefeld, a small publishing consulting company, found that the sales of 192 small book publishers were up 12.5 percent in 1981 over 1980. These publishers were optimistic about 1982, predicting "an average growth rate of 19.3 percent." Furthermore, "nearly 74 percent ... operated at a profit."[5] Few large publishing houses could match either this growth rate or profit picture. One ironic finding is that 66 of the smaller houses categorized as "not-for-profit" outperformed their profit-minded counterparts.

So, a fact which deserves closer examination--and celebration --is that one of the healthiest phenomena is the proliferation, growth, and geographical dispersion of small publishing enterprises.

CHARGE: <u>Conglomerates are taking over book publishing. Big publishers are buying up smaller ones. The end of literature is in sight.</u>

Understandable anxieties exist everywhere in the community, especially among authors, who feel underappreciated, and among publishers, who see many books going down the drain instead of up the charts. One of the most unreasonable fears, however, grows out of the automatic assumption that anyone not already in book publishing is therefore not fit to publish. When an executive from Western Pacific Railroad attempted to gain control of Houghton Mifflin not long ago, its authors rose up in a body and threatened to leave the company if this Ghengis Kahn from the West took over. From the authors' statements to the press, it was clear that no one knew much about the man. He could have been as cultured as anyone now heading up a book publishing company. But this is a possibility that authors in heat cannot conceive of, let alone entertain. Their elitism was extraordinary--and went largely unremarked.

A similar alarm, raised when American Express attempted to buy into a well-known publishing company, evoked the ludicrous image of a commercial "giant" gobbling up a pitiful little press called McGraw-Hill. Book publishers, after all, have to come from somewhere else at the outset. To be sure, several prominent publishers are descendants of publishing ancestors, inheritors of publishing companies and sometimes fortunes. But most people in publishing were not "in publishing" before they crossed the line. And not all of publishing's backing came from book sources to begin with. The initial funding for two of the most prestigious publishing houses in the country came from profits in steel and in girdles. But people spoken of as "nonbook" types are subject to prejudices that, if applied to religious groups, would bring out the shock troops of antidefamation leagues.

It seems to me that the real risk when "nonbook" people come into publishing is not that they know so little about books, but that they know so little about money. At no time has general book publishing ever contributed profits consistently to its mother company that could measure up to conservative investments in safe securities--money that could be earned without work and with relatively little risk. Their shortsightedness as investors, as businessmen, should characterize their unfitness, not their supposed lack of taste or assumed inability to read intelligently or to understand editorial talk (which at best can be difficult to translate).

The big buying trend is over, but the contradictions linger on. There is virtually no mention of the publishing houses and imprints that would simply have disappeared without the intervention of larger and more successful companies. Antiliterary charges are duds. Random House bought Knopf and Pantheon, and this complex was in turn bought by RCA, which later sold it off. This seems to have produced nothing more notable than a flow of capital and, presumably, memos. Despite all fears, there is no documented evidence that CBS ownership has done any damage to the Holt list.

These comments are no argument that Big (or Different) is Beautiful. But one of the built-in contradictions for antibigness authors is that the best known of them require publishing institutions of some size to do precisely what the authors want done.

CHARGE: The major problem is distribution.

Intellectuals, even more than marketing men, love to focus on the "distribution problem." If only publishers would set to rights the distribution mess in their own houses, all problems would be solved.

Publishers, in fact, do not control the means of distribution. It would be a far more efficient business if we did, and definitely more dangerous, as it is in countries--such as Italy and France-- where a few major publishing houses essentially own the engines of book distribution. Publishers operate only at the front end of the distribution chain. We are, in terms used for earth-moving equipment (which is sometimes what the work resembles), "front-end loaders." We move the books, in essence, toward the distribution channels, trying to get them through.

As a matter of fact, distribution is getting better, and we owe the improvements in part to electronic machines--which are, of course, resisted by those who see themselves as creative or intellectual and who therefore must protest the depersonalization brought about by computers.

CHARGE: Bookstores are dying out. Big chains are grinding the good shops into the ground.

Add to this the comment of the respected head of a university press: "Most books are being bought in this country by two computers." Given the fact that most university presses get their books into the bookstore chains only with the greatest difficulty, his frustration is understandable--but inaccurate. Computers don't buy books. People program them to provide information on book sales, levels of inventory, and the kinds of information bookstore owners have needed for centuries to run their exceedingly complicated businesses. The same chains the director criticizes employ dozens of individual book buyers for special categories of books.

Yes, booksellers large and small (and publishers, including the university press director) use computers. The failure to bring in such tools to aid in the management of the book business would be a much greater "sin." As for the decline of the small shop, look first at the comment, "The new shops, and the healthiest survivors of the old, are not the well-stocked personal shops of the 20's." This was in the Winter 1963 issue of Daedalus, before the growth of the large chain bookstore operations.

The big bookstore chains, notably B. Dalton and Walden, have become imposing presences, and independent bookshops have felt the heat of their competition. Any poorly located or lackluster shop is likely to be damaged by the arrival on the scene of a bright, "well-merchandised" chain store. At the same time, any well-run, intelligently managed independent bookstore is not likely to yield its customers to what is seen as the impersonality of a chain branch shop.

Just as fiction is a perennial invalid, so too is the good "personal" bookshop. It has been disappearing since it first began. The small bookshop goes out of business for the same reasons that many new small businesses expire. Many shops that are poorly run and inadequately financed are owned by people who would rather buy books than sell them, who love books but do not love the gritty details of managing a retail business with hundreds of "suppliers," all offering different terms. Constant problems of inventory, turnover, cash flow, credit, and erroneous shipments compound the difficulty, and the results are, in good years, a modest profit at best.

The well-stocked bookshop, operated by a perceptive owner, is a treasure, an asset to any community. There never have been very many of this kind. The jewel of a shop is just that: rare, precious, hard to find--and, often, expensive. Chains compete vigorously with such shops. Discounters, in particular, give them trouble, at least when the discounter first opens up. But the best bookshops do more than survive. They compete effectively with the chains by providing what is uniquely theirs to offer: personal service and attention; well-chosen inventories of books, old and new; gift wrapping; amiable return or exchange privileges; and so on.

It is not as if the personal bookshop presents no problem of its own; for one, the highly opinionated prejudices of its owner. If you share the same opinions, fine. If not, the selection of books on hand will seem decidedly limited.

The bigger chains--Dalton, Walden, Crown, Caldor--are sharply competitive and decidedly unsentimental in certain aspects of their operations. The pride of one or two of them in their computers, category buying, and advertising is excessive. Chains put pressure on publishers, in addition to other bookshops, as all big-muscle retailing tends to exert pressure on its "vendors." Whether there are illegal discriminatory practices underway has yet to be tested. (One has to stress illegal. Otherwise, that's what buying is--discrimination.) It is inaccurate to say that there are no "book people" in the chain stores. The chains still find themselves employing clerks who are more responsive to books than to systems. More than one manager runs a chain store as if it were a personal shop.

Unmentioned in the complaints about chains are the smaller or middle-sized bookstore groups: Kroch's and Brentano's in the Middle West; Doubleday, nationally; and others. These include some of the best bookshops in the country.

In any case, there are facts. The number of bookstores in the United States has nearly doubled since 1972. Bowker, publishers for the book trade, notes an increase in the number of retail book outlets from about 10,000 to around 19,000 in that period. Some are chain outlets. But the big two chains taken together number less than 3,000 shops. Thus, thousands of other stores have come onto the scene even as the chains have been undergoing their greatest growth. For years before large group retailing threatened to bind us, as some see it, in chains, the call was for booksellers who could sell books, as one solution to the distribution problem. The chains, for better and worse, provide some of that. Hundreds of shops are open where none existed before. Considered as a plus, as extra sales situations, they are valuable. They represent a large share, but not necessarily the essence, of the business.

The inspired, informed, informal bookseller is a sometimes delicate, sometimes hardy plant to be cherished. But the healthy ones become so because they are smart, not just sentimental. They know books, and they know their trade. Can they compete? Yes, and they do. They compete with group buying and big backing by using their own trusted methods; with their knowledge of books, authors, and customers; by risk-taking; and, by guerrilla warfare, taking advantage of their speed, mobility, training, and, the strongest motive of all, their will to survive.

CHARGE: There are 40,000 books published every year. Too many.

Book people persist in using balloon figures. For years, people have been saying that 40,000 new books are published each year, and that this causes stillbirth, that stores cannot accept that many, that reviewers cannot cover them, that the bad drives out the good. . . .

First, it should be noted that when the number of books published went <u>down</u>, as it did from 1979 to 1980 (from 45,182 to 42,377), no one seemed to notice. Sooner or later, however, the total will pass 50,000.

So what? Such numbers miss the mark and send up clouds of dust. Of the 40,000-plus books published each year, between 7,000 and 9,000 titles are not new books at all but reissues. Of the rest, over 5,000 are in science and medicine, and of these, most are not general books, by any stretch of the definition, but technical. The largest category published is sociology and economics, more than 6,000 titles per year, and few of these are aimed at the general reader, reviewer, or bookstore.

Fiction has soared--from 2,313 titles in 1979 to 5,003 in 1981. But what are they, especially given the decrease from 1979 to 1980? Many are "genre" or "category" novels, new releases in the seemingly endless stream of paperback romances, with varying degrees of spice, ranging, as in a Chinese restaurant, from bland to hot. These do not compete for review space, they have increased the profitability of stores who sell them, and they constitute something more akin to magazine than to book publishing.

In addition, many books in the numerical tallies are scholarly or other specialized monographs. No one knows, in fact, how many of the books published are aimed at the general reader, and thus beamed at bookstores and reviewers along the way.

One source separates "literary books" from "practical and professional books." In 1979 there were said to be 8,416 "literary books" and 22,777 "practical and professional" ones. In the period 1959-79, the number of practical and professional books very nearly doubled, while the increase in literary books went from a little over 5,000 titles to over 8,000.

In terms of allover U.S. book production, the United States produced 12,000 titles in 1914 and did not come up with this total again until 1956. Thereafter, the period of most rapid growth was 1960-64, followed by a slowdown in 1969-70.[6]

A steadily swelling stream of "too many books"? No. Too many indifferent, insufficient, unsatisfactory, or redundant books-- which the public often ignores or rejects. The marketplace is the final editor.

CHARGE: <u>Authors are poorly paid and live on the edge of poverty</u>.

To the New York, Washington, or Los Angeles newspaper reader, this would seem a curious claim, since the reader is treated occasionally to accounts of million-dollar contracts. He tends to see author in the same category as rock or sports stars, as indeed a few are. The author, on the other hand, tends to see himself/herself as inadequately compensated, possibly cheated, and certainly working at below the minimum wage, especially reckoned on an hourly basis. Indeed, most authors would be better off if they were paid hourly--at any rate--because most writers are writing nearly all the time, one way or another.

The Authors' Guild constantly surveys publishers' contracts and authors' earnings, to the extent of their ability to determine these figures. The New York Times carried the following front-page headline--based on a survey made for the Authors' Guild Foundation by the Center for the Social Sciences at Columbia University: "Average U.S. Author's Writing Brings in Less Than $5,000 a Year."[7] Following which, an author, James Lincoln Collier, wrote a piece for Publishers Weekly, entitled, "Can Writers Afford to Write Books," charging that the publishing industry exists "only by the grace of subsidies provided by writers."[8]

Curtis Benjamin responded to the Times story. "The Columbia survey was narrowly focused and hence misleading."[9]

Benjamin's first discovery was that the sample was "badly skewed because it included largely authors who were likely to write only Trade books.... Much larger categories of authors, such as those of educational and professional or practical books, were all but ignored." The sample, he said, was confined to 3,200 of the 5,000 members of the Authors' Guild, plus about 1,900 other writers "who had been invited to join the Guild but declined to do so," and got a 54 percent response. But the report claimed that the survey was "unmatched" in its number of respondents, "its intention to represent the full population of book writers in America," and so on. Benjamin asked: Approximately how large is the total population of American authors? The surveyors had to acknowledge that the size and composition of that population remained "largely a mystery."

In addition, authors' earnings, frequently, are a second (and, if the spouse works, a third) income. Indeed, many authors are academics. Whether one teaches to subsidize writing or writes to enlarge the compensations of teaching is an individual decision. But candid academics point to the surprising range of rewards that can issue from the publication of even the least successful book--fellowships, grants, symposia and speaking invitations, travel, and opportunities for career advancement. Far from publish or perish, it is more apt to be publish and prosper, when everything is added in.

That there are undercompensated authors, as there are unrecognized ones, is all too plain. That most authors live well below poverty levels is a "documented" charge that is all too silly.

MISCELLANEOUS CHARGES: Publishers want only blockbusters. Wrong. Publishers want blockbusters, but they also want good books that will sell in the middle range, and we want interesting new authors to publish. Anyone who goes about it otherwise is not planning to be in publishing for very long. Publishing is no longer an occupation for gentlemen. Partly true. For one thing, women are exceedingly important throughout the business. For another, there is the question of whether it ever was. The first publisher was the Church, whose members might have been part of an aristocracy, but who were not, in the conventional sense, gentlemen. Subsequently, publishers grew up out of booksellers and printers, that is, tradesmen. The fact that on occasion gentlemen and gentlewomen have participated in publishing makes for an interesting cultural and commercial footnote but not for a characterization of the whole business. Fiction is dead. Fiction is always dead or dying and, like the theater and the bookshop, remains one of our hardiest invalids. More fiction is published than any other category. Nonfiction sells better than fiction. Wrong. The word "nonfiction" identifies nothing, except books that are, or pretend to be, not fictional. Some of the biggest selling books every year are novels, and the mass market paperback and book club businesses are founded on fiction. It is when hardcover sales alone are used to compute the sales of fiction versus nonfiction that the deception sets in.

Let's look briefly at two of our common concerns--reading and, that neglected and maligned figure, the reader.

Reading

> If reading is done off a "green screen" as some predict will be commonplace in the 1990s, [Secretary of Education Terrel H.] Bell said, that makes the teaching of literacy "even more important."[10]
>
> --Publishers Weekly

The "teaching of literacy" evokes considerable concern in the community--as well it should. Of the various forms of poverty, the worst are to be starved for food or love, to be denied the vote or voice, and to be unable to read. Recently we have learned to worry about "functional illiteracy." A number of our citizens are able to read, that is, they are able to make out letters and words, but cannot make the imaginative leap toward meaning and comprehension. We have now begun to speak of "semiliteracy"--which can mean either the disinclination of "today's youth to read for their own enjoyment" or the tendency to be satisfied with "shallow interpretations of what they do read"--and of "aliteracy," knowing how to read but not wanting to. Townsend Hoopes, president of the Association of American Publishers, describes this as an indication of the "widening gap between the leadership elite and the general public."[11]

As a nation, we have the notion that we have been spectacularly unsuccessful in combatting illiteracy. Indeed, it appears that we have been more ingenious at inventing new forms of illiteracy than in curing it. And we are generous in awarding blame. No wonder: there is plenty to go around, with dozens of suitable scapegoats. Parents and college administrators blame it on the teachers, primary and secondary schoolteachers blame it on the parents, everyone blames it on television. We hear of the latest learning disabilities; and, of the oldest teaching inabilities. Authors and publishers worry, but most do next to nothing about it, except to use the widely debated "readability" levels and word lists.

Not nearly as easy as assigning blame is recognizing the genuine difficulties of learning to read in less than auspicious circumstances. We have the inspiring example of Abraham Lincoln reading by firelight; there are fewer case histories of learning to read without books at hand, or where English is not the family's first language. Robert Coles and others have shown that learning to read can be extraordinarily difficult when the student does not come out of "natural reading circumstances." But it is more entertaining and makes better copy to give short shrift to the complexities of reading and to decry public education, Archie Bunker-like home life, and "The Dukes of Hazzard."

In What Was Literature? Leslie Fiedler writes that, although he does so for a living, "it is an odd enough notion ... to 'teach,' say, the plays of Shakespeare or the novels of Dickens and Twain, works written to move and titillate: to require, in effect, a pleasurable response from a captive student audience." (Fiedler adds: "The whole enterprise is a little like giving a course in making love."[12] In this, he is surely correct. A required response, even for pleasure, can induce impotence.)

Parents, publishers, and writers are too quick to blame teachers when there is ample evidence that children who see and possess books and periodicals in their homes, who are asked friendly questions about their reading, and who are read to, are the ones who become lifelong readers. Teachers are too quick to blame parents when part of the problem, at least, is the unwillingness of teachers to assign writing projects and to mark them carefully and sensitively. Or who concentrate on "skills" when we could be offering love, fantasy, reality, escape, understanding, surprise--the eternal gifts of reading and writing, of self-expression, and the discovery of the lives of others.

Characteristically, the community sees disaster everywhere. Taxpayer revolts distress liberals, who fail to understand that decades of reporting only the bad news--especially the "news" that the millions of dollars spent on education over the years have produced only widespread illiteracy--is reason enough for taxpayers to demand a slowdown. Instead of recognizing that the news is not all bad, that each year millions of youngsters are transformed into readers, we unvaryingly forecast poor educational weather, with more to come. Instead, we might offer, as energetically as we do the bad news, the good news that free libraries, schools, trained and sometimes gifted professionals, book reviews and book chats, television and movie versions of books, and the increasing availability of the best in children's literature at attractive paperback prices, all conspire to create a climate for literacy that is unparalleled in human history.

There are, too, unrecognized or unstated appeals in reading. No civilized person loves pornography. Yet more than a few people have become enthralled by reading when they discovered that sexual excitement could be found in books. Certainly, this is not an injunction to produce porn, but it could open the way for the recognition that what some people see in books is what others have seen in photography and art. Erotic arousal testifies to the pleasure and especially to the power of the written word--a not quite respectable approach, perhaps, but worth consideration. There are unquantifiable qualities in reading that draw people to print.

Meanwhile, the enormous advantage of the "new technology" is not the microchip but rather that video games teach children to associate the flickering green panels with pleasure. A voluntary commitment of time and learning gives them action, control, and reward. Just as many younger Americans have grown up feeling that the paperback book is not a hardcover, hardnosed, required textbook but a friendly, spontaneous, portable, informal, disposable device, so the new games are teaching kids not just to blow up planets and blow away enemies, but that there is joy in the interaction between hand, eye, and screen.

Ours is referred to as a time that is becoming increasingly visual, as if this were uniquely an era of images rather than an age of print. Yet there never were eras wholly devoted to print, which has existed simultaneously with paintings, posters, engravings, Chautauqua lecturers, opera, radio, motion pictures, newsreels, cave paintings and other graffiti. Do we live in a time dominated by pictures, by symbols, a semiotic soup without an alphabet? Words are abstract art, are symbols. In the litanies about literacy, as elsewhere, we should stop looking back at a golden age that never was.

Readers

Americans simply "don't read books"; to others, slightly less apocalyptic, Americans don't read "enough" books or "good" books. The question of who reads and why involves a web of motives; the transmission of messages, intended or accidental; and atmospherics as well as education. The situation is not helped by most surveys.

Such studies as we do have--and these, in the main, reflect jaundiced opinions--appear to argue that readers are declining or that new readers are not being created. Comparisons are made to the sales of certain leading titles of yesteryear, or yestercentury, but such comparisons fail to take account of yesteryears' fewer titles, when there were fewer popular authors, fewer forms of alternative entertainment, and less competition for the reader's time and money (though no one need minimize the appeals of sex, whist, or weariness to absorb hours and sometimes money).

On the other hand, when a respectable study is done, questionable interpretations follow. In 1978 the research team of Yankelovich, Skelly, and White made public the results of a study they had conducted for the Book Industry Study Group. As reported--and interpreted--by the New York Times, "Study Finds that Nearly Half in U.S. Do Not Read Books." The Library of Congress came to a different conclusion: "Contrary to popular opinion, over 90 percent of the U.S. population constitutes a reading public--a significant number of them readers who find time for ten or more books over a six-month period."[13] At about the same time, a Gallup poll, sponsored by the American Library Association, released its results. Among them: "Fiction was still the most popular reading," and "One-fourth of ... [the] respondents said television influenced their book selection."[14]

All this was interesting, but none of it was new, nor, sadly, were polls designed to elicit much additional needed information. Most surveys conclude that just under half of all adult Americans read a book sometime or other. The differing interpretations are standard, too. Is the glass half full or half empty?

The book publishers and the library association, with the best will in the world, had underwritten research that merely confirmed what every serious study has shown over the past forty years. Many people like fiction. Book reading tends to correlate with several characteristics, among them education and income. In 1974 a report, "Books and Leisure Time," by the Newspaper Advertising Bureau, indicated that nearly six out of ten (58 percent) Americans over eighteen had purchased one or more books in the previous year. Among those with "some college or more," 83 percent were book buyers. A study done by W.R. Simmons and Associates in 1975-76 showed the relationship between reading, education, and income, as did a survey by the National Advisory Committee on Libraries in 1967 and a study of book-buying behavior in 1966 by the National Industrial Conference Board.

In 1963, in an article for the New York Times Book Review, I pointed out that Gallup had made the dismal discovery that "just over half of American adults did not read a single book all the way through in the past year," and noted that for some, this nourished the notion that we were a nation of nonreaders. But Gallup's findings also meant that as many as 40 or 50 million Americans had read a book in 1962, over twice the number who had seen a pro basketball or football game; that well over $1 billion had been spent on books and maps in that year, more than we put down in movie theaters or at parimutuel windows.

At any rate, what few reliable data there are go back to Bernard Berelson's pioneering work in libraries in 1949 and are astonishingly consistent. Reinventions of the wheel have a certain charm, but they do not advance the cart or the art.[15]

If the community is to become better at diagnosing, prescribing, and pursuing cures for the several illiteracies, perhaps we had first better improve our own reading, including survey results that Gallup to conclusions.

The survey done by the Book Industry Study Group did turn up a few promising leads. I had always assumed, for instance, that the higher incidence of book reading among the "educated" meant the college-educated, as indeed it does. But those with a high-school education show up remarkably well as readers. Why? Are high-school graduates continuing their education? Are they seeking self-improvement? Or are they less satisfied than college graduates with their jobs and thus reading out of the almost universal need to escape? Skeptical as I am of "motivational research," it is essential to learn more about the healthy reader if we are to help the person who does not or cannot read.

Further, if we are to use statistics, let us insist at least on their disciplined development. Studies usually measure book readers against the total population, sometimes against only the total adult population. Which of these studies recognize that 18 million, or 11 percent of our people, speak a language other than English at home, that 8 million speak Spanish, for instance?

If readership studies start with a total population of 226 million, and that number is reduced by those under age nineteen, we are at 154 million in a single step. If, in a search for the center of the matter, we deduct those people over seventy-five, the working number becomes 144 million. Subract non-English-speaking people and the number becomes something like 126 million--not the 226 million frequently spoken of as "our" population. Then remove the blind and other handicapped who cannot read, or read easily, and factor in not just hardcover book sales but book club memberships, the readership of paperback reprints, books in other forms (magazine serials or excerpts, for example), books borrowed not only from libraries but from friends, and, in addition to complexity, a kind of usefulness and humanity begins to bleed into the otherwise bloodless statistics.

What do we make of the greatly increased number of working women? Women have always been assumed to be the major readers in this country, to the extent that anyone will admit that we have readers. Does their presence in the work force mean that they have more money to spend on books but less time to read? Or do they find time to read regardless of their limited leisure hours? The common assumption that women are the readers is supported by the gender evidence in book club rolls. Yet what are we to make of the study in 1979 which showed that the most frequent visitors to libraries (about once every two weeks, or more than twenty-five trips per year) tended to be men, aged eighteen to thirty-four?[16]

Why speak of television as a minus, a deterrent, or a drain, when almost every survey tells us that book readers are not passive or bookish, that their interests are not confined to books? Book readers watch television, go to movies and ballgames, eat "fast" as well as "gourmet" foods, play records, go to concerts, and in general use more time than they think they have.

America has a long way to go toward universal literacy. But underestimating or undervaluing what we are accomplishing is a waste of time and energy. For years, expenditures for books increased while money spent for magazines, newspapers, and movies decreased. The number of book publishers has grown markedly and at a much faster rate than the formation of television and radio stations, newspapers, or periodicals.

Despite recent declines in the unit sales of individual books, we are still doing better than we were in the fifties, and not just because of increased population. The last time I looked at a comparison of unit sales of popular novels, Herman Wouk's Marjorie Morningstar of 1954 and Peter Benchley's Jaws of 1974, the former had sold a little under 2 million copies in its original hardcover, paperback, and book club editions, while the latter sold, in the same three forms, around 10 million. And these numbers do not include what magazine people call "pass-along" readership--the reading of one copy by more than one person.

The popular perception persists--there are not many book readers in America. By what measure can we count ourselves a "nation of readers" (in the phrase used by the Center for the Book at the Library of Congress)? One hundred percent of all Americans reading how many books per year? Eighty percent? Anything over fifty percent? What number would you use to designate "book people?" Five million? One million? One hundred thousand?

Many authors feel that they know more writers than readers. Publishers mutter that if all the people who write poetry would buy one book of poetry per year, the entire aspect of poetry publishing would change over the weekend.

Yet over 5 million books are bought in this country per day. To be sure, this includes book club members, paperback readers, schools, libraries, and the rest. But institutions do not diminish the implications of this number; rather, they increase it, because an institutional copy is apt to be read by more than one person.

Such numbers are offered neither as proofs or puffs. They only underline the idea that the community worries but doesn't wonder; it criticizes energetically but investigates perfunctorily; threatened by unknowns, it issues pronouncements as if they were facts. The leading spokespeople for books, citizens of at least some education, display dizzying naivete, gullibility, and credulity.

A report that S.A.T. scores are rising brings out the scoffers immediately. When there is clear proof that the regularly

maligned American is reading a book, he (or she) is accused of
reading "trash." They don't read what they "should," what is good
for them, and surely they cannot be reading both popular literature
and Literature. Literary people may like pizza and popcorn as
well as paillard de veau and Corton Charlemagne, but they cannot
believe that others do, too. Such concessions could be upsetting.
Just when you have them safely stereotyped, tucked away in categories, American readers are revealed as pluralistic pigeons who
refuse to stay holed.

A Roots, a Godfather, a Garp, a Hailey, a Wouk, a Uris,
regularly reach readers in the millions. Instead of dismissing this
fact as unrelated to serious book reading, those concerned with
reading habits should ask: Why them? What does it take to rouse
the reader? The evidence is fuzzy that this is a nation of nonreaders. We appear to be a nation that can be excited by a book--but
not easily.

Within the community, a deep and divisive schizophrenia
exists about whether we want to select and sell only The Best, even
if that means selling to the fewest, or bring out books for the many,
with the understanding that the popular fare will help to subsidize
some of the best and also might lead readers from one kind of book
to another. Underlying the conflict is the issue of whether we really want all sorts of books for all sorts of people, or just books for
Our Kind, Our Crowd. No amount of cultural overlay or the laying
down of sophisticated smokescreens from on high can obscure the
fact that the views of certain elements within the community are
not notably democratic.

Then, too, we cannot shift all problems to the reader or the
nonreader or the teacher. We should go back to origins also.
Poorly written, uninteresting books might well cause indifferent
audiences. As Richard Poirier puts it, "Bad things may indeed be
happening to books these days, including, one might add, much of
the writing that is found in them."[17]

It could be that it is not so much a matter of the disappearing individual reader as the disappearing singularity of books. One
of the publishing industry's rare, thoughtful, and studious analysts,
Per Gedin, put it succinctly in his little-noted book, Literature in
The Marketplace. Citing the Euromonitor Book Readership Survey
of 1975, Gedin writes, "Books are becoming another form of mass
media and entertainment and are losing their individual appeal."[18]
If book reading has slowed, it might not just be a matter of Reaganomics or red-neck six-pack pleasures, but a decline of the book itself. Successful or not, some books are becoming faceless in the
crowd. Perhaps, given the difficulties, diversions, disappointments,
and depression, it is remarkable that people read at all.

The arguments are familiar and fatiguing. As with disarmament, everybody's right and everybody's wrong. Still, the problems will not go away. A number of automatic antagonisms ought

Communication and Education

to be reexamined, and others replaced. This is the time for an end to easy assumptions. Books are good? Some books are. Good books are neglected? Not usually. Great books are rare? Great everything is rare. Let us confront a few newer notions, for ancient arguments only camouflage what could be more important matters. Consider, for example:

Television and Reading--It is time to set aside simplistic notions that television is the enemy of reading or that television must be enlisted to "save" reading. Reading is not an isolated experience; it is ailing or alive in the culture and gets substantial aid and interference from other sources. Television has a push-pull influence: it conceivably attracts some readers; claims for its own non-readers who would not read even if there were no television; and takes others away some, but not all, of the time. Even more obviously, television stimulates interest in reading on occasion, through its several techniques, intended or accidental. People are driven to books by good television programs made from those books; people are also driven back to books out of boredom with the small screen.

As, one suspects, they are drawn to seeing more movies or plays after having been to (or heard about) a very satisfying movie or play and later stay away from films or the theatre for a time after being disappointed--and perhaps return to (or do more) reading. We need to recognize and study the ecology of the media. Currents of attraction swirl among minds, competition for attention is intense, and there are notable as well as minor distractions and substantial or trivial differences in pleasures offered to the individual. Scholars searching for suitable subjects could find in media ecology, relatedness, independence or interdependence, much to chew on. One medium has an impact on another, and all of them react to all others. For the first time since commercial television began, the total viewing audience is not growing rapidly. Does book readership decline when television and motion picture audiences increase? Does the record business run parallel with book publishing --or counter to it? Should authors and publishers attempt to adapt to the world of fast-moving images--or stay with what books do best, what moving images cannot do? Television news was once broadcast in "ghetto" hours; now it is prime time entertainment. What conclusions does this suggest for books, which are in part a journalistic, news-bringing medium, or for the novel as "news," one of its classic roles? Television people devote a good deal of attention to slotting, the sequence of programs, to how one program feeds interest in another, and to the competition in the same time period. Publishing devotes little, if any, effort to considering sequence, and knows next to nothing about what the competition is doing, except for the most obvious big, popular books coming up. Can one book feed another--or does one highly touted, but ultimately disappointing, book diminish the audience temporarily?

Part of the community's anxiety about television is a fear of what might be happening to print, especially when the argument enters the TV-versus-newspapers stage. Everyone "knows" that American newspapers are dying, that most Americans get their news from television, and so on. A recent article by Leo Bogart in The Wilson Quarterly shows that newspapers have better circulation ratios to population in cities where TV news ratings are high rather than low; that what kills off newspapers is not a lack of readers but a lack of advertising revenue for the number two paper in any market; that the birth of new newspapers has approximately balanced the death of old ones (twelve dailies stopped publication in 1980-81, and twenty-five new ones were started); that daily newspapers are now published in 1,560 American towns, more than ever before; that during the 1978 strike of New York newspapers, television news viewing went down, not up.[19]

Needed--A solidly based study of the incomes and economic support systems of writers, publishers, scholars, and others to disperse the dust of both old claims and new ones. The survey of writers' incomes cited earlier failed to take adequately into account many factors of considerable consequence, including (as noted) the total population of writers in the United States; the incomes of technical, scientific, textbook, or scholarly authors; patronage apart from publishers; and the fact that, for most authors, writing provides a second income. What can be considered fair compensation for those for whom writing is a second, part-time job, performed, in some cases, in a second-rate manner and in others (Wallace Stevens, for example) in stunning, singular fashion?

Needed--More specific information on the several kinds of publishing so that it can be sorted out, and textbooks, general books, monographs, and so on, no longer lumped together indiscriminately or ignored.

Needed--Educational projects to bring the young and old of publishing together--to give the young some sense of history and a knowledge of antecedents, so that they will not buy every bargain apocalypse offered them, and to encourage the older members to contribute reliably to a credible history of a useful and little-understood industry. Hundreds of publishing courses are taught to people hoping to get into publishing; meanwhile, many of the people in publishing know little of the history of the book, misunderstand or misuse the few facts they have, and misreport the process in which they participate.

The literature of publishing is sketchy, scattered, and simply appalling. In the main, it is written not by publishers, but by authors. Thus the "history" of publishing is seen by privileged and sometimes victimized participants. Barthes writes that "for a very long time--probably for the entire classical capitalist period, i.e., from the sixteenth to the nineteenth century, in France--the uncontested owners of the language, and they alone, were authors.... If we except preachers and jurists (enclosed moreover in functional languages), no one else spoke."[20] Most publishing history is still written by the "owners" of the language. Apart from the distortions or biases of authors, when editors, agents, and publishers do write their memoirs, they are usually a collection of boastful or trivial unreliable recollections (and almost always disorganized and in desperate need of editing).

On Censorship, Book-Banning, and Book-Burning--All our energies are given over to stamping out fires. Time should be devoted too (as with crime and poverty) to uncovering the root or hidden causes of resistance to books--the desire, say, in some textbook cases, to have a voice in the education of one's children. Or to go on believing in the Bible. As Paul Cowan wrote of a textbook adoption controversy in Charleston, West Virginia, "It is not an isolated battle ... it is nothing less than a fight over America's future ... it is a holy war between people who depend on books and people who depend on the Book."[21] Or the chance for self-aggrandizement of some of the publicity-hungry censors. Some of those on the other side of the line, who see themselves on the side of the angels, are decent people, trying to do the right thing as they understand right.

Know your enemy. He could turn out to be a misguided friend. Further, to use the language of the intelligence community, you might be able to "turn" him.

And let us give up overestimating the opposition. Liberals eager to leap to a defense of virtue, including their own, and evereager to find new monsters to scourge, contribute to the power of right-tilted, media-minded evangelists who claim vast followings but do not always have them.

The issues of censorship, textbooks, and pornography go beyond mere distaste for red-neck opposition to Darwin or J.D. Salinger. How can we fight fire with fire but also with education, to help people understand that banning books usually means banning freedom, and that good books (by any measure) are inevitably burned with the bad? How can we celebrate the heroism of those who stand up for freedom or those who help calm the fears of their frightened neighbors, neighbors who don't always buy sophisticated versions of science, religion, or morality? Not everyone, after all, grew up nurtured on the First Amendment--for all they know, every Amendment is important (a point lost on some First Amendment "groupies," who are less concerned about the Sixth, say, as long as they are not on trial for their lives). Granted, we have to accept grotesque distortions of the First Amendment to go on enjoying its benefits, but those feeling dismay have no constitutional duty to remain silent.

Let us look for issues under or behind the usual issues, for the "reticences and resonances of this society," as someone said. Are there legitimate inhibitions to publication? Should there be? What are authors' and publishers' self-imposed standards? Are there _any_ limits worth considering?

On the Courts' Call for the Notes of Writers--Let us fight

this at the same time we look for considerations beyond the ordinary. If the recent interpretations of some courts are to be construed as law, a reporter's hasty scribblings are now to be taken as gospel. This is somewhat like issuing a subpoena for a person's mind, his or her free associations, rough drafts, privileged impressions, private thoughts, and harmless mistakes.

Public Lending Rights, Copyrights and Copycats, etc.--When will we take these questions--the possible payment to authors and publishers for their investment, by tiny fees paid for books borrowed from libraries or photocopied--to the public? They deserve to know both sides, the desirability of payments from one point of view, and the respectable opposition to it from others, including the inhibition of free libraries and the necessary policing and paperwork by librarians at a time when they are strapped for funds, staff, and time. Except for an increasing awareness of the question of justice in the copying of records and videocassettes, this issue is not even in the public consciousness. Yet it is the public who will pay--or not--and it is time to bring them into the act.

Relevant, Useful, Economical Technology--This brings us to the decades of technological backwardness in printing and papermaking. Despite the proliferation of calculators and computers, progress in both activities is glacial. Few devices, processes, or products have been invented in decades to affect materially the costs of "goods" produced. Offset lithography made easier the reproduction of photographs. The word processor is excellent for "keyboarding" copy, particularly reference works that need regular revision; for "typesetting" manuscripts into reproducible form--perhaps especially--for short-run publishing, including scholarly monographs. (The author is already doing the work anyhow--i.e., composing-- and the possibilities are, as possibilities are almost always said to be, endless. But there are as yet no universals, no established standards for the hardware, and, as with booksellers/wholesalers/ librarians, and publishers, system-to-system matching remains a difficulty. Excellent, too, are the potentialities for disaster, with instant erasure or deletion. The opportunities to save both time and money are real. Still, for the editing of books, in the sense of what happens between an author and editor, the word processor does not yet show many advantages, except for producing clean copies of the manuscript when the author revises after editing.) But for too long, the basic costs--of paper, printing, binding--have not been reduced materially. The nation suffers a shortage of technical as well as social invention.

In 1976 I said that publishing is not suffering from Future Shock, that supposedly onrushing future overwhelming us with technological changes and improvements. Rather, it is hampered by a receding technological future as the technology of the past weighs us down. In this vein, Joan Manley, vice-president of Time, Inc., asked the Book Manufacturing Institute: Where are the "innovators and inventors who should be easing the weight of past technology? Are they not there in the numbers we need because we think we cannot afford them?" She reminded the manufacturers that technological breakthroughs do not come on the cheap, that other industries recognize the importance of research and development. The National Science Foundation, she said, reports that all industries spent in general about 2 percent of their gross receipts on R&D in a recent year, when printers and publishers spent only 0.6 percent on the same effort.[22]

In the end, or in the future, it may not matter, for conventional printing is being overtaken by electronic reproduction, and printers may find themselves, like coopers and blacksmiths, technologically obsolescent. And we are still tearing down trees to make paper. Can our vaunted technological community come up with nothing better?

The Politics of Publishing--What are they? Not just those of altered textbooks, responding to market or ethnic pressures (often at odds--too few black faces; too many black faces, not enough yellow or white ones; etc.), but the politics of "general publishing," where most lists appear to be predominantly left of center, with only one or two houses identified as on the right? Publishers profess to have no politics, but their lists belie their claim.

Why do we divide literature into the two categories of "fiction" and "nonfiction"? What is nonfiction, after all? It includes poetry, which at its best is truth, but is not limited to the factual. It includes biography, history, belles lettres, religion, instruction, sciences (soft, social, hard, practical, theoretical). It includes, in short, everything that the word "fiction" does not. It is, in other words, "everything else." Thus nonfiction is an inept, inappropriate, inelegant, nondescript nondescription.

Who is reponsible for facts, claims, charges, in a book? This unresolved debate flares now and then. The author alone is responsible, says the publisher; there is no way for us to know. The publisher, says the author; there is no way for me to accept full responsibility alone. (This issue is at the heart of contractual questions about who shall insure whom, when one party tries to hold the other responsible or tries to be held harmless.)

What of the increasing tendency to blur the lines that once defined fiction, history, the memoir, journalism, biography? And should there be a truth-in-packaging law applied to authors and publishers? Can the public be protected about reckless claims or mislabeling, even if it cannot be defended against hyperbole? Not only a few cynically commercial publishers practice deception; university presses tend to put definitive titles on narrow gauge studies. Publishers and writers, especially journalistic ones, enjoy First Amendment freedoms designed for the reader, the public, and regularly abuse them. This is part of the reason for the rage expressed against reporters, writers, editors, publishers, and broadcasters from right and left, in polls, and from the bench.

This condition is aggravated by publishing's refusal to follow the proscriptions proffered by literary watchdogs, or antiliterary vigilantes, and other counselors who push prescriptions for narrowness, blandness, or bankruptcy. Writers and publishers will never be above suspicion; we must try not to lose even more respect for our work, our wares, and ourselves. Those who flourish in freedom, unfettered by formal and fixed responsibilities, must be the most responsible people of all.

If the community of the book is to progress beyond its usual limits, we must challenge the usual prejudices--about reading and the reader, about the writer, the book, the publisher, and the bookseller, and other related people, practices, processes. If we are to raise the standards of performance, we have to set aside the standard presumptions--our elitism, defeatism, the mind-set of We Happy Few, the usual airy "data."

The assumptions that most need shaking are those we hold near and dear. One is the unhappy tendency to divide all controversies within the community into "we" versus "they." Of the industry, those who are inside are considered "book people"; all others are not, and are, when they come close, beyond the pale, beyond consideration. Of publishers, there are said to be "good" publishers or "commercial" publishers, "literary" or "serious" publishers versus all others. Unfair biases still exist, notably the conviction on the part of editors, reviewers, and authors that editors are the soul and substance of the business, a belief reinforced by agents, librarians, and others, when they are, momentarily, not inflamed over some editorial insufficiency. The editor über alles reflects an underappreciation of what is done by sales, promotion, rights, and business departments. Inventory management, that is to say, setting printings, is the third most difficult decision in publishing after the first two, editorial judgment and the publisher's decision about whether to publish or not. Nevertheless, the unfortunate assumption persists that "noneditorial" people in publishing are semiliterate and are at the service of editors, rather than publishing specialists in their own right, with their own rights.

To be sure, imbalance of any kind is a poor idea, no matter in what direction a house may be tilting. When one executive arrived to take charge of the publishing division of a national religious organization, he found that they had more accountants on the payroll than editors. "Ah," said Werner Mark Linz, the new publisher, "I see we're in the accounting, not the publishing business." Still, defamations of accountants are commonplace, as if all accountants must be minimally human, interested only in The Numbers and unable to read anything except balance sheets. In a healthy publishing house, many opinions are taken into consideration, if not taken as definitive, because each person's opinion is worth something--as reader, as citizen, as a member of the firm.

Such "class" distinctions are at times well founded but more often are based on ignorance. Such attitudes constitute an unattractive form of occupational discrimination, the sort of prejudice that the prejudiced themselves find hateful when based on race or nationality. Publishing is not an equal opportunity employer when one function or department--finance, sales, editorial, rights selling, administrative or managerial--is ascendant, dominant over others.

None of the arguments above suggests that the substitution of my opinions and examples for those of others has any importance. What could be important, and are vitally needed, are serious, substantial additions to our skimpy body of knowledge and insubstantial literature. Instead of the babble and the incoherence, we need more structured debates, more disciplined inquiries. We need more information and less opinion, and more skepticism about our own convictions. Not least, there is a need for the parties to come reasonably well prepared for discussion. We can serve the book in no better way than to read and think, to refuse to be glib, and to allow no more unexamined "facts" to pass.

We neither fully understand our successes nor successfully diagnose our illnesses. Not every slip is a landslide, not every miss a mile. What is needed are centers for the study of the book, reading, reproduction, and so on, and journals to publish the results --as we have in Daedalus, Book Forum, The Wilson Quarterly, The Annals, Publishing History, Scholarly Publishing--although we have no one journal to consistently publish the results of work in our several related fields. We need to collate and sift and sort the results of research and various sources of information, not work in separated fiefs. Perhaps we need a General Theory of the Book. What we do not need are more facile declarations, or glimmering, glowering generalities.

Where are we to get this information? From library schools (who have some of the best research), the associations of publishers and librarians, bookseller records, the studies done continually by newspaper and magazine publishers. Book club information is among the best and "hardest" in the business, and although closely guarded, sometimes can be extracted or shared. One book club expert said, for instance, that the members of a military book club are not "heavily veterans of World War II." They are younger. The members of specialty book clubs, devoted to interests like cooking, science-fiction, mysteries, and so on, are not as "upscale" as members of general book clubs. What are the implications of this information? If there are more female names on book club rolls than male, are men under-reading or are they underrepresented? Do women buy for men, sign the checks? Are men closet readers, who admit to reading biography or history but not fiction? We need limited and linked studies, done on a manageable scale.

Who is putting together the work of gifted-reading teachers with the work of those dealing with reading and learning difficulties, and with the work of researchers in optics, motor difficulties, ethnic and cultural considerations? Where is the center for more than just discussion or promotion of the book? What prospects are there for a center for advanced study of democratic reading and writing institutions?

Here and there, excellent research is under way. Robert Darnton, professor of history at Princeton, has written a publishing history of the Encyclopédie, and his article, "What Is the History of Books?" (Daedalus, Summer 1982) is a model inquiry, serious but not grim, especially his wonderful work on the trade records of one bookseller attempting to corner the new market in Voltaire.

Beyond study, we need a genuine sense of community. American writers sometimes lament their dispersal, as if it were displacement. American booksellers, librarians, and publishers see themselves as separate parishes. The sociologist Lewis Coser and his associates found that editors spend less and less time with authors.[23] We are more preoccupied with the practice of publishing. The less we see of each other, the more misunderstandings arise.

Perhaps we are not a community after all; perhaps we merely populate Pluto's Republic, "each according to our own prejudices," as Sir Peter Medawar puts it. Pluto's Republic, Anthony Tucker says in a review of Medawar, is "the foggy intellectual underworld of misperception ... the fuddled underworld we all inhabit from time to time," marked by an "absence of logic, philosophical philanderings and misconceptions, ... failures to confront reality or sift order out of chaos." Within the Republic "are all thinkers who regard rhapsodic intellection as an adequate substitute for the process of ratiocination."[24]

It is convenient and comforting to think of our republic as the Community of the Book. But perhaps we are destined to remain a series of separate states, warring factions in a cultural/commercial Middle East, shouting imprecations at each other across borders, with occasional skirmishes and now and then a six-day war. I hope not. For we are bound up in common concerns and causes; we do need each other, and for the usual reasons--because we are mutually dependent. "The word community," writes Henri J. M. Nouwen and co-authors,

> expresses a certain supportive and nurturing way of living and working together. When someone says, "I miss a sense of community here; something should be done to build a better community," she or he is probably suffering from alienation, loneliness, or lack of mutual support and cooperation.... It is therefore not strange that for quite a few critical observers of the contemporary scene, the word community has become associated with sentimentalism, romanticism, and even melancholy.[25]

Nouwen writes of the Christian community, but such thoughts apply to the Community of the Book as well. A community exists or comes together for the purpose of sustenance, shelter, support, safety, convenience, comfort, common values. Communities are based, wrote Leslie J. Vaughan, "on blood, family, kin, clan, race, ideology, love, shared goals."[26] All communities have their factions and their problems, and we are not lacking in ours. The factions take up positions. Snipers are posted in the trees. We send out scouts. But our reconnaissance, our intelligence gathering, is faulty.

We are eloquent on our weaknesses and fail to recognize our strengths. We are so concerned with calamity that we cannot see continuity. It has often been said, Eric Larrabee noted, "that the struggle of American consciousness has been to reconcile independence with interdependence, the one with the many."[27]

The search for community is not new, as Charles Handy writes: St. Benedict praised the idea when he founded his first monastery in the seventh century: "a community in which all were equal yet each was different, a community where each person's effort contributed to some common task or mission ... where privacy and mutual aid were both important."[28]

Nonetheless, ours is a community of sorts, a pleasant place, even with (and in part because of) our problems. Such frictions feed the fires of the community's power, providing light, heat, energy, and, on occasion, genuine warmth. Without crisis we feel threatened. Our institutions are smaller than they seem, our total numbers larger and of more significance than we think. We have our urban centers, suburbs, ghettoes, lords of the manor, and houses on the hill. Most of our officials are self-appointed, including those who, like myself, militantly issue armchair generalizations. Our time and talents are taken up, much of the time, with activities of interest and importance--the transmission of ideas and analyses, the telling of tales. The community has its attractions and its attractive people, and an ebullient optimism, coupled with a streak of fatalism, that are among its most appealing, foolish, and basic features. The mass of work produced is middling; the overall conduct and character of the community is characterized, falsely, by what happens at the extremes. Here, the norm is no more interesting than elsewhere, and the good news is no news.

Where is this place? Some say it is a state of mind. At moments, it looks like a state of mindlessness. Sensitivity is everywhere, but sense is uncommon, and many of our outstanding citizens are brilliant but not smart. Indians are always thought to be circling out there in the dark, and around here, everybody sees almost everybody else as an Indian.

Yet we like it. If we ever learn to love each other as much as the work we do, the people of the book will turn out to be a community as varied and vital, as valuable and enjoyable as the book itself.

N.B.: This is a thoroughgoing revision by the author of the paper that originally appeared in Daedalus.

References

1. The figures available always seem large. John P. Dessauer (Publishers Weekly, December 17, 1982) places "relevant 1981 domestic consumer purchases at 1.34 billion units, yielding $5.76 billion in retail level sales and $4.12 billion in publishers' revenues." But as Dessauer and other industry analysts often point out, total sales of all book publishing of all kinds often amount to less than the net profits of any one of a number of truly large U.S. individual companies.
   AT&T and Exxon, for instance, in 1981 had net profits of over $6.8 billion and $5.5 billion (Forbes, May 10, 1982). Again, publishing industry sales are said to be big--but every company that made the Forbes "500" list had sales of over $1 billion, and 110 of them now have more than $5 billion.
   The few publishing companies that make the Fortune and Forbes 500 lists are those which include other and more profitable activities--magazines, broadcasting, and so on; i.e., Time, Inc.; The Readers Digest; McGraw-Hill; Times-Mirror (and Doubleday, whose figures, as a private corporation, are not published).
   What is more interesting is that book publishing's influence, reach, range, presumed power, and prestige, for greater or lesser good, are out of all proportion to its dollar-ranking as an industry.
2. Dessauer sums up the "explosive growth" of small publishing houses (as had Doebler) in Publishers Weekly, December 17, 1982.
3. See also "Small Publisher Power," by Judith Applebaum, Publishers Weekly, September 10, 1982.
4. Ibid., pp. 24, 25.
5. Ibid., pp. 25-26.
6. "American Book Title Production," Publishers Weekly, October 1, 1982, p. 40. The fiction totals can be misleading, thanks to what Bowker's Weekly Record confesses is "a considerable undercount of mass market paperbacks" in 1979 and 1980.
7. June 15, 1982.
8. July 27, 1982.
9. Unpublished version of a manuscript by Benjamin, later revised for Publishers Weekly.
10. September 24, 1982, p. 16.
11. Publishers Weekly, October 1, 1982. Also, Association of American Publishers Newsletter, October 1982. The gap between publishers' concern and action is footnoted in a summary of "The Year in Review" for the AAP: "A major initiative undertaken during the year was the effort to find a special niche for publishers in the widening war on illiteracy, low reading skills, and low reading motivation." After letters to President Reagan urging a "Business Committee for Literacy," and pledges by twenty publishers, "at year's end the committee had not been established and no pledged money had been collected or spent."

12. Leslie Fiedler, What Was Literature?: Class Culture and Mass Society (New York: Simon and Schuster, 1982).
13. Herbert Mitgang, New York Times, November 14, 1978. Library of Congress Information Bulletin 37 (46) (November 17, 1978).
14. Saturday Review, "Trade Winds, America's Reading," Walter Arnold, January 20, 1979.
15. Samuel S. Vaughan, "The Quest for the 'Average Reader' is an Endless Game of Fiction," New York Times Book Review, December 29, 1963. Bernard Berelson, The Library's Public (New York: Columbia University Press, 1949).
16. Information on U.S. households where English is not spoken or is not the first language is from American Demographics, July/August 1982; on library use, from "The Good News about Library Visitors," pamphlet published by the American Library Association, based on a study for the White House Conference on Libraries and Information Services, 1979.
17. Poirier quote is from Raritan.
18. Revised edition, 1958, Faber & Faber, London, p. 7. First published in the United States in 1977 by Overlook Press.
19. Dr. Bogart has written extensively on print, especially vis-à-vis television, in The Wilson Quarterly issue on media, 1982, and in The Age of Television.
20. From "Authors and Writers," in A Barthes Reader, edited by Susan Sontag (New York: Hill and Wang, 1982), p. 185. Reprinted from his Critical Essays.
21. Paul Cowan, "A Fight over America's Future," in The Tribes of America, chapter 4 (New York: Doubleday, 1979), p. 77; previously published in The Village Voice.
22. Reported in Publishers Weekly; followed by a report, December 3, 1982, entitled "1982 Was a Year of 'Technological Restraint.'" See also, "Technology, Enterprise, and American Economic Growth," in Jordan D. Lewis, Science, March 5, 1982, abstracted in The Wilson Quarterly, Autumn 1982, to the effect that the United States leads in corporate R&D as a percentage of industrial output at 1.9 percent--but "Americans concentrate on products for the immediate future, while leading foreign companies look decades ahead."
23. Lewis A. Coser, Charles Kadushin, Walter W. Powell, Books: The Culture & Commerce of Publishing (New York: Basic Books, 1982).
24. Anthony Tucker, "Poor Pluto," The Guardian, October 14, 1982.
25. Donald P. McNeil, Douglas A. Morrison, and Henri J.M. Nouwen, Compassion (New York: Doubleday, 1982).
26. In a letter to the author, November 1982.
27. Buffalo Courier-Express, August 10, 1980.
28. Charles Handy, Gods of Management (London: Souvenir Press, 1978; reprinted London: Pan Books, 1979).

Part III

THE SOCIAL PREROGATIVE

ACCESS AND DISSEMINATION ISSUES

CONCERNING FEDERAL GOVERNMENT INFORMATION*

Marc A. Levin

Ever since the first successful Soviet venture into space in 1957, a national debate has ensued concerning federal policies to improve national information services. Initially, discussion revolved chiefly around scientific and technical information, expanding more recently to encompass the entire spectrum of national information needs and priorities. Evidence of this growing national concern can be seen in the recent plethora of information-related legislation introduced before the U.S. Congress. The result has been increasing interest throughout the federal government concerning the development of policies to guide federal agencies in the dissemination of information to the public.

The traditional presumption underlying U.S. information policy has been the "open availability of and ease of access to information ... of interest to or concern[ing] the welfare of American citizens," based on broad principles enunciated in the First Amendment to the U.S. Constitution.[1] Historically, however, there has been no comprehensive national information policy and no consensus about instituting one, either in Congress or the executive branch. This lack of centralization has led to a mosaic of public and administrative laws and varying policy interpretations within the government, with departments and agencies pursuing their own missions and often developing their own information policies.

The issues surrounding federal information demand close and immediate scrutiny, especially in light of recent trends which may significantly alter the traditional free flow of information. While it is true that there has been no comprehensive national information policy, one is now developing which poses some dangerous precedents. First, it runs counter to our tradition of open availability of information, and second, it is being developed "through the back door." This developing information policy is being devised by aggressive private-sector interests, without proper oversight from

---

*Reprinted by permission of the author and publisher from Special Libraries, 74:2 (April 1983) 127-37. Copyright © 1983 by Special Libraries Association.

Congress or input from the library community, and promises easy concurrence by the Reagan administration. Furthermore, many people now argue that new technologies and philosophies are making the current patchwork dissemination system obsolete. These combined reasons illustrate why access and dissemination issues are now particularly relevant and demand urgent attention by the library and information community.

The Federal Information Milieu

Economist Marc Porat's classic study revealed that by the mid-1970s, approximately one half of the U.S. Gross National Product was devoted to information activities, and that this proportion of the economy had doubled during the last 30 years.[2] These findings motivate the argument that the United States is now an information-based economy. Indeed, if an information-based society is one in which planning and bureaucracy have become widespread, according to Porat's definition, then nowhere is this more evident than in the federal government, where information-related activities consume the majority of expended resources and energy. Our massive, modern federal bureaucracy has evolved into an information producing, distributing, and consuming organism concerned with planning, coordinating, communicating, and processing information.

In a recent policy statement, the Office of Management and Budget defined "public information" as that

> which is collected, produced or created by or for the Federal Government, with federal funds, primarily for the purpose of communicating with, educating or informing one or more segments of the public. The distinguishing characteristic of public information is that the agency actively seeks, in some fashion, to disseminate such information or otherwise make it available to the public.[3]

Thus, the federal government encourages public dissemination of the information it generates or maintains by providing press releases, reports, publications, exhibits, audiovisual materials, advertising, and facilities for answering public inquiries. The mechanisms used to meet this responsibility include, but are not limited to, the Government Printing Office's sales and depository library programs; the National Technical Information Service; individual agency clearinghouses, information centers, and sales programs; and private dissemination services. In fact, some statutory provisions compel agencies to disseminate information upon petition or request in order to insure the public's right to learn about the workings of the federal government.

The heart of federal information dissemination is the Government Printing Office (GPO), created by the Congressional Joint Committee on Printing (JCP) more than 120 years ago to be the single and central source of printing for the U.S. government and the solution to problems plaguing federal printing since the country's founding.[4] Among these were the need to curb opportunistic printers and to arrest a system based on political patronage and unscrupulous business practices. Since then, the character of government publishing and printing has altered drastically.

During the nineteenth century, Congress was the predominant branch of government. The executive branch was still small and did a limited amount of publishing. With the advent of two world wars, and the New Deal in the 1930s, the executive branch expanded enormously; its publishing activities now overshadow those of the legislative branch. Yet, the central agency responsible for government printing still remains under legislative control.

The GPO, described as the world's largest printer, is to provide printing, binding, and distribution services for all three branches (legislative, executive and judicial) of the federal government. To fulfill its mission, the GPO performs four major functions: procurement, production, distribution (including cataloging and indexing), and administration. Distribution is managed by the Superintendent of Documents, which administers the 26 GPO bookstores nationwide, mail order sales service, depository library, and free distribution programs. The major distinction between these services is that the sales program is required to recover all costs through sales revenue, whereas the depository and free distribution programs are funded through congressional appropriations and subsidies.

Another federal agency assigned a significant role in the dissemination process is the National Technical Information Service (NTIS), operated by the Department of Commerce under a 1950 congressional mandate. The NTIS acts as a central clearinghouse for technical information considered useful to American business and industry, and as such is the cornerstone of the technological publishing structure in the United States. It is also one of the world's leading processors of specialty information. As stated in the 1981/82 Government Manual, NTIS is the "central source for the public sale of U.S. Government-sponsored research, development, and engineering reports as well as foreign technical reports and other analyses prepared by national and local government agencies, their contractors, or grantees."

Since its publications are paid for by customers, the NTIS is entirely self-sustaining and not tax-supported. As a general rule, its publications are more expensive than they would be if distributed by the GPO. Thus, the NTIS and the GPO are competitors in the acquisition and dissemination of publications that have borderline jurisdiction. One congressional study of the publications practices of selected executive agencies found that many nontechnical and nonscientific publications were made available only through the NTIS.[5] This kind of competition not only diminishes the overall effectiveness of government information dissemination; it also results in public confusion.

Problems and Proposed Changes

In 1978, the Joint Committee on Printing appointed an Ad Hoc Advisory Committee on Revision of Title 44 to identify contemporary policy issues confronting government information dissemination. Since the present system was codified in 1895, technological advances have changed the way government information is generated, produced, and disseminated, and there has been growing public demand for improved access to this information. Two central themes emerged with unanimity: the need to overhaul the outmoded 1895 Printing Act and the need to develop a policy to assure public access to federal information.[6]

The Committee recommended the establishment of a central coordinating office to administer public information policy for the government. This central information office, combining the functions of GPO, NTIS, and OMB, would facilitate improved public access, eliminate duplication of effort, and serve as an information "ombudsman" on behalf of the public. In its review of the federal depository library program, the Advisory Committee learned that numerous publications are never sent to the GPO, and that agency noncompliance with the depository requirements are rampant, if not often intentional. Moreover, many government agencies specifically permit private contractors to copyright the results of federally funded research and consultant studies, thereby disregarding the public's right to this information. The Committee concluded that the present distribution system was too cumbersome, diverse, and complex and served to inhibit rather than encourage public access.

As a result of the Committee's recommendations, a National Publications Act of 1980 (H.R. 5424) was introduced in Congress to "provide for the introduction of modern printing and distribution management techniques, a greater degree of public participation in the decision-making process," along with needed improvements to the depository program.[7] A major provision involved drastic restructuring of the archaic GPO to modernize its operations. The new entity would be renamed the National Publications Office (NPO), and a six-member commission would act as a "board of directors." This would replace the Joint Committee on Printing, with members chosen from the printing and publishing industries, organized labor, and the library/information community.

A major goal of the bill was to ensure that government information is available to taxpayers as inexpensively as possible. Despite strong, united support from professional library groups and organized labor, this legislation was ultimately defeated in Congress. Opposition from well-financed pressure groups representing the private printing establishment, as well as antiunion interests, assured its defeat.

Despite the bill's downfall, the GPO today is undergoing major, substantive changes, due to policy leadership under the

Reagan Administration. Under the stewardship of Danford L. Sawyer, the current Public Printer, GPO faces great change and redirection. Sawyer's attitude regarding the future of GPO can be best summarized in the following remarks made before the American Library Association.

> As with many government organizations these days, it is essential that GPO prove its need to exist. President Reagan has made it quite clear that unnecessary programs and overhead have no home in his Administration.... Therefore, it is one of my first responsibilities to prove the worth of such GPO efforts as the Documents' Sales and Distribution Programs, or if their value can not be substantiated, to eliminate them.[8]

A massive realignment of GPO's priorities has resulted due to policy shifts in conjunction with agency budget cuts, which threaten the future of access and dissemination to government information. Sawyer has proposed closing 23 of GPO's nationwide bookstores, reducing wherever possible the number of GPO employees, and increasing the lease of printing contracts to private firms.

Perhaps the most disconcerting action implemented was the policy not to offer for public sale government publications that were not expected to yield annual revenues of at least $1,000, thus scrapping thousands of slow-moving titles. The irony of this situation is that the GPO was not created to be a profitable organization but to serve the government's printing needs. Suddenly, its aim is to conduct business on a cost-recovery basis, disregarding the public's right to have easy access to federally financed information.

Today the future of NTIS also remains uncertain, even though it pays for itself. The Reagan Administration is currently studying various proposals regarding its future, including one submitted by the Information Industry Association which advocated abolishing NTIS in favor of contracting this function to the private sector.[9]

It is imperative that Congress establish a workable and enforceable information policy that encompasses the entire realm of government information, especially in light of increasing private-sector initiatives which may restrict the flow of federal information. To be successful, such a national policy must accommodate technological, political, and social realities and be able to clarify the appropriate role of the private sector in dissemination of government-generated information.

The Federal Statistical Milieu

Unlike most industrialized nations, the United States produces statistical data in a highly decentralized fashion. The initial core of the system was the constitutionally mandated decennial census. Now 38 core agencies operate major programs to collect or analyze statistics. These agencies have expanded tenfold over the past 30 years, developing model statistical programs to serve the needs of policy-makers and other users. They represent a collective budget of $945 million in FY 1979 and employ more than 30,000 civil servants.[10]

While this decentralized system worked well for many years, a landmark 1978 federal statistics planning document noted that users of federal statistics often feel confused and exasperated when trying to locate existing statistics, and are demanding a more centralized, coordinated facility for determining what data are available.[11] Consequently, one priority reflected in the 300 recommendations was to improve public access to data in the process of achieving a more integrated and effective statistical network.

Because computers are so widely available today, and many users of federal statistics can afford to process statistical data themselves, there has been a growing demand for the federal government to provide statistical information in the form of machine-readable data files (MRDFs). MRDFs offer the advantage of permitting agencies to prepare data much more cheaply and quickly than for conventional publication. For the user, MRDFs facilitate the ease of data manipulation and analysis. However, providing MRDFs to users would pose serious drawbacks, among them lack of system compatibility and unequal access to public data. Many users would not necessarily have the resources to handle data provided in the form of MRDFs. Moreover, users without computer facilities or expertise would be deprived of equal access to public data relative to users with computers.

Since American society presently is better equipped to handle information disseminated in a print rather than a machine-readable format, it is essential that the federal government improve the more traditional methods of data transmission in order to assure equal access to information while continuing its efforts to meet the demands of new technology in the area of data transmission.

Most statistical agencies report an increasing demand for data access and improved user services, yet their budget allocations are insufficient to meet it. Some agencies have begun to use NTIS and the National Archives and Record Service (NARS) to distribute statistical data files deposited with them. The recent NTIS publication of a <u>Directory of Federal Statistical Data Files</u> represents a pioneering effort to consolidate a comprehensive listing of all major federal statistical data files that have been designated for public use. Unfortunately, such cooperative efforts are vulnerable to agency budget reductions. The Reagan administration's determination to trim the budgets of non-defense agencies threatens to dismantle many crucial statistical programs. This has prompted grave concern among users of federal data, leading the <u>Wall Street Journal</u> to proclaim in a front-page article, "there is increasing evidence that Washington's number mills are beginning to break down."[12]

Statisticians and analysts lament the demise of numerous statistical programs due to budget cutbacks at the Bureaus of the Census and Labor Statistics and also fear elimination of smaller, less visible statistical activities. For example, the Bureau of the Census reportedly has reevaluated its anticipated release of data from the 1980 census, and plans to release selected data only in computer tape or microfiche formats as an economy measure. This decision gives credence to the growing contention that federal data dissemination is rapidly slipping from paper to microfiche to computer tape-only formats. Finally, users fear the potentially devastating long-term consequences of program eliminations, since future resurrection of eliminated programs would most likely be prohibitively costly.

Recent Legislation and Legal Implications

As stated earlier, the First Amendment to the Constitution provides the foundation for U.S. information policy. While the First Amendment is not itself a national information policy and does not guarantee widespread dissemination of information, it is part of a value system that gives high priority to a well-informed citizenry. It thus represents one of a number of constitutional traditions, statutes, and customs that define the general treatment of information in the United States.

Many federal statutes, either directly or indirectly, require the government to disseminate certain information to the public. Years of debate in Congress regarding the public's right to know culminated in the 1966 enactment of the Freedom of Information Act (FOIA), which serves as a check on the entire process of government decision-making by allowing the public to understand how decisions are made.[13] By requiring disclosure of agency documents upon citizen request, except those containing specified information of a personal or damaging nature, the FOIA promotes access to government information. It may also be considered a dissemination law since it requires federal agencies to publish specified information concerning their mission, organization, procedures, and policies.

Principles such as those expressed in the First Amendment and the FOIA engender conflicts concerning the government's need to balance civil liberties and personal privacy against its need for information availability. The Privacy Act of 1974 was designed to guarantee individuals' protection from disclosure of sensitive, government-held information, made increasingly necessary by the continuing development of sophisticated computers, telecommunications, and surveillance technologies which exacerbate the problems concerning privacy. Nonetheless, tension will always exist between the interests served by full public access to government-held information and the interests served by restricted access since these invariably are difficult to balance and maintain in equilibrium. The Reagan administration has attempted to weaken the FOIA on grounds that increased government secrecy is vital for national security.

Thus far, an adamant Congress has resisted his initiatives in this area.

In 1977 Congress, under the Carter administration, established the Commission on Federal Paperwork to make recommendations concerning elimination of needless paperwork within government operations. The Commission estimated that the Federal government was spending more than $100 billion annually on data collection, paperwork, and information-handling activities.[14] As a result of the Commission's numerous recommendations, Congress passed the Paperwork Reduction Act of 1980 which introduced for the first time the concept of information resources management. This could have a great impact on all federal information acquisition and distribution activities.

The major criticism of the Act concerns its consolidation within the Office of Management and Budget (OMB)--both information management and policy oversight. Besides developing statistical policy, OMB's newly created Office of Information and Regulatory Affairs, with a staff of 12 full-time employees, is responsible for managing the paperwork budget, administrative records, and records management; regulating federal automatic data processing and telecommunication facilities; setting regulatory policies; and providing the cost-benefit analysis of regulations associated with these duties for the entire federal government.[15] This attempt to improve information policies has been less than successful due to OMB's inadequate staffing, and concentration on regulatory reform and budget cuts. It is clear that information management and policy are not considered high-priority issues in the current administration.

Impact of Emerging Technologies

During the past decades, computers have become a major technological tool of American society. Recent advances in computer and telecommunication technology promise an even more drastic revolution in the way information is collected, stored, used, and disseminated. It is now practical to provide public access to massive amounts of information held in government databases all around the country through computerized data communication networks.

With each new technological advance, economic or social tensions may surface. As noted, computer and telecommunication technologies raise important policy issues related to guarantees of personal privacy and equal access to government databases.[16] Although the government has compiled personal information about individuals for quite some time, the current potential for abuse, with the prospect of extensive government-controlled data banks, is raising widespread attention and concern.

A major concern involves the potential secondary use of personal information contained in federal databases; increasingly sophisticated technology will enable public access to this information via "intelligent" (modified) telephones and televisions located in offices and homes. Privacy rights could be impaired substantially if confidentiality is diminished because of widespread distribution of information.

As the federal government continues to use cost-effective technologies, such as micrographics and video display terminals, as alternatives to printing information, it should also strive to provide equal access to the information at reasonable cost. On the other hand, the government needs to recover costs and also wishes to encourage the private sector. Thus, the debate continues concerning the issues of "fee" or "free" government information and the appropriate levels of subsidy and pricing to improve access to the government's resources.

An information "gap" would result if federal databases were only available to people via the private sector, at a price that discourages equal access on economic grounds. These are the conflicting issues federal policymakers must address in setting a uniform information policy.

Current Executive Policy Directions

The election of Ronald Reagan to the Presidency in 1980 ushered in a new era for the American federal system, characterized by drastic budget cutbacks, further private industry encroachments into the public sector, and new executive and legislative initiatives which together will deeply affect both library and citizen access to information.

In April 1981, the President imposed a moratorium on the production and procurement of new federal periodicals, pamphlets, and audiovisual products. Subsequently, OMB issued Bulletin 81-16, providing "procedures and guidelines for eliminating unnecessary Federal spending for the development and printing" of information products. Besides establishing a moratorium on all new government publications, this directive mandated federal agencies to review all existing publications, develop plans consistent with policy guidelines to control their production, and minimize federal spending by charging user fees to recover costs. Ensuing dollar savings were to be used to offset supplemental appropriations and/or applied towards agency salary increases. According to American Library Association estimates, by November 1981 more than 900 government publications had been eliminated and a myriad of other titles were being reviewed for transfer to the private sector for future publication.[17] (Of course, not all of these publications may have warranted federal expenditure.)

Current federal information restrictions are based on specific policy decisions centering on the administration's interpretation of the 1980 Paperwork Reduction Act and austerity budgeting.

Not surprisingly, in a climate in which some government information activities are considered unnecessary frills, information-dissemination programs are the first to be eliminated when agencies are faced with severe budget cuts. But the Reagan retrenchments go much further than simple agency budget cuts, reaching deep into the government's information-dissemination programs in ways that could fundamentally damage public access to information for decades.

Another significant administration proposal involves the institution of more user fees as an economy measure. This decision represents a sharp policy shift since the government traditionally has not charged for information-dissemination services, viewing them as serving the important societal function of informing citizens. Furthermore, the recipients of this information are taxpayers who have already paid once for its preparation. Heavy reliance on user fees could severely limit wide dissemination of information believed to be in the public interest. It could also create an information elite of affluent citizens who alone can afford access to expensive government information.

Although the federal government has always encouraged the private sector to serve the public interest by collecting, cataloging, indexing, reproducing, and disseminating government information, the extent to which private commercial activities are now being promulgated raises serious concerns. The philosophy and presumption of OMB policy directives, first issued in 1955 in Circular A-76, are that "in a democratic free enterprise economic system" the government should "rely on competitive private enterprise to supply the products and services it needs," and "should not compete with its citizens." While previous administrations have shared these presumptions and followed OMB directives more or less loosely, President Reagan has made implementation an integral part of his economic recovery program.

The strict application of this policy raises serious conflicting views concerning the appropriate role of government in providing information resources, products, and services--especially where the objective of relying on the private sector appears to conflict with the need to provide important services to the public. How such issues will be resolved when they arise is open to question.

Some recommendations concerning access to federal information consistent with OMB directives were made in 1981 by the Public/Private Sector Task Force of the National Commission on Libraries and Information Science (NCLIS), following a two-year study of the interactions between government and private-sector information activities. Generally, the Task Force urged the government to provide policy leadership in facilitating the development and use of information products and services, while at the same time encouraging private-sector investment to promote wide dissemination. More specifically, the Task Force favored open access to federal information, made widely available to the public; greater reliance on libraries and private-sector organizations to make federal information available; and limited direct government intervention in the marketplace unless there are clearly defined reasons for doing so, such decisions subject to periodic review.[18]

Conflicts between public and private information-dissemination services will inevitably surface as government information increasingly becomes a market commodity. The Reagan administration has a strong, ideological bias in favor of the private sector and advocates rigid interpretation of federal procurement policies. This philosophy, combined with pressure exerted by groups such as the Information Industry Association (IIA), is leading to sharp curtailment of government information available to the public.

One example was the recent attempt by Excerpta Medica, a private medical database producer, to limit the role of the National Library of Medicine (NLM) in promoting its subsidized database service (MEDLINE). Excerpta Medica sees NLM as a damaging competitor in the medical information business because of its low-cost subsidized services which overlap and duplicate their own commercial product.

IIA, a trade organization representing influential corporate information interests, has argued since its inception that the public sector should not be operating any enterprise that the private sector can run. This doctrine has been incorporated explicitly into official government policy, raising legitimate fears that "our national stock of information is being removed from government custodianship and transferred to private ownership and control."[19]

Agenda for Action

The preceding discussion of federal policies and initiatives concerning information dissemination and access depicts a scenario rife with special interests and/or executive benign neglect. Neither the executive nor legislative branches have ever established a comprehensive national information policy that would address the multitude of issues involving public access to federal information. Now, however, under the Reagan administration, a national information policy is beginning to emerge. Unfortunately it is designed to cater to the private information sector, with little regard for ensuring citizen or library access.

The irony of this situation, especially given the philosophy behind it, is that the change involves a violation of American tradition. This tradition has always viewed information as having a public value and asserted the public interest inherent in a free flow of information. Thus, the government's historic failure to formulate a comprehensive national information policy has presented corporate special interests with an excellent opportunity to develop their own policy, with full executive-branch cooperation.

Many professionals in the library and information communities are perturbed by the encroaching information gap that threatens to deny citizen access to information due to a combination of factors, such as technological illiteracy, lack of economic resources, and assorted federal policy directions. It can be argued that the lack of access to government information deprives American taxpayers of the "fruits" of their taxes. The question remains, should government information be treated as an economic good to be dealt with in purely economic terms, or as a social good to be dealt with in social terms, or as a combination of both? Perhaps we should consider the suggestion to establish a "National Information Constitution" designed to address the needs of individuals, industry, labor, libraries, and the government.[20] Indeed, the current confusing array of laws and regulations, with their overlapping strengths, contradictions, and deficiencies, is greatly in need of an overall structural framework.

The time for action is now, involving a dual approach by concerned information professionals. The first set of actions may be taken individually and involves traditional modes of political influence --lobbying elected officials, letter-writing, phone calls, personal visits to elected representatives, and most important, voting--all represent effective methods to inform and influence members of Congress.

The second set of actions involves organizational activities and programs. Professional groups, such as Special Libraries Association, should provide more leadership and direction to focus members' attention on issues likely to profoundly affect the future of information services. It is imperative that information professionals assume a proactive rather than a reactive role and fully participate in influencing legislation and policies that affect the profession. Since nonprofit organizations such as SLA are restricted from direct political involvement, it is recommended that a political action committee be established under the auspices of information organizations, dedicated to ensure a hearing and a presence in Washington. The majority of other professional associations and groups (i.e., realtors, bankers, publishers, organized labor) have already established political action committees to channel money and influence into the political arena with the goal of obtaining favorable commitments from elected leaders. As an initial step, SLA should establish a Washington office, comparable to American Library Association's Washington office, to coordinate its legislative and political activities.

The modern information professional is fast assuming the role of ombudsman between the information seeker and the available resources. Access to information is now the key issue. To influence developments in the national information scene we must enter the political arena, in which we have not formerly participated, or face the prospect of disenfranchisement. Federal shedding of information services and products in favor of the private sector threatens to drain library financial resources. More importantly, it may eventually diminish the nation's capacity for self-government. An informed and enlightened public remains a central foundation of democracy. The information community must vigilantly monitor federal information policy developments to ensure continued and improved access to the nation's vast federal information resources, so vital to our professional and personal lives.

References

1. Yurrow, Jane H., et al. Issues in Information Policy. National Telecommunication and Information Administration, NTIA-SP-80-9. Washington, D.C., U.S. Government Printing Office, 1981. 102p.
2. Porat, Marc Uri. The Information Economy: Definition and Measurement. Office of Telecommunications, OT Special Publication 77-12. Washington, D.C., U.S. Government Printing Office, 1977. 9v.
3. 45 Federal Register 38461.
4. U.S. Government Printing Office. 100 GPO Years, 1861-1961: a History of United States Public Printing, by Harry Schecter. Washington, D.C., U.S. Government Printing Office, 1961. 164p.
5. Library of Congress. Congressional Research Service. 1978 Survey of Selected Publications Practices of Executive Branch Agencies: Findings, by Sharon S. Gressle. Washington, D.C., U.S. Government Printing Office, 1979. 36p.
6. U.S. Congress. Ad Hoc Advisory Committee on Revision of Title 44. Federal Government Printing and Publishing: Policy Issues. Washington, D.C., U.S. Government Printing Office, 1979. 120p.
7. U.S. Congress. House. Committee on House Administration. National Publications Act of 1980. (House Report 96-836, Pt. I), 96th Cong., 2d Sess. Washington, D.C., U.S. Government Printing Office, 1980. 179p.
8. Sawyer, Danford L., Jr. "Remarks from the Public Printer." Government Publications Review 9(no. 3):243-246 (1982).
9. Reid, T.R. and Charles R. Babcock. "Private Firms Ready to Score Kill on Printing U.S. Studies." Washington Post: p. A-29 (Nov 20, 1981).
10. "Improving the Federal Statistical System: Report of the President's Reorganization Project for the Federal Statistical System." Statistical Reporter 80-8:197-212 (May 1980).
11. U.S. Office of Federal Statistical Policy and Standards. A Framework for Planning U.S. Federal Statistics for the 1980's. Washington, D.C., U.S. Government Printing Office, 1978. 387p.
12. Malabre, Alfred L., Jr. "Budget Cutting Hurts Quality of Data." Wall Street Journal: 1 (Aug 30, 1982).
13. Gordon, Andrew C. and John P. Heinz, eds. Public Access to Information. New Brunswick, N.J., Transaction Books, 1979. 278p.

14. U.S. Commission on Federal Paperwork. Final Summary Report. Washington, D.C., U.S. Government Printing Office, 1977. 74p.
15. U.S. Congress. House. Committee on Government Operations. Legislation and National Security Subcommittee. Paperwork Reduction Act of 1980: Hearings ... on H.R. 6410 ... February 7, 21, and 26, 1980. 96th Cong., 2d Sess. Washington, D.C., U.S. Government Printing Office, 1980. 353p.
16. U.S. Congress. Office of Technology Assessment. Computer-Based National Information Systems: Technology and Public Policy Issues. Washington, D.C., U.S. Government Printing Office, 1981. 166p.
17. American Library Association. Less Access to Less Information by and About the U.S. Government: II. Washington, D.C., ALA Washington Office, 1982. 4p.
18. U.S. National Commission on Libraries and Information Science. Public Sector/Private Sector Interaction in Providing Information Services: Report to the NCLIS from the Public Sector/Private Sector Task Force. Washington, D.C., U.S. Government Printing Office, 1982. 88p.
19. Schiller, Anita R. and Herbert I. Schiller. "The Privatizing of Information: Who Can Own What America Knows?" The Nation 234(no. 15):461-463 (Apr 17, 1982).
20. Lee, Ted. "Unsolicited Proposal: Why the Nation Sorely Needs an 'Information Constitution.'" Government Executive 10(no. 11):56-59 (Nov 1978).

THE INVERTED FILE*

Jeff Pemberton

A BACKWARD AND FORWARD LOOK AT THE NEW YORK TIMES
INFORMATION BANK--A TALE OF IRONIES COMPOUNDED ...
AND AN ANALYSIS OF THE MEAD DEAL

This is the story of one of the most costly database ventures in the history of the online information business. It is a story of pioneering vision, of daring technological reach, of management blunders that brought scorn from the remainder of the information industry. It is the story of the New York Times Information Bank. I am telling the story at this particular time because the database may be endangered by a change in its production and distribution that is now being implemented. Moreover, this change has evoked the strongest, most angry response from users toward information suppliers that I have seen in my 15 years in the computerized information business. Since the problems that have beset the Information Bank have largely been management policies and marketing difficulties I will focus attention on those two areas.

Before beginning, however, there are a couple of underlying personal beliefs to be noted. First, it is my firm conviction that the New York Times newspaper is incomparably the finest newspaper in the world ... bar none. I read it religiously, almost to the exclusion of other news sources, I must confess. Second, it follows that the database that is derived from this newspaper is in my judgment the best database of current affairs information that is obtainable. And while I have long been critical of certain features of the controlled vocabulary that is used for the database, I am convinced that the overall quality of that file is among the finest in our business. In terms of richness of indexing and abstracting and general attention to quality, it has few peers among databases in any subject area.

Regrettably, the future of that database (in the form in which we have known it for a decade) is now in doubt ... in my judgment. In January of this year the New York Times Company announced

---
*Reprinted by permission of the author and publisher from Online, 7:4 (July 1983) 7-15. Copyright © 1983 by Online, Inc.

that by mid-year it would transfer the mounting of the database and the marketing of it to Mead Data Central, a subsidiary of the Mead Corporation, a paper company. Mead was the founder of the LEXIS legal database and the NEXIS current affairs file. Shortly thereafter, the 65 members of the indexing staff and the 40 people on the marketing staff were dismissed. Data processing personnel were kept on longer, to effect the transfer of the database to the Mead computer. As of this writing that transfer has not yet been made. The indexing for the bibliographic database (Information Bank versions I and II) has been moved to the Times Building in Manhattan. So far, major customers who use the Infobank heavily have reported some (but not a lot of) discernible change in the frequency of updates or the appearance of the abstracts. I think that situation could well change ... for reasons that I will explain later.

First, however, let me trace the history of the Information Bank. It was a database whose origins differed in several significant respects from other online files. Conceived in the mid-Sixties by John Rothman, then the Editor of the printed New York Times Index, the Information Bank was far more than just a simple spin-off of computerized typesetting tapes, as were most databases at the time. Instead, the Information Bank was to be a totally vertically integrated system that would include automated microfiche retrieval and display on special "digital/analog" terminals. This microfiche subsystem--available only inside the Times headquarters on 43rd Street in Manhattan--was to enable the paper to eliminate its costly and inefficient clipping "morgue." The substantial savings from the morgue were to be applied to the Information Bank's balance sheet, thus giving it a mighty leg up on the way to profitability.

Alas, the microfiche system never worked reliably. It was the notorious Foto Mem (whose foibles I recounted in an earlier column). Suffice to say here that the failure of the Foto Mem--coupled with a perception on the part of Times reporters that the Information Bank indexing left something to be desired--meant that the morgue replacement scheme was never even attempted. Thus, the Information Bank started life without benefit of the hefty revenues that were supposed to accrue from morgue savings.

There were other strikes against it, too. It was about a year and a half behind schedule. Management was itchy for some income that would offset at least part of the heavy outlays. At first the database had only three years of the New York Times in it, plus a smattering of non-Times journals ... hardly a great enticement for potential customers--98 percent of whom had no experience whatsoever with an online system. The system could only be accessed by a special, highly expensive terminal (thanks to a cagey IBM strategy which endowed the software with only one compatible terminal, the obsolete EBCDIC-code 2260--a situation hastily remedied by resorting to a $5,000 programmable unit that could be made to emulate an ASCII terminal).

The initial market for the Information Bank was perceived to be among government agencies in Washington, simply because their thirst for current affairs information was often so strong as to overcome the thinness of the initial three year database. Unfortunately for the Infobank this was Richard Nixon's Washington and his minions regarded the New York Times--the newspaper that published the Pentagon Papers--as an actively hostile force. Into this challenging situation I sallied forth as the original Infobank sales representative. It was 1972, the dawn of the online age.

The first task was to attend to those customers already waiting in line to be the first kid on their block with a new toy--"cherry picking" as we say. Who was the very first Information Bank customer? Who was so anxious to get electronic research that they installed a dedicated line into the Times computer? The Central Intelligence Agency. The terminus of the line was in Langley, Virginia. Not far behind was the National Security Agency and the Defense Intelligence Agency. And, speaking of spies and spying, I must here recount my most amusing Information Bank anecdote (and it is completely true).

The setting was the anteroom of the Soviet Embassy in Washington. On hand were over 40 Russians from the embassy staff headed by Ambassador Dobrynin himself. I was to give a live demonstration of this new tool that would make their intelligence gathering a bit easier. I logged on to the system and brought up my first abstract. It was barely readable ... garbage. So many characters were out of place that it almost looked like a Cyrillic alphabet. I guessed the cause and it was irremediable. So I played it cool and announced, "Gentlemen, we have a connection with the computer and I will be able to give you a demonstration of the Information Bank but I fear that you will have to overlook a certain amount of disorder among the characters on the screen. I suspect we have a bit of interference on this particular line." Their reaction was a unanimous, sustained and mighty guffaw. Interference, indeed! That line was bugged ... bugged by every spook in Washington--the CIA, the NSA, the FBI, the DIA, the works ... plus the KGB. When the laughter died down I gave them some nice little Boolean searches, linking Henry Kissinger to just about every world leader he had met.

When the cherry picking was over and the spies and other agencies with deep pockets were trained to use the Infobank's arcane vocabulary, the real marketing began. I became marketing manager and hired a small staff. It was tough sledding. The U.S. was in a recession ... not a bad one by today's standards but enough to make a Ford Motor Co. management decree that all new services such as the Information Bank were to be terminated. But basically the Infobank's initial marketing problem was one shared by all new services whose sale requires--beyond the arguments concerning the service itself--a fundamental departure from the way a customer performs a certain task. You had to sell the basic concept of online searching before you could sell the database. It was a problem faced by all of the early online systems.

The Information Bank, however, also suffered from problems imposed by upper levels of Times management. Later, after moving to Parsippany, New Jersey, it was to suffer from problems made by its own manager. One of the early problems concerned subscription requirements. You couldn't simply install a terminal and sell connect hours. You had to get the customer to sign a year's subscription at a minimum of $675 a month, or unlimited service for $1,350 a month. Senior management was adamant in hewing to this demand. As one Vice President put it, "we may not have very many customers but at least we know we're going to get money from the ones we've got." Another Vice President opined that, "you can always lower prices but you can't raise them." My own view is just the opposite: lure the customer with low prices and when the worth of the product becomes obvious, raise them.

Some of these problems stemmed from the retirement of Ivan Veit, Executive Vice President and the man to whom John Rothman originally reported. An excellent businessman, Veit was a friend of the Information Bank and he was in a high place. His successor, Sidney Gruson, had risen through the editorial side of the *Times*. A fine reporter, he had once come close to winning a Pulitzer Prize. But a businessman he was not. Impatient with details, he avoided doing his homework and never really understood what the information business was all about. As a result, the Infobank was launched without firm direction from top management.

In all fairness, however, it should be said of the early Information Bank that everybody was breaking fresh ground ... and fresh ground sometimes contains hard rocks and sinewy roots. The really serious blunders, it seems to me, came after the operation was turned over to a new manager whose blend of Harvard MBA, IBM apprenticeship and aggressively brisk demeanor had captivated Gruson and his associates. With a strongly Teutonic visage, Karl Keil took over the Information Bank in such an authoritarian manner that he was variously referred to by subordinates as "Sieg Keil" or "The Man With The Monocle."

As he arrived it was the mid-Seventies. Online searching had progressed to the point where sales representatives no longer had to do two selling jobs. Lockheed's Roger Summit had correctly perceived that the real marketing force in winning new converts to online was not massive drumbeating but massive amounts of data and he was scouring the world to recruit new databases. Once people became converts to online searching their appetite for additional databases became insatiable. Summit's idea of an information "supermarket" found favor and his DIALOG system came to dominate the world of online information.

In this world of multi-database systems the Information Bank was increasingly becoming something of an anomaly, what some people in the industry refer to as a "boutique" approach to database marketing. As the operator of a host system, it bore the high costs of its own high powered computer and a data processing staff to go with it. But as the marketer of a single database, it could only increase its revenues by gaining new password holders or by persuading existing customers to perform more and/or longer searches. Both avenues were highly labor intensive; it was not by accident that the Information Bank came to have the largest sales and training staff in the online industry ... all for a single database (and four small ancillary files). Summit's DIALOG and other multi-database systems, however, could avail themselves of a simple strategy. If DIALOG was already selling the Compendex engineering database and it added the INSPEC database of electronics, computers and physics information, all he had to do was send out a "blue sheet" which told people how to search INSPEC and his existing scientific and technical customers would flock to try the new file.

Although the Times did, in time, prepare some ancillary databases to the Information Bank, such as AMI and Medab, these were small and highly specialized ... not the big files of broad appeal that would bring in large revenues.

One of the databases that Roger Summit would have liked to add to DIALOG was, of course, the New York Times Information Bank. And, in fact the idea was discussed by Times executives up to and including the Board of Directors. Yet at this point--sometime in 1976--Karl Keil, the new manager, still held absolute sway and was able to veto the idea. It was easy to see why. Had the Infobank gone up on DIALOG those searchers who were frustrated by the time-consuming, menu-driven original IB software would have moved over to DIALOG and Times upper management might have wondered why they were paying for an expensive computer of their own. Keil, of course, could have been left high and dry. Keil was, if nothing else, a supreme empire builder and he was not about to let anybody jeopardize his empire. So the DIALOG deal never got off the ground.

Another strategy that could have offered profitability to the Information Bank was the simple one of giving their sales force more to sell ... namely more databases. With a field sales force larger than DIALOG and ORBIT combined, the Times was in a unique position to become an information supermarket itself.

At first, however, this was not a feasible alternative; the original Infobank software simply did not have the capability to cope with the complexities of many of the more popular scientific and technical databases. The software had been designed for Times reporters to use with minimal training and it led them along in step-by-step fashion that was supposed to be idiot-proof.

Regrettably, it lacked a free text search capability and when Times reporters wanted to search newly coined jargon, slang, acronyms or technical terms that had not been incorporated into the Infobank Thesaurus they were frustrated to find zero postings ... even though the terms were plain to see in the abstracts. This lack of free text searching was to dog the Infobank for years, until the advent of the Information Bank II. It impeded the acceptance of the IB by the Times own reporters. It frustrated outside searchers to the point where the head of the Systems Department of a large West Coast library told me that, "I don't even want to be in the same room when somebody's running an Information Bank search."

Curiously, and ironically, this retrieval system, which evoked such a negative response from an adult information professional, could be learned by a child with no instruction whatsoever. I once watched a Times sportswriter bring his 10-year-old son into the newsroom and use an Information Bank terminal as a babysitter. The father did not know how to use the IB and there was no instruction book around. But in a few minutes the lad had learned the system and was having a grand time. But, as Paul Berthiaume, the last full time Infobank manager, confided to me once, "the trouble with this software is that once people get proficient with it they get to hate it."

So the original Infobank software precluded the possibility of an information supermarket approach ... but only temporarily. It was not too long before an opportunity came up that could have put the Times squarely in the information supermarket business with a hard core of solid databases, an excellent piece of software and a loyal band of customers in an area where the Times was weak. It was the chance to buy Bibliographic Retrieval Services--"BRS." Begun in 1977 by three veterans of the State University of New York's online retrieval service, BRS had quickly emerged as the major rival to DIALOG. Its customer base was largely academic librarians, a natural market for the Infobank, but one that the IB had priced itself out of. But, by constructing a subset of the database with citations only, prices could have been lowered enough to tap this market and public libraries as well. But the real nugget at BRS was not a customer base nor a software package. It was Janet Egeland. She was the tireless, hard-driving Vice President of Marketing who had put BRS on the map ... and in a very short space of time, BRS also possessed an excellent professional executive in its President, Ron Quake, and a superior software team. All this could be had for about three or four million dollars. Keil turned it down.

You can't blame him. These BRS people outclassed him by a country mile and he knew it. Let them have access to the 14th floor executive suite of the New York Times Company and his days would be numbered in single digits. The irony here is that the Times did--and I suspect still does--desperately need top flight female executives. Unwittingly, the company had bought a smallish subsidiary that was under federal guns for its discriminatory hiring and promotion policies. The purchase brought sex discrimination woes to the Times in buckets and it was not unusual for a manager to summarily be told that he would hire a female to fill his next opening--period. And the final irony of this particular situation was that the purchase of BRS would have brought an uncommonly attractive woman to the Times--a plus that Sydney Gruson would especially enjoy. A connoisseur of the female form, Gruson had once summoned me to his office to discuss Infobank marketing and when the conversation turned to my next sales representative, named Sally, he had but a single question concerning her qualifications. "Is she pretty?"

As the seventies waned, the Information Bank made a number of changes. Originally housed in the Times' 43rd Street headquarters in Manhattan, the operation was moved to an office park in Parsippany, New Jersey in 1975. Part of the reason was to relieve overcrowding on 43rd Street. Part was to achieve a solution to the union problem in the Indexing Department. In the beginning, dating all the way back to when the paper was founded in 1851, there had been a printed index ... at first in careful strokes of a quill pen, then typeset and bound in the familiar red volume we have all used in college or public libraries.

The people who do this work today take considerable pride in their ability to reduce a complex, far-ranging page-one story into a cogent, tersely written abstract. They also believe that this cannot be done on a production line basis and that they must be protected against management efforts to rush the job. Their protection is the Newspaper Guild, a feisty union that has not been reluctant to strike the Times. During the four years that I worked for the Information Bank there were frequent brush fires and skirmishes between management and the unionized indexers. Parsippany was to end that. The indexing department on 43rd Street was to be gradually phased out and eventually all indexing--for both print and electronic products --would be done in non-union Parsippany. It is another major irony in the saga of the Information Bank that the 65 indexers in Parsippany were dismissed and their work transferred back to the 20-person staff of the New York Times Index. We will discuss later the curious aspects of dumping the work of 65 on a staff of 20.

Certainly the most important change for the Infobank was the departure of Karl Keil. In the beginning he had enjoyed the faith and confidence of Gruson and others on the 14th floor. But by 1979 this capital was expended. Some people in the company's management came to feel that he had not only made poor business decisions but was, in the words of one Times executive I talked to, "a mean little S.O.B."

Keil's successor, Paul Berthiaume, was poles apart. Outgoing and candid, patently honest, he lifted staff morale mightily. He was a genuine leader. He ordered new software, complete with free text search capability. Plans were laid for a full text database of the Times. It seemed that the Information Bank was again on the march. I met him shortly after he took over. I liked him immediately. And I think that, were he alive today, the Information Bank would have had a good chance of surviving on its own, without recourse to the Mead deal. Tragically, Paul Berthiaume had a congenital heart defect. He had already suffered one massive

heart attack; his father and brother had died before 45. Paul died
at 46 in October of 1981.

    Since then the Information Bank has never had a leader who
was recruited for the specific job of running it. Instead, it has had
a succession of managers borrowed from the parent company. None
of these have had a reason to plead the IB's case on the 14th floor.
Except for a brief period, it has always lost money. The amount
of net loss (money invested in the enterprise and not recovered by
revenues) is probably somewhere between 10 and 15 million dollars.
It is no surprise, then, that the bean counters took over and de-
creed that the time had come to end the losses. But where were
the bean counters when Keil was turning down the proposals that
could have stemmed the red ink?

    Onto the sea of red ink sailed a new boat that was supposed
to rescue the Times: Mead Data Central, a company that had successfully convinced lawyers to sideline their law clerks' tedious book
research in favor of its LEXIS online database. LEXIS had been
followed by NEXIS, a full-text database of a number of newspapers.
As far as I can tell from the people I have interviewed, LEXIS was
a huge success and NEXIS was a money-losing failure. Mead may
have needed the Times more than vice versa.

    Unlike the original Information Bank, which had been founded
on the principle of rigorous indexing and comprehensive abstracting,
NEXIS not only eschewed both but disdained both. Searching was by
free text only; Mead management's feelings, voiced through its sales
representatives, were clear: indexing and abstracting were frivolous
luxuries, fit only for fusty "librarians." NEXIS' market was to be
comprised of corporate and media people who would gravitate toward
a simplistic search system accessed by a dedicated terminal in
which function keys made the whole process as foolproof as possible.
The irony here is that these are the same people who are buying
microcomputers in droves and are learning to use a whole arsenal
of sophisticated programs such as VisiCalc, dBase II and Peachtext.
Even the new Apple LISA, while simplifying some of the basic steps,
nonetheless lifts its users to heights of computer expertise that is
light years beyond the little NEXIS terminal.

    Looking at the situation from my vantage point it seems to
me that Mead is going to face a major dilemma in the not too distant
future. Most of the professional online searchers I have talked to
who use NEXIS, say they use it as little as possible. They cite a
confusing pricing structure and a difficult retrieval system as their
principal reasons. Listen to this NEXIS user talking. She is in
the library at the New York headquarters of one of the largest U.S.
news operations. "I use NEXIS as little as possible. They try to
tell us that it's simple to use but searching NEXIS is a real pain
... some searches cost us $2 and others go up to $250 and there's
no way to tell in advance if you're going to have a $250 search that
just isn't worthwhile." But Mead really isn't courting the professional searcher. They have always marketed principally to end

The Social Prerogative 297

users. The dilemma I see for NEXIS is this: they think the numbers of end users will grow. But, as they grow in number, they will also begin to use other systems than NEXIS and, as they compare its retrieval system to the speed and flexibility of professional grade systems they will begin to hold NEXIS in the same contempt that Paul Berthiaume reported among end users who had outgrown the simplistic Information Bank I.

So, as this issue of ONLINE goes to press, the Infobank is near to being transferred to the Mead computer and the stage is set for some interesting developments. Questions abound. Will the Times Index staff of 20 be able to perform the indexing and abstracting chores previously handled by the 65 Parsippany indexers? Will the bibliographic Information Bank, in fact, survive, since Mead has no stomach for indexing, and the Times is alternatively available as a full text file? Will Mead continue to insist that users take on its own terminal regardless of whether the user wants it or not? Will some other database producer, looking at the high prices charged by Mead, try to produce a database competitive with the Information Bank?

Let's take the questions in order. Can the staff of 20 that produces the printed Times Index also index and abstract both the Times and the 59 non-Times journals that comprise the Information Bank? And maintain the same update frequency as before? They say they can. As of this writing (early May) my inquiries have not proved conclusively whether or not the update frequency is yet suffering as a result of the Parsippany shutdown. One of the difficulties in measurement is that the time lag on entering non-Times material has always been somewhat erratic, according to heavy users of the database. So it would be possible to let the non-Times material slip further behind in the interests of maintaining currency of updates of the New York Times. I have been told by major users, however, that the abstracts are starting to look shorter than when they were produced at Parsippany. Another sign: the Times Index has reduced the number of descriptors in the controlled vocabulary in an effort to speed up production. I don't know whether they plan to inform users of that fact and list the deletions or not.

Without waiting for an exhaustive survey of updating, however, it is possible to make some observations about the Information Bank indexing operation based on pure logic. I think there is an either/or situation that prevails. Either ... (1). The Times Index staff of 20 cannot handle the workload formerly done by 65 people in Parsippany (in addition to their own workload) and will inexorably slip behind--particularly in the non-Times material--to the point where the database becomes dangerous to use ... dangerous in the sense that the user will lack confidence that articles that are supposed to be in the file are, in fact, in it. Once this confidence is lost, the database is, as a practical matter, useless.

Consider this: the Parsippany indexing operation handled between 12 and 15,000 abstracts per month. Figure it averaged in between--13,500/mo. Divide that by 65 people--208 abstracts per person. Divide by 22 working days in a month--9.5 abstracts per day. Now perform the same arithmetic with 20 people. They will have to average 30.7 abstracts per day. After deducting for lunch, coffee breaks, bathroom breaks and general time slippage, I think we can figure a productive day of about 6 hours. That means the Times Index staff will have to average one abstract every 12 minutes. Considering that some of the articles can barely be read in 12 minutes, let alone indexed and abstracted, and you have the basis for some skepticism.

Isn't it true, though, that the Times Index is already producing a database of abstracts of the New York Times for the printed index and that this can also be used for the online database? Were that it was so simple. The Times Index, for some arcane reasons that should have been reexamined long ago, does not publish a complete abstract for each major story. If Reagan holds a press conference and touches on arms control, monetary policy, abortion and job training there will be four index entries and four abstracts, each of which covers only the subject to which it is indexed. Consolidating these disparate parts into a single cohesive abstract can involve more than just pushing a button. I'm sure it's been streamlined somewhat, but when I worked at the Times it was a messy proposition.

OR Choice No. 2. The Times Index proves that it can, in fact, handle the extra work on a permanent basis. If this is the case, one has to ask the logical question, why did they have those 65 people in Parsippany in the first place? No wonder the operation was losing money! Example: in 1977 the Information Bank had $2.2 million in revenues and expenses of $3 million--an $800,000 shortfall.

The rule of thumb at the Infobank was that expenses were about equally divided between the three major components: indexing, data processing and marketing. That would make the indexing costs about $1 million ... $200,000 more than needed to erase the deficit had the indexing been done in New York. Personally, I think $1 million is low. I don't see how you can pay an indexer a salary plus fringe benefits and equip and house the person for less than $25,000/year each. That would total $1,625,000 for the 65 person staff ... enough for a nice little profit if, indeed, the New York indexing staff of 20 can really handle the whole job. If the maintenance of an indexing staff of 65 in Parsippany was simply part of Karl Keil's empire building, where was the oversight management from the Times' 14th floor?

Next question: will the Information Bank as we know it survive? Hard to tell. I doubt if the Mead people really care. I suspect that if fresh bibliographic input to the Infobank were to stop tomorrow Mead would simply keep the backfiles up for retrospective searching and tell people to use the New York Times On-Line (the full-text database) for new material. So the real question is, how much does the Times, itself, really want to keep the database going? Now, if the 20 indexers on the staff can handle the load and are willing to keep soldiering on, then it's a moot point; management will let them do it. But if they can't handle it, then my guess is that the Information Bank will be allowed to die. It has no one to argue its case within the Times and the Mead people certainly aren't going to do it.

Now to the question of the Mead terminal. It is called the UBIQ. Supposed to be short for "ubiquitous." There are a couple of models, varying in rental charge between $50/mo. or $200, depending on printer features. More on this will be found in Maureen Corcoran's article farther back in this issue. It is this terminal, more than any other factor, that has aroused the wrath of the professional information community. "We're horrified," exclaimed the head of computerized research at one of America's largest research labs. "They're trying to stuff a dedicated terminal down our throats when the whole trend is toward multi-purpose terminals and micros," he said. Last week Mead sent two sales representatives to his office to try and persuade him to install a UBIQ terminal. He resisted. They said he could have it for nothing. "No dice, I told them I just don't have room for another terminal," he told me after the meeting. "We're going to make do without the Times and use substitutes," he said.

To understand this situation, you have to consider the background. Mead started its online business in the legal field with its LEXIS database of case law. Lawyers had no terminals at that time. Lawyers also had neither the time nor patience for anything but the simplest search system. The answer: a system that put many of the commands on plainly labelled function keys. It worked. It was only natural, then, that the same philosophy would be followed with the NEXIS database, particularly since the primary markets were judged to be corporations and news media, not librarians, and the former generally lacked terminals a few years ago.

Now all markets are changing. The end result is clear. Everyone will do computer searching with a microcomputer. Dumb terminals are obsolescent and dedicated dumb terminals are dinosaurs. Will Mead change? They may change somewhat, but in a way that could exacerbate the situation rather than relieve it. In a letter to Mead, which included a question on their intentions on terminals I received the following answer from James P. Roemer, Vice President of Product Development:

> We believe that the MDC terminal is one of the best values in the industry today. However, our most recent evaluation indicates that there are several models of terminals which have the potential to provide an acceptable level of service for an experienced user. It's now practical to provide the necessary interconnections to a selected number of terminals.
>
> We intend to provide our users with a choice of the

MDC terminal or an optional, certified, industry standard model. We will make the final choice of the industry terminals carefully and thoughtfully so as to maintain the high standard of quality and service our customers enjoy today.

Frankly, I am baffled. An ASCII code terminal is an ASCII code terminal. All it has to do is make the interconnect and get the correct characters up on the screen. But Big Brother Mead is going to make the "final choice" of a "certified, industry standard model." What if I don't have a "certified" model? What if I have an old puce-colored Telewidget? Or what if I have the latest Apple LISA micro and my Fujitsu hard disk drive is all set up for downloading the Infobank so that I can format the results in with others from Dow Jones, Disclosure and ABI/INFORM? I bet it will be a while before Mead "certifies" that rig. I must say that this kind of an approach smacks of a haughtiness that I and a number of our readers have observed in Mead Data Central's dealings with professional information people. This is not meant as a blanket indictment of all Mead employees. But there have been enough negative vibrations emanating from Mead to make it a point for discussion.

Last question: will somebody else attempt to compete in the current affairs database marketplace if there is no longer competition between Mead and the Times? Let's examine some of the potential players. Start with Ziff-Davis, publisher of both popular and business publications and owner of Information Access Corporation ("IAC"). IAC produces the National Newspaper Index, a citation-only file on DIALOG which counts the New York Times as its core source for general current affairs.

In its present form NNI leaves a lot to be desired compared with Information Bank II. Its descriptors are the archaic Library of Congress subject headings (want "Cooking"?--try "cookery"). Its titles are actual newspaper headlines, which may or may not be descriptive of the contents of the article. It lacks abstracts. Users report a degree of general sloppiness in the records. I'm sure that Ziff-Davis is attempting to rectify this latter condition but that is the reputation the database has gained. NNI is, however, a force in the marketplace. Because of its much lower cost of production, it is much lower in price than the Infobank. And this price gap may widen.

One of my sources--at one of America's largest libraries, where both the IB and NEXIS are used--keeps a careful record of their relative costs. He reports that for a long time the average cost of a NEXIS search was less than an Infobank search. But, starting a little over a year ago, NEXIS costs rose to more than 22 percent higher than the IB, he reported. Specifically, during 1981 the library's NEXIS searches averaged 10 minutes and $15 each while Infobank searches averaged 12 minutes and $19 each. By 1982, NEXIS searches had dropped in time to 9.4 minutes but the average cost had risen to $21. Infobank searches in 1982 had dropped to 9.5 minutes and the cost had dropped to $17. In the case of the IB, the average time had dropped significantly because of the efficiencies brought by Information Bank II. The rise in NEXIS billings, despite a slight drop in search times, came because of the intrinsic nature of the NEXIS pricing structure.

NEXIS employs a three-way pricing structure: (1) connect time (which varies with usage); (2) line charges for printing off of your terminal; (3) "search unit" charges, which are based on the number of occurrences of your search terms in the database. Inevitably, as the NEXIS database grows, with both updates to existing journals and the addition of new journals, the number of occurrences of a term will rise and the search unit charges will rise. It's like "bracket creep" in your income taxes. Although a theoretical case can be made for search unit charges, the practical effect at the user level is a continual and unseen rise in prices. At one large federal library, search unit charges "were eating us alive," according to an official. They asked Mead to drop them. Mead did. But when a major TV network asked for the same relief, it was refused.

Mead representatives have been telling Infobank users that once the IB is added to NEXIS that it will be maintained as a separate "library" (that's Meadese for database) and that this will keep costs down because the search unit charges will be applied to a smaller file. We'll see. Personally, I would expect them to maintain price parity between the Infobank and NEXIS. In any event, when search unit charges are applied to the IB, the growth of the database will make a continual rise in per-search costs inevitable.

So we will be left with a low cost NNI at the bottom of the product spectrum and a very high cost Infobank at the top ... and nothing in the middle. I can't believe that this situation will prevail indefinitely. And if I was in charge of IAC I would certainly be gearing up to occupy that middle ground. How? A modern vocabulary, terse abstracts, close quality control. Certainly the parent company has the money to fund such an effort if they choose.

Now to another possible competitor. Again we have a rich irony. The company is the H.W. Wilson Co., publisher of the venerable Readers' Guide to Periodical Literature, and the irony is that they are now busily engaged in readying their own host computer system ... the same course that proved to be so expensive for the Times. It may be that the future will be filled with small- to medium-sized host systems, all feeding through common "gateway" communications networks. But that's not what is happening NOW. And, having been way late in jumping on the online bandwagon, I think it is equally foolish to leap into an unknown future.

The Readers' Guide, of course, is primarily magazines, not newspapers, but the point is that the Wilson company possesses an organization accustomed to processing current, popular literature. They already index the New York Times Book Review and the Sunday

Times Magazine. They are also interviewing a number of ex Information Bank employees. So, if they chose to, they, too, could gear up to occupy that middle ground. Will they do it? Only if pushed, I think. If they hire enough ex Times people these veterans might become a force urging Wilson to have a go at it.

Any others? Well, there are a number of companies that are involved in current affairs databases in one way or another. All it takes is money and motivation. Some will be more tempted (or driven) than others. The name Byron Falk and Roxbury Data Systems comes to mind. Byron was the first Operations Manager of the Information Bank. He left the Times, formed Roxbury as an indexing/abstracting company that contracted with the Infobank to supply a substantial portion of the non-Times portion of the IB database. Later, an independent publishing project of his involving Times material infuriated the Times to the point of litigation. Bad blood flowed copiously. Byron would not mind twisting the lion's tail at all. So what is the bottom line of all this? For the Information Bank user, the immediate bottom line is the possibility of an increase in search costs, the necessity of taking on an obsolete UBIQ terminal (or investing in a new "certified" terminal), the probability of a slippage in update frequency and a reduction in the number of descriptors--not a very enticing package.

The bottom line for the Times is that, instead of washing their hands and forgetting about the Information Bank, as was their hope, they have lurched into a situation that could end up with more than a little loss of face and some messy loose ends. Item: the Summit, N.J. library signed up for the Infobank last Fall. On the Infobank's recommendation they leased a TI 745 terminal. Now, Mead tells them they can't use it for the IB come July. They sent a letter to the Information Bank's Park Ave. office petitioning them for reimbursement for their terminal lease cancellation penalties and miscellaneous other small losses. The letter came back. "No longer at this address." Evidently the Times did not arrange to forward Information Bank mail. I suspect the billing department's mail room is not closed down, though. So the little library gave up on the matter, and all that is left is a bad taste in the mouth because they think they were misled. A small matter? Yes. And messy. And needless.

But the main question is this: if the 20 people in the Index cannot cope with the 150,000 abstracts per year that have to go into the database, then the database will begin to lose customers. Eventually it will get to the point where revenues to Mead will not be sufficient to offset their royalties to the Times and still make a decent profit. Mead will want to dump the Information Bank and keep the "New York Times On-Line." And the Information Bank will ignominiously be sent to the grave. And the really unfortunate irony here is that a decade after it began, after years of complaints and derision by information professionals, the tide had turned. By 1982 a typical comment about the Information Bank was, "You know the Times has really got their act together now." I heard it often enough to say that that was the prevailing opinion prior to the Mead deal.

For my part, I do not want to see the Information Bank disappear ... for both professional and personal reasons. Full-text databases with natural searching, such as the New York Times On-Line, have their place. But there is no real substitute for good indexing, and this is particularly true in a current affairs database that covers such a wide range of topics as the New York Times.

Let me offer an example. Ten years ago I was trying to sell the Information Bank to the market research library at General Mills. Because the library's patrons are trying to figure out what products the company should be making 10, 20 and 30 years from now, they have a compelling need to spot emerging trends in the lifestyles of their customers. I was asked if the Times would consider adding the word "lifestyle" to the Thesaurus. We did. I checked some of the articles that were assigned that descriptor. One sticks out in my mind. It was a story on an American couple and their child taking a vacation; the article made a point of documenting the changes that were taking place in the holiday desires and habits of young American families. In short, it was an article on changing lifestyles. Yet, nowhere in the article was that telltale word used. It took a skilled human indexer and a comprehensive Thesaurus to make this article accessible. It would NOT have been accessible through the New York Times On-Line. And that, Mr. Mead, is what indexing is all about.

Now there is one final thing to say. Since I have voiced a number of criticisms about various people's decisions throughout this essay I think it only fair to state what I would do if I were (or had been) in charge. As far as the past of several years ago is concerned, I would have bought BRS and gone into the information supermarket business. Had I been in charge six months ago I would still have tried to buy BRS; I have been told by a leading figure in the information industry that the Baron Thyssen-Bornemisza (owner of Indian Head/owner of Information Handling Group/owner of BRS) has become disenchanted with the American online business. Maybe, maybe not. But I would have taken a shot at it. If I were put in charge right now, given the realities of the Mead deal, I would do the following:

1. Try to amend the Mead contract to allow nonexclusive rights to the Information Bank, while allowing them to retain exclusive rights to the full-text database.

2. Scrap the non-Times portion of the Infobank. Over the long run I think there will be copyright problems with this, anyway. The only exception would be if the Morgue replacement scheme was revived (which would be technically feasible now with videodisk technology).

3. Make the records in the printed Times Index and the Information Bank identical so that everything is a clean operation.

4. Stick with the present indexing staff; augment it if necessary.

5. Mount the database on DIALOG, BRS, Mead and the European Space Agency's IRS system.

I think that the above plan would earn a profit, satisfy the needs of the Information Bank's 2,000 plus users and restore some direction to the enterprise. Whatever action is taken, my hope is that Walter Mattson, the President of the New York Times Company and a man I regard as an astute businessman, will take a more direct part in the fate of this uniquely valuable database. If any of our readers would like to communicate their thoughts on this matter to Mr. Mattson, he can be addressed at The New York Times Company, 229 W. 43rd St., New York, N.Y. 10036.

THE RISE AND PAUSE OF THE U.S. FREEDOM OF INFORMATION ACT*

Harold C. Relyea

In 1966, the United States became the third country to legislate a presumptive right of public access to the records of agencies of the national government. Such law had existed in Sweden, with only a brief interruption, since 1766 and in Finland since 1951. The new American statute, called the Freedom of Information Act,[1] had been undergoing development for at least a half dozen years prior to its enactment and congressional inquiry into the need for such a law had begin in 1955.[2]

The Freedom of Information proposal had not been greeted with universal acceptance within the Federal Government. No executive branch official testified in support of the legislation during congressional committee hearings on the measure and the White House successfully pressured for a House report on the bill which, in its interpretation of the provisions, appeared at places to be inconsistent not only with the Senate report, but also with the explicit language of the statute as well. As a consequence of such powerful opposition to the bill, advocates could not risk subjecting it to clarifying amendments for fear that opponents might seize the opportunity for their own inroads. Thus, although administrators and judges should have been guided by precise statutory language supported by an instructive legislative history, considerable adjudication became necessary under the F.O.I. Act as a consequence of its occasionally indefinite language and confusing legislative history.

The President reluctantly signed the bill, indicating to top officials a lack of sympathy for its requirements; an Attorney General's memorandum interpreting the statute reflected a bias against the true spirit of the law; and the departments and agencies, in allocating resources for the administration of the Act, failed to regard its dictates seriously. These and other deficiencies soon became apparent to congressional overseers. A 1972 report on the implementation of the F.O.I.A. concluded: "The efficient operation

---
*Reprinted by permission of the author and publisher from Government Publications Review, 10 (January/February 1983) 19-33. Copyright © 1983 by Pergamon Press, Ltd.

of the Freedom of Information Act has been hindered by 5 years of foot-dragging by the Federal bureaucracy, ... obvious in parts of two Administrations."[3]

Subsequently, both houses of Congress began developing legislative remedies which resulted in the Freedom of Information Act Amendments of 1974.[4] Executive branch officials repeated their earlier performance of withholding support for the corrective legislation and President Ford vetoed the measure. Bipartisan support was sufficient, however, for an override of the Chief Executive's opposition and the amendments became law. Among the more significant changes made to improve F.O.I. Act operations were requiring that a requester only "reasonably describe" the records being sought; allowing an agency to furnish documents without charge or at reduced cost if it determined that such action would be in the public interest; allowing a court to conduct an *in camera* review of contested materials to determine if they were being properly withheld; establishing specific response times for agency action on both initial and appellate requests as well as lawsuits filed in federal courts; allowing a judge to award attorney fees and litigation costs where a private complainant had "substantially prevailed" in seeking records from an agency; prescribing that a court may take notice of "arbitrary and capricious" withholding of agency documents and require that a civil service investigation take place in order to determine if disciplinary action is warranted; expanding and clarifying the definition of agencies covered by the F.O.I. Act; and specifying that any record containing segregable portions of withholdable information, shall be released with the necessary deletions. In addition, exemptions pertaining to classified information and law enforcement materials were narrowed and made more specific in terms of their application.

The Freedom of Information Act was amended once again in 1976 by a special provision in the Government in the Sunshine Act, another open government law.[5] This modification overturned a judicial misinterpretation of the F.O.I.A.'s third exemption to disclosure by narrowing the types of intervening secrecy statutes falling within its scope.[6] There have not been any subsequent additional direct changes in the F.O.I. Act.[7] Nonetheless, various kinds of efforts have been made during the past six years with a view to further amendment of the statute. One avenue of exploration has been the possibility of applying the provisions of the Act to Congress.

Congressional Application

There are at least two historical reasons why the initial proponents of the Freedom of Information Act did not consider applying it to Congress. In 1955, interest in examining the factors affecting the availability of government information centered in the House Committee on Government Operations. This panel had general responsibility for monitoring the efficiency and economy of executive branch programs and activities, but had no jurisdiction over Congress or the federal courts. When the chairman of the committee chartered a Special Subcommittee on Government Information, it concentrated upon the availability of information from the departments and agencies.[8] This focus seems to have been deemed appropriate at the time because the executive branch was viewed, particularly by the press, as the most grievous withholder of information.[9]

Later, when it was verified that many departments and agencies were misconstruing the public information section of the Administrative Procedure Act to cloak their records and activities in secrecy,[10] new information disclosure legislation was designed to overcome the discretionary withholding authority of the A.P.A. section. Indeed, when the F.O.I. Act was adopted, it amended the public information section of the Administrative Procedure Act by totally displacing it. However, in choosing this legislative strategy, the F.O.I. Act became part of a larger statute which applied exclusively to the Federal departments and agencies.

Although recent discussions of applying the Freedom of Information Act to Congress appear to have ignored these historical explanations for the scope of the statute, they have identified other longstanding and rather formidable constitutional barriers to requiring immediately that Congress comply with the requirements of the F.O.I.A.

By 1974, in the course of legislating for government possession of and access to the records and tape recordings of President Nixon,[11] a national study commission was created to explore "problems and questions with respect to the control, disposition, and preservation of records and documents produced by or on behalf of Federal officials, with a view toward the development of appropriate legislative recommendations and other recommendations regarding appropriate rules and procedures with respect to such control, disposition, and preservation."[12] Popularly known as the Public Documents Commission, this panel reported a variety of findings and recommendations in the spring of 1977. With regard to the matter of public access to legislative branch records, a majority of the Commission urged that "All institutional records of Congress should henceforth be subject to the provisions of the Freedom of Information Act and the principles of the Privacy Act."[13] A minority within the panel, including its chairman, found themselves in disagreement with most of their colleagues over "profoundly different philosophies and approaches to law and government."[14] However, there was little disagreement between the two groups over the means for providing public access to the official records of all three branches, the minority camp urging that they "be open to the public in accordance with the present terms of the Privacy Act and the Freedom of Information Act except as Congress shall modify the Privacy Act and the exemptions of the Freedom of Information Act for the President, the Congress and the Judiciary."[15]

Legislation in conformity with these views was introduced in both Houses of Congress the following year.[16] Both bills sought to apply certain laws pertaining only to the executive branch to the entire legislative branch and, in some instances, to the federal judiciary as well.[17] These proposals did not receive formal consideration during the 94th Congress and were offered again in 1979. [18] A similar bill was introduced in 1980 in the House to make the F.O.I.A. and the Privacy Act applicable to "any authority of Congress."[19]

Hearings on the Senate measure were held in September 1979, before the Subcommittee on Oversight of Government Management, a subunit of the Committee on Governmental Affairs. Subcommittee Chairman Carl Levin, in probable reference to the F.O.I.A. provision, acknowledged at the outset of the proceeding that "the bill raises some constitutional questions regarding the separation of powers and the speech-and-debate clause" as well as more general "practical problems in terms of the enforcement and the cost of compliance which must be considered in determining the impact of the changes proposed in the bill."[20]

In testimony before the Subcommittee, Professor Vincent Blasi of the University of Michigan School of Law commented upon the obstacle which the speech or debate clause (Article I, Section 6, Clause 1) posed for applying the F.O.I. Act to Congress, but observed, as well, that the courts had set limits as to the types of activities which the provision governs.[21] He also noted that:

> the Freedom of Information Act was drafted with all of the specific exceptions to deal essentially with the decision-making of the independent regulatory agencies and the executive departments, and it doesn't have a nice fit to congressional decision-making and that insofar as there are aspects of congressional decision-making that are protected under speech or debate that are not protected under the exceptions to the Freedom of Information Act, those will be hammered out case by case in interpreting speech-or-debate clause defenses to Freedom of Information actions.[22]

Deputy Attorney General Larry Simms raised both a constitutional and practical issue when he suggested "that the Department of Justice represent Members of the Congress in suits that arise under this statute."[23] This position was affirmed later by the Department along with the view that "a significant number of FOIA actions can be expected," including a variety of lawsuits to determine "the applicability of the various FOIA exemptions to the different categories of congressional documents...."[24] The recommendation of the Department raised a question as to whether or not it is constitutionally appropriate or politically desirable to have executive branch attorneys defending members or officials of Congress in F.O.I. Act lawsuits.[25]

Finally, while generally in favor of the bill being considered by the Subcommittee, Common Cause President David Cohen seemed to be willing to forego the F.O.I. Act provision in the face of constitutional and practical problems, saying "that at this stage, the Freedom of Information Act is not a high-yield item for this committee, and it would be far better to focus on the discrimination part and to show that you're serious about addressing a double-standard question."[26]

After one day of hearings, the Subcommittee took no further action on the bill. Neither of the counterpart proposals pending in the House received any formal consideration. All three measures expired with the conclusion of the 96th Congress. Although similar legislation has been introduced since 1980, it has not received any serious congressional attention. This situation may result, in part, from the omnibus nature of this measure as well as the multiplicity of accommodations it suggests.

The House and the Senate developed the Freedom of Information Act in a climate of opinion which was devoid of any consideration of including Congress within its scope. The statute was drafted, refined, initially adopted, and later amended with only the executive branch departments and agencies in mind. Given this legislative perspective and history, the courts have interpreted the law accordingly.[27]

In any attempt to apply the F.O.I. Act to Congress, it would appear that some reconciliation would be necessary with certain constitutional obstacles as well as some rules of the two legislative chambers.[28] It also appears likely that special exceptions to disclosure, not now available in the statute's current exemptions, would have to be perfected. In addition, a variety of operational and administrative problems would have to be addressed. However, in general, there appears to be far more interest in perfecting the F.O.I. Act as it applies to the federal departments and agencies than there is in adapting it to embrace Congress.

Oversight and Evaluation

In the aftermath of legislating the 1974 and 1976 amendments to the statute, Congress continued to monitor F.O.I. Act administration and operations through oversight proceedings, support agency studies, and other informal tracking methods. During the autumn of 1977, the Senate Subcommittee on Administrative Practice and Procedure examined executive branch implementation of the 1974 amendments.[29] A subsequent report by the panel's staff indicated that the most frequent and continuing problems found were "interminable delays in responding to requests, arbitrary imposition of excessive fees, and unexplained denials or deletions" together with the need for "a change in agency attitudes as well as practices regarding Government information."[30] To remedy the situation, over 100 recommendations were offered concerning certain exemptions of the Act, its general administration, its implementation by specifically cited agencies, and its oversight by both the executive branch and Congress.

Various aspects of F.O.I. Act administration were explored during the summer and autumn of 1980 by the Senate Subcommittee on Intergovernmental Relations.[31] Because the November elections gave the Republicans a majority in the Senate, Subcommittee Chairman James Sasser was forced to relinquish his leadership position on the panel. However, he subsequently developed and released a personal report on his F.O.I. Act investigation and offered over two dozen recommendations regarding the statute. He prefaced these suggestions with the view that the Subcommittee's oversight proceedings "clearly indicate that some changes are in order for the Freedom of Information Act," but that "there is no need to overhaul the statute drastically; the vast majority of recommendations which I have made to effect administrative improvements will not require legislative amendment of the Act." The report offered the concluding comment that "the F.O.I. Act is basically sound law as it stands, requiring only some fine tuning with regard to agency implementation and management."[32]

In the House of Representatives, the Subcommittee on Government Information and Individual Rights, the lineal successor to the Special Subcommittee on Government Information created in 1955, also was a close observer of F.O.I. Act operations during this period. Formal hearings were held on the classified materials exemption and the implications of President Carter's new executive order on security classification policy and procedure [33]; the business information exemption and so-called reverse-F.O.I. Act lawsuits [34]; Federal Bureau of Investigation compliance with the statute [35]; the availability of government contractor records [36]; the impact of the Act on federal law enforcement [37]; and the effect of the statute on the Central Intelligence Agency.[38] Most recently, in July 1981, the panel held general oversight hearings exploring experiences and problems with the F.O.I. Act.[39] In the spring of 1982, the Reagan Administration's new executive order on security classification was scrutinized.[40]

Elsewhere in Congress, however, there were indications that at least two subcommittees were not so favorably disposed to the Freedom of Information Act. During 12 days of hearings, beginning in July 1977, and concluding in May 1978, the Senate Subcommittee on Criminal Laws and Procedures heard almost exclusively negative testimony concerning the impact of the F.O.I. Act on law enforcement intelligence and public security.[41] General Accounting Office investigators, asked to look into this situation by the Subcommittee, gave a report which, in part, said:

> We asked the agencies for examples of how the [F.O.I. and Privacy] acts have affected their investigative operations. Although several agencies provided examples

showing the legislation's impact in specific cases, no agency could document the total impact the laws have had on overall investigative operations. Furthermore, it was difficult for them to distinguish between the impact resulting specifically from the FOI/PA provisions and the impact from other laws or regulations, misinterpretations of laws and regulations, or from a general distrust of law enforcement agencies.[42]

Nevertheless, the Subcommittee subsequently issued a report which, among other strictures, criticized the F.O.I. Act and recommended that the statutorily allotted time for responding to an initial request be expanded to 60 days; that rosters of investigative personnel or of employees in sensitive government agencies or sensitive positions be exempted specifically from disclosure; that agencies not be required to process requests under the F.O.I. Act from foreign nationals; that the confidentiality of all information received from foreign governments be assured by specifically exempting it from disclosure; that law enforcement training manuals, investigative handbooks, and manuals dealing with investigative technologies developed through confidential research contracts be exempted specifically from disclosure; that persons making F.O.I.A. requests be required to indicate the number of previous such requests they have made and the dates of same; that Congress consider limiting the number of requests a person may make per year; and that agencies not be required to reproduce public record or published materials such as newspaper clippings when responding to an F.O.I. Act request, but simply identify such items by a bibliographic citation.[43] The Subcommittee also sought amendments to protect information provided by third agencies from automatic disclosure; to not make it mandatory for federal law enforcement agencies, in withholding information from active investigative files, to inform the subjects of these files that they are, in fact, under active investigation; and to more effectively protect the identity of and information provided by informants and cooperative citizens to law enforcement agencies.[44]

Responding to complaints from the federal intelligence community concerning the adverse impact of the Freedom of Information Act and the Privacy Act on their activities, the Subcommittee on Legislation of the House Permanent Select Committee on Intelligence held one day of hearings on this matter in April 1979. Representatives from the Central Intelligence Agency, the National Security Agency, and the Federal Bureau of Investigation were the only witnesses. Legislative proposals giving them relief from certain of the requirements of the F.O.I. Act were aired by the CIA and the FBI. The Subcommittee, however, took no action on these measures.[45]

Indeed, during the past few years, various assessments of the Freedom of Information Act and suggestions for modifying it have evolved from the executive branch. In December 1978, Attorney General Griffin Bell initiated "a comprehensive review" of F.O.I. Act implementation with a view to determining "if any administrative or legislative changes may be necessary or desirable."[46] Almost two years elapsed before a package of amendments was finalized by the Department of Justice. The situation was then overtaken by events. With President Carter's electoral defeat in November 1980, Attorney General Benjamin Civiletti formally transmitted the collection to the Office of Management and Budget as a draft bill for consideration and review, indicating he intended to acquaint his successor with its contents.[47]

During 1979, the FBI and CIA aired proposals to amend the F.O.I. Act which were designed to provide them with some relief from complying with the statute. Congressional subcommittees explored these propositions, but no further action was taken regarding them.[48] In October 1980, the Justice Management Division issued a report criticizing the way the Department of Justice internally administered the F.O.I. Act and the manner in which it coordinated government-wide compliance with the requirements of the law.[49] Earlier in the year, the Comptroller General of the United States had suggested that "specific policy setting responsibility for the Freedom of Information Act" be vested in the Office of Management and Budget to provide "much-needed executive direction and oversight."[50] Recently, the Drug Enforcement Administration, another Department of Justice unit, issued a report explaining the adverse effects of the F.O.I. Act on its law enforcement activities and suggesting some relief from the requirements of the statute might be in order.[51]

Shortly after President Reagan assumed office, Attorney General William French Smith initiated another "comprehensive review" of the F.O.I. Act, primarily because, in his view, "years of experience have made clear that many persons are employing it in ways Congress did not intend." Other reasons cited as prompting the study were "the cost of administering the Act and the volume of litigation it spawns."[52] Draft amendments resulting from this examination were transmitted to both Houses of Congress in October of 1981.[53]

Legislative Developments

As this recent history of studies and recommendations suggests, an awareness has existed for some time, both within and outside of government, that the Freedom of Information Act might be further perfected through both legislative refinement and administrative improvement. The question before the 97th Congress was not if, but what, modification of the F.O.I. Act was necessary. Approximately a dozen bills to amend the statute directly were introduced during 1981 and 1982. Amost all of them would have had the effect, if enacted, of restricting the availability of records under the Act. Although most of the measures were narrow in scope--e.g., modifying the statute only with regard to business records, intelligence materials, or proper requesters--two of them were comprehensive or omnibus bills. One was developed by the Reagan administration and the other was produced by Sen. Orrin Hatch (R.-Utah), Chairman of the Subcommittee on the Constitution of the Senate Committee on the Judiciary. From July to December of 1981, the Subcommittee held extensive hearings on F.O.I. Act operations and problems.[54] In late December, the panel marked-up the Hatch bill (S. 1730), incorporating many provisions from the Administration proposal (S. 1751), and reported it on a 3-2 vote to the full committee for further consideration. The resulting composite measure contained a number of F.O.I.A. limitations and seemingly would have transformed the Act from being exclusively an information disclosure law to being a combination records disclosure and withholding statute.[55]

To opponents of the measure, the Subcommittee vote, which was very close and totally bipartisan, suggested the proposal was vulnerable to remedial amendments or even defeat. Because it had a crowded legislative calendar, the Senate Committee on the Judiciary did not take immediate action on the Hatch bill. Opposition forces, consisting largely of press groups, sought to negotiate with Sen. Hatch's staff on objectionable provisions while simultaneously enlisting the support of other Senators for the changes they desired.

Although agreements were reached on some disputed provisions, a number of points of conflict remained unresolved. When Sen. Hatch attempted to obtain committee agreement to a modified version of the subcommittee-adopted text of his bill, he was forced to accept additional amendments within the panel. When a compromise measure was reported unanimously from the Committee on the Judiciary in mid-May, it was legislation which no one seriously wanted to push for enactment in its existing form. However, if the original supporters of the proposal sought to bring it before the Senate and to restore its restrictive provisions through floor amendments, considerable debate, or perhaps even a filibuster, probably would have ensued. Favorable outcomes for any such reconstructions were not assured and the majority leadership of the Senate very likely was not eager to lose valuable time through these efforts. Indeed, any such further action on the bill seemingly would have served no useful purpose. No counterpart legislation of any kind had been given a hearing in the House because the chairman of the Subcommittee on Government Information and Individual Rights, Rep. Glenn English (D.-Okla.), was waiting until the Senate had completed or nearly finished its action before beginning any proceedings on this matter. Thus, the Hatch bill was held in abeyance.[56]

Apart from this series of events, the Senate Select Committee on Intelligence considered a bill (S. 1273) exempting certain files of the CIA and other intelligence agencies from the provisions of any law requiring search, review, and disclosure of their contents. Introduced by Sen. John Chafee (R.-R.I.) as an amendment to the Central Intelligence Agency Act of 1949, the legislation would have removed from F.O.I. Act process and release those files designated by the Director of Central Intelligence as containing material concerned with systems for the collection of foreign intelligence information, special activities and foreign intelligence operations, investigations of potential foreign intelligence sources, and intelligence and security liaison arrangements with foreign governments and intelligence services. Although a hearing was held on the proposal, with intelligence community witnesses testifying favorably on the measure and private sector witnesses expressing opposition to it, the committee had taken no further action on the bill by the final weeks of the 97th Congress.[57]

During 1981 and 1982, various indirect amendments to the F.O.I. Act were attempted through legislation establishing confidentiality for a particular category or type of information in accordance with the criteria of the third exemption of the Act concerning intervening secrecy statutes. By the time of the October congressional recess, two of these "backdoor" amendments had been successfully enacted and others were embedded in bills nearing a final vote. The Omnibus Budget Reconciliation Act of 1981 contained a provision prohibiting the Consumer Produce Safety Commission from disclosing information containing or relating to a trade secret or subject to the fourth exemption of the F.O.I. Act concerning trade secrets or confidential commercial or financial information.[58] A similar prohibition had been imposed on the Federal Trade Commission in 1980.[59]

The Department of Energy National Security and Military Applications of Nuclear Energy Authorization Act for 1982 provided authority for the Secretary of Energy to protect certain unclassified information from disclosure under the F.O.I. Act.[60] Similar restrictive powers had been granted to the Nuclear Regulatory Commission in 1980.[61] In the final weeks of the 97th Congress, conferees for the N.R.C. authorization bill for fiscal years 1982 and 1983 reported a measure containing three clarifications of the Secretary of Energy's authority to protect unclassified information: limiting it specifically to atomic energy defense program matters, providing that the Secretary's determinations are subject to judicial review, and requiring quarterly reports on the exercise of this restrictive power.[62]

When a bill authorizing funds for the federal intelligence community emerged from the Senate Select Committee on Intelligence in the spring of 1981, it contained a provision stating that no law could be construed to require the disclosure of the organization or any function of the Defense Intelligence Agency, of any information with respect to the activities of that entity, or of the names, titles, salaries, or number of persons it employed.[63] The House version of the legislation did not contain this language. Conferees deleted the provision in the course of reconciling the differing versions of the proposal as initially adopted by each congressional chamber.[64]

By the time of the October recess, both houses of Congress had approved legislation extending the Commodity Exchange Act

The Social Prerogative

containing quite different information confidentiality and disclosure provisions. In brief, the Senate bill prohibited the Commodity Futures Trading Commission from disclosing, except as otherwise narrowly specified elsewhere in the Commodity Exchange Act, any records containing or based on confidential information or proprietary information that would not customarily be released to the public by the person from whom it was obtained.[65] The House bill created procedures for notifying submitters of information of requests for disclosure before the Commission actually released the material. A submitter could offer written argument against the release of the information. The Commission was directed to issue implementing regulations specifying additional procedural details.[66] If the legislation is to be enacted before the conclusion of the 97th Congress, these differences among others, must be reconciled in conference committee.

Finally, when the Senate Committee on Appropriations reported a bill allocating funds for the Department of the Treasury, the U.S. Postal Service, the Executive Office of the President, and certain other independent agencies, it appended a provision creating a tenth F.O.I. Act exemption for records maintained by the Secret Service in connection with its presidential and vice presidential protective functions.[67] No such amendment of the F.O.I. Act was included in the companion appropriations measure passed by the House. It remains to be seen as to whether the provision will be continued or rejected, or transformed into a confidentiality allowance within the scope of the third exemption, as Congress moves toward a final vote on this funding legislation.

E.O. 12356

Although the Reagan Administration was not successful in its attempt to alter the Freedom of Information Act through direct legislative amendments, it did effect a change in the statute indirectly by revising the policy and procedures for creating official secrets. The first exemption of the F.O.I. Act allows the withholding of information and records that are "(A) specifically authorized under criteria established by an Executive order to be kept secret in the interest of national defense or foreign policy and (B) are in fact properly classified pursuant to such Executive order."[68] In April 1982, President Reagan issued a new executive order establishing broad categories of classifiable information, mandating that information falling within these categories be classified, allowing reclassification of previously released materials, and eliminating automatic declassification arrangements.[69] If, as it appears, more government records and documents may be classified under this directive, then those same materials will be exempt from disclosure under the F.O.I. Act.

Security classification policy and procedures have been prescribed since 1940 through a series of presidential executive orders. Since 1953, succeeding orders have narrowed the bases and discretion for assigning official secrecy to agency records. In many regards, the new Reagan directive reversed this trend and left congressional opponents in a quandary.

The Constitution of the United States vests all legislative power in Congress and prescribes the manner in which statutes shall be created. In exercising its lawmaking authority in an area specifically entrusted to it, Congress, on rare occasions, has repealed some presidential policy directives. However, the legislature may not divest the President of a constitutional function. Consequently, there are areas of power shared by the two branches. Exercising general executive authority (Article II, Section 1, Clause 1) and purusing his responsibilities as Commander-in-Chief (Article II, Section 2, Clause 1), the President may prescribe policy and procedures for the protection of department and agency records for reasons of national defense or security. Congress, relying upon its mandate to provide for the common defense (Article I, Section 8, Clause 1), to "make rules for the government and regulation of the land and naval forces" (Article I, Section 8, Clause 14), and to "make all laws which shall be necessary and proper for carrying into execution the foregoing powers" stipulated in the Constitution (Article I, Section 8, Clause 18) also seemingly may legislate on this subject. Indeed, during the past few years, varying suggestions have been made from within Congress that a statutorily-based security classification system be pursued.[70] However, to date, the House and the Senate have been willing to defer to the President to determine such policy.

The Reagan administration began its effort to develop a new executive order on security classification a few months after the inauguration. By late summer, an initial preliminary version of a new directive was circulated among selected department and agency officials by the Deputy General Counsel of the CIA. During the autumn and winter of 1981 and into the first months of the new year, the process of refining the draft security classification order continued within the executive branch.

In early February, the tentative text of the directive was made available for the first time to selected congressional committees. They were allowed approximately two weeks to comment on the draft. Somewhat angered, eight chairmen of committees or subcommittees of the House of Representatives signed a letter to the President protesting the brief comment period, requesting that the imposed deadline be extended, and declaring that no changes should be made in the operative security classification order "without allowing for thorough review."[71]

The administration agreed to extend the comment deadline by a few weeks, but declined to send witnesses to mid-March hearings on the draft order scheduled by the House Subcommittee on Government Information and Individual Rights. As a consequence of this development, the chairman and two other members of the panel took the unusual step of sending a letter directly to the President asking that a spokesman be sent to testify soon on the draft order.[72] Two administration representatives, neither of whom held policy-making positions, subsequently appeared before the Subcommittee in early May, but by that time the directive had been signed by the President.[73] Subcommittees of the House Committee on Science and Technology holding a joint hearing on the impact of national security considerations on science and technology also had been denied an Administration witness for their late March proceeding.[74]

Effective August 1, 1982, E.O. 12356 appears to reverse a trend of the past 30 years during which succeeding presidential classification directives narrowed the bases and discretion for assigning official secrecy to executive branch documents and materials. Under the new order, the protection of information is emphasized disproportionately over the public accessibility of government records, some previously valued limitations on classification criteria and judgment are eliminated, and other new broad conditions for classification are established.

Gone is the "identifiable" damage standard of the predecessor order so that classification is premised merely upon the expectation that disclosure "reasonably could be expected to cause damage to the national security." Unlike its two immediate precursors, E.O. 12356 establishes no basic classification time period(s) leading to automatic declassification or selective continuation of protection for a limited quantity of materials. Its primary policy premise is that records "shall be classified as long as required by national security considerations." A discretionary allowance is made for the establishment of a specific date or event when declassification shall occur, but only if sufficient evidence or information exists to allow such a determination. Finally, E.O. 12356 also abandons an earlier prohibition on classifying a product of nongovernmental research and development that does not incorporate or reveal classified information to which the producer or developer was given prior access until and unless the government acquires a proprietary interest in the product; an earlier specification that the declassification of official secrets be given emphasis comparable to that accorded classification; and a predecessor requirement that all special access programs be reviewed regularly and, with the exception of those required by treaty or international agreement, be terminated automatically every five years unless renewed in accordance with prescribed procedures.

Added are three new classification categories pertaining to information concerning "the vulnerabilities or capabilities of systems, installations, projects, or plans relating to the national security," "cryptology," and "a confidential source." In addition, E.O. 12356 allows the reclassification of "information previously declassified and disclosed if it is determined in writing that (1) the information requires protection in the interest of national security; and (2) the information may reasonably be recovered." The predecessor order explicitly prohibited reclassification.

With E.O. 12356, both a greater quantity and variety of information seems destined for security protection. Resort to classification is encouraged; conditions and criteria for applying classification are broadened; and discretion for imposing classification is increased. The policy changes effected by the new order are likely to result in more classification, less declassification, and the longer duration of official secrecy. The consequences of these developments, in turn, seemingly will be much greater administrative expense to the government and less public access to agency records under the F.O.I. Act.

A House report on E.O. 12356 took issue with the elimination of the "identifiable" damage standard for applying security classification and viewed the new classification categories as overbroad, of uncertain need, and "not qualified or defined."[75] In addition, it was suggested that, even though a presidential executive order on security classification policy and procedures may be developed and issued without being subject to the public notice and comment requirements of the Administrative Procedure Act,[76] both the government and the public would be better served by adherence to the spirit of that provision.[77]

Legislation was introduced in the Senate to mitigate the effect of E.O. 12356 on the F.O.I. Act. In brief, the bill (S. 2452) would have established two standards regarding the withholding of classified information: that its release could reasonably be expected to cause identifiable damage to the national security and that the public interest in disclosure be weighed against the government's reasons for imposing official secrecy. This measure did not receive any consideration during the 97th Congress.[78]

Looking Ahead

During the 98th Congress, efforts to amend the Freedom of Information Act begin anew. There is a strong likelihood that certain legislative proposals will emerge once again, perhaps in an atmosphere of greater favorability to ultimate adoption. At the moment, the final outcome for any of them, of course, is uncertain. The ultimate acceptability of each measure probably will depend upon accommodations, compromises, and modifications made during the course of progress through the legislative process. To state this observation in another way, given the high degree of controversy involved, any bill to amend the F.O.I. Act probably will undergo considerable change before it is finally enacted into law. Thus, recognizing that this discussion is confined to beginning proposals, what kinds of measures seem viable?

First, some version of the Hatch bill (S. 1730) very likely will be introduced, not necessarily one with provisions exactly like those of the compromise prescription reported by the Senate Committee on the Judiciary but, perhaps, closer to the text of the original Hatch measure or the version of it reported from subcommittee which embodied administration modifications.

The Social Prerogative 319

Second, a bill affording better protection for business records and commercial information may emerge. At a minimum, such legislation seemingly would amend the F.O.I. Act to establish a procedure whereby submitters could challenge disclosures of their records before an agency or a court or both. Such a measure also might seek to change the language of the fourth exemption of the Act to broaden its application so that more commercial and financial records could be withheld. Early enactment of this type of legislation might preclude the adoption of more sweeping amendments limiting the effects of the F.O.I. Act. There is some reason to believe that better protection of business information is viewed as an area of F.O.I. Act reform in need of primary, if not, in some minds, exclusive attention. Thus, the realization of modifications in this regard may be seen as sufficient to forego protracted deliberation over a more extensive and controversial revision measure.

Third, a bill granting the federal intelligence community or the CIA alone some relief from the requirements of the F.O.I. Act may be offered. To be generally acceptable, such legislation probably would not provide intelligence agencies complete immunity from the Act by placing them outside the statute's definition of "agency," but, instead, would allow certain kinds of intelligence information to be not subject to F.O.I. Act review or disclosure.

Finally, although it is possible that a bill extending and strengthening the disclosure provisions of the Freedom of Information Act might be introduced, the appearance of such legislation is not probable. Discussion of and debate over amendments to the Act during 1981 and 1982 suggest there are only a few "strengthening" proposals that are viable at present. Chief among these possibilities are provisions clarifying and easing the granting of fee waivers or offsetting some of the effects of the new security classification executive order upon the Act. Proponents of these reforms need not resort to some idealistic separate bill, but seemingly could pursue them more effectively as committee or floor amendments, if necessary, to other legislation amending the F.O.I. Act.

It also might be mentioned that new statutory provisions establishing confidentiality for certain classes and kinds of information probably will appear in various bills offered during the course of the 98th Congress. If enacted, these authorities may indirectly amend the F.O.I. Act by falling within the scope of its third exemption. Types of information which may be granted protection through this arrangement, however, are not obvious at the moment.

In addition, discussion of and debate over direct amendments to the Freedom of Information Act during 1983 may be affected somewhat by legislative deliberations on another matter. Over the past two years, executive branch officials increasingly have sought to control, for reasons of national security, the communication of certain scientific information to citizens of selected foreign countries. One of the authorities relied upon for this controversial regulation--the Export Administration Act of 1979, as amended [79]

--will expire automatically at the end of September 1983. It will be necessary for Congress to renew this law in some form early in the year. Deliberation over information controls in this context may affect some of the efforts to amend the F.O.I. Act. The Hatch bill (S. 1730), for example, contained a proposed new exemption protecting technical data that may not be exported lawfully outside of the United States without an approval, authorization, or license from an agency, unless the requester had obtained the necessary clearance.

Of course too much controversy or the lack of a proposal to which a majority in both houses of Congress can agree may result in no legislation being enacted. This is a possibility in the case of F.O.I. Act amendments. Indeed, as recent history well indicates, Congress has been cautious and thoughtful when called upon to modify the Freedom of Information Act.

Notes and References

1. 5 U.S.C. 552.
2. See U.S. Congress, House, Committee on Government Operations, Availability of Information from Federal Departments and Agencies, Hearings, 84th-86th Congresses, 1956-1959, 17 parts.
3. U.S. Congress, House, Committee on Government Operations, Administration of the Freedom of Information Act. H. Rept. 92-1419, 92nd Congress, 2d Session, 1972, p. 8.
4. 88 Stat. 1561.
5. 90 Stat. 1241.
6. See Administrator, Federal Aviation Administration v. Robertson, 422 U.S. 255 (1975).
7. Indirect changes in the statute, however, may occur with the enactment of laws containing prohibitions on information disclosure which fall within the scope of the F.O.I. Act's third exemption (5 U.S.C. 552(b)(3)). There also have been judicial interpretations of the Act which have prompted some to suggest legislative correctives or clarifications might be in order. Chief among these court decisions inspiring reform efforts was Chrysler Corporation v. Brown, 441 U.S. 281 (1979); also see Kissinger v. Reporters' Committee for Freedom of the Press, 445 U.S. 136 (1980); Forsham v. Harris, 445 U.S. 169 (1980).
8. See U.S. Congress, House, Committee on Government Operations, Availability of Information from Federal Departments and Agencies, Part 1, Hearings, 84th Congress, 1st Session, 1956, pp. 1-3.
9. See, generally, Herbert Brucker, Freedom of Information (New York: Macmillan, 1949); Harold L. Cross, The People's Right to Know (New York: Columbia Unniversity Press, 1953); Francis E. Rourke, Secrecy and Publicity (Baltimore: The Johns Hopkins Press, 1961); James Russell Wiggins, Freedom or Secrecy, rev. ed. (New York: Oxford University Press, 1964, originally published 1956).

10. 5 U.S.C. 1002 (1964 ed.).
11. 88 Stat. 1695.
12. 88 Stat. 1698, 1699; the formal name of the panel was the National Study Commission on Records and Documents of Federal Officials.
13. U.S. National Study Commission on Records and Documents of Federal Officials, Final Report, (Washington: GPO, 1977), p. 34.
14. U.S. National Study Commission on Records and Documents of Federal Officials, Alternate Report (appended to Final Report), 1977, p. 105.
15. Ibid., p. 99.
16. S. 3086 was introduced on May 15, 1978, by Sen. Patrick Leahy; see Congressional Record, v. 124, May 16, 1978, pp. S7522-S7525; H.R. 12937 was introduced on June 1, 1978, by Rep. Andrew Jacobs for himself and 17 co-sponsors.
17. The bills sought to apply the Freedom of Information Act to "any unit of the Legislative Branch of the Federal Government" and not just the two Houses of Congress.
18. S. 1112 was introduced on May 10, 1979, by Sen. Patrick Leahy; see Congressional Record, v. 125, May 10, 1979, pp. S5659-S5664; H.R. 3571 was introduced on April 10, 1979, by Rep. Andrew Jacobs.
19. H.R. 6870 was introduced on March 19, 1980, by Rep. Dan Quayle; see Congressional Record, v. 126, March 18, 1980, p. E1327; it was not clear if the bill was intended to apply the Freedom of Information Act to only the two Houses of Congress or to the entire legislative branch.
20. U.S. Congress, Senate, Committee on Governmental Affairs, Subcommittee on Oversight of Government Management, To Eliminate Congressional and Federal Double Standards, Hearing, 96th Congress, 1st Session, 1979, p. 1.
21. Ibid., pp. 22-23.
22. Ibid., p. 28.
23. Ibid., pp. 68, 71-73.
24. Ibid., pp. 69-71.
25. See U.S. Congress, Senate, Committee on the Judiciary, Representation of Congress and Congressional Interests in Court, Hearings, 94th Congress, 2d Session, 1976.
26. U.S. Congress, Senate, Committee on Governmental Affairs, Subcommittee on Oversight of Government Management, To Eliminate Congressional and Federal Double Standards, op. cit., p. 74.
27. The nature of congressional exclusion from the coverage of the Freedom of Information Act may be appreciated when considering a recent case involving a committee hearing transcript in the possession of the Central Intelligence Agency. Under the provisions of the F.O.I. Act, plaintiffs had sought access to all CIA records pertaining to the legislative history of the National Security Act of 1947 and the Central Intelligence Agency Act of 1949. A dispute arose over two documents, one of which was an unpublished transcript of an executive (closed) session hearing held by a House committee which had marked

the record "secret." The CIA withheld the transcript, arguing it was not an "agency record" covered by the F.O.I. law. The District Court agreed with this decision and the Court of Appeals affirmed this judgment, saying in part: "We base our conclusion both on the circumstances attending the document's generation and the conditions attached to its possession by the CIA. The facts that the Committee met in executive session and that the Transcript was denominated "Secret" plainly evidence a Congressional intent to maintain Congressional control over the document's confidentiality. The fact that the CIA retains the Transcript solely for internal reference purposes indicates that the document is in no meaningful sense the property of the CIA; the Agency is not free to dispose of the Transcript as it wills, but holds the document, as it were, as a "trustee" for Congress. Under these circumstances, the decision to make the transcript public should be made by the originating body, not by the recipient agency.

We hold, therefore, that the Hearing Transcript is not an "agency record" but a Congressional document to which the FOIA does not apply. We reach this conclusion because we believe that on all the facts of the case Congress' intent to retain control of the document is clear. Other cases will arise where this intent is less plain. We leave those cases for another day." Goland v. Central Intelligence Agency, 607 F.2d 339 at 347-348 (D.C. Cir. 1978); cert. denied 445 U.S. 927 (1980).

28. See, for example, House Rule 11 pertaining to investigative hearing procedures; also see House Rule 29 and Senate Rule 30 concerning closed chamber sessions; also see House Rule 37 and Senate Rule 30 on the withdrawal of papers presented to each chamber; of interest as well regarding public access to congressional records is H.Res. 288, 83rd Congress, 1st Session, and S.Res. 474, 96th Congress, 2d Session.
29. See U.S. Congress, Senate, Committee on the Judiciary, Subcommittee on Administrative Practice and Procedure, Freedom of Information Act, Hearings, 95th Congress, 1st Session, 1978.
30. U.S. Congress, Senate, Committee on the Judiciary, Subcommittee on Administrative Practice and Procedure, Agency Implementation of the 1974 Amendments to the Freedom of Information Act, Committee print, 95th Congress, 2d Session, 1980, p. 23.
31. U.S. Congress, Senate, Committee on Governmental Affairs, Subcommittee on Intergovernmental Relations, Oversight of the Administration of the Federal Freedom of Information Act, Hearings, 96th Congress, 2d Session, 1980.
32. Senator Jim Sasser, Oversight of the Administration of the Federal Freedom of Information Act: A Personal Report, November, 1981, pp. ii-iii, 4, 64-65.
33. See U.S. Congress, House, Committee on Government Operations, Security Classification Exemption to the Freedom of Information Act, Hearings, 95th Congress, 1st Session, 1979.
34. See U.S. Congress, House, Committee on Government Opera-

The Social Prerogative

tions, Business Record Exemption of the Freedom of Information Act, Hearings, 95th Congress, 1st Session, 1977; also see U.S. Congress, House, Committee on Government Operations, Freedom of Information Act Requests for Business Data and Reverse-FOIA Lawsuits, H. Rept. 95-1382, 95th Congress, 2d Session, 1978.

35. See U.S. Congress, House, Committee on Government Operations, FBI Compliance with the Freedom of Information Act, Hearings, 95th Congress, 2d Session, 1978.

36. See U.S. Congress, House, Committee on Government Operations, Information Policy Issues Relating to Contractor Data and Administrative Markings, Hearings, 95th Congress, 2d Session, 1979; also see U.S. Congress, House, Committee on Government Operations, Lack of Guidelines for Federal Contract and Grant Data, H. Rept. 95-1663, 95th Congress, 2d Session, 1978.

37. See U.S. Congress, House, Committee on Government Operations, The Freedom of Information Act: Federal Law Enforcement Implementation, Hearings, 96th Congress, 1st Session, 1981.

38. See U.S. Congress, House, Committee on Government Operations, The Freedom of Information Act: Central Intelligence Agency Exemptions, Hearings, 96th Congress, 2d Session, 1981.

39. See U.S. Congress, House, Committee on Government Operations, Freedom of Information Act Oversight, Hearings, 97th Congress, 1st Session, 1981.

40. See U.S. Congress, House, Committee on Government Operations, Executive Order on Security Classification, Hearings, 97th Congress, 2d Session, 1982; also see U.S. Congress, House, Committee on Government Operations, Security Classification Policy and Executive Order 12356, H. Rept. 97-731, 97th Congress, 2d Session, 1982.

41. See U.S. Congress, Senate, Committee on the Judiciary, Subcommittee on Criminal Laws and Procedures, The Erosion of Law Enforcement Intelligence and its Impact on the Public Security, Hearings, 95th Congress, 1st and 2d Sessions, 1977-1978.

42. See U.S. General Accounting Office, Impact of the Freedom of Information and Privacy Acts on Law Enforcement Agencies: Report by the Comptroller General of the United States, GGD-78-108, November 15, 1978, Appendix I, p. 3; appears in U.S. Congress, Senate, Committee on the Judiciary, Subcommittee on Criminal Laws and Procedures, The Erosion of Law Enforcement Intelligence and its Impact on the Public Security, Committee print, 95th Congress, 2d Session, 1978, p. 146.

43. See U.S. Congress, Senate, Committee on the Judiciary, Subcommittee on Criminal Laws and Procedures, The Erosion of Law Enforcement Intelligence and its Impact on the Public Security, Committee print, 95th Congress, 2d Session, 1978, pp. 70-71.

44. Ibid., pp. 71-72.

45. See U.S. Congress, House, Permanent Select Committee on Intelligence. Subcommittee on Legislation, Impact of the Freedom of Information Act and the Privacy Act on Intelligence Activities, Hearings, 96th Congress, 1st Session, 1980.
46. U.S. Department of Justice, Office of Attorney General, Letter to Heads of All Frederal Departments and Agencies Re: Freedom of Information Act Study (Washington, D.C.: December 11, 1978).
47. U.S. Department of Justice, Office of Attorney General, Letter to Hon. James T. McIntyre, Jr. (Washington, D.C.: December 18, 1980).
48. See citations at notes 37, 38, and 45.
49. See U.S. Department of Justice, Justice Management Division, Evaluation of the Department of Justice Management of the Freedom of Information and Privacy Acts (Washington, D.C.: October, 1980).
50. See U.S. Congress, House, Committee on Government Operations, Paperwork Reduction Act of 1980, Hearings, 96th Congress, 2d Session, 1980, p. 37.
51. See U.S. Department of Justice, Drug Enforcement Administration, Office of Planning and Evaluation, The Effect of the Freedom of Information Act on DEA Investigations (Washington, D.C.: February 5, 1982).
52. U.S. Department of Justice, Press release (Washington, D.C.: May 4, 1981).
53. See Congressional Record, v. 127, October 20, 1981, pp. S11702-11713.
54. See U.S. Congress, Senate, Committee on the Judiciary, Subcommittee on the Constitution, Freedom of Information Act, Hearings, (2 volumes), 97th Congress, 1st Session, 1982.
55. See Richard C. Ehlke and Harold C. Relyea, "FOIA Proposals Would Fundamentally Transform Act," Legal Times of Washington 4 (February 8, 1982) pp. 11, 15-17.
56. See, generally, Harold C. Relyea, "Modifying the Freedom of Information Act: Ideas and Implications," Journal of Media Law and Practice 3 (May 1982) pp. 54-85.
57. See U.S. Congress, Senate, Select Committee on Intelligence, Intelligence Reform Act of 1981, Hearings, 97th Congress, 1st Session, 1981.
58. See 95 Stat. 357 at 713-715.
59. See 94 Stat. 374 at 385-388.
60. See 95 Stat. 1163 at 1169.
61. See 94 Stat. 780 at 788-789.
62. For the pertinent portions of the conference committee report, see Congressional Record, v. 128, September 28, 1982, pp. H7673, H7682.
63. See U.S. Congress, Senate, Select Committee on Intelligence, Authorizing Appropriations for Fiscal Year 1982 for Intelligence Activities of the U.S. Government, the Intelligence Community Staff, the Central Intelligence Agency Retirement and Disability System, and to Provide Certain Personnel Management Authorities for the Defense Intelligence Agency, and for Other Purposes, S. Rept. 97-57, 97th Congress, 1st Session, 1981, pp. 21, 27.

64. See U.S. Congress, House, Committee of Conference, Intelligence Authorization Act for Fiscal Year 1982, H. Rept. 97-332, 97th Congress, 1st Session, 1981.
65. See U.S. Congress, Senate, Committee on Agriculture, Nutrition, and Forestry, Futures Trading Act of 1982, S. Rept. 97-384, 97th Congress, 2d Session, 1982, pp. 90-91, 152-154.
66. See U.S. Congress, House, Committee on Agriculture, Futures Trading Act of 1982, H. Rept. 97-565 Part 1, 97th Congress, 2d Session, 1982, pp. 94-95, 139-141, 205-207.
67. See U.S. Congress, Senate, Committee on Appropriations, Treasury, Postal Service, and General Government Appropriation Bill, 1983, S. Rept. 97-547, 97th Congress, 2d Session, 1982, p. 45.
68. 5 U.S.C. 552(b)(1).
69. See E.O. 12356 in Federal Register, v. 47, April 6, 1982, pp. 14874-14884; also see Ibid., April 12, 1982, p. 15557; Ibid., May 11, 1982, pp. 20105-20106; Ibid., June 25, 1982, pp. 27836-27842.
70. See U.S. Congress, House, Committee on Government Operations, Executive Classification of Information--Security Classification Problems Involving Exemption (b)(1) of the Freedom of Information Act (5 U.S.C. 552), H. Rept. 93-221, 93rd Congress, 1st Session, 1973, p. 104; U.S. Congress, House, Committee on Standards of Official Conduct, Report on Investigation Pursuant to H. Res. 1042 Concerning Unauthorized Publication of the Report of the Select Committee on Intelligence, H. Rept. 94-1754, 94th Congress, 2d Session, 1976, pp. 43-44; U.S. Congress, Senate, Committee on the Judiciary, Subcommittee on Administrative Practice and Procedure, Agency Implementation of the 1974 Amendments to the Freedom of Information Act, Committee print, 95th Congress, 2d Session, 1980, p. 36.
71. This letter appears in U.S. Congress, House, Committee on Government Operations, Executive Order on Security Classification, Hearings, 97th Congress, 2d Session, 1982, pp. 317-318.
72. See Ibid., pp. 324-326.
73. See Ibid., pp. 129-220.
74. See U.S. Congress, House, Committee on Science and Technology, Subcommittee on Science, Research and Technology and Subcommittee on Investigations and Oversight, Impact of National Security Considerations on Science and Technology, Hearings, 97th Congress, 2d Session, 1982, p. 1.
75. See U.S. Congress, House, Committee on Government Operations, Security Classification Policy and Executive Order 12356, H. Rept. 97-731, 97th Congress, 2d Session, 1982, pp. 13-20.
76. 5 U.S.C. 553.
77. See H. Rept. 97-731, op. cit., p. 35.
78. See Congressional Record, v. 128, April 28, 1982, pp. S4210-S4216.
79. 50 U.S.C. App. 2401-2413.

CENSORSHIP IN THE EARLY PROFESSIONALIZATION OF AMERICAN LIBRARIES, 1876 TO 1929*

Frederick J. Stielow

> As good almost kill a Man as kill a good Book; who kills a Man kills a reasonable creature, God's Image; but he who destroys a good Book, kills reason itself, kills the Image of God, as it were in the eye.... We should be wary therefore what persecution we raise against the living labors of public men, how we spill that seasoned life of men preserved and stored up in Books; since we see a kind of homicide may be thus committed, sometimes a martyrdom, and if it extend to the whole impression, a kind of massacre.[1]

John Milton's stirring attack upon censorship in the Areopagitica accurately prefigures the opinions of many librarians today, but it is in direct contrast to the dominant feelings expressed during the first half-century after the founding of the modern library movement in 1876. During those early years, censorship in the form of book selection and removal policies was a basic fact of life in American libraries. Yet, it would be simplistic to suggest that librarians blithely accepted their roles as censors; censorship was actually recognized from the start of this period as one of the most serious and vexing issues of the profession.

As will be seen, the complexity of this issue belies any rigid moral judgments; rather we must examine such a policy in the context of its time. We should also view it in regard to the nature of the library in society--in both theory and reality. In this article, censorship will be specifically investigated in relation to the printed opinions of librarians in three somewhat overlapping periods: the Gilded Age to 1900, the Progressive Era to 1921, and the Twenties.

Censorship was a firmly established practice with centuries of acceptance by the time the American Library Association organized in 1876--the beginning of our first period of study. The word itself

---

*Reprinted by permission of the author and publisher from The Journal of Library History, 18:1 (Winter 1983) 37-54. Copyright © 1983 by the University of Texas Press.

dated from fifth-century-B.C. Rome. The concept drew its philosophical legitimacy from the doctrine of the general good, which was first propounded in Plato's Republic and more fully enunciated in Thomas Aquinas's thirteenth-century Summa Theologica. With Gutenberg's invention, the controlled dissemination of the written word took on more urgency for Western church and state leaders; they formally codified the principles of censorship and created mechanisms to regulate the flow of information even before its publication. Thus a long tradition of control was ready to greet the explosive expansion of printed materials, which followed the development of inexpensive pulp paper in the second quarter of the nineteenth century. [2]

The nineteenth-century emergence of a mass press produced immediate responses around the world, including the United States. Here, federal action in 1842 was accompanied by numerous state obscenity laws. But the heyday of control awaited the North's victory in the Civil War. As David Pivar's Purity Crusade has shown, censorship grew dramatically in the aftermath of the war. This country soon gained a new term--"comstockery"--to describe the phenomenon. Led by Anthony Comstock, concerned citizens promoted the installation of the stringent American postal regulations of 1873--The Comstock Law--and secured anti-obscenity legislation in thirty states by 1900. The courts were not lagging in support of such statutes and by 1879 had adopted the Hicklin test, which judged the culpability of materials by their effects upon the most susceptible members of society. These legal actions would frame the librarians' positions during our period of inquiry. [3]

In addition to technological determinism and tradition, the reasons for a rise of censorship during the Gilded Age are not difficult to discern. Industrialization, urbanization, and immigration contributed not only to fabulous wealth and ostentatious displays, but also to the threat of instability or revolution. The fears engendered coupled with Victorian-era status and sexual anxieties to underline efforts to educate an emerging proletarian class into proper "American" industrial work habits and morals.

Following the lead of English historian E.P. Thompson and French philosopher-historian Michel Foucault, American scholars-- such as Herbert Gutman, Michael Katz, and David Rothman--have shown the pervasiveness of these educational efforts for a broad range of American institutions, from schools and prisons to mental asylums and factories. Although clearly delineated in Sidney Ditzion's Arsenals of a Democratic Culture and indicated in Robert Weibe's seminal Search for Order, the linkage of the campaign for order to the public library movement was only firmly established in library literature by the work of Michael Harris in 1973. [4] To Harris, the elitist and authoritarian nature of library leaders and backers allowed them to become naively convinced of the institution's potential as a "conservator of order": for example, Andrew Carnegie's 1894 statement that the effect of libraries could only be --"to make men not violent revolutionairies [sic], but cautious evolutionists; not destroyers, but careful improvers."[5]

Yet, we must avoid any overly moralistic or simplistic interpretations based upon such statements, for the motivations behind the campaign for order extended beyond Machiavellian manipulations. For example, Joseph F. Wall--Carnegie's major biographer --argues that his subject's largesse in the foundation of the modern library stemmed from a combination of factors. These included the control of unruly elements and ideals of scientific philanthropy, as well as egotism and the example of childhood experiences in the library of Colonel Anderson. Carnegie's plans built not only from fear, but on the duty and desire to improve humanity and also on long established traditions of <u>noblesse oblige</u>. His primary concerns were at least verbalized in the direction of improving class ties and building the "race," without exposing it to the dangers of "energy-sapping" charity.[6] As he argued in the <u>Gospel of Wealth</u>, Carnegie was also concerned with reconciling the imbalance of riches in the Gilded Age: "the problem of our age is the proper administration of wealth, that ties of brotherhood may still bind together rich and poor in harmonious relationship."[7]

Moreover, the actions and beliefs of early library supporters --like Carnegie--were in keeping with the most respected intellectual, medical, and scientific opinions of the period. In particular, such efforts reflected the growing triumph of evolutionary thought during the last quarter of the nineteenth century. Not only secular thinkers, but even religious leaders of the Social Gospel Movement, and (through an often perverted Spencerianism) businessmen accepted the tenets of this thesis.[8] As famous educator Francis A. Walker noted in 1890: "I must deem any man very shallow in his observation of the facts of life and utterly lacking in the biological senses, who fails to discern in competition the forces to which it is mainly due that mankind has risen from stage to stage, in intellectual, moral, and physical power."[9] One facet of this acceptance of evolutionism was a belief in the possibility of perfecting humanity by manipulating the environment. In particular, proponents of such manipulation touted the mechanisms of education, which extended to the "self-enlightening" use of libraries. Again, such thoughts were not specifically based upon fear, but relied upon calls for positive action. As Andrew Carnegie said at the dedication of a library in Pittsburgh in 1895:

> What we must seek, then for surplus wealth, if we are to work genuine good, are uses which give nothing for nothing, which require cooperation, self-help, and which, by no possibility, can tend to sap the spirit of manly independence, which is the only sure foundation upon which the steady improvement of our race can be built. We were soon led to see in the free Library an institution which fulfilled these conditions, and which must work only for good and never for evil. It gives nothing for nothing.[10]

While undeniably racist, sexist, and paternalistic, such self-help statements undoubtedly appealed to Carnegie's fellow leaders in the public library movement. These pronouncements provided the library with a mission and social function beyond the preservation of books. Libraries were conceived as educational adjuncts, places where people could continue their studies--that is, betterment-- after schooling, or learn the skills needed for their place in society.

Yet, difficulties also existed, for the power of the word also held a threat; trash novels and socialist tracts might undermine the glorious edifice that was to be. Melvil Dewey noted this threat in his auspiciously titled "Libraries as Related to the Educational Work of the State":

> To teach the masses to read and then turn them out in early youth with this power and no guiding influence, is only to invite catastrophe ... the world agrees that it is unwise to give sharp tools and powerful weapons to the masses without some assurance of how they are to be used. [11]

The twin dangers of debased literature and uncontrollable knowledge produced a paradox with a logical solution--censorship. The librarian as a professional was entrusted with the duty of ensuring the flow of "correct" materials to the proletariat; indeed, this task helped define his or her duties as a professional.

In addition to the dangers of unsupervised reading, members of the fledgling American Library Association were quite cognizant of the theoretical benefits that could accrue to society through the librarian's role as moral arbiter and custodian. Beginning in the 1870s, articles on censorship--or exclusion as it was sometimes called--were frequently featured in the Association's organ, the Library Journal: for example, the 1879 "The Evil of Unlimited Freedom in the Use of Juvenile Fiction" and the 1885 "Free Libraries and Unclean Books," or such promotional efforts as the 1896 "The Librarian's Duty as a Citizen" and the 1897 "What May a Librarian Do to Influence the Reading of a Community." By February of 1882, this same magazine published one of the first national surveys on censorship, the A.L.A. Co-operation Committee's "Report on Exclusion," and in 1895 reported the results of the Association's Denver Conference symposium--"Improper Books: Methods Employed to Discover and Exclude Them."[12]

From this type of material we can discern several general patterns in this era. Clearly, as other scholars have shown, librarians felt that they possessed the ability, duty, and position to control controversial titles. As Ditzion later suggested, librarians normally joined in contemporary community standards and took part in the dissemination of the dominant social theories of the period, as well as acquiescing to societal pressures. Most librarians were especially concerned with the effects of objectionable materials upon youth. They tried to limit potential dangers through careful selection policies, the development of separate children's facilities, and the controlled circulation of adult holdings--especially in so-called inferno collections. To further circumvent the prospects of unintentional contact with unprepared minds, major works by foreign authors were purchased in untranslated editions.[13]

Many librarians also felt justified, or relieved, because of budget constraints, for "by this negative censorship the library can to a large extent solve the problem of the undesirable book, simply because there are so many books above suspicion which it is unable to buy."[14] The arguments posited by librarians do not reveal malicious intent, but suggest a sense of social responsibility and duty, such as that indicated by Walter Learned in 1896:

> Each institution represented here exerts in its community a mighty tough silent influence, greater, I fancy, than even some of us imagine. We cannot err in this line of exclusion if we are alive to this responsibility.... The maxim for the public library in this regard might well read--"When in doubt, leave it out."[15]

Yet, this same source of literature also reveals a previously overlooked consciousness of the complexity of this issue, and opposition to the implementation of censorship practices. Even F. B. Perkins, the errant father of Charlotte Perkins Gilman, in his strident 1885 attack against "prurient literary dirt-eaters" was forced to disavow certain anti-censorship positions:

> 1. Any book ought to be supplied to any applicant.
> 2. Adult readers should be allowed to read any books they choose.
> 3. "Classics" should be delivered out, even if they are dirty.
> 4. The regulations of the library should be broken, if necessary, to suit newspaper men, in order to avoid their revenge.
> 5. If the books now in question are to be refused, a great many other books now delivered without reserve, including the Bible, should also be refused.[16]

However grudging, Perkins's stand was not alone in early library literature. In the very first volume of the Library Journal, William F. Poole, one of the most highly regarded librarians of the time, actively defended the library's right to maintain suggestive novels of literary merit.[17] Also within the same volume A. R. Spofford, head of the Library of Congress, in a more pointed fashion could speak out against at least one form of censorship:

> But another ancient abuse--the odious and narrow-minded system of licensing books, of permitting some works to be printed and refusing the privilege to others--has been kept up in nations commonly called enlightened.... That entire and absolute freedom of the press which prevails, and has always prevailed, in the United States, has been known until of late years to no other nation.[18]

Writers on censorship should not ignore another indication within the preceding excerpt--the hallowed place of intellectual freedom in the myth structure of Anglo-America. For opposition to censorship was also a part of the intellectual climate of opinion in the Victorian era. Some librarians were willing to support a tradition that drew upon the writings of John Milton, John Stuart Mill, Thomas Jefferson, and Thomas Paine--as well as the symbolic significance of the American Revolution and the Bill of Rights. The contradictions between these facts and the imposition of exclusion were especially clear in Lindsay Swift's 1899 criticisms, "Paternalism in Public Libraries":

> I cannot see how other professional restriction differs from theological restriction. The world has certainly combated eccesiastical domination with some measure of success; but how shall we fairly decry the influence of priestcraft if we concede the right of any other interference with perfect intellectual freedom?... Nobody today deliberately purposes to subjugate freedom in the public libraries, but there is nevertheless a tendency to regulate and decide for others, which is antipathetic to the democratic principles of least possible government.[19]

No doubt partially motivated by the economic and social troubles of the late 1890s, Swift managed a thoughtful and remarkably modern attack against his elitist fellow librarians. He was able to disparage American proponents of exclusion by comparing them to the horrific censors of tsarist Russia. In addition, he argued, "We must be brave in our own virtue; if strong meat is not injurious to us, need we be too solicitous about the effect on the people?"[20] To Swift, simple honesty and courage were needed in matters of book selection, and he was not above sarcasm to make his points:

> In regard to the vexatious question of the so-called sex problem I have little to say, but experience tells me that those who are the most actively concerned over improper literature are not those whom I would most implicitly trust in the wider realms of morals.[21]

While Swift's article represents one extreme position of the debate, he was not alone in his sentiments. Some felt that their professional abilities conferred the right to exempt most nonfiction from censorship's scrutiny; the social sciences and sciences, for example, were generally measured by more utilitarian standards. Many librarians differed with stringent censorship stands on matters of aesthetics, particularly in dealing with acknowledged literary classics. Limited opposition was also offered by F.M. Crunden of the St. Louis Public Library, who recanted his decision to withdraw the works of recently arrested Oscar Wilde in a simply stated--but published--note: "After glancing through Wilde's books ... I put them back on the shelves."[22] Librarians were even willing to differ with the underlying assumptions of the nation's legal stand on obscene works; many believed that adult reading materials should be considerably more sophisticated than those aimed at children-- the most susceptible members of society. Thus, Walter Learned in his previously mentioned and essentially pro-censorship article, "The Line of Exclusion," could still state:

> I think it may be safely assumed that the books in a free public library should not be limited to those which are fitted to the young and immature mind. To so limit it would be to exclude from the public library much that is important in English literature, much that is vital to it, much that is proper and healthy reading for the adult ... occasional coarseness of expression might seem to suggest a doubt; but the same doubt might arise concerning the Old Testament, frankly a book which, could we ignore its religious character, is not in places fitted to the comprehension and reading of the young.[23]

The complexities of the censorship issue were further heightened by periodic stands against outside forces in the Purity Crusade. Librarians were prepared to defend their primacy in the selection of books, and their position was fortified by their professional allusions and the prestige of their institutions. The most famous of such cases in the late nineteenth century occurred in Boston in the 1880s. James M. Hubbard's attacks on the "immoral" novels in the Boston Public Library received nationwide notoriety in the pages of the North American Review. Boston library officials responded in terms that indicated concerns beyond moral indoctrination:

> The library, as has been stated, is maintained as a great popular metropolitan institution. It is not a goody-goody Sunday School library, such as many seem to wish to make it; it is not kept up expressly for the benefit of the Puritan New Englander ... but it is also intended to meet the requirements of the Roman Catholic Irishman, the atheistic German, the radical Frenchman, all of whom are citizens of Boston, paying their proportion of the taxes which support the institution, and therefore equally entitled to be considered in the selection of books and periodicals. [24]

The library's responsibility to the taxpayers, which was stressed in the preceding quotation, was one of several countervailing factors in reality that served to limit the library's theoretical place in the crusade for moral uplift and order. As librarians Phyllis Dain and Evelyn Geller indicated in their challenges to Michael Harris's revisionist critique, and further supported by the above quotation, the elitist forces in the library were still able to respond to the needs of the lower classes. Moreover, many librarians realized that they might have to pander to common tastes in order to induce people to enter their establishments. Such well-known figures as Justin Winsor and William Poole were outspoken in their attempts to popularize the library, and such steps obviously required reduced standards of censorship.[25]

The very structure of the library further restricted the institution's capacity in the crusade for order. We must recognize that the library could never function as an active agent for social change in this period; rather it must be seen as an essentially passive institution. This characterization is in keeping with its essentially voluntary, not coercive, nature, as well as the public's longstanding interpretation of the library as a repository and preserver of culture. In addition, fragmentized control at the local level effectively thwarted the bureaucratic regimentation of centralized state authority, which figures so heavily in the results of Michel Foucault-inspired studies. Indeed, the socially active role envisioned for libraries clashed with the increasing technical orientation of librarians, as well as the last clear tendency to emerge from late nineteenth century writings--the repeated desire to avoid publicity over censorship cases.[26]

In spite of such mitigating factors and opposition, the dominant opinions in the library continued to favor exclusion throughout the last quarter of the nineteenth century and into the Progressive era. Yet subtle changes were occurring in this second period of inquiry, and the anti-censorship position began to gain more strength.

The exclusionist stand retained many of the justifications suggested for the earlier period, but moved steadily away from the elitist framework of genteel America into the more "scientific" rhetoric of the Progressives. Thus, we find in the literature repeated attempts to objectify and isolate the distinctive features of "objectionable" items within an evolutionist framework. Even Arthur E. Bostwick's now infamous 1908 presidential address to the American Library Association, "The Librarian as a Censor," reflected this orientation. Bostwick presented a tripartite model for the classification of printed works and then noted: "I have tried to set down regarding them data ... for the purpose of impressing upon you the fact that disagreement is not so much regarding the data as regarding the application to them of principles."[27] He argued that some characteristics were condemned by immutable laws, yet a larger category contained offensive aspects of a more transitory nature: "Impropriety or indecency, on the other hand, is purely arbitrary.... Impropriety is a violation of certain social customs, and although I should be the last to question the observance of customs, we must grant, I think, that they rest on foundations other than those of right or wrong."[28]

But Bostwick's article also represents the extremist position in favor of censorship in the library. Ironically ignoring its original satirical intent, Bostwick borrowed a quotation from Shakespeare to stress the heroic possibilities for the librarian:

> "Some are born great; some achieve greatness; some have greatness thrust upon them." It is in this last way that the librarian has become a censor of literature.... As the library's audience becomes larger, as its educational functions spread and are brought to bear on more and

more of the young and immature, the duty of sifting its materials becomes more imperative.[29]

The author was able to extol the virtues of a professional who was able to resist the enticements of lascivious literature: "Thank heaven they do not tempt the librarian. Here at last is a purveyor of books who has no interest in distributing what is not clean, honest, and true. The librarian may ... say to this menacing tide, 'Thus far shalt thou go and no farther.'"[30]

In response to Bostwick's address, the Library Journal published a two-part survey that was drawn from throughout the nation and designed to be representative of the "librarian's standpoint." Despite the suggestive title--"What Shall Libraries Do about Bad Books?"--the respondents exhibited a wider divergence of opinion over the question of exclusion than seen in the late nineteenth century. In addition, their replies mirrored many of the ongoing developments within the country and the libraries themselves.

Bostwick and the others were especially concerned because of their perceptions of an increasing volume of questionable literature that had arisen since the turn of the century. Even rural America was not spared this curse. Although fortunately comforted by the moral superiority of the countryside, Lutie Stearns of Wisconsin's Traveling Library Department, for example, in a splendid example of the rural/urban split declared: "We realize that the standard of such libraries sent to rural communities is much higher than for the average city library, as country dwellers, praise be, will not 'stand for' the sort of things read by many city borrowers."[31]

Some of the essayists clearly agreed with Bostwick's general stand. George H. Tripp stated, "that books which are questionable in tone should be excluded from public libraries must be assumed." [32] Tripp was also grateful for the aid provided by the A.L.A. Committee on Bookbuying with its lists of recommended works. Most continued to feel that the main danger lay with children, arguing: "In the library which gives free access, the guarding of the morals of the young becomes an active responsibility."[33]

Yet by the turn of the century much of the problem of children's access to suggestive materials had been solved by the growing presence of separate youth collections. Thus the majority of those queried spoke to the need to provide the mature urbanite with a more sophisticated variety of literature. The dilemma presented by this type of book was often solved by some form of restricted shelving, however grudgingly: "Newark Free Public Library--A few books which are nasty according to present-day notions are placed on restricted shelves and are issued to adults only; they are given unhesitatingly to such adults as ask for them."[34]

While it must be stressed that these librarians generally favored some sort of censorship, the presence of dissenting opinions is still highly suggestive, especially in regard to the underlying premises of their forum. For example, Frances Rathbone of East Orange even questioned the applicability of restricted shelving, noting that--"the attitude that innocence is preserved by ignorance seems impossible in this day of the newspaper, magazine and problem novel, if it ever was wise."[35] Similarly, Samuel Ranck of Grand Rapids, Michigan, decried the entire notion of social control through the manipulation of reading materials:

> In fact, to the minds of certain persons, any book which is a criticism of, or whose purpose is to change, the present social order is regarded as unwholesome, if not immoral, and therefore should have no place on library shelves, inasmuch as it is likely to awaken or engender class strife. To deal with books of this character it seems to me is not a difficult problem at all. Representatives of all shades of views on social, economic, and religious questions should have a place on library shelves. The policy of the library should be sympathetic, catholic, toward all political, economic, social, and religious questions.[36]

Such statements were in keeping with the liberal tinge of many of the social reform movements of the era. Despite current historiographic emphasis on social regulations and scientific management, there was also a push toward civil liberties and against the perceived restraints of Puritanism in the Progressive Era. The late nineteenth and early twentieth century witnessed the rise of yellow journalism and also "muckraking" journalists and authors, who exposed corruption in all levels of the power structure. In these "progressive" times, George Santayana and others in the intelligentsia were able to vilify even the basic genteel and Calvinist roots of American society. The idea of censorship was also attacked. Theodore Schroeder, Hutchins Hapgood, and Lincoln Stephens, for example, successfully founded the Free Speech league, and literary and legal circles in general began to show increasing uneasiness over and opposition to vice societies and censorship. As Henry F. May later described in The End of American Innocence, the first decades of the twentieth century were a transitional period for American intellectuals. While not in the vanguard of these changes, the librarians still had to cope with the demands of changing tastes and the appearance of controversial, but undeniably valuable production by the likes of Stephen Crane and Theodore Dreiser.[37]

While we should not expect to discover librarians in active support of the radical message of a Randolph Bourne, the presence of any opposition to conformity in library circles during the war years is notable. Yet, in 1916 ALA President Mary White Plummer issued a call for openness and the need to combat censorship. Further, while Mary L. Hunt was dismissed from the Portland, Oregon, library because of a pacifist stance against the purchase of war bonds, she was immediately invited to work by another library. Such instances should not be overstressed. As Frances C.

Sayers and others have made clear, the paranoid pressures of the Home Front with its liberty cabbage and Creal Committee became far too intense. The liberalizing trend of the prewar years was effectively reversed. As evidenced by the willing embrace of government-issued censorship lists for ALA-managed military libraries, most librarians were undoubtedly anxious to sacrifice liberal gains for the war effort.[38]

Wartime fervor and censorship did not die with the armistice, and this contradiction helped prepare the way for the liberalizing movements in the Twenties. If librarians had accepted wartime suppression of individual liberties, they were still affronted by the trauma of the Red Summer of 1919 and the activities of such groups as the Ku Klux Klan and American Legion. Perhaps more significant to the eventual opposition to exclusion was the changing intellectual climate of the period. Librarians, in particular, were forced to acknowledge the growing stature of the modern novel and the appreciation of continental culture that burst on the scene after the war. Librarian Helen Haines commented in a 1924 article:

> It seems to me that fiction was never so varied, so stimulating, so revealing of life in myriad phases, so illuminating of the hidden springs of impulse and character, as it is at the present time.... We are steadily widening our mental horizons and diminishing our provinciality under the inflow of European fiction in English translation that has come to us in steadily mounting volume since the war made Americans realize the existence of the World.[39]

These effects added to the general ambiance of the Twenties (in historical terms the years between 1922 and 1923 and the start of the Depression in 1929) as the most contradictory age in American history and the start of our modern era. Since Frederick Lewis Allen's Only Yesterday, historians have been fascinated by this truncated decade of Freud, flappers, Fords, and speakeasies. For librarians this period is doubly important as marking the start of modern library education under the Williamson Report of 1923.

Paralleling concerns over library education and the failure of Progressive reforms were similar uncertainties regarding the propriety of censorship. These doubts emerged from the confusion of the Library Journal's 1922 survey, "Questionable Books in Public Libraries," to which one librarian could only reply--"Our present state of mind in regard to it is so chaotic, and subject to change, that there would be no use in trying to record it."[40] The only area of seeming unanimity was "that it is inadvisable to give general publicity in their communities to the fact that certain works are not approved by them for acquisition."[41] In spite of this silence, the report reveals that librarians were now evenly divided over the issue of censorship; the selections chosen by editor Louis N. Feipel showed a continuation of such practices as restricted collections or the marking of offensive materials, but in a like number of instances found librarians belatedly admitting that--"it is hardly

The Social Prerogative 337

for the library to say who is fitted to take out a book, and who is not."[42] As Chicago Public Library authorities stated, the major reason behind this latter trend was the emergence of a responsible adult readership:

> In the larger public tax-supported libraries ... this problem is affected by the rapidly increasing element of the population that has both the taste or interest to desire and the maturity and discretion to appraise and appreciate the work of reputable, often the best writers.[43]

From the confusion of 1922, the movement toward civil libertarianism expanded rapidly. The following year, Mary U. Rothrock unleashed a storm of debate at the annual ALA convention with her mild criticisms of censorship and suggestions that "The function of the library is to bring to all the people the books that belong to them."[44] Rothrock made certain to exclude the guarding of children's reading from her suggestions. Her position was phrased with the detachment of the social sciences and in keeping with evolutionary thought:

> Expressed in terms of psychology, a book is an association test, affecting each member of a group of people who read it in accordance with his own dominant thought.... In other words, the morality or immorality of a book depends upon what the reader brings to it and of that he alone can be the judge.[45]

In heated opposition to these sentiments rose M. E. Ahern, the editor of Public Libraries. Ahern at the convention and in a later series of editorials called upon librarians to "walk in lofty purpose and valuable service unmoved by the roar of distasteful ideas around them."[46]

But in the changing climate of opinion in the Twenties, Ahern's arguments could no longer carry. As Paul Boyer has detailed, librarians rapidly abandoned their exclusionary stands in this period, especially in response to the perceived threat of the Clean Book Campaign (1923-1925). That blatant effort to regulate the public's taste forged an "anticensorship coalition" of authors, critics, booksellers, publishers, and librarians--even among those favoring exclusion.[47] So rapid, though hardly total, was the victory of the anti-censorship stance among librarians that Helen Haines of the Los Angeles Public Library could write in 1924, "I know no more depressing indication of the librarian's attitude toward literature than may be found in Mr. Feipel's elaborate inquiries into 'Questionable Books in Public Libraries,' printed in the Library Journal about two years ago."[48] To Haines and a growing majority of librarians, it now appeared that the profession had seriously miscalculated with its support of exclusion:

> In its ideal, such censorship may be sound; in official actuality it must be futile, impracticable, and dangerous:

> futile, because it instantly rouses interest in and demand
> for the forbidden; impracticable, because it cannot be consistently or fairly applied; dangerous, because the imposition of official restriction or prohibition on the expression
> of thought, the freedom of literature, is in itself a far
> greater menace than the evil it seeks to prevent.[49]

One may argue from such a quotation that the results it advocates are far from liberating, since the conditions of tolerance are utilized to maintain the overall structure and functions of society. As philosopher Herbert Marcuse suggests, even "progressive movements threaten to turn into their opposite to the degree to which they accept the rules of the game.... In such a case Freedom (of opinion, of assembly, of speech) becomes an instrument for absolving servitude."[50] However ineffective its role as a censor, the library should still be viewed within a pattern of social control. To French thinker Michel Foucault, it becomes essential to study such actions as part of a broader history of detail:

> It is rather a multiplicity of often minor processes, of
> different origin and scattered location, which overlap, repeat, or imitate one another, support one another, distinguish themselves from one another according to their
> domain of application, converge and gradually produce the
> blueprint of a general method.... Describing them will
> require great attention to detail: beneath every set of
> figures, we must seek not a meaning, but a precaution;
> we must situate them not only in the inextricability of a
> functioning, but in the coherence of a tactic.... Discipline is a political anatomy of detail.[51]

Such arguments as these and those of Michael Harris are essentially correct--but limited and unidirectional. They assume a direct Machiavellian effect from the "top down," without recognizing a multiplicity of motives and the ability of the "down" to alter the situation. Initially librarians embraced the professional status of censors, and their institution was designed to participate in an elitist campaign for moral order and uplift. Yet, though the library may be viewed as a penultimate creation within the superstructure, the inherent contradictions between the library's theoretical place as an agent of control and the reality of its voluntary nature required a solution. Similarly, the irony of an establishment created as an "arsenal for democracy" serving as a censor suggested the need for change. Out of these dialectics and a combination of the technical training of librarians, changing public tastes, and outside threats came a questioning of the value of censorship. By 1925, censorship policies, while not totally dismissed, had been altered from an accepted standard into an issue to be attacked or at least challenged in public--a substantial development in the history of librarianship.

References

1. John Milton, Areopagitica, quoted in John McCormick and Mairi MacInnes, Versions of Censorship (Garden City, N.Y.: Doubleday, 1962), p. 9. I have modernized the spellings.
2. Harold C. Gardiner, Catholic Viewpoint on Censorship (Garden City, N.Y.: Hanover House, 1958), p. 24; Plato, Dialogues of Plato (New York: Pocket Books, 1950), pp. 254-255; McCormick, Versions, pp. xiii-xv.
3. George Bowerman (ed.), Censorship and the Public Library (New York: H.W. Wilson, 1931), pp. 15-17; Robert Haney, Comstockery in America: Patterns of Censorship and Control (Boston: Beacon Press, 1960), pp. 16-20; David Pivar, Purity Crusade, Sexual Morality, and Social Control, 1868-1900 (Westport, Conn.: Greenwood Press, 1973).
4. Herbert Gutman, Work, Culture and Society in Industrializing America (New York: Knopf, 1976); Michael Katz, Class, Bureaucracy and Schools: The Illusion of Educational Change in America (New York: Praeger, 1975); David Rothman, The Discovery of the Asylum: Social Order and Disorder in the New Republic (Boston: Little, Brown, 1971); Michael Harris, "The Purpose of the American Library," Library Journal 98 (1973): 2509-2514. It should be noted that Harris only touches upon the subject of censorship.
5. Quoted in Joseph F. Wall, Andrew Carnegie (New York: Oxford University Press, 1970), p. 821.
6. Ibid., pp. 106, 400, 515; also from private discussions with Dr. Wall, December 1979.
7. Andrew Carnegie, The Gospel of Wealth and Other Timely Essays (New York: Century, 1900), p. 1.
8. Paul Boller, Jr., "New Men and New Ideas," in H. Wayne Morgan, The Gilded Age: A Reappraisal (Syracuse, N.Y.: Syracuse University Press, 1963); Merle Curti, The Growth of American Thought, 3rd ed. (New York: Harper and Row, 1964), ch. 22-24.
9. Curti, American Thought, p. 540.
10. Burton Hendrick (ed.), Miscellaneous Writings of Andrew Carnegie (Freeport, N.Y.: Books for Libraries, 1933), p. 210.
11. Quoted in Sidney Ditzion, Arsenals of a Democratic Culture (Chicago: American Library Association, 1947), p. 74; see also Burton Bledstein, The Culture of Professionalism (New York: Norton, 1976), pp. 56-77.
12. M.A. Bean, "The Evil of Unlimited Freedom ...," Library Journal 4 (1879): 341-343; F.B. Perkins, "Free Libraries and Unclean Books," Library Journal 10 (1885): 396-399; A.L. Peck, "What May a Librarian Do ...," Library Journal 22 (1897): 77-90; C.K. Bolton, "The Librarian's Duty ...," Library Journal 21 (1896): 219-222; A.L.A. Co-operation Committee, "Report on Exclusion," Library Journal 7 (1882): 28-29; "Improper Books," Library Journal 20 (1895): 32-37.
13. See also Dee Garrison, "Cultural Custodians of the Gilded Age," Journal of Library History 6 (1971): 327-336; and Garrison, Apostles of Culture: The Public Librarian and

American Society, 1876-1920 (New York: Free Press, 1979); Esther Jane Carrier, Fiction in Public Libraries, 1876-1900 (Metuchen, N.J.: Scarecrow, 1965).

14. Samuel Ranck in "What Shall Librarians Do about Bad Books?" (Library Journal 33 [1908]: 353).
15. Walter Learned, "The Line of Exclusion," Library Journal 21 (1896): 323.
16. Perkins, "Free Libraries," p. 397. While the following evidence stresses the opposition to censorship, the reader is again advised that this was the exception to the rule.
17. William F. Poole, "Some Popular Objections to Public Libraries," Library Journal 1 (1876): 49-51.
18. A.R. Spofford, "Copyright in Its Relations to Libraries and Literature," Library Journal 1 (1876): 85.
19. Lindsay Swift, "Paternalism in Public Libraries," Library Journal 24 (1899): 610.
20. Ibid., p. 615.
21. Ibid.
22. F.M. Crunden, Letter to the Editor, Library Journal 20 (1895): 198.
23. Learned, "Line of Exclusion," pp. 320-321.
24. Quoted in Ditzion, Arsenals, pp. 184-185.
25. Phyllis Dain, "Ambivalence and Paradox," Library Journal 100 (1975): 261-265; Evelyn Geller, "The Librarian as Censor," Library Journal 101 (1976): 1255-1258. A reading of these two actually adds very little and shows little variance from Harris's position on the late nineteenth century.
26. See note 13; Michael Harris, "The Purpose," p. 2512. He makes the intriguing point that by 1900 the librarians' devotion to technical detail made them increasingly ignore theoretical and philosophical matters.
27. Arthur E. Bostwick, "The Librarian as a Censor," Library Journal 33 (1908): 263.
28. Ibid., p. 260.
29. Ibid., p. 297.
30. Ibid., p. 264; see also Electra C. Doren, "Action upon Bad Books," Library Journal 28 (1903): 167-169.
31. "What Shall Librarians Do," p. 352.
32. Ibid., p. 350.
33. Ibid., p. 352.
34. Ibid., p. 351.
35. Ibid., p. 392.
36. Ibid., p. 354.
37. Paul Boyer, Purity in Print: The Vice Society Movement and Book Censorship in America (New York: Scribners, 1968), pp. 40-52; George Santayana, The Genteel Tradition: Nine Essays, edited by Douglas L. Wilson (Cambridge, Mass.: Harvard University, 1967).
38. Frances C. Sayers, "If the Trumpet Be Not Sounded," Wilson Library Bulletin 39 (1965): 659-662. Sayers sees a wavering line on censorship from 1896 and mentions that during the war she and a friend lost their jobs at the New York Public Library due to such hysteria. Also see Arthur P. Young, Books

for Sammies: The American Library Association and World War I, Beta Phi Mu Chapbook No. 15 (Pittsburgh, Penn.: Beta Phi Mu, 1981). This book is a revision of "The American Library Association and World War I" (Ph.D. dissertation, University of Illinois at Urbana-Champaign, 1976).
39. Helen Haines, "Modern Fiction and the Public Library," Library Journal 49 (1924): 458.
40. Louis N. Feipel, "Questionable Books in Public Libraries," Library Journal 47 (1922): 859. Boyer, Purity in Print, badly misrepresents the results of the Feipel survey.
41. Feipel, "Questionable Books," p. 909.
42. Ibid.
43. Ibid., p. 859.
44. Mary U. Rothrock, "Censorship of Fiction in the Public Library," Library Journal 48 (1923): 455. She also agrees that the Feipel survey showed a marked swing from censorship.
45. Ibid.
46. Boyer, Purity in Print, p. 116.
47. Ibid., pp. 125-127.
48. Haines, "Modern Fiction," p. 458.
49. Ibid., p. 460.
50. Herbert Marcuse, "Repressive Tolerance," in Eleanor Widmer (ed.), Freedom and Culture: Literary Censorship in the 70's (Belmont, Cal.: Wadsworth, 1970), p. 28.
51. Michel Foucault, Discipline and Punish: The Birth of the Prison (New York: Vintage, 1979), pp. 138-139.

● ● ●

I would like to thank Dan Bergen, Jon Tyron, L.B. Woods of the University of Rhode Island, and Deborah Johnson of the University of Southwestern Louisiana.

ISLAND TREES v. PICO: THE LEGAL IMPLICATIONS*

Robert D. Stone

The purpose of this paper is to analyze the June 25 decision of the United States Supreme Court in the Island Trees school library case (Board of Education, Island Trees Union Free School District No. 26, et al. v. Pico, et al., _____ U.S. _____, 50 Law Week 4831 [1982]).

While attending a conference of a conservatively oriented educational organization, three members of the Island Trees board of education obtained excerpts from allegedly objectionable books. Upon returning to the district, those board members examined the school library card index to determine whether the books in question were in the school libraries. It was eventually determined that nine of them were in the high school library, one was in the junior high school library, and one was used in the curriculum. The books included The Fixer, by Bernard Malamud, Slaughterhouse Five, by Kurt Vonnegut, The Naked Ape, by Desmond Morris, Down These Mean Streets, by Piri Thomas, Best Short Stories of Negro Writers, by Langston Hughes, Go Ask Alice, of anonymous authorship, Laughing Boy, by Oliver LaFarge, Black Boy, by Richard Wright, A Hero Ain't Nothin' But a Sandwich, by Alice Childress, and Soul on Ice, by Eldridge Cleaver.

At a meeting with the superintendent of schools and the principals of the high school and junior high school, the board of education gave an "unofficial direction" that the books in question be removed from the library shelves and delivered to the board's offices so that board members could read them. When that directive was carried out it became public knowledge, and the board issued a press release justifying its action. It characterized the removed books as "anti-American, anti-Christian, and anti-Semitic, and just plain filthy" and concluded that "It is our duty, our moral obligation, to protect the children in our schools from this moral danger as surely as from physical and medical dnagers."

A short time later, the board of education appointed a "Book

---

*Reprinted by permission of the author and publisher from Collection Building, 5 (Spring 1983) 3-8. Copyright © 1983 by Neal-Schuman Publishers.

The Social Prerogative

Review Committee," consisting of four Island Trees parents and four members of the district staff, to read the books in question and to recommend to the board whether they should be retained in the libraries, taking into account the books' "educational suitability," "good taste," "relevance," and "appropriateness to age and grade level." That Committee recommended to the board that five of the books be retained in the libraries and that two others be removed from the shelves. As for the remaining books, the Committee could not agree on two, took no position on one, and recommended that one be made available to students only with parental approval.

Following submission of the Committee's report, the board substantially rejected it, concluding that only one book should be returned to the high school library without restriction, that another should be made available to students, subject to parental approval, and that the remaining nine books should be removed from the school libraries of the district and from any use in the curriculum. The board gave no reasons for rejecting the recommendations of the Committee.

The board's decision precipitated a lawsuit, brought by students and their parents, in the United States District Court for the Eastern District of New York. The plaintiffs contended that the board had ordered the removal of the books in question from the libraries of the Island Trees district and had prohibited their use in the curriculum "because particular passages in the books offended their social, political and moral tastes and not because the books, taken as a whole, were lacking in educational value."

Judge Pratt, the District Court judge, dismissed the action, relying on a decision of the United States Court of Appeals for the Second Circuit, to which I shall refer in a moment. He said, "Here, the issue is whether the first amendment requires a federal court to forbid a school board from removing library books which its members find to be inconsistent with the basic values of the community that elected them." Judge Pratt concluded that the First Amendment does not have that effect.

The decision upon which Judge Pratt relied was rendered by the Court of Appeals for the Second Circuit in the so-called Presidents Council case (Presidents Council, District 25 v. Community School Board No. 25, 457 F. 2d 289, cert. den. 409 U.S. 998 [1972]). In that case, the Second Circuit held that a school library book that was improperly selected "for whatever reason" could be removed "by the same authority which was empowered to make the selection in the first place." In the words of Judge Mulligan of the Second Circuit, "... some authorized person or body has to make a determination as to what the library collection will be. It is predictable that no matter what choice of books may be made by whatever segment of academe, some other person or group may well dissent. The ensuing shouts of book burning, witch hunting and violation of academic freedom hardly elevate this intramural strife

to first amendment constitutional proportions. If it did, there
would be a constant intrusion of the judiciary into the internal affairs of the school. Academic freedom is scarcely fostered by the
intrusion of three or even nine federal jurists making curriculum
or library choices for the community of scholars."

Judge Pratt's Island Trees decision predictably was appealed
to the Second Circuit. Not so predictably, in view of its <u>Presidents
Council</u> decision, the Second Circuit reversed Judge Pratt and remanded the matter for trial (638 F. 2d 404). The reason for the
reversal was clearly a concern on the part of the appellate court
with both the apparent motivation of the Island Trees board of education in directing removal of the books in question, and the procedures used by the board in making its determination. In the
words of Judge Sifton:

> Where ... as in this case, evidence that the decisions
> made were based on the defendants' moral or political
> beliefs appears together with evidence of procedural and
> substantive irregularities sufficient to suggest an unwil-
> lingness on the part of the school officials to subject
> their political and personal judgments to the same sort
> of scrutiny as that accorded other decisions relating to
> the education of their charges, an inference emerges that
> political views and personal taste are being asserted not
> in the interests of the children's well-being, but rather
> for the purpose of establishing those views as the correct
> and orthodox ones for all purposes in the particular com-
> munity.

And so the case went to the United States Supreme Court.
The questions there can be expressed rather succinctly: Does the
First Amendment prohibit boards of education from removing books
from school libraries? The Supreme Court, in its June 25 decisions, answered the question with a thundering "maybe."

While probably not unprecedented in their diversity, the responses of the Court to the question before it were remarkably divergent. Seven of the nine judges wrote separate opinions. No
more than four judges concurred in any one opinion. One would
assume that the opinion embraced by four judges was the prevailing
opinion. Not so. The single opinion which got the most votes was
a dissenting opinion. Only three judges fully concurred in Justice
Brennan's opinion, which reflected the official decision of the Court,
but the Brennan view prevailed because two judges joined in his
conclusion, while not fully agreeing with his reasoning.

<u>What Was the Island Trees Decision?</u>

If we are to attempt to seriously seek instruction from the Supreme
Court's Island Trees decisions--and of course we must--I think we
are required to approach the task from these standpoints:

The Social Prerogative

1. What a majority of the Court held.
2. What the Court did not hold.
3. What the various justices said.

The decision of five justices (Brennan, Marshall, Stevens, Blackmun, and White) was that the Circuit Court of Appeals was right when it remanded the case for trial before the District Court. A judicial decision that a trial is required means, by definition, that there are issues of fact which need to be determined. The issue of fact which both the Court of Appeals and the Supreme Court found in this case is the motives of the members of the Island Trees board of education in deciding that certain books should be removed from the school libraries. In the words of Justice Brennan, who wrote the prevailing opinion, "... whether [the school board's] removal of books from their school libraries denied [students] their First Amendment rights depends upon the motivation behind [the board's] actions. If [the board members] intended by their removal decision to deny [students] access to ideas with which [the board members] disagreed, and if this intent was the decisive factor in [the board members'] decision, then [the board members] have exercised their discretion in violation of the Constitution."

In concluding that a trial was required, Justice Brennan found that "The evidence plainly does not foreclose the possibility that [the board members'] decision to remove the books rested decisively upon disagreement with constitutionally protected ideas in those books, or upon a desire on [the board members'] part to impose upon the students of the Island Trees High School and Junior High School a political orthodoxy to which [the board members] and their constituents adhered." In a word, Judge Brennan concludes that there is some limit on the authority of boards of education to remove books from school libraries, and that the motivation of the board in deciding that books should be removed from the library is the pivotal factor in determining whether the board's action did or did not violate the First Amendment rights of students.

If Justice Brennan's decision had simply concluded that the motivation of the board members was essential to a determination of the case, and had stopped there, the decision of the Court would probably have been a rather simple five-four. That is precisely what Justice White would have had him do. However, Justice Brennan went much further, and wrote a rather extensive treatise on the extent to which the First Amendment limits the discretion of school boards to remove books from school libraries. The result is that we have to do some more work in order to understand the decisions.

Before looking at what the seven justices had to say about the subject of library books and the First Amendment, we need to get out of the way those things which the justices said were not involved in the case.

Justice Brennan perceived that the issue before the Court was a limited one, and that it did not involve any issues relating to specific teachings or curricula. "On the contrary," he said "the only books at issue in this case are library books, books that by their nature are optional rather than required reading. Our adjudication of the present case thus does not intrude into the classroom, or into the compulsory courses taught there."

Nor, as Justice Brennan sees it, does the case involve the acquisition of library books, as distinguished from their removal.

Not even textbooks are involved, the Court agrees, but only library books.

And there seems to be no question in the minds of the justices who prevailed that the removal of books from school libraries because of vulgarity or lack of educational suitability is entirely proper.

Thus we come to the central question: What is the United States Supreme Court likely to see, in the future, as the limits-- if any--on the authority of a board of education to direct the removal of books from a school library?

Perhaps the most important message to emerge from at least six of the seven opinions in the Island Trees case is that boards of education may--and indeed are expected to--seek to instill community values in their students. Judge Brennan said "We are ... in full agreement with [the board of education] that local school boards must be permitted 'to establish and apply their curriculum in such a way as to transmit community values,' and that 'there is a legitimate and substantial community interest in promoting respect for authority and traditional values be they social, moral, or political.'" Justice Blackmun made the point several times in his opinion. "... [A]s we all can agree," he said, "the Court has acknowledged the importance of the public schools 'in the preparation of individuals for participation as citizens, and in the preservation of values on which our society rests' ... Because of the essential socializing function of schools, local education officials may attempt 'to promote civic virtues'" "... [S]chool officials may seek to instill certain values 'by persuasion and example' or by choice of emphasis."

As one might expect, Justices Berger, Powell and Rehnquist enthusiastically agreed. It is a "truism," said Justice Powell, that the schools are highly important "in the preparation of individuals for participation as citizens," and as vehicles for "inculcating fundamental values necessary to the maintenance of a democratic political system." And Justice Rehnquist observes that it is "permissible and appropriate for local boards to make educational decisions based upon their personal social, political and moral views."

What then is the problem? Why does a majority of the Court see any difficulty at all with the actions of the Island Trees board of education?

Justice Brennan, joined by Justices Marshall and Stevens in what is referred to as the "plurality" opinion, held that a school board's right to inculcate community values in its students is limited by a right on the part of the students, under the First Amendment, "to receive information and ideas." That right, said the plurality, "is an inherent corollary of the rights of free speech and press that are explicitly guaranteed by the Constitution, in two senses. First, the right to receive ideas follows ineluctably from the sender's First Amendment right to send them.... More importantly, the right to receive ideas is a necessary predicate to the recipient's meaningful exercise of his own rights of speech, press, and political freedom."

If that is the law of the land, the question for school boards, school administrators, and school attorneys throughout the country is how to distinguish between those decisions concerning library books which are simply a permissible exercise of the school board's freedom to inculcate community values in its students, and those decisions and actions which infringe the right of the student to receive information and ideas. Justices Brennan, Marshall, and Stevens say that the test is the motivation for the school board's action. "If [the school board members] intended by their removal decision to deny [to students] access to ideas with which [the school board members] disagreed, and if this intent was the decisive factor in [the school board's] decision, then [the school board members] have exercised their discretion in violation of the Constitution."

And apparently by way of explanation and limitation of that conclusion, the plurality accepted the view of the Island Trees students that "an unconstitutional motivation would not be demonstrated if it were shown that [the school board] had decided to remove the books at issue because those books were pervasively vulgar ... or if the removal decision was based solely upon the 'educational suitability' of the books in question."

Justice Blackmun, while concurring in the result reached by the plurality, does not agree that there is a constitutional right to receive information, or that there is anything constitutionally unique about school libraries. Instead, he sees the issue in these terms: While it is entirely appropriate that the State use public schools to inculcate fundamental values necessary to the maintenance of a democratic political system, "it is beyond dispute that schools and school boards must operate within the confines of the First Amendment.... [S]chools, like other enterprises operated by the State, may not be run in such a manner as to 'prescribe what shall be orthodox in politics, nationalism, religion, or other matters of opinion.'"

Apparently sensing that the distinction he was making might be a bit difficult for the average citizen to quickly comprehend, Justice Blackmun restated his point several times, using different words. At one point he said, "In starker terms, we must reconcile the schools' 'inculcative' function with the First Amendment's bar on 'prescriptions of orthodoxy.'" At another point he said, "Concededly, a tension exists between the properly inculcative purposes of public education and any limitation on the school board's absolute discretion to choose academic materials." At still another point he said that while school officials may seek to instill certain values in their students by persuasion and example or by choice of emphasis, he warned "That sort of positive educational action, however, is the converse of an intentional attempt to shield students from certain ideas that officials find politically distasteful."

Thus, four justices of the United States Supreme Court--and only four--conclude that there is a constitutional limitation on the right of boards of education to remove books from school libraries; and only three of them agree on the rationale by which that limitation is found to exist. What of the other five justices?

Justice White became the swing vote by concurring in the conclusion of Justice Brennan and three others that the case should be remanded to the District Court for a trial. However, Justice White's vote was motivated solely by the fact that he agreed with the Circuit Court of Appeals that it might be important to know the reasons underlying the Island Trees school board's decision to remove the books in question. He expressed regret at the fact that "the Court seems compelled to go further and issue a dissertation on the extent to which the First Amendment limits the discretion of the school board to remove books from the school library." He would have saved that task for another day.

We come then to the dissents. The disagreement by the Chief Justice and by Justices Powell, Rehnquist, and O'Connor with the views of the plurality can only be described as intense. Each of the dissenters believes strongly that the educational decisions of school boards ought not to be subject to judicial review. Proceeding from that base, the Chief Justice and Justices Powell and Rehnquist each wrote opinions highly critical of both the reasoning and the conclusions of Justices Brennan, Blackmun, Marshall, and Stevens.

In tone, the opinions of the Chief Justice and Justice Rehnquist were among the most critical I have read of the views of other members of the Court. The Chief Justice became downright testy when he said that one of the principal issues in the case is "whether local schools are to be administered by elected school boards, or by federal judges and teenage pupils." Justice Powell said: "The plurality's reasoning is marked by contradiction." And Judge Rehnquist said that among his reasons for disagreeing with Justice Brennan's opinion is that "it is analytically unsound and internally inconsistent."

On a loftier plane, Justices Burger, Powell, and Rehnquist dealt critically with the two principal conclusions upon which the plurality opinions were constructed: that the First Amendment accords students a constitutional right to receive information and ideas; and that the existence of that right somehow places a limitation on the authority of school boards to seek to transmit community values to students.

On the "right to receive" notion, the dissenters believe that no such right has ever before been recognized by the United States Supreme Court, and they find no basis now to conclude that such a right exists. While a scholarly analysis of both sides of that question might be interesting, such an effort is beyond the scope of this paper.

Far more important for us, I believe, is to hear what the dissenters have to say about what they perceive to be the logical flaws in the plurality opinions.

With respect to the plurality's notion that there are constitutional limits on the authority of school boards to seek to inculcate values, the Chief Justice said this:

> How are 'fundamental values' to be inculcated except by having school boards make content-based decisions about the appropriateness of retaining materials in the school library and curriculum. In order to fulfill its function, an elected school board <u>must</u> express its views on the subjects which are taught to its students. In doing so those elected officials express the views of their community; they may err, of course, and the voters may remove them.

Perhaps the most perceptive criticism on the part of the dissenters has to do with the standards by which the "motives" of a school board in removing books from a library would be judged.

The plurality indicated that removal would be permissible if a book were found to be "educationally unsuitable." The Chief Justice finds educational suitability to be "a standardless phrase."

The plurality held that a school board's discretion "may not be exercised in a narrowly partisan or political manner." Both the Chief Justice and Justice Powell conclude that such a standard provides no guidance at all to school boards, to their counsel, or to the Courts.

The plurality held that although it found a First Amendment limitation on the right of school boards to <u>remove</u> books from school libraries, there is no such limitation on the school board's authority to decide what books will be <u>placed</u> in the library in the first instance. Both the Chief Justice and Justice Rehnquist found that distinction illogical. As Justice Rehnquist put it, "The failure of a library to acquire a book denies access to its contents just as effectively as does the removal of the book from the library's shelf."

Justice Rehnquist summed up in these words the conclusion which all the dissenters seem to have reached.

I find the actions taken in this case hard to distinguish from the myriad choices made by school boards in the routine supervision of elementary and secondary schools. "Courts do not and cannot intervene in the resolution of conflicts which arise in the daily operation of school systems and which do not directly and sharply implicate basic constitutional values" ... In this case [the students'] rights of free speech and expression were not infringed, and by [the students'] own admission no ideas were "suppressed." I would leave to another day the harder cases.

What of the future? The Supreme Court obviously has not spoken clearly. The four dissenting justices are far more unified in their points of view than are the five justices who voted to send the case back to the District Court for trial. The almost unanimous reaction thus far to the Island Trees decision is that the Court has failed to resolve the issue, that the Court was "deadlocked," and that the Court has failed to provide any useful guidelines for school boards and for the lower Courts.

While four justices have held--and a fifth has implicitly agreed--that local school authorities may not remove books from school library shelves simply because they dislike the ideas contained in them, the Court has not told us what grounds for removal --other than "vulgarity"--are permissible.

There is an old expression among lawyers that "Hard cases make bad law." In the words of a University of Chicago law professor, the Island Trees decision proves that "particularly hard cases make no law."

The difficulty of the issue is well illustrated in a June 30 editorial in the usually logical The New York Times. In the lead paragraph, the editorial characterized the Island Trees decision as holding that boards of education "may not deny students access to ideas only because they are offensive to the community"; and two paragraphs later it observed that "The purpose of local control of education is precisely to let the community standards shape the curriculum."

There may or may not be a trial in the Island Trees case. And if there is a trial, Island Trees may or may not get back to the United States Supreme Court.

But whatever the future history of Pico v. Island Trees, it is completely certain that at some point in the future, the issue of the removal of books from school libraries will be back before the United States Supreme Court. While it is by no means clear how the Court will rule the next time, I think it is fair to predict that any future constraint on the authority of school boards with respect to library books will be narrower in scope and clearer in application than the decision in Island Trees.

ARE SCHOOL CENSORSHIP CASES REALLY INCREASING?*

Kenneth I. Taylor

A current notion that schools are experiencing "capricious and irrational" censorship pressures at an increasing rate is, by now, all but taken for granted by a good segment of the American population. Librarians' appeals for help against censorship by the public, according to one source, rose 500 percent after President Reagan was elected. Censorship, according to another, is "real, nationwide, and growing," while a third warns, "America may be experiencing one of the worst waves of censorship this country has known." Like a ritualistic chant in which the word becomes real, constant repetition has given the notion such a high degree of credibility that we have come close to losing sight of its origins.

While there is little doubt that censorship occurs, we also know that it has been present at every point in American history, including several infamous, nationally organized examples. Should today's public be censoring at an increasing rate that is reaching an all-time high, we must then be experiencing an unprecedented alienation of those people whose support and participation we now so badly need.

Whenever we make charges of censorship, we are making statements about national behavior and adding critical judgment as well. As professionals, we have a moral and ethical responsibility to determine whether or not they are accurate. The purpose of this article is to examine the evidence of three nationally prominent sources of the notion of increasing censorship, which represent professional and commercial interests. Their data, it is proposed, reflect, to an appreciable degree, the perception and apprehensions of persons who are most intimately involved in providing and using school materials and, to an unreliable extent, the actions of community members. For more helpful information, it is recommended, we should be looking directly to the public in order to learn about its inquiries regarding school programs and materials.

---

*Reprinted by permission of the author and publisher from School Library Media Quarterly, 11:1 (Fall 1982) 26-34.

ALA Office of Intellectual Freedom

For a decade and a half, the Office of Intellectual Freedom of the American Library Association (ALA) has reported on censorship of library materials. Established in 1967, it compiles records of censorship activities, reports on court decisions, and provides information and assistance to librarians who are encountering censorship difficulties. In philosophy, it appeals to authority, namely the U.S. Constitution as a guarantee of student rights and professional reviewing media as assurance of collection quality. Its distinctions between school and public library objectives are minimal.

In speeches, talk-show appearances, and press releases that provide content for sources as diverse as Ellen Goodman and the Wall Street Journal, the staff cites titles of classics, Pulitzer Prize winners, and dictionaries as its stock-in-trade proof of the irrationality of censorship. Catcher in the Rye, Diary of Anne Frank and Huckleberry Finn rank among their favorites, whereas titles, such as Sensuous Woman and Valley of the Dolls, which have also been censored, receive scant notice.

In an analysis of the Office's bimonthly newsletter to its subscribers, Woods found ninety-one individual titles cited as having been censored at least twice in academic, public, or school libraries from 1966 to 1975.[1] When we compare Woods' list, however, with those of national citizens groups in the late 1940s, we find that the Friends of the Public Schools of America, one of the most powerful and numerous antischool groups, listed, within a span of three years, ninety individuals in its Bulletin, apart from textbook writers and corporate entries, whose entire works were to be banned from libraries throughout the country. In this one instance, we have evidence of greater attempted censorship activity by a single group than is being reported by ALA today on American citizens as a whole.

The Office of Intellectual Freedom conducts few, if any, behavioral studies but bases its estimates of increasing censorship instead on staff perceptions, informal counts of pleas for help, and anecdotal case histories. A well-publicized count states that requests for information rose from "about" four a week to "about" four a day, or a rise of "500 percent," after President Reagan's election.[2] This, the Office surmises, is evidence of increasing conservative power and hostility toward public education.

It is clear that frequency counts of this order constitute dubious evidence of a rise in censorship. Like the compilation of national statistics on health and crime, figures rise as an agency's data-gathering techniques improve and respondents become more accustomed to reporting. A comparable increase in librarians' requests for assistance could have been predicted as the Office publicized the availability of its services. While the Office of Intellectual Freedom provides a useful service by helping those in need and periodically furnishes good copy for journalists, its statistics and press releases should not be accepted as valid indexes of censorship rate.

The National Council of Teachers of English

According to the National Council of Teachers of English (NCTE), censorship is increasing in frequency and intensity, is more prevalent, and may be at its highest point in American educational history. Its position is based on two member surveys made in 1966 and 1977, each of which asked respondents whether they had experienced "objections" to books or magazines. There were, respectively, 608 (38 percent) and 630 (30 percent) returns.

Council members reported a higher frequency of objections in 1977. These results and accompanying articles were published in a best-selling monograph, Dealing with Censorship. [3] According to the report, which equates "objections" and "book censorship pressure,"

> If book censorship alone is considered, the 1977 survey shows that slightly over 30 percent of the returns reported book censorship pressures. In raw numbers, 188 respondents reported objections to books used in their schools; 427 respondents reported no objections. In contrast, the NCTE survey of 1966 showed just over 20 percent of the returns reporting censorship pressures on books. The 10 percent increase seems [sic] a significant difference. [4]

This last sentence and personal judgments of other writers in the monograph form the only basis of the Council's well-publicized conclusion that censorship had increased over an eleven-year period. Press releases announced findings to the national news and professional media and supplied content for countless articles, including a feature in Parade, the most widely circulated periodical in the U.S.

"After a lapse of several years, cries of 'Ban the book' are rising again," exclaims U.S. News and World Report. "Books and periodicals that some groups find offensive are the targets of a renewed effort at censorship in the nation's schools and libraries." Quoting James E. Davis, editor of Dealing with Censorship, they continue, "Censorship demands have intensified markedly in recent months. There isn't a teacher or school board member in the country that isn't being compelled to take books out of the curriculum."[5]

In Dealing with Censorship, Davis and others refer to what they call the "benchmark" citizens' quarrel with the West Virginia Kanawha County (Charleston) School Board, which began in April 1974 and erupted in violence that drew national attention. Starting with textbooks up for adoption, the controversy developed into a county-wide class struggle wherein one group of citizens and educators was perceived as imposing subject matter and values on others who were markedly different. While the controversy was a reminder of the national pattern of community outbreaks in the McCarthy era, it did not spread, as predicted, to other school districts. Council leaders cite this event and the NCTE's two surveys as evidence of an upsurge in censorship after a brief but deceptive lull. "In my estimation," writes Edward Jenkinson, chairman of the NCTE Committee against Censorship, "there are more attempts at censoring now than ever before."[6] According to Robert T. Rhode, in the same report, "Today, America may be experiencing one of the worst waves of censorship this country has known."[7]

We do, of course, have censorship pressures, but they are in no manner as powerful or unified as the purge of pro-British materials from the Chicago and New York City schools, as well as states such as Wisconsin, Oregon, and Oklahoma, that was inspired by the Hearst newspaper chain in the 1920s. Nor do we have employment boycotting of blacklisted writers, like Lillian Hellman and Ring Lardner, as we did after World War II.

Certain problems in the design of the two NCTE surveys are often found in others in education and related behavioral fields. We have no follow-up sampling of nonrespondents to see how they differ from or are similar to those who did respond, nor do we know their reasons for not replying. We also have a problem when comparing two surveys that are taken eleven years apart. If we were to apply statistical treatment, we would have to assume, as we would hesitate to do, that cultural and social factors in the U.S. had remained the same. This principle of statistical analysis applies also to informal interpretations of survey data, as was done by the NCTE. Did English teachers feel as free to report on community pressures in 1966 as in 1977? We have no way of knowing.

More serious, however, is the ambiguity of the term "objection" and its use by the Council to mean "book censorship pressure." An objection to a book on grounds of quality or place in the curriculum need not constitute an attempt to censor, even when it is replaced by another. Addressing English teachers and the problems they encounter in selecting materials, Allan Glatthorn writes, "Some of our choices seem just not for all the young adolescents in our classes ... I do think that some of us have made some foolish mistakes in the hope of finding relevant literature."[8] In order to establish validity, the designers of the NCTE surveys should have defined closely related terms for respondents and field-tested the questions for clarity.

Because of these problems, the Council report is uneven in value for anyone who seeks information on public and teacher roles in appraising materials. Several of the articles are over-reactive, already dated, and, occasionally, inaccurate. For example, Robert F. Hogan's undocumented portrayal of the typical censor as a blue-collar worker, who is undereducated and fundamentalist in religion, promotes a stereotype.[9] From what we know of the McCarthy period and more current examples, critics of the schools are often successful, politically influential members of the business community or the professions, who are articulate, highly persuasive, and regard themselves as equal or superior to educators.

Several articles in the NCTE report provide psychological and behavioral insights that should be helpful to beginning teachers. One, by Allan Glatthorn, is on selection of materials and the values, rights, and privacy of the student.[10] Another is Robert C. Small's article on respect for the citizen who raises questions about materials and teaching.[11] Both are likely to be important long after the data of the two surveys.

AAP-ALA-ASCD Survey

In 1980, the Association of American Publishers (AAP), American Library Association, and Association for Supervision and Curriculum Development (ASCD) undertook a survey of school administrators and librarians that they have called "the most extensive study that has been undertaken to date."[12] Its purpose was "to provide comprehensive data on the relationship between the censorship problem and the larger selection process." Of 7,500 questionnaires sent to administrators and librarians, 1,891, or 25 percent, were returned. As in the case of the two NCTE surveys, we have no information on nonrespondents. Respondents were asked for the number (or an approximation) of separate items that had been "challenged" since September 1, 1978. Administrators were asked to report on classroom and library materials. Librarians were to respond on library materials only.

Shortly upon receipt of the returns, the researchers found that respondents had encountered difficulty in defining the term "challenges." Several replied that they were reporting only on challenges that had involved formal complaint procedures, whereas others said they were reporting on formal and informal challenges combined. Designers of the instrument said in their summary report that they had had both in mind.

Strikingly different views of "challenges" emerge from the two groups of respondents. Whereas one in five administrators reported challenges to materials in their schools, one in three librarians did so; and whereas administrators reported that 10 percent of the challenges had come from the teaching staff, librarians reported 31 percent. Although no reasons are proposed by the researchers for these discrepancies, we might suppose, for the moment, that librarians had encountered more informal challenges from parents and teachers, whereas administrators were more aware of formal complaints. The actual reason is less important than the evidence here that questionnaire data often bear a closer relationship to the experiences and perceptions of the respondents themselves than to actual facts. In this study, we have 577 librarians proportionately reporting a much higher incidence of challenges originating inside and outside the school than did 1,314 administrators. This point is especially important to keep in mind wherever we find the researchers combining the data of the two groups, as they do, for example, in their treatment of responses on rate of challenges to materials between two two-year periods.

Referring to 1978-80, the instrument asked both groups, "How does this rate compare with the rate of challenges in the two-year period preceding September 1, 1978: lower, about the same, higher, not certain?" The treatment given these responses results in a surprisingly misleading impression of widespread increase from one two-year period to the next.

Data given on reported challenges in 1978-80 and changes in rate from 1976-78 are as follows:

- 1,891 administrators and librarians responded.
- 1,387 or nearly 74 percent did not report challenges of any kind.
- 494 or 26 percent did report challenges.

Of the 494 above who reported challenges,

- 68 or 13.8 percent were uncertain if a change in rate had occurred.
- 250 or 50.6 percent perceived no change.
- 131 or 26.5 percent perceived an increase.
- 45 or 9.1 percent perceived a decrease.

From these data, we can formulate for ourselves a straightforward conclusion of our own making (but not one made in the report): <u>Nearly 7 percent of 1,891 school administrators and librarians perceived an increase in the number of challenges to school materials over a four-year period, whereas 93 percent did not.</u>

The press release to the news media and the professions, however, reports only on the responses of the 176 persons who perceived some kind of "change," either lower or higher. By combining the 45 who reported a decrease and the 131 who reported an increase, and without furnishing raw data for independent reader analysis, the five-page press release statement for July 31, 1981, presents the following as one of its "salient survey findings":

> Nearly 75 percent of the respondents who indicated any change in the rate of challenges between the 1976-78 and 1978-80 periods reported that the rate had increased.[13]

This has become one of the most frequently quoted findings of the study in the national press, an instance in which a 6.9-percent response has been elevated to a more newsworthy 75 percent. Given the researchers' acknowledgment of the ambiguity of the word "challenge," the obvious perceptual nature of the two sets of responses, and what may well become a classic example of data mistreatment, we cannot begin to conclude from these reported findings that an increase in challenges to materials actually occurred (a) in the schools of the respondents when taken as a group, (b) in the survey sample, or (c) in the nation at large.

We also find more than one viewpoint in the report and its accompanying press release, providing curiously divergent interpretations of the findings. In the body, we are properly cautioned against regarding challenges to be the same as censorship attempts:

> While the frequency of challenges reported in the survey is of concern ... it is important to emphasize that challenges to instructional and library materials do not necessarily constitute a threat to freedom of speech or the ability of our schools to provide quality education. On the contrary, such challenges--whether by professionals within the schools or by parents and other members of the community outside--have a legitimate place in a democratic educational system.[14]

We are also advised in the introduction, "Neither the report itself nor the survey data should be taken as precise indicators of the rate or impact of censorship pressures nationwide."[15] Despite this precaution, the researchers (or others) then offer, in the next paragraph, an inexplicable generalization about national behavior: "What the experiences reported here do indicate is that censorship pressures on books and other learning materials in the public schools are real, nationwide, and growing."[16]

The press release, which is all that many editors and journalists receive, carries the word "censorship" in its heading: "NATIONWIDE SURVEY INDICATES GROWING CENSORSHIP IN THE U.S. PUBLIC SCHOOLS."[17] Each of these unsupportable statements has been published by news and professional publications without data or clarification for the general reader.

The AAP-ALA-ASCD survey should not be accepted as a report on the American public. It is, inadvertently, a significantly arresting perceptual study of two groups of educators who may be perceiving, experiencing, and reacting to public inquiries about materials in very different ways. With this in mind, readers should disregard any survey conclusions based on combined responses of librarians and administrators. They should also interpret findings on "reported" behaviors as "perceived" behaviors.

The report, which has been distributed by the Washington office of the Association of American Publishers, may be useful as a source of ideas for more-sophisticated perceptual studies. Among these might be an inquiry into what appears to be an unconscious or compulsive desire, by this and other professional sources, to raise the specter of increasing censorship pressures in the absence of appropriate data.

The report also contains several briefly stated but possibly helpful recommendations on selection policies, procedures for handling complaints, and community education programs. All of these, it reminds the reader, are best implemented before problems arise.

The Public and Its Schools

We find it impossible to assert from the data of any of these three sources that censorship pressures are increasing either in frequency or intensity. We learn more from these studies and articles about the perceptions of the respondents and writers than we do about the public itself. Many of them see the schools and their communities engaged in adversarial relationships, like labor and management of earlier decades. The public creates crises by exerting unwelcomed pressures on teachers and librarians.

We should be careful that our studies do not constitute what Robert Asahina calls "social science fiction," wherein an investigator begins with a notion, gathers factual and anecdotal data that concur, and interprets them to obtain a foregone conclusion. Like the Hite reports on human sexuality, to use a popular and patent example, such studies seem to elicit responses from those who are most deeply involved with or enamored of the subject and share the predispositions of the researchers. We will do better by observing and defining public behavior as precisely as possible, using historical and contemporary perspective.

Even a modest knowledge of twentieth-century history indicates that censorship has been far more powerful than at present. Although the NCTE report refers to censorship in the colonial seventeenth century, it does not mention the 1920s or late 1940s when school personnel could and did lose their positions because of "anti-American" ideas, membership in blacklisted organizations, or "anarchistic intent." While the conservative right wing might be growing in political effectiveness today, it is in no way as powerful and influential as business, religious, and patriotic groups that joined forces to launch nationwide attacks on education. We have nothing even remotely like their efforts to remove titles from every school in the nation, as was done successfully with the Rugg social studies texts in 1939 and the Building America series in 1947, both of which ceased publication because of the unified pressures.

There are also important differences between the public attitude toward schools in the first half of this century and today. In the 1920s and 1940s, the public feared schools on ideological grounds and turned to national citizen groups for leadership. The Hearst newspaper syndicate, the Daughters of the American Revolution, and the Conference of Small Business Organizations were among a sizable number of powerful special interests that encouraged attacks on public education. In 1950, Fulton J. Lewis, Jr., one of the nation's most powerful radio broadcasters, was able to begin his evening commentary with full assurance that the listening public shared his opinion about the subversive state of education, by announcing,

"Now getting around to our study of un-Americanism in the textbooks of the schools and colleges of this nation ..."[18]

Public concerns about the schools are now largely economic and related to teacher and student performance. Requests to cover religious doctrine, such as creationism, are overshadowed by an insistence on high performance in reading and related basic skills. We can be thankful that, when the public questions professional choices in materials, it turns to the schools rather than outside authority. It does not invite outsiders in to plead a local case. Most inquiries come from individuals rather than groups, and, instead of charging teachers with subversive purposes, it asks why certain materials are being used in relation to student maturity or school objectives.

Teachers, in turn, will be more effective if they respond without appealing to authority, either to the opinions of "experts," institutional pronouncements, or the First Amendment, and speak in terms of the individual student and parent. Nationally distributed selection tools, book reviews by persons unknown in the community, and book lists from professional and commercial sources are poor arguments as a defense of local school decisions. Librarians and teachers should be the first to point out problems inherent in national reviewing processes and acknowledge that powerful commercial influences are exerted on school libraries and textbook committees. The public wishes to know instead how educators work together in the selection process, what criteria they follow, and how they relate programs to community needs.

A mistake made by educators after World War II was to ignore early attacks on the schools, assuming that they were isolated and of little consequence, whereas they were symptomatic of a nationwide fear of foreign subversion. Today's concerns are nationwide expressions by individuals who are inquiring in the personal interest of their children. They are not anonymous faces in the community who are trying to use schools to justify their own failings, as more than one of the professional organizations in this article have publicly charged.

Schools need not fear that the public is about to turn to super-patriotic groups for help, although it may, history tells us, should the country become involved in an international conflict. Schools should be concerned instead about the public's turning to alternative programs and home instruction for the teaching and materials it regards as best, a phenomenon, interestingly enough, that may signify a decreasing need for censorship pressure.

We should be able to understand some aspects of the public's search for alternatives by examining the activities of prominent personalities, such as the much-maligned Gablers. Norma and Mel Gabler have long been known as leaders of conservative educational thought, with fans who see them as charming, attractive, and devoted individuals unafraid to speak out on controversial matters.

The Gablers are not enemies of the schools, like the Lucille Cardin Crains or Allen A. Zolls of thirty years ago. They do not seek to destroy public education or replace the curriculum. They ask instead for a place for their views in the school program, not an unreasonable position to take in a democratic nation.

They do their homework thoroughly, know textbook content in impressive detail, and share their information with others. They use official state channels to make their views known in Texas at selection time, and, by their own admission in their story, Textbooks on Trial, often fail in their attempts to have a textbook accepted or rejected.[19] Their reviewing processes might withstand public scrutiny better than those of many school systems. Komoski reports that 45 percent of nearly twelve thousand teachers indicate that they had not taken part in reviewing the materials they were using. Fifty percent of those who said they had participated reported spending less than an hour in the process.[20]

Activities of public figures like the Gablers tell us that those who inquire about school decisions have a high respect for the influence of materials on young minds. The Gablers believe, as did many of our Founding Fathers, that ideas in school materials can influence young readers and affect their behavior as citizens. There was a distinct preference for American-written materials in the post-Revolutionary period over those of British origin. Men, like Thomas Jefferson and Benjamin Rush, who devoted much of their writing to education, wanted schools that taught moral values and prepared students to be effective citizens. They would have been less impressed by present-day authority appeals to the First Amendment, which say that children, "theoretically at least," should have access to any and all ideas, than by our knowledge of Piagetian principles of moral, intellectual, and social development in children and youth.

Many members of the public are also worried, as educators should be, about the inferior quality of many school texts, a concern shared by Frances Fitzgerald who writes from the position of historian as scholar.[21] Librarians and others are on weak ground when they question the power of materials to influence young people adversely. Educators have an excellent opportunity instead to point to the advantages in using original sources, such as the Federalist Papers and Tocqueville's Democracy in America, or, for younger readers, colonial diaries and letters, in lieu of the secondary accounts of texts.

Parents and community members in the past have been active supporters of school library and classroom supplementary collections, as demonstrated by financial support from the local to the federal level. They have a right to inquire why and how materials are being selected for school use, whether on the basis of classroom activities in response to children's needs or because of their listing in nationally distributed selection tools. Is Catcher in the Rye, said to be the most frequently censored title, in the school library because it has a place in the instructional program or because it constitutes a part of what someone outside considers to be an ideal collection? Are stories of little girls masturbating used by the teachers and counselors or does the library media collection comprise an independent, quasi curriculum of its own in response to commercial interests?

These are the kinds of real but difficult questions that parents are asking. When they do, they are not necessarily challenging the responsibility of teachers or librarians; nor, when they inquire about the relationship of materials to the conceptual and affective development of children, are they rebuking student rights. According to Robert Small, too often "resolutions are made and passed condemning censorship with almost no understanding that protesting citizens are to a very considerable extent fulfilling the role assigned to them by the historical development of the American school."[22]

It is probably time for research on or the development of a taxonomy of questioning behaviors that can help us identify and define the multiple meanings behind the asking of why. Perhaps such behavioral inquiry will help us distinguish between serious public inquiry on the one hand and a fearful perception of censorship pressures on the other.

Acknowledgments

This article was submitted during preparation to M. Frances Klein, associate professor, University of Southern California; Robert E. Clasen, professor and chairperson, Extension Programs in Education, University of Wisconsin; and P. Kenneth Komoski, executive director, Educational Products Information Exchange. The writer gratefully acknowledges their comments by correspondence and telephone.

References

1. L. B. Woods, "The Most Censored Materials in the U.S.," Library Journal 103:2170 (1 Nov. 1978).
2. "Books and TV--New Targets of Religious Right," U.S. News and World Report, 8 June 1981, p. 43.
3. James E. David, ed., Dealing with Censorship (Urbana, Ill.: National Council of Teachers of English, 1979).
4. Lee Burress, "A Brief Report of the 1977 NCTE Censorship Survey," in Davis, Dealing with Censorship, p. 16.
5. "Censorship on Rise Again in Schools," U.S. News and World Report, 4 June 1979, p. 51.
6. Edward B. Jenkinson, "Dirty Dictionaries, Obscene Nursery Rhymes, and Burned Books," in Davis, Dealing with Censorship, p. 5.

7. Robert T. Rhode, "Legal Decisions and Censorship: A Game of Chance," in Davis, Dealing with Censorship, p. 76.
8. Allan Glatthorn, "Censorship and the Classroom Teacher," in Davis, Dealing with Censorship, p. 52.
9. Robert F. Hogan, "Some Thoughts on Censorship in the Schools," in Davis, Dealing with Censorship, p. 86-95.
10. Glatthorn, "Censorship and the Classroom Teacher," p. 48-53.
11. Robert C. Small, "Censorship and English: Some Things We Don't Seem to Think about Very Often (but Should)," in Davis, Dealing with Censorship, p. 54-62.
12. Association of American Publishers and others, Limiting What Students Should Read (Washington, D.C.: The Association, 1981).
13. AAP-ALA-ASCD press release (31 July 1981), p. 2.
14. Association of American Publishers, Limiting, p. 11.
15. Ibid., p. 2.
16. Ibid.
17. AAP-ALA-ASCD, p. 1.
18. Robert A. Skaife, "They Want Tailored Schools," Nation's Schools 47:35 (May 1951).
19. James C. Hefley, Textbooks on Trial (Wheaton, Ill.: Victor Books, 1976).
20. P. Kenneth Komoski, Report on a National Study of the Nature and the Quality of Instructional Materials Most Used by Teachers and Learners (Epie Report no. 76 [New York: EPIE Institute, 1977]), p. 7-8.
21. Frances Fitzgerald, America Revised (Boston: Little, Brown, 1979).
22. Small, "Censorship and English," p. 61.

A WALK ON THE WILD SIDE: A CONVERSATION WITH

"SEX-POSITIVE" PUBLISHER JOANI BLANK*

Celeste West

<u>Celeste West</u>: As publisher of Down There Press, your nine titles are famous, even notorious, for being the most "out there" sex titles this side of pornography. Yet you are an ardent feminist--in fact, one of the most successful and respected women in feminist publishing. A lot of people would feel that combining pleasure and politics makes for strange bedfellows, so to speak. How did this come about?

<u>Joani Blank</u>: I founded Down There Press seven years ago simply because there is such a dearth of really good, enlightening sex education books. I am a sex therapist and educator by profession, and most of my colleagues will tell you that there are very few "sex-positive" books we can recommend without reservation to the layperson.

<u>CW</u>: You mean books which are free of sex-role stereotyping, exploitation, homophobia, and just silly mis-information?

<u>JB</u>: Yes. Many authors of sex books can't resist the temptation to be provocative, to write something titillating or sensational, or "cute" and trite. You can count the worthwhile books practically on one hand: <u>Our Bodies, Ourselves</u>; works by Shere Hite, Lonnie Barbach, and Betty Dodson; <u>Joy of Sex</u>; one or two sex education books for gay men; and a few good feminist press lesbian titles like <u>Loving Women.</u>

<u>CW</u>: Of course, <u>Our Bodies, Ourselves</u> was first brought out by courageous feminists at the Boston Women's Health Collective who had to publish it themselves. I still have my beloved, original 35¢ newsprint copy. I remember we just couldn't believe someone telling it like it is. And now it's the so-called Moral Majority's favorite book to hate.

<u>JB</u>: High recommendation! But people are actually starved

---

*Reprinted by permission of the author and publisher from <u>Collection Building</u>, 5 (Spring 1983) 36-39. Copyright © 1983 by Celeste West.

for honest material. We know that almost everyone has concerns
about sex during some part of their lives. You'd think that publishers would be persuading sexperts to turn out dozens of such
books.

CW: Lonnie Barbach, noted sex therapist and author, says
studies find that 62 percent of "happily" married women are sexually dissatisfied. I hate to think about the unhappily married ones....

JB: Or the single ones, or the men. Thousands of men (and
women) who have no sexual dysfunction are bored, uninspired or totally uninterested in sex. So the books I publish for adults and
children are informational and give people permission to explore
more and new ways of enjoying themselves.

CW: Your "Playbooks" about sex do more than describe the
plumbing then?

JB: Yes, they actively celebrate sex. They encourage loving
experiment strongly based in self-love (sexual and otherwise) and
self-assertion. You know, how to have a four-star juiceful good
ole time. I take the words "play" and "sex play" very seriously.
Lots of folks have forgotten how to play at and with sex. Maybe
we should be calling what many people do in bed, besides sleep,
"sex work!"

CW: Well, I can't tell you how much I've enjoyed playing with
your photo-essay book, I Am My Lover. I mean, if I could only
take one exquisite four-color centerfold with me to a desert island....

JB: Unfortunately, I Am My Lover is out-of-print. The
printer went off to Mexico with the originals and the plates, so it's
not possible to reprint it either.

CW: Sic transit gloria. On the subject of printers, there are
porn printers and also very conservative ones. I know printers who
won't do lesbian novels or menstruation poems. Have you had any
hassles in getting your books printed?

JB: Oh, have I! When I begin getting printers' bids for a
job, I tell them immediately that my books are sexually explicit.
At first, they say, "No problem." But then they always add, "No
photographs, are there?" When I had to say with Men Loving Themselves: Images of Male Sexuality, "Oh yes, there are 135 photos of
sexually aroused men, with narratives of how they got that way,"
nine out of ten printers just freaked out.

CW: I'm sure they are shocked that a woman has the audacity
to publish explicit sex material. That's supposed to be the Hefner/
Mafia male prerogative. But what are they afraid of? You don't
put the printer's name on the book, and printers certainly need all
the business they can get now. Besides, most of them print tons
of schlock, subliminal sex images, and come-ons every day.

The Social Prerogative 365

<u>JB</u>: Yes, but the need to censor up-front sexuality is very powerful. Usually, my contact in a print shop deals with it by blaming someone else's prudery. The estimator will say he's certainly liberal regarding sexual mores, but the owner isn't. Or the owner will say the workers on the line wouldn't like it or are women, or that other clients would be offended. (By the way, I've never been turned down by a woman owner or estimator.) I have only had one owner frankly tell me that he personally couldn't deal with the subject matter. I thanked him for his honesty.

<u>CW</u>: Have you ever had to use porn printers?

<u>JB</u>: No. But I have had to pay premium prices to "respectable" printers. The economical, short-run book printers in the Midwest, which most small publishers use, won't touch some of my stuff.

<u>CW</u>: Perhaps if you did something more textbookish--without those beautiful photographs?

<u>JB</u>: Nope. My latest book, which looks and reads like a textbook and has no photos, was rejected by more than a dozen printers the moment they heard the title: <u>Anal Pleasure and Health.</u>

<u>CW</u>: Joani Blank meets the anal taboo--would it be a mixed metaphor to say, "face to face?" I remember when you had the book party for <u>Anal Pleasure</u> in San Francisco. My friends, some of whom own and love your other books, were too freaked out by the subject to go to the party with me.

<u>JB</u>: You didn't even come!

<u>CW</u>: Well, that's because I was embarrassed to go by myself. I mean, I knew it was just a book party, and I guessed anal sex might be preferable to banal sex, but gee.... Now, I've since read the book, I can say for the record that Jack Morin really turns on the light at the end of the tunnel. It is quite an amazing book, especially for some people like me who think they've heard it all....

<u>JB</u>: I guess you could say all these cute asshole jokes are the equivalent of the nervous laughter that seems to accompany most discussions of the book. But the work is extremely important because it deals with the whole nature of taboo itself. And Jack has so many valuable things to say about how to communicate sex needs generally, and how to deal with the power struggles inherent in all relationships.

<u>CW</u>: Plus all the serious health aspects.

<u>JB</u>: Would you write a review of <u>Anal Pleasure</u>?

<u>CW</u>: Sure. I ran a review of <u>Good Vibrations,</u> your vibrator guide, when we were publishing <u>Booklegger Magazine.</u> We reviewed

a lot of tasty, racy stuff, and librarians loved it. But I found out later that most librarians bought those kind of books for themselves rather than for their libraries.

JB: Well, maybe the books influenced those librarians' lives for the better or enabled other good books to get in that seemed milder by comparison. Now that Booklegger Magazine is gone, who would publish a review for libraries?

CW: I know this is a family magazine, but Arthur Curley may allow us to go so far as to provide you a blurb here like: "Anal Pleasure and Health may be your gateway to a holesome, new meta-physical experience."

JB: Now tell that to Library Journal.

CW: Listen, I've found that, with certain notable exceptions, virtually all of them women, library lit editors are a pretty pusillanimous bunch. For example, I just found out with American Libraries that a writer (me) can't criticize the Association of American Publishers regarding conglomerate control; their members pay for so many ads, I guess. Now I don't know if these editors are also infected with what you term "sex-negativity," but they certainly spread the terminal boredom of general life-negativity and fear.

JB: Well, I find that amazing since I think libraries are some of the most exciting places in the world. I understand when Reagan was governor of California he tried to dismantle them here. He was right--libraries can lead you to free inquiry. I would give anything to get my books into libraries so all kinds of people could use them. And the books would be cared for and conserved.

CW: So do libraries ever order your books?

JB: In a word, no. Well, except for when I published Period, the first book on menstruation ever written for young girls --believe it or not in 1979! I got a flurry of library orders from a review in School Library Journal. But that book doesn't say a word about sex. Anyway, I sold the rights to Period, which has now been translated into three languages, and I don't publish it anymore, Volcano Press does.

CW: What about university libraries or psychology or medical libraries ordering?

JB: No. Especially not medical libraries. Doctors' information on sexuality is carefully kept Dark-Age.

CW: I guess that's pretty well substantiated in the work feminists are doing to counter the atrocities the medical establishment has perpetuated against women in general and women's sexuality in particular. A friend of mine in medical school at Stanford says the sexuality training is abysmal: one part ignorance and one part arrogance.

The Social Prerogative

JB: That's one reason why it is so important for laypeople to be able to get good information elsewhere. I have tried getting Down There publications into libraries, but like any small press, it's hard to get reviewed. When I do mailings to libraries, they don't seem to buy much either.

CW: Well, a few of your books, the Playbooks, are workbook format. That's a problem for libraries, no matter the topic. If a reader participates and fills in the blanks, it changes the book for other people.

JB: Of course, that might be provocative.

CW: But like graffiti--only if it's pretty original.

JB: Well, I am doing a non-workbook version of the Kid's Playbook because of a nice review in School Library Journal pointing out the problem. And most of my books are not in the workbook format at all.

CW: It comes down to, I think, only about one librarian in ten acts on the courage of his or her convictions. Some would say one in a hundred, but I'm the eternal optimist. Consider that a librarian has to be a pretty creative cataloger even to assign accurate headings to Down There books. Sandy Berman published a wonderful discussion of cataloging your vibrator book. You'd think from the paucity of sensible sex subject headings, virtually no one at Library of Congress or Sears ever does "it."

JB: I checked out a book called Sex and the Undecided Librarian (Scarecrow, 1974), and it was really depressing.

CW: The title is depressing enough.

JB: It seems even "liberated" librarians are afraid of confrontation. They fear that the world is full of Mrs. Grundys who will sweep down on a library, fire everybody for moral turpitude, and cut the funds forever.

CW: I'd say that's true; librarians are deathly afraid of the real or imagined censor to whom they ascribe immense power. There is almost a compulsion for libraries to project themselves, much as the school or church establishment, as bastions of publicly funded decency.

JB: Well, we all know sexual "decency" is about as relative as time. As a librarian, would you ever censor anything?

CW: Well, I never had a real chance. I got censored first. But at San Francisco Public, for example, I would have nipped most of the expensive American Rifle Association death-wish material, the investment services, the non-books (celebs, preppies, etc.), probably a lot of the mass market stuff. And then--substitute my own biases, of course. The problem is that librarians have limited funds, so we do, in effect, "censor" something every time we select another.

JB: Yes, but there always seems to be money to select some things and not others.

CW: Exactly. It all comes down to a matter of one's personal politics and professionalism, the latter I would define as "fairness" in this conversation. I think librarians "select out" quality, explicit sex books like yours because they are very puritanical people or else they are cowards. Or, god help us, both. They may say a sex book will just get stolen, but that's usually a cop-out. I remember when SFPL had to put all the astrology and Zen books on reserve. So what? It's a sad commentary on human thievery, but at least the books circulated.

JB: I really think that if most librarians could see my books they would judge them to be affirmative and joyful, just the opposite of destructive, obscene. But I don't know how to reach the cowardly "liberal...."

CW: I guess you could publish an accompanying self-defense kit like the Boston Women's Health Collective did for libraries and schools who get hassled for Our Bodies, Ourselves. Library diversity and freedom of speech have lots of allies, but librarians surely need some political savvy to know how to mobilize this support.

JB: Maybe the library schools could teach that as a specialty, like you say they do with cataloging or kids' books or computers. Train some sort of censorship shock-troops. These folks could be on the staff to defuse "well-meaning" censors with education, or blast away at the hardcore intellectual/sexual fascist.

CW: But Joani, that philosophical foundation is what everyone is supposed to get by doing time at a library school in the first place. We're professional book and media workers because we're trained to select the best, fairest material, know the reason why, and stand by it.

JB: So what goes wrong--if you get only your one out of ten who has some kind of professional code?

CW: I don't know. I guess it's like what I found in law school, too; they don't teach justice or ethics there. They focus on the jargon and the props. People go to get a union card basically.

JB: Well, I've still had better luck with the American Library Association--getting the "intellectual freedom" material--than I've had with the really up-tight American Booksellers Association.

The Social Prerogative

CW: I know their membership is furious that ABA won't fight the large publishers in court for unfair trade practices subsidizing the chain bookstores, but what's happened with Down There?

JB: This year I had to go to war with the ABA staff to exhibit my books at the ABA Convention. Apparently, I already had a reputation with them.

CW: But the ABA follies are infamous for showcasing all kinds of real excess! They finally had to forbid large publishers from hiring "tits 'n ass" to pander their wares because the milling around was hurting floor sales. So this year we had male models in leather lingerie strutting their stuff. And lots of sex books exhibits--even a beefcake row for gay men.

JB: I guess it's real obvious when someone publishes only sex books like me. I can't prove they gave me a hard time because of the nature of my books, but all indicators point that way.

CW: Are they worried actual porn publishers will demand space if they give it to you?

JB: Oh, those guys aren't going to waste a minute promoting their books to regular booksellers. They wouldn't get any orders. A lot of the porns don't even have company names, and they have a system of book manufacture and marketing that is totally separate from the rest of the book world. The new Canadian documentary Not A Love Story shows how porn marketing works. According to the film, the typical sex book store earns $10,000 per day!

CW: Too bad we can't tax them to pay for library service. Anyway, I would say you, at least, have the sweet god Eros on your side. I join many other people in admiring your courage, tenacity, and sense of humor in confronting all the "sex-negatives." But it must be exhausting and sad sometimes. How do you keep going?

JB: Oh, it's fun being a big frog in a small pond; you know, being the only one who dares ... And working in the sex field is, after all, sexy.

(Note: For a free copy of the Down There Press catalog, write DOWN THERE PRESS, Box 2086, Burlingame, CA 94010.)

Notes on Contributors

WILLIAM BAUMOL, noted economist, is at Princeton University and New York University.

JAMES BENSON teaches at the Graduate School of Library Service, University of Alabama, and is a frequent contributor to library literature.

SUE ANNE BATEY BLACKMAN is at Princeton University.

MARY LEE BUNDY is a Professor at the College of Library and Information Services, University of Maryland, College Park (Amy Bridgman and Laura Keltie are her students).

CAROLE HASTINGS CARPENTER is Reference Librarian at the Senior High School Library, Milford, Delaware.

MARY K. CHELTON is a teacher and co-editor of Voice of Youth Advocates, P.O. Box 6569, University, AL 35486.

AUDREY EAGLEN is head of the Order Department, Cuyahoga County Public Library.

RICHARD DE GENNARO is Director of Libraries at the University of Pennsylvania and often contributes to this volume.

CONNIE EPSTEIN, formerly editor-in-chief of Morrow Junior Books, teaches a workshop in writing for children at Hofstra University.

WM. R. ESHELMAN is President of Scarecrow Press.

CAROLE HASTINGS see Carpenter.

DAVID HARTWELL is editor in chief of Timescape Books, published by Simon & Schuster.

ESTELLE JUSSIM is a well-known authority on photography and teaches at the Graduate School of Library and Information Science, Simmons College.

MARC A. LEVIN is with the Institute of Governmental Studies, University of California at Berkeley.

MAURICE LINE often contributes to this volume, and is Director General of the British Library Lending Division.

GUY A. MARCO, noted bibliographer, lives in Washington, D.C.

J.B. MILLER, poet and founding editor of Empyrea magazine, received the Hopwood Award for poetry in 1976.

ASHLEY MONTAGU is a world-famous anthropologist and author now at Princeton University.

JOE MOREHEAD teaches at the School of Library and Information Science, SUNY/Albany, and is a frequent contributor to this collection.

KARL NYREN is Senior Editor at Library Journal.

DANIEL O'CONNOR teaches at the School of Communication, Information, and Library Studies, Rutgers University.

JEFF PEMBERTON is editor and publisher of Online.

DARBY PENNEY is Law Librarian in the Counsel's Office of the New York State Department of Mental Hygiene, Albany.

HAROLD C. RELYEA is with the Congressional Research Service at the Library of Congress.

ANTHONY SMITH is director of the British Film Institute, London.

NORMAN STEVENS is University Librarian at the University of Connecticut and a well-known contributor to library literature.

FREDERICK STIELOW teaches at the College of Library and Information Services, University of Maryland, College Park.

STEPHEN STOAN is Social Science Librarian at Wichita State University.

ROBERT STONE is Counsel and Deputy Commissioner for Legal Affairs at the New York State Education Department.

KENNETH TAYLOR is an Industrial Training Manager for International Signal and Control Electronics.

SAMUEL S. VAUGHAN is Vice-President and Chairman of the Editorial Board at Doubleday & Co., Inc.

CELESTE WEST is a freelance librarian and journalist from San Francisco.

LUO XINGYUN is with the Institute of Scientific and Technical Information of China, Beijing.